The Straits Philosophical Society & Colonial Elites in Malaya

The **ISEAS – Yusof Ishak Institute** (formerly Institute of Southeast Asian Studies) is an autonomous organization established in 1968. It is a regional centre dedicated to the study of socio-political, security, and economic trends and developments in Southeast Asia and its wider geostrategic and economic environment. The Institute's research programmes are grouped under Regional Economic Studies (RES), Regional Strategic and Political Studies (RSPS), and Regional Social and Cultural Studies (RSCS). The Institute is also home to the ASEAN Studies Centre (ASC), the Singapore APEC Study Centre, and the Temasek History Research Centre (THRC).

ISEAS Publishing, an established academic press, has issued more than 2,000 books and journals. It is the largest scholarly publisher of research about Southeast Asia from within the region. ISEAS Publishing works with many other academic and trade publishers and distributors to disseminate important research and analyses from and about Southeast Asia to the rest of the world.

The Straits Philosophical Society & Colonial Elites in Malaya

Selected Papers on Race, Identity and Social Order 1893–1915

EDITED BY

LIM TECK GHEE

CHARLES BROPHY

YUSOF ISHAK INSTITUTE

First published in Singapore in 2023 by
ISEAS Publishing
30 Heng Mui Keng Terrace
Singapore 119614

E-mail: publish@iseas.edu.sg
Website: <http://bookshop.iseas.edu.sg>

All rights reserved. No part of this publication may be reproduced, stored in a retrieval system, or transmitted in any form or by any means, electronic, mechanical, photocopying, recording or otherwise, without the prior permission of the ISEAS – Yusof Ishak Institute.

© 2023 ISEAS – Yusof Ishak Institute, Singapore

The responsibility for facts and opinions in this publication rests exclusively with the authors and their interpretations do not necessarily reflect the views or the policy of the publisher or its supporters.

ISEAS Library Cataloguing-in-Publication Data

Name(s): Lim, Teck Ghee, editor. | Brophy, Charles, editor.
Title: The Straits Philosophical Society & colonial elites in Malaya : selected papers on race, identity and social order 1893-1915 / edited by Lim Teck Ghee and Charles Brophy.
Description: Singapore : ISEAS-Yusof Ishak Institute, 2023. | Includes index.
Identifiers: ISBN 978-981-5011-33-3 (soft cover) | ISBN 978-981-5011-34-0 (pdf) | 978-981-5011-35-7 (epub)
Subjects: LCSH: Great Britain—Colonies. | Malaya—Social conditions—20th century. | Malaya—History—British rule, 1867-1942.
Classification: LCC DS596.6 S89

Cover design by Lee Meng Hui
Index compiled by Raffaie Nahar
Typesetting by International Typesetters Pte Ltd
Printed in Singapore by Mainland Press Pte Ltd

CONTENTS

Preface ix

About the Editors xii

1. Introduction 1

I The Ideological Basis of Colonial Rule

2. Dutch and English Administration in the East 43
   Walter J. Napier, 13 January 1894
   Criticism *by Henry N. Ridley*

3. The Influence of Europeans Abroad upon Native Races 58
   W.R. Collyer, 16 April 1898

4. The Doctrine of the Survival of the Fittest as Applied to Man 71
   Henry N. Ridley, 15 December 1900

5. The Disadvantages of Education for the Lower Classes 79
   Gilbert E. Brooke, 11 November 1904
   Criticism *by Tan Teck Soon*

6. East and West 93
   Henry N. Ridley, 12 April 1907

7. Utilitarianism 103
   Henry N. Ridley, 9 October 1908
   Criticism *by* G.E. Venning Thomas

8. The Influence of Climate on Character 116
   W.M. Runciman, 11 May 1915

II Governing the Colony: Race, Crime, Opium, and Law

9. On the Contagious Diseases Acts 127
   David J. Galloway, 9 July 1893
   Criticism *by* G.D. Haviland

10. The Opium Problem in the Straits Settlements 148
    The Rev. George M. Reith, 12 August 1893

11. The Relation of the Opium Traffic to Local Revenue 153
    Arthur Knight, 12 August 1893

12. The Prevention and Repression of Crime 159
    C.W.S. Kynnersley, 14 October 1893
    Criticism *by* Tan Teck Soon

13. The Application of English Law to Asiatic Races: 188
    With Special Reference to the Chinese
    Walter J. Napier, 9 September 1899

14. The Administration of Law and Order in the 198
    Colony in its Early Years
    W.R. Collyer, 18 April 1903

15. The Reformation of British Malaya 212
    James Aitken, 15 November 1907
    Criticism *by Arthur Knight*

III The Colonial Order and the Chinese

16. Chinese Local Trade 233
    Tan Teck Soon, 10 August 1901
    Criticism *by J.M. Allinson*

17. Local Educational Problems 247
    Tan Teck Soon, 16 August 1902
    Criticism *by Mr. A. Knight*

18. Opium versus Alcohol 262
    Lim Boon Keng, 10 July 1908
    Criticism *by J.G. Campbell*

19. The Chinese in British Malaya 278
    Lim Boon Keng, 10 February 1910

20. The Chinese Revolutionary Movement in Malaya 292
    Lim Boon Keng, 11 July 1913
    Criticism *by J.H. Roberts*

21. Socialism among the Chinese 305
    Lim Boon Keng, 12 December 1913

IV Studying "the Malays" and their Religion

22. "Latah" 319
    D.J. Galloway, 11 September 1897
    Criticism *by Henry N. Ridley*

23. Christianity and Mohammedanism 338
    Rev. G.M. Reith, 12 February 1895

24. Our Duty to the Malays 356
    C.W.S. Kynnersley, 13 April 1901

25. The Future of the Malay Race 363
    H. N. Ridley, 13 September 1902
    Criticism *by R. Hanitsch*

26. The Influence of Modern Civilization on the Malay 375
    Rev. W. Murray, 8 January 1909
    Criticism *by David A. Bishop*

27. Moslem Influence on the Malay Race 385
    W.G. Shellabear, 12 September 1912
    Criticism *by J.L. Humphreys*

28. Mohammedanism, as Revealed in its Literature 413
    W.G. Shellabear, 7 May 1915
    Criticism *by Tan Teck Soon*

29. Conclusion: 437
    The Afterlives of the Straits Philosophical Society

Index 446

PREFACE

This book has had an unusually long gestation period. It all started in 1976 when Lim Teck Ghee, at that time teaching at the University of Penang as it was then known, was working in the Penang Library in 1976 and stumbled across a box of old papers that the library staff intended to dispose of. The papers included what were the original copies of some of the proceedings of the Straits Philosophical Society, a society founded in 1893 by colonial officials with the objective of engaging in critical discussion on matters related to philosophy, history, literature, science and the arts.

The value of the papers was recognized and communicated to the Library management to ensure that they would be properly handled and preserved for posterity.

Further examination of the papers—there were 17 sets—revealed that some of them had never been published and that it would be worthwhile to reproduce them because they provided insights into the thinking of some of the most influential people in the Peninsula on a variety of subjects and issues of importance during that period. The fact that their subject matter was still being debated, and in some instances arousing controversy in academia and the public sphere, attested to the need to make them available to a larger audience.

Since then, the publication of the papers has been a challenge. The first choice of publisher—the Malaysian Branch of the Royal Asiatic Society—was not successful as it was then felt that too much emphasis was being given to the publishing of colonial sources. At the same time, a number of early collaborators in the publication dropped out in part because of the common inability to commit time to the research. More time was lost with Lim Teck Ghee's departure from the academia world and Malaysia in 1996.

A chance meeting between Lim Teck Ghee who returned to Malaysia in 2005 and Timo Kortteinen, Professor with the Department of Sociology, University of Helsinki when the latter was undertaking field research in Malaysia in 2007 revived the prospect of a publication on the papers. The two decided to conduct further research on the papers and to collate a selection of Penang and other located papers that would be suitable for publication.

Unfortunately Timo who played an important role in shaping the structure of the book and who also provided notes for the initial draft introduction was not able to see his contribution through to this end product.

His untimely death in 2009 resulted in a further delay to the publication as the collection of materials for the publication was returned to his family in Helsinki.

Fortunately, a colleague of Timo, Professor Timo Kaartinen with the Department of Cultural Anthropology at the University of Helsinki, was able to step in at this difficult stage to obtain the materials from his widow. He arranged for them to be sent to Malaysia and was also instrumental in helping the project obtain funding assistance from the Academy of Finland to defray the costs of further archival work, and editorial assistance to publish the book.

Although Timo Kortteinen is not with us at this final stage of the enterprise, we think he will be happy with the outcome of his efforts here. We are hopeful that the book is seen to fit well with Timo's larger corpus of scholarship which has helped advance the boundaries of social science in Southeast Asia.

Special appreciation is due to Matti and Katriinan Kortteinen and Timo Kaartinen without whom this book would not be possible. Also to the Academy of Finland for its grant assistance in the finalization of the book. Universiti Pulau Pinang provided a modest grant which enabled the typing of the original papers found in the Penang library.

Lastly we want to thank the two reviewers of the draft book for their useful suggestions which have helped us in improving the manuscript for publication as well as Wang Gungwu and Anthony Reid for providing their endorsements to appear in the published book.

Lim Teck Ghee
Charles Brophy

ABOUT THE EDITORS

Dr Lim Teck Ghee's career has straddled academia and international development organizations. He has held a Social Science Chair at the University of Malaya and was a Visiting Fellow and Professor at various universities. Following his departure from academia, he worked with UNESCAP and the World Bank. His works include *Peasants and Their Agricultural Economy in Colonial Malaya, 1874-1941* (1977), *Reflections on Development in Southeast Asia* (1988, editor), *Multiethnic Malaysia: Past, Present and Future* (2009, as co-editor). More recent works include *Challenging the Status Quo in Malaysia* (2017), *Anatomy of an Electoral Tsunami* (2018, as co-editor) and *Dark Forces Changing Malaysia and Malaysia Towards GE15 and Beyond* (with Murray Hunter, 2022).

Charles Brophy is an independent scholar with a focus on the political and intellectual history of modern Malaysia and Singapore. He holds a Masters in Colonial and Global History from the University of Leiden. His work has featured in *Modern Asian Studies*, *Mekong Review*, *Imagined Malaysia Review* and *New Mandala*.

1

INTRODUCTION

The Straits Philosophical Society and Colonial Elites in Malaya: Perspectives on Race, Identity and Social Order

Founded in Singapore in 1893, the Straits Philosophical Society was, in the tradition of other learned societies throughout the British Empire, a space within the colony for the "critical discussion of questions in Philosophy, History, Theology, Literature, Science and Art".[1] With a membership restricted to graduates of British and European universities, fellows of British or European learned societies and those with "distinguished merit in the opinion of the Society in any branch of knowledge",[2] it was a meeting place for the educated elite of the colony made up of colonial civil servants, soldiers, missionaries, businessmen, as well as prominent Straits Chinese.

Colonial associations have been increasingly recognized in colonial historiography as important sites in the lifeworld of the colony.[3] Sports clubs, church associations, charitable groups and educational institutions have been studied as spaces in which the social life of the colony, the political, social, and economic ideologies and the ordering of colonial rule, particularly along racial lines, were reproduced and reinforced. The clubhouse, in particular, has been shown by historians to be a pivotal institution—becoming a sacred ground for Europeans as a bastion of racial prestige, whilst also reinforcing the mystique of the ruling caste.[4] The limited, but politically significant, integration of colonial subjects it permitted was similarly a vital wellspring of colonial hegemony.[5]

More recently scholarly societies have been studied as important centres in the intellectual and ideological life of the colony. Firstly, as spaces for the dissemination of colonial knowledge and systems of thought; and secondly, as spaces in which the colonized learned and responded to the thinking of the representatives of colonial power. Su Lin Lewis, touching on the Straits Philosophical Society, the Siam Society and the Burma Research Society, has argued for the colonial learned society as a site of "sociability and intellectual exchange" producing independent intellectual cultures which would later contribute to the rise of social reform movements and early nationalist movements.[6] These societies, she argues, "contributed to an emerging intellectual culture of libraries, public lectures, and universities" and the flow of intellectual ideas through "correspondence, travel, and exchanges of publications".[7] Carol Ann Boshier's work on the Burma Research Society has also provided an in-depth analysis of the intellectual exchanges between colonial officials and Burmese thinkers which the Society fostered.[8] The earlier Society for the Acquisition of General Knowledge in Bengal, and the Young Bengal movement around it, has similarly been highlighted as a space in which Western knowledge and philosophies were being appropriated and modified for the local conditions of colonial India.[9]

Unlike other colonial learned societies, the Society was more exclusive in its membership. The founding members of the Society, with one exception, were European men from the colonial administrative elite in Singapore.[10] From among the founding members, Mr (later Sir) J.W. Bonser was a leading jurist in the colony. Mr A. Knight was a Straits civil servant and Secretary of the Society for twenty years who, among other pursuits, had a lifelong commitment to the Presbyterian Church alongside Reverend G. Reith and Reverend J.A. Lamont, both of whom made contributions to missionary work and education in the Straits Settlements. Dr D.J. Galloway was a prominent medical authority in the Straits Settlements. Dr G. Haviland was appointed the Raffles Library and Museum curator in 1893 and was also a member of the

Committee of the Library and Museum, as were Mr T. Shelford and Mr R.W. Hullett. Mr Hullett was one of Singapore's leading educators. His students included Mr Tan Teck Soon, social reformer and activist, the only non-European founding member of the Society, and one of the longest-serving founding members, as well as future member Dr Lim Boon Keng, a prominent physician and social reformer. Also connected to Hullett was Mr (later Sir) H.N. Ridley with whom Hullett shared a passion for botany. Ridley was the Director of the Botanical Gardens from 1888 to 1911 and a stalwart of the Society. Mr R.N. Bland and Mr C.W.S. Kynnersley were senior officers of the colonial administration. Among the founding members of the Society was also Mr J. McKillop from the business community and an employee of the Straits Trading Company. Finally, among the prominent founders of the Society, there was Sir Charles Warren who was the Society's first president and a distinguished military official and a scholar. It is noteworthy that throughout its existence the Society had no representation of Jawi Peranakan or Malay members, or any women members.

The origins of the Society lay in a meeting at the house of Sir Charles Warren in March 1893. Present were Warren, Rev. G.M. Reith, J.W. Bonser, W.J. Napier and H.N. Ridley, who agreed on the need for a "local association to discuss the many important questions that press upon modern thought and life". A committee was formed and Warren was appointed president. Membership was capped at fifteen and a small list of corresponding members from outside of Singapore was established.[11] Charles Warren's presidency was, however, brief. He would be replaced in 1894 by W.R. Collyer, a prominent lawyer who had earlier served in Sierra Leone, the Gold Coast and Cyprus. In 1903 Collyer would become the Attorney-General of the Straits Settlements. He would serve as president of the Society between 1894 and 1901 and then from 1902–6 before leaving the colony. He was replaced as president by H.N. Ridley who served from 1907–12. In 1912, A.W. Still, a journalist and prominent editor of the *Straits Times,* assumed the presidency. It would appear that at some point after Still, Lim Boon Keng would assume the position of president.[12] By 1901 the Society also expanded outside of Singapore, when an attempt to form a branch of corresponding members in Penang led to the formation of the Penang

Philosophical Society. The first president was C.W.S. Kynnsersley who had relocated there from Singapore, though he would later return to Singapore. Penang members visiting Singapore could attend the meetings of the main Society. Around 1913 the rules of the Society also changed, allowing for an expansion of the membership and the formation of a Kuala Lumpur branch. We know, however, little about the functioning of these branches.

It is unclear for how long the Society was in operation. It appears that it was still functioning as late as 1923, before slowly entering into decline.[13] Speaking in 1935 to the Raffles College Union, then Colonial Secretary Sir Andrew Caldecott located the Society's demise "in the first years of the war".[14] Yet in response in the pages of the *Singapore Free Press*, F.C. Peck, a prominent merchant, suggested that papers of the Society continued to be printed until 1918 and he would recall reading papers to the Society as late as 1921 and 1923.[15] During the last three years of the Society's life, the members produced only "two essays between them" before the Society entered into demise. Yet, as no records of the proceedings have survived beyond 1918 it can be assumed that the Society met regularly between at least 1893 and 1918.[16]

The format of the Society's meetings appears to have been consistent throughout most of the Society's life. Membership was limited to fifteen in number and members, meeting on the second Friday or Saturday of every month, took it in turns to read a paper. This was followed by a critique of the paper by another member before a general discussion ensued, chaired by the president.[17] Whilst the choice of topic was open to members, three principles structured their discussions. One was that the speakers were expected to provide amusement as well as knowledge. A second was that the papers be of general, and not merely specialist, interest. Finally, there was a request that "so far as is practicable, our geographical position may influence our labours and give colour to our thought, so that each subject in our papers may be affected by local circumstances".[18] This was intended to encourage members to apply their knowledge and research to the colony in which they lived and worked.

Although the Society was not exclusively European, and many of its members did not hold full-time administrative office, many had some direct responsibility for public policy. Yet, notwithstanding the privileged

FIGURE 1.1
Members of the Society at the farewell banquet to W.R. Collyer at the Singapore Club on 19 January 1906

Back row (left to right): Tan Teck Soon; Lieutenant-Colonel Sankey; Rev. W. Murray; W.R. Collyer; H.N. Ridley; A. Knight; Lieutenant-Colonel Pennefather; G.E. Brooke; H.F. Rankin; Dr D.J. Galloway.
Front row (left to right): R.W. Hullett; Dr Lim Boon Keng; R. Hanitsch; Lieutenant J.N. Biggs; G.E.V. Thomas; C. Emerson; P.J. Burgess; Major Ritchie.

Source: Gilbert Edward Brooke, Roland St. John Braddell, and Walter Makepeace, *One Hundred Years of Singapore*, vol. 2 (London: John Murray, 1921).

position of its members, the papers of the Society are important for the candour with which the issues that dominated colonial policy were discussed. One of the few constraints on discussion, particularly in the early years of the Society, was that it was "strictly private", and members were forbidden to divulge the content of proceedings to the colony's press without permission. The after-dinner discussions following the talks were designed to institutionalize "freedom of thought and expression", outside of the gaze of the colony's developing public sphere.[19] This allowed the members to stray into more controversial territory. F.C. Peck would later recall reading a paper on Christianity and Christian morality which "was, and still is, unsuitable for publication" based on views which "if not universally accepted in 1935, were very unpopular and even 'disloyal' and 'seditious' in 1923".[20]

Nevertheless, some of the papers did later appear in print, especially in the *Straits Chinese Magazine* (*SCM*), one of the first organs of local opinion in Malaya, which was co-founded by prominent member Lim Boon Keng. The lively public debates to which the *SCM* gave expression helped to insert the more private discussions of the Society into the mainstream social and political debates of the time. The *SCM* also highlighted important interactions between the European members of the Society and Straits Chinese elites. Another outlet for the Society's papers was a collection compiled by Henry Ridley, then president of the Society, and published in 1913 as *Noctes Orientales*. This collection printed those papers of local interest and, as Ridley suggested, many of the papers were as relevant in 1913 as at their time of being read to the Society.[21] The proceedings of subsequent years 1911–16 were made available in pamphlet form by the Methodist Publishing House of Singapore.

The aim of the present volume is, however, to make widely available a broader selection of papers from the Society, particularly those which touch on themes important to the intellectual history of British Malaya from the end of the nineteenth century. As Tim Harper has noted, large swathes of the intellectual history of Singapore and Malaya remain untold.[22] Whilst in recent years some key gaps have been filled, this collection includes some previously unpublished and less easily available papers to provide a more detailed and revealing view of colonial thought, especially on the themes of race and government in British Malaya. This provides an important background and context to understanding and unravelling the policies that have continued to be crucial to the political and social development of Malaysia and Singapore.

Race and the New Imperialism

The intellectual world in which the Society was situated was that of the era of the "New Imperialism". The period from the 1870s had been marked by several factors which demarcated a new age in colonial rule: new rounds of imperial expansion, emerging economic globalization through an expanding capitalist world economy, a growth in global connectivity through new technologies such as the telegraph and developments in shipping, and a growing interaction between colony and metropole. This entailed a move from a more indirectly ruled, distant and diffuse empire, towards a more modern and systematic imperial project.

The reduction in physical and non-physical distance heightened European concerns over the ends and means of empire. Frederick Cooper and Laura Ann Stoler have noted that by the last quarter of the nineteenth century, European empires were now

> taking pains to reassure each other that their coercion and brutality were no longer frank attempts at extraction but reasoned efforts to build structures capable of reproducing themselves: stable government replacing the violent conflictual tyrannies of indigenous polities; orderly commerce and wage labour replacing the chaos of slaving and raiding; a complex structuring of group boundaries, racial identities and permissible forms of sexual and social interaction replacing the disconcerting fluidities of an earlier age".[23]

What they term the "embourgeoisiement"[24] of imperialism in the late nineteenth century marks the greater focus placed on the modernization of the colony (only sometimes including the colonized), an emphasis on new systems of administration, new programmes of colonial economic development and a growing concern with bourgeois morality in the exercise of colonial rule.

As Hobsbawm has noted, by the late nineteenth century this trend was part of a wider transition ongoing in European society. The growth of mass democracy, mass working class movements and the Long Depression were unsettling the bourgeois liberal order which had dominated mid-nineteenth century Europe with its belief in progress, reform, and moderate liberalism.[25] European politics with the rise of Germany—an illiberal economic and technological power—became increasingly statist, conservative and anti-democratic. Whilst in an earlier period a liberal bourgeoisie had reconciled itself to imperialism on modernizing grounds and had embraced a nationalism that remained in touch with universal bourgeois aspirations, by the end of the nineteenth century both imperialism and nationalism, and the struggle between nations and races, became ends in themselves.

This transition towards a more conservative and statist bourgeois order gave a central place to the question of race. By the mid-nineteenth century ideas of race had come to develop alongside new scientific theories of heredity, phrenology, and Darwinian evolution. Whereas before, "race" had been a relatively general term, denoting varying groupings of people—in the way for example that Raffles would talk of the Malay race—the concept of "race" was gradually used as a narrower biologically-defined classification and would generate a series of essentialist and fixed assumptions. Prominent intellectuals such as Herbert Spencer and Francis Galton would apply Darwinian thinking in the emerging fields of sociology and eugenics respectively, both to understand the functioning of human society and as a moral discourse. Spencer, the most prominent sociologist of the late nineteenth century, coined the term "survival of the fittest" to denote both the struggle for survival that underlay human society, as well as the role of this struggle in producing a higher and more civilized society. The categories of breeding, inheritance and environmental determination emerged then as characteristics that would define a particular society.[26]

This process has been understood by Partha Chatterjee in terms of the "rule of colonial difference" which largely centred on a new importance given to the category of race in the exercise of colonial rule.[27] Late nineteenth-century colonial rule, according to Chatterjee, took Europe's "modern regime of power"—its new tools of administration, classification, and economic development—to modernize the administration in the colony. However, in asserting the racial and developmental difference between Indians and Europeans, colonial states also maintained a paternalistic and despotic power over the colonized. The colonized, it would be argued, could not simply be made in the image of the colonizer and emphasis should be placed on managing the border between the colonized and colonizer, rather than on projects of liberal reform.

Linked to the focus on race was also a growing focus by the colonial state on the category of community as primordial and fixed,[28] defined not only by race but also by religious, national, or linguistic grouping.

Sudipta Kaviraj has understood this transition in terms of the move from "fuzzy communities" to "enumerated communities"[29] in which, through new practices of classification and counting by the colonial state, increasingly fixed rigid boundaries were established between groups based on "scientific" and bureaucratic criteria. Anderson has talked of the emergence of a totalizing classification in which new tools of "census, map, museum" would produce totalizing identities that would supersede an earlier fluidity of identity.[30] The census, in particular, would emerge as an important tool for the government and its classifications of colonial populations.[31] More recently, the works of Karuna Mantena[32] and Mahmood Mamdani[33] on late nineteenth-century liberal imperialism highlight the way in which a new focus on customary law in the work of Henry Maine encouraged the preservation and codification of custom within modern colonial frameworks. This, in turn, required greater attention to anthropological study, ethnography and knowledge production within colonial rule. Such a development entailed significant criticisms of liberal, modernizing, and reforming ideas of empire. It also increasingly encouraged British power to exercise itself indirectly over colonial populations. This reasoning would influence later British expansions in Fiji as well as in the Malay Peninsula.

Philosophically this late nineteenth-century focus on race and community also implied the suspension of the universal claims of liberal thought and generated a discourse of liberal exceptionalism. This entailed the common idea that liberal principles of government could not be applied to all societies equally. John Stuart Mill in his treatise on representative government would complain that earlier utilitarianism had ignored the stage of advancement of societies:

> The recognition of this truth, though for the most part empirically rather than philosophically may be regarded as the main point of superiority in the political theories of the present above those of the last age; in which it was customary to claim representative democracy for England and France by arguments which would equally have provided it the only fit form of government for Bedouins or Malays.[34]

Such an idea entailed the belief that colonized populations could be governed in non-liberal ways which were more natural to their condition.

It also formed the basis for the development of liberal communitarian thought which, based on the influence of social Darwinism and the growing role of the state, gave a greater role to national, religious, and racial communities within liberal thought both in Europe and in the colonial world.[35]

The Malay Peninsula in the History of Colonial Thought

The Straits Philosophical Society was a part of this intellectual history of late nineteenth-century colonial thought, caught up in its broader political and intellectual developments. In keeping with global transformations, the Straits Settlements were increasingly moving in status from an outpost of empire to that of a more integrated colony. In 1867 the Straits Settlements would become a Crown Colony, governed directly from London not via Calcutta. By the 1870s the opening of the Suez Canal was increasing trade through the Straits, whilst telegram and postal ships increased communication. Economically, the period saw the consolidation of the agency houses over individual merchants, and the spread of Chinese capital from entrepôt trade to investing capital in the interior, particularly in the tin trade. Linked to this was a growth in labour migration. This heightened connectivity would also stimulate the intellectual life of the colony. European members of the Society would regularly refer to ongoing debates in Europe over political and social reform, the rise of socialism and new trends in colonial policy. The Straits Settlements were also a site through which scholars and an emerging regional nationalist intelligentsia would pass (from Rabindranath Tagore to Kang You Wei), alongside a growing regional press and book trade, via Europe, China, India, and Egypt. Mark Frost has noted that in 1876 the post offices of the Straits Settlements received just 21,241 books (including trade circulars and pamphlets) and dispatched 5,481, but by the year 1891, two years before the founding of the Society, they received 137,500 books and dispatched 59,000.[36] These connections served as the basis for an emerging diasporic public sphere for the colony in the 1890s and early twentieth century.[37]

The 1870s also saw colonial attention drawn to the interior of the Malay Peninsula and to the development of British intervention in the

Malay States. In doing so the periphery of the empire also came into contact with broader trends in imperial thought. This included ideas of indirect rule, concepts of racial difference, the counting and specification of "native" communities, the instrumentalization of anthropological and ethnological knowledge, as well as critiques of modernization and reformist ideas of colonial rule.

This defined the terms of British intervention. On the one hand, it was driven by a moralized image of the Malay sultanates as spaces of lawlessness, violence, caprice, tyranny, and waste which could only be improved on contact with British civilization. On the other hand, it was marked by a belief that colonial control and attempts to reform or modernize the Malay sultanates too quickly, would serve only to invite rebellion. This was most evident in the fall-out from the Perak War and the debates around debt-slavery and toll collection which saw Hugh Low assume a more gradualist and measured policy in the aftermath of Birch's killing.[38] In keeping with the feudal image of the Malays developing amongst the British, this ideology of colonial intervention became focused not only on the maintenance of racial difference but on something more akin to a paternalistic management of modernization which drew upon critiques of liberal and reformist ideas of empire; and which suggested that colonial populations should be improved on their own terms.[39]

Spearheading these endeavours was a new generation of colonial officials, who ventured into the Peninsula combining the tools of colonial knowledge production with the expansion of British administrative control—a process in which the colonial administrator could be said to be "making a slow transition from the status of social engineer to that of social conservator and anthropologist-as-legislator".[40] Much has been written about the role of Frank Swettenham (whose brother J.A. Swettenham was a member of the Society) as a central ideologue of the British forward-march across the Malay Peninsula. Swettenham was representative of this new figure of the "anthropologist-as-legislator" who was keen to study the Malays and to understand their ways as a basis and further justification for British intervention. The same was true of officials such as Hugh Clifford (a corresponding member of the Society in 1893) and Hugh Low, as well as scholar-administrators represented by William Maxwell and William Walter Skeat,[41] who were mixing ethnographic studies of the Malay language and customs, with bureaucratic forms of data collection, from census taking[42] to land registration.[43] Within the Society, figures including H.N. Ridley, W.G. Shellabear and C.W.S. Kynnersley—with their concern with the anthropology of the Malay Peninsula and the consolidation of British rule—were important to this link between the production of colonial knowledge on the Malay Peninsula and the development of political ideologies of colonial rule.

Race and the Critique of Liberalism

The role of the Straits Philosophical Society within this new discourse on race and colonial rule was two-fold. It was firstly a space in which earlier liberal and reformist approaches to empire were criticized, and secondly a space in which the category of race was being constructed in colonial Malaya.

Whilst earlier figures such as Raffles and John Crawfurd had drawn from Enlightenment ideas of progress and liberalism, the papers of the Society highlighted a rejection of this earlier thinking.[44] Raffles and Crawfurd had centred their "enlightened" approach to empire on the criticism of the mercantilism of the Dutch. Yet in the Society figures such as Walter J. Napier and Ridley, in early contributions in 1894, would criticize British rule in Malaya for its overtly laissez-faire approach and would speak in favour of the more authoritarian approach of the Dutch in Java. Others like Gilbert E. Brooke in his essay on education, in 1904, would build upon the thought of Herbert Spencer to criticize liberal and reformist approaches to mass education both in Britain and in Malaya. Brooke would advocate for the maintenance of social hierarchy as dictated by what he termed the "necessities of modern social and political economy". Other essays reflected a broader critique of utilitarian thinking that was in keeping with the revaluation of figures like John Stuart Mill. In contributions in 1908 and Venning Thomas would engage more directly with liberal thought and criticized utilitarianism for its emphasis on equality and on the rule of the majority which they associated with the rule of the mob. To buttress his position Ridley highlighted the happiness of the old English and Malay peasantry who existed without either development or the vote. For Venning Thomas a paternalistic definition of utilitarianism allowed for the removal of the vote from the mob and the removal of the *keris* from the Malays.

These critiques of the liberal and reformist ends of the empire also reflected the growing concern with race in the Society. A figure such as W.R. Collyer in his 1898 Presidential Address would argue pessimistically that the civilizing mission of European empires increasingly came up against the reality of racial difference.

> We ... have become sceptical as to the universal mission of our race. Of its steady progress and vitality we may have no doubt, but as to its missionary force and its power of assimilating other races, we feel that there is a good deal to be said on both sides.

"Every race", he would note, "seems to receive impressions in a way peculiar to itself, according to its natural receptivity", and this to him was evident by a comparison of British influence in India and China. Whilst in China Western civilization had had a negligible influence, in India the British had been able to have some "civilizing" impact on educated, upper-class Indians, although for the Indian masses it had achieved far less impact—a fact which justified an increasingly paternalistic approach to British rule.

> How little European precept and example has influenced the life of the masses in India is shown by the present position of Bombay, the main lesson of which seems to be how unfit the people of India are for any kind of self-government, and how necessary it is, for the preservation of order and peace, that some white race should rule them.

In China, on the other hand, Western civilization was seen to have had a negligible influence and this failure seemed to Collyer to entail a need to revise the civilizing mission itself. Suggesting that it should not be aimed at overarching projects of reform and modernization of colonial societies, he argued for colonial powers to deal with colonized peoples "honestly, openly, and considerately" to spread the benefits of Western civilization over time through gradual persuasion rather than forced imposition.

Other figures in the Society remained, however, more pessimistic about the ability to fundamentally change Eastern societies through contact with Western culture and civilization. In H.N. Ridley's 1907 piece, "East and West" he argued, highlighting a biological metaphor, that:

> By cultivation you may improve or modify thorns and thistles, but you will never be able to gather grapes off thorns or figs off thistles. The inherent qualities of the species remain the same to the end of time.

Ridley's contribution to the Society reflected his broader interest in American racism and social Darwinist thought.[45] This led to the argument that, whilst the British could help to produce a better quality of Indian, African, or Malay, such races would continue to be defined by their particular racial characteristics. Against liberal doctrines of improvement and progress, Ridley's writings would constantly reject what he regarded as artificial interventions in the operation of the law of the survival of the fittest. His basic argument was that such attempts to counteract its effects were only leading to the production of weak and degenerate races. In other contributions to the Society, Ridley would call for an approach to politics that balanced the interests of the individual with that of the race. This justified, in the name of racial progress, illiberal forms of government. Yet Ridley's particularly biological and Darwinist approach did not always dominate the Society's proceedings. Another member, W.M. Runciman, would also highlight the impact of climatic influences on racial characteristics. Yet unlike Ridley, he would emphasize the possibility through moral and religious influence of counteracting the effects of climate to improve groups such as the Malays. Such questions over race and the improvement of non-European races became central to the discussions of the Society, particularly in the discussions of the future of the Malays.

The "Real Malay"

Central to the critique of liberal ideas of empire was the growing relationship between colonial thought and anthropology. This increasingly tied the imposition of colonial modernity to the anthropological study of the colonized, both in terms of the body (physiognomy, race, social Darwinism, and climatic and environmental determinism) and culture (language, custom and society). Linked to this was also the growing importance of the discipline of psychology to colonial thought in problematizing the mindset or character of colonial peoples.[46] In the debates of the Society this gave particular emphasis to the study of the Malays, in keeping with the emergence of the new "anthropologist-as-legislator". Thus, officials such as Swettenham and Clifford published anthropological accounts of the Malay character and Malay society and these writings highlighted the need to understand the current character and future potential of the Malays as a basis for colonial policy.

Syed Hussein Alatas has highlighted the presence within colonial writings of pop-psychological analyses of the Malays and their mindset which were based on simple observation and stereotype. In the Society such a tendency was evident across many of the papers of the European and, as we shall see, non-European members. This trend was evident in D.J. Galloway's essay on *latah*, a nervous condition seen as particularly prevalent amongst the Malays, which was discussed in terms of their racial and psychological character—notably their higher susceptibility to external stimuli and a lack of inhibition. Yet this anthropological and psychological image was also regarded as subject to change. As Galloway and his respondent Ridley would come to argue, with education and urbanization *latah* was disappearing amongst the Malays, suggesting that their character was changing with developments on the Peninsula.

Daniel P.S. Goh has highlighted how the image of the Malays in late nineteenth-century colonial thought came to be defined not in terms of an irredeemable oriental otherness, which would have positioned the Malays completely outside the colonial modern, but rather in developmental terms, which saw the Malays as biologically, culturally, and historically behind Europe. Central to this was an idea of the feudalism and medievalism of the Malays.[47] As Goh has argued, such medievalism was related to Darwinian notions of evolution and thus evolutionist notions of social development. This situated the Malays as pre-modern and underdeveloped but also as having the potential under British tutelage for a measure of development and modernization.[48]

As Clifford would argue of colonial intervention through a biological metaphor,

> one cannot but sympathise with the Malays, who are suddenly and violently translated from the point to which they had attained in the natural development of their race, and are required to live up to the standards of a people who are six centuries in advance of them in national progress. If a plant is made to blossom or bear fruit three months before its time, it is regarded as a triumph of the gardener's art; but what, then, are we to say of this huge moral-forcing system which we call "Protection"? Forced plants, we know, suffer in the process; and the Malay, whose proper place is amidst the conditions of the Thirteenth Century, is apt to become morally weak and seedy, and to lose something of his robust self-respect, when he is forced to bear Nineteenth-Century fruit.[49]

The practical effects of this image can be seen in the British development of a traditionalist and protectionist approach to Malay politics and society. Policies were enacted which sought to protect the Malays from economic competition from immigrant races and from what was seen as the onslaught of modernization. Economically this occurred through the exclusion of the Malays from the commercial plantation economy, particularly through colonial land policy,[50] whilst politically it rested on the preservation and extension of what was viewed as the age-old customs of Malay political culture that emphasized the centrality of the sultans and the Malay aristocracy.[51] It is in the Society's debates over the protection and modernization of the Malays that we can see these ideas in their process of formation.

We can detect in the Society's discussions on the relationship between the current racial character of the Malays and their potential for progress several differing interpretations. Rev W. Murray, for example, argued in his 1909 paper, "The Influence of Modern Civilisation on the Malay" that the Malays had been left lazy and unambitious on account of the climate of the Malay Peninsula as well as the nature of the pre-colonial system of governance, which had reduced incentives for hard work. The British presence had been able in part to counteract this and, by providing a system of peace and law and order, had been able to effect external changes in the Malays. This, he observed, could be translated into internal changes that could modify the Malay from a pirate and warrior to a lover of peace and order. David Bishop, on the other hand, who viewed this in terms of the domestication and taming of the Malay character, did not agree that the Malays would modernize fully. Their character and nature would rather require their continued dependence on British tutelage.

> Civilisation works on him slowly in charges external and internal, but it has not inspired him with a spirit of self-confidence or self-help. He is not likely to be exterminated by the nations of the West, but rather to increase under their influence.

Bishop would offer a more critical take on the modernization of the Malays under British influence which idealized their feudal character. Rather than the improvement of the Malays, he argued that there had been a deterioration of character under British rule:

> The ordinary, Malay of today, as compared with his ancestors, suggests the poor, tame, spiritless lion born and bred in a cage at the Zoo, contrasted with the grand and noble animal which has never suffered bondage... Meaner qualities have replaced the grander, and the modern Malay is less simple, less sincere, less trustworthy, less noble than his ancestors.

This suggested to him that the modernization of the Malays was producing moral deterioration and not progress.

The question of immigration and its impact on the Malays was also important in the Society's deliberations. C.W.S. Kynnerslay would offer a more positive account of the potential for Malay development by arguing that in those states where the Malays were in a majority, they showed an ability to govern themselves and develop their states. Hence, he noted that the British importation of clerks and civil servants was preventing them from advancing. Kynnerslay went on to argue for the British to train and recruit Malays into the civil service. Ridley, however, emphasized a more social Darwinist approach to the question of immigration. Believing that the Malays lacked the character and racial biology to prevent subsumption by immigrant races, in particular the

Chinese, Ridley pointed to two trends that might delay this subsumption. One was the presence of Islam as a differentiating factor between the Malays and Chinese. The second was the presence of the British who could for some time artificially protect the Malays from external competition. In response, Hanitsch would argue that protection of the Malay race might be possible but only based on the restriction of immigration and through a system of education, which would build upon existing trades and protect the current state of Malay society. As Hanitsch would argue:

> The Malay is in many ways so childlike that for a long time he will require careful training and nurturing. If we left him alone, and all Europeans took passage for home to-day, I really believe he would turn to-morrow again into the bloodthirsty pirate he was before. But duly taken care of for some generations to come,—and I don't think ever any native race required more careful handling, I believe that the Malays would have a bright and prosperous future before them.

These calls for the protection of the Malays, on account of their character and competition from more advanced races, were not isolated: they came into the debates over immigration, civil service employment, economic protection, native upliftment, and other subjects and would continue to influence debates over Malayness and key matters relating to government and administration in the late-colonial and post-colonial period.

The Malays and their Religion

In both Murray and Ridley's essays, we also see discussion of another aspect of the Malay character—Islam—which as a religious ideology was argued to stand in the way of the modernization of the Malays.

Islam held a problematic place in relation to colonial assumptions around Malayness and this was clearly reflected in the Society's proceedings. As adherents of Islam the Malays, rather than being isolated and disconnected, were part of a global religious, monotheistic, discourse. At the same time, Islam offered an alternative religious, philosophical, legal, and cultural system to that of the Western modern. The reaction to this in colonial thought was often to downplay the importance of Islam, as a religious and cultural doctrine, within Malay society. Thus, in the work of officials such as Raffles, Marsden, Skeat, and R.J. Wilkinson, we see the privileging of the importance of pre-Islamic customs and society in the definition of Malayness.[52] Such privileging was based on two further assumptions. The first was an attempt to racialize and particularize Islam within the Malay world, tying it to Arabness and Arab culture.[53] The second was the assumption that the Malays had adopted Islam superficially and ritualistically, thus rendering Islam a "veneer" over true Malay traditions and customs.[54] This assumption, mirroring assumptions around their superficial reception of Western values, suggested that the Malays lacked an intellectual character and education which would allow them to adopt and fashion ideas of their own accord.[55]

At the same time, European discourse on Islam in the colony was defined by ongoing discussions within the Christian community, and particularly in its missionary variant. The discussions of the Society were taking place during a period of change in the church due to the influx of Methodists and Presbyterian missionaries. The composition of the Society itself reflected the escalation of this missionary work. W.G. Shellabear was the founder of the Methodist Publishing House and a gifted scholar of Malay. G.M. Reith, Archibald Lamont, as well as Murray, worked at the Presbyterian mission in Singapore. Lamont specialized in educational work in the Amoy dialect and worked with Tan Teck Soon to found the Eastern School. Murray had only limited knowledge of Chinese but had learned Malay during a period in Penang (1893–99) and had baptized one Munshi Othman. In Singapore, he operated the Baba Mission and introduced the Boys Brigade into the colony.

Early missionary thought was hostile to Islam, on account of the theological challenges it posed to Christian thinking, and the experiences of missionaries in their work among Muslims which tended to produce hostility between the two.[56] This tension, which often hampered the role that missionaries played in the colony, was reflected in the discussions on missionary work that took place in the Society.[57] At the same time, the discussions on Islam in the Society can be seen to mirror the debates taking place in colonial and missionary circles between liberal and conservative schools. These in turn contributed to broader debates on the modernization of the Malays.

Three papers that highlighted these trends were G.M. Reith's 1895 paper on "Christianity and Mohammedanism" and W.G. Shellabear's papers on "Moslem Influence on the Malay Race" (1913) and "Mohammedanism, As Revealed in Its Literature" (1915). Reith's paper represented a more liberal tendency in the Church and, building upon Darwinian terminology and ideas of race, he highlighted the similarities rather than the differences between Islam and Christianity. So too would he suggest that the aim of missionaries should not solely be the conversion of Malays to Christianity, but the development of a critical intellectual spirit amongst the Malays that would mirror the critical re-adjustment which had occurred in Christianity. This suggested the possibility of a modernization of the Malay character beyond the narrow discourse on Malayness which dominated discussions of the Society.

This revaluation of Islam and the Malay character was also evident in the contributions of W.G. Shellabear. As Robert Hunt has argued, Shellabear was central to the revaluation of the role of Islam in Malay society by challenging the assumption of Islam as a mere veneer over Malay society, and in arguing for the need for missionaries to understand the true nature of Malay society to contribute towards its modernization and development.[58] In so doing, Shellabear would take up an Orientalist focus upon language and texts[59] to better understand the Malays, a position also prominent in his subsequent essay "Mohammedanism, As Revealed in Its Literature". Here Shellabear was reproducing assumptions that Islam played a limited role in civilizing Malay society. Comparing a list of Malay words derived from Arabic and Sanskrit, he argued that Hinduism was "by far the more effective civilising agency". He would also observe that the influence of Islam on the Malays was largely restricted to the sphere of religion, and the terminology for books and writing, but not to the language of government and commerce. To him, the adoption of words from European and Chinese languages suggested that "the Chinese and European peoples have done infinitely more than the Arabs to give the Malays the fruits of civilisation". This suggested to Shellabear that the reform and modernization of the Malays was to come from the influence of non-Islamic cultures, and not from Islam or the Malays themselves. An extension of this analysis was the role the British Empire was to play in the development of the Malays.

> I would suggest that what Islam has failed to do for the Malay race, Christian civilisation, as represented by the British Government and British commercial enterprise, has already gone far to accomplish.

Yet Shellabear's essay is important also for the contemporary reflections it would make on the role of Islam in the development of a modern nationalist identity among the Malays. Arguing that for them "Islam is not so much a religion as a nationality"—his was an early work identifying ideas of *bangsa* with Islam. Another observation was that of the influence of Turkish nationalism on the Malays which he saw in the development of an Islamic public sphere in the colony, one which was in contact with Islamic writings from the Middle East and South Asia. In doing so he was highlighting a process of modernization which, as we will similarly see amongst the Straits Chinese, broke with colonial assumptions of racial identity, and proposed an alternative model of modernization and social reform. This lay the groundwork for the advance of Islamic and nationalist movements in the period after the Society.[60]

Governing the Colony: Race, Crime, Opium and Law

Colonial concern towards the urban life of the colony was an experience common throughout the empire.[61] Urban government and planning were spheres in which ideas of "colonial difference" were confronted with the daily, and intimate, contact of Western and non-Western populations, and spaces within which Western morality and sensibility were confronted with transgression. Urban life produced a whole series of anxieties and concerns around sanitation, hygiene, crime, construction, sexuality, and migration, problematizing for colonial administrators how they should intervene in what was perceived as chaotic and transitory urban spaces in the name of colonial order. In this regard, the Straits Settlements, and particularly Singapore, were no exception.[62]

In keeping with the racialization of colonial thought, the "urban problem" was commonly identified as a "racial problem" and in Singapore, the "racial problem" was significantly seen as a "Chinese problem". From the 1830s onwards the Chinese formed the largest ethnic group in Singapore. By 1849 they formed over half of the population, and by the end of the nineteenth century over 70 per cent of the population was Chinese.[63] Of this population the vast majority were new migrants participating in a migration boom which, from the 1870s, saw a dramatic increase in Chinese immigrants to the colony, rising four-fold by the time the Society began meeting in 1893,[64] with only around 10 per cent of Chinese in the colony having been born there.[65] Of this population three divisions were stark. The first was the segregation along dialect and clan lines, which formed the basis for the self-organization of the Chinese in the colony through clan associations or *kongsi*. The second was the gender division with a particularly high ratio of Chinese men to women—as high as 14 men to 1 woman in the 1860s, before steadily declining in the 1870s to 6 men to 1 woman and then to 4 men to 1 woman in the 1890s.[66] Even after the major influx of Chinese after the 1870s, it was still believed by colonial officials that no "respectable", i.e. married Chinese women had migrated to the colony.[67] Finally, the third division was along class lines, between the new migrants of the coolie trade and petty traders, and the more established, and wealthier, traders and businessmen of the colony who were increasingly English educated and often more loyal subjects of the British Empire.

Such divisions brought with them problems for the colonial administrators. The Chinese were a population that British colonial administrators were largely unused to governing. The fact that in the early years many of the European administrators and traders had arrived in the colony via India, and the fact that the Straits Settlements were under the Government of India, meant that Europeans, who were familiar with Indian and Islamic law and customs, had no such familiarity with Chinese law, language, and customs. This was the source of constant dissatisfaction amongst the Chinese community when they turned to British courts for justice.[68] Indeed a figure such as Governor Blundell feared that any attempt to translate English law into Chinese was "utterly hopeless" on account of the nature of the language.[69]

The background history of this problem was addressed by W. Napier in his *Introduction to the Study of the Law Administered in the Colony of the Straits Settlements* which was published in 1898. In the following year Napier addressed the Society on "The Application of English Law to Asiatic Races, With Special Reference to the Chinese". As Napier would note the problem lay in the initial declaration of the Settlements as unoccupied thus allowing for the wholesale importation of English law without clear mention of the accommodation of customary law. This in effect allowed judges to apply English statute in the colony without consideration of local conditions. Napier noted the impact of this on the Chinese:

> The wholesale introduction of English law disappointed Chinese expectations and ideas on three points at least — (i) in its non-recognition of adoption, (ii) in its giving the wife and the daughters a large, and in the case of the latter an equal share with that of the sons, and (iii) in the impossibility of tying up property for several generations with a view to the due performance of the "sinchew" or ancestral worship. All these questions have been fought out in the Courts of the Colony, and in each instance have those Courts refused a recognition of the native custom.

Even though by the 1890s in the Malay States, Chinese law had attained a degree of recognition and a draft code on Chinese customary law was being developed, the legacy of the division between colonial administration and the Chinese population had already laid the groundwork for the Chinese to adopt a system of self-government for the resolution of disputes and the regulation of social life through the secret societies.

This system of self-government had long unsettled colonial administrators and merchants, and was perceived to be at the root of a whole series of issues: popular unrest and violence, petty crime, abuses in the coolie trade and the sex trade. These perceived transgressions had led to constant demands for the Chinese to be brought "to heel".[70] A key argument was that the majority of the Chinese who migrated to the colony never came into contact with the colonial state and that this reality was not conducive to law and order. In the aftermath of the Penang Riots of 1867, intervention began in the form of the Dangerous

Societies Suppression Ordinance 1869, with the intent of recognizing and registering secret societies. In 1876, an incident resulting in the ransacking of a post office in Singapore was seen by the colonial authorities as the work of Chinese secret societies and lent urgency to the establishment of the Chinese Protectorate in the colony in 1877.

The office of the Protector was initially established under William Pickering to handle matters related to the Chinese population of the settlement and to replace the previous dependence of the colonial government on prominent community leaders.[71] The main tasks of the Protector reflected the significant social problems which were seen to emanate from and impacted the Chinese. The Protector was tasked with the regulation of immigration, particularly male coolie labourers and female sex workers, the regulation of the sex trade and the regulation of secret societies. To respond to these concerns, a new bureaucracy was established for the registration, categorization, and surveillance of the Chinese with an emphasis placed on the regulation of the ports, brothels and lock hospitals, intervention in labour contracts and medical examinations. The Chinese Protector was also appointed as the Registrar of Societies to negotiate with the secret societies and bring them under the control of the colonial state.

How intervention should occur was a long-running debate in the colony.[72] In the end, the nature of the Chinese Protectorate was significantly shaped by Pickering's sensibilities and his experience mediating between warring Chinese secret societies in the Malay States in the 1860s and early 1870s. Drawing upon his long stint working in Hong Kong where he learned Mandarin and the southern Chinese dialects, Pickering, as with other moral reformers in the colony and wider empire, made the Protectorate an extension of his Christian morality and the "civilizing mission". His establishment, with the assistance of prominent Chinese and European missionaries, of a refuge and rehabilitation centre for women who had turned to sex work in 1878 was testimony to this moral drive.

Yet as the papers of the Society highlight, the role played by the category of race in this moral discourse was key. In the debates of the Society, these issues were particularly evident in the papers of D.J. Galloway on sexual disease, George M. Reith, and Arthur Knight on the opium trade and C.W.S. Kynnersley on the prison system in Singapore. All of these papers highlighted the governance of the Chinese, yet they are also prominent for their emphasis on the racial characteristics of the Chinese and their supposed susceptibility in the Straits to crime, sex work and opium smoking. This led to criticisms of liberal and moral reformers—in keeping with the writings of Brooke, Ridley and Collier outlined above—and the suggestion that such reform was inapplicable to the Chinese in the colony.

For Galloway, in the case of the sex trade, and Kynnersley, in reference to prison reform, they suggested the need for firm interventions to reform Chinese society in the Straits. Actions such as the detention of sex workers and petty criminals were therefore deemed desirable. Reith, who was a minister with the local Presbyterian church, regarded the smoking of opium by the Chinese as inevitable "The Chinaman will have his opium somehow; if not with the consent of the Government, then without it". He pointed out that its suppression would only lead to violence in the colony which justified for him the continuation of the opium trade.

Yet questions of urban government produced another practical question for colonial officials—namely, the extent to which the colonial government had any role to play in developing or facilitating the formation of a society in the Straits Settlements, or whether it was to be restricted only to governing "alien" populations. This was not only a significant area of debate within the Society amongst its European members, but it also was a major point of contention between its European and Straits Chinese members. This was evident in the contribution of W.R. Collyer to the Society in 1903 which pointed out that, if in the early years of the colony the distinction lay between the diverging application of law to European and non-European populations, by the turn of the twentieth century, the contradiction lay between the interests of business in the colony and legal order.

This, to him, raised the question of whether the colony was simply a place to make money or a place in which legal order had intrinsic value. This consideration was evident also in James Aitken's essay of 1907, "The Reformation of British Malaya", which contained a broad dissection of what he saw to be the failings of British policy in

Malaya and which, in his view, called for the British to generate for the colony a fuller level of economic and social development. The debate would, inevitably, also focus on the position of the Malays, and British responsibility to include them within the development of the colonial economy and colonial society. Aitken was an associate of Song Ong Siang, a prominent Straits Chinese lawyer who, together with Dr Lim Boon Keng, a society member, had started the *Straits Chinese Magazine*. It is very probable that the journal, the first English language one edited and published by the local community, provided both material as well as ideas for Aiken in his call for a more modernizing and developmental ethos within colonial policy.

The Colonial Order and the Chinese

It was through such debates over colonial policy in the Society that the English-speaking Straits Chinese could offer to the European members alternative perspectives on the colony's Chinese community. So too would they bring into question racial assumptions around Chineseness which structured the Society's discussions.[73] The presence within the Society of well-educated members of the Chinese community: Lim Boon Keng, Tan Teck Soon and later Choo Kia Peng, gave a prominent perspective on Chinese issues and subjects of concern. This was reinforced by the fact that their educational credentials and social standing often surpassed those of many of the European participants. The biographies of Lim Boon Keng and Tan Teck Soon, in particular, are informative as to their impressive political achievements and intellectual capabilities.

First educated at Raffles Institution, after his time as a Queen's Scholar in Edinburgh, Lim Boon Keng returned to Singapore in 1892 to establish a medical practice and was soon named a member of the Legislative Council. During this time, he emerged as a prominent social reformer and proponent of Chinese nationalism and Confucianism. He co-founded the Singapore Chinese Girls' School, together with Song Ong Siang, the Chinese Philomathic Society, and the Anti-Opium Society, as well as the *Straits Chinese Magazine*. Despite his Chinese roots and concerns, he was also a figure fiercely loyal to, though not uncritical of, the empire.[74] Aside from membership of the Society, he was also a founder of the Straits Chinese British Association, to give the Straits Chinese British a collective voice in the colony. He was also the colony's representative at the two royal coronations in 1902 and 1911, and an advocate of the British war effort through the Straits Volunteer Corps.[75] He was also a founding member of the Tongmenghui in Singapore, the precursor to the Kuomintang branch, whilst with the formation of the Chinese Republic he became a private secretary and personal physician to Sun Yat Sen and an Inspector-General of hospitals in Beijing. So too with Tan Teck Soon, who was also educated at Raffles Institution, before leaving for China on the Guthrie Scholarship to study at the Anglo-Chinese College in Amoy. In the years after his return, he became the editor and proprietor of the *Daily Advertiser*, a newspaper which covered news from mainland China. He was also an educator through the Singapore Chinese Educational Institute, an institute for adult education; the author of *Bright Celestials* with Reverend Arthur Lamont; and subsequently the manager of the Chinese-language newspaper *Thien Nan Shin Pao*. Alongside Lim Boon Keng he was also a regular contributor to the *Straits Chinese Magazine*.

Both these personalities highlight some common trends in the intellectual life of the Straits Chinese in the period. The first was loyalty to the British Empire through organizations such as the Straits Chinese British Association and the Straits Volunteer Corps. The second was the belief in the importance of modern science, medicine, technology, and education, and thus the progress that Western societies could offer to the societies of the East. The third was their committed participation in the development of a public sphere in the colony in which they contributed to a proliferation of print media in English, Malay and Chinese, as well as through their active role in the formation of new intellectual societies.[76] Finally, they were also participants in a diasporic nationalism and a cultural sense of Chineseness which provided a basis for differentiating themselves from Western and colonial thought and was also the starting point of a Malayan consciousness.[77]

These trends formed the basis for a complex political identity,[78] and their critical discussions in the Society, as well as their contributions to other forums such as the *Straits Chinese Magazine*, reveal that their accommodation to colonial thought was an uneasy one. In one of his most well-known contributions to the *Straits Chinese Magazine*, titled "Our Enemies", Lim Boon Keng sought to define the approach which the Straits Chinese should take in their interaction with Western knowledge:

> the Chinese-born British subjects are now in the state of transition, socially and intellectually, between the old ways of our forefathers and the new doctrines of European civilisation. Naturally, we are interested in the criticisms advanced in favour of or against the ancient systems and institutions, which had served our ancestors so well. It is excusable for us to be anxious to uphold these in the face of all attacks, but, however apt we are to act rashly and to regard influences which threaten to change our views as hostile to the integrity of permanence of our institutions, social or religious, we should conduct our defence intelligently and reasonably.[79]

This dynamic of accepting "the new doctrines of European civilisation" whilst "intelligently and reasonably" defending traditional institutions was not unique. It was also a theme common to the experiences of the creole and "middling" classes in the colonial world, who, while accepting the modernizing framework of colonial thought, attempted to differentiate themselves from it on the basis of their own national culture.[80]

This was perhaps most evident in the themes and concepts which the Straits Chinese intellectuals utilized in their discussions in the Society in which they mobilized ideas of liberalism, nationalism, race, and evolution, yet in ways that countered European doctrines of racial superiority, racial difference and illiberal models of colonial government.[81] Their challenge occurred in three key ways.

The first took the form of social reform movements, which sought to bring the Straits Chinese society in line with modern values. This was expressed in Tan Teck Soon and Lim Boon Keng's advocacy for education, and opposition to the queue and opium consumption as contained in the pages of the *Straits Chinese Magazine,* as well as in their contributions to the Society. In Lim Boon Keng's essay on "Opium versus Alcohol", themes of race, political economy, and medicine would be mobilized to call for the prohibition on opium use.[82]

The second was an attempt to link traditional Chinese society, culture, and religion with modern forms of knowledge; and in effect, highlighting a culturally Chinese basis for modern systems of thought. This resonated with Tan Teck Soon's revaluation of traditional Chinese thought as highlighted by Christine Doran who pointed to Tan's emphasis on themes of "change, dynamism, progress and popular sovereignty in his conception of the centuries-long development of Chinese society".[83] This was evident too in Lim Boon Keng's writings on Confucianism in which he sought to continuously highlight the compatibility between Confucian thought and modernity.[84] He would not only see a Confucian basis for liberal, socialist and evolutionary thought. He also posited Confucianism as a universal and rational religion, applicable to all societies which could provide for an alternative way of thinking the new category of "race", beyond questions of supremacy.[85] For Lim this formed part of a broader criticism of racial discrimination within the British Empire.[86] Attending the Universal Races Congress in London in 1911 Lim argued that Chinese society did not have any "race-prejudice which would make the colour line a question in their country".[87]

Finally, this took the form of a critique of Western ideas of modernity, often in terms of its materialism, nihilism, and lack of spirituality; and the ensuing argument that non-Western cultures offered a more ethical form of modernity. The resulting logic was a long-running theme in Lim Boon Keng's thought. Earlier, in 1894, Lim was discussing the issue of the degeneration of the Baba, arguing that in their emulation of European culture and materialism, the Straits Chinese had "deteriorated morally" and lost their Chinese culture.

> The Baba class, as young men, chiefly engaged themselves as clerks to merchants. Their ambition was to dress, to be stylish and in every way to emulate the airs and graces of the Europeans. This led them into extravagances wholly foreign to their forefathers. Money-making became the chief aim. ... If they wished to progress at all, their only hope lay in keeping to the lines laid down by China centuries ago, instead of endeavouring to assimilate an exotic civilisation.[88]

These themes of Baba degeneration and the regressive effects of commercial life in the Straits was a theme found in the *Straits Chinese*

Magazine. It was also central to Lim's essay on "The Chinese in British Malaya" which was read to the Society in 1910. Here he would again argue that the pampered life in the Straits and the mixing of Chinese blood with Malay blood had led the Straits Chinese to "despise labour, and prefer the easy-going dependence of a clerkship to any kind of work involving toil". This was a theme that would also emerge in Lim's war-time lectures, where he argued that the Straits Chinese had become "machines of the merchants", their business houses had entered into decay and they had inherited from the Malays a distaste for hard work. This mirrors similar themes of degeneration that emerged in colonial Bengal in the mid-nineteenth century. In the same manner that Bengali intellectuals came to oppose British modernity to the ethical culture of Hinduism, for Lim the solution to the degeneration of the Baba was adherence to Confucianism.[89]

Confucianism was here understood by Lim as a system of morality and education that provided the basis for an ethical society and one which could account for economic and social development whilst maintaining order and the importance of traditional customs. As he would argue in "The Chinese Revolutionary Movement in Malaya" and "Socialism Among the Chinese", adherence to Western political thought had led extremists in China towards ideas of nihilism and anarchism, the abolition of religion and the advocacy of equality in all things. To combat these, Lim advocated Confucian values and Confucian forms of socialism as a path that would avoid such extremes. This ideological position would later lead Lim into disputes with more radical nationalists in China who rejected a Confucian basis for a modern Chinese nation. Lim who remained unconvinced would continue to advocate for a Confucian basis for modern Chinese nationalism.[90]

Hybrid Identities

In the case of Malaya, the nationalist schema was complicated by the fact that the Straits Chinese were a community in a multi-ethnic society. This fact placed them outside of monolithic discourses of nation, identity and belonging.[91] What is discernible in the writings of the Straits Chinese on modernity and nationalism was both a transnational concern with China and Chineseness, as well as a concern with local culture and politics, which formed the basis of a hybrid social and political identity.[92]

This hybrid identity was evident in the public sphere of the Straits Chinese. In their early literary endeavours, the Straits Chinese pursued predominantly Malay literary forms, the *pantun* and the *syair*, whilst the Straits Chinese press pursued publications in Romanized Malay, in particular the *Surat Khabar Peranakan* (Straits Chinese Herald), *Bintang Timor* and the *Malaysia Advocate*. Such papers, which featured national and international news, opinion, and literary pieces, formed the basis for the interaction between the Straits Chinese and Malay communities. *Bintang Timor*, for example, received sponsorship and contributions from the Dato' Bentara Luar of Johor, whilst the paper also ran opinion pieces on Malay issues. Most notably this occurred in a series of eleven articles in 1894 under the title "*Mengapa Melayu Layu?*" (Why are the Malays Withering Away?) in which the author, writing under a pseudonym, "offered a scathing analysis of the alleged reasons for Malay economic and educational backwardness", which reproduced many of the terms of European criticism of the Malays, and in return received a scathing reply from the *Jawi Peranakan* newspaper.[93]

As this exchange evidenced, the dynamics of hybridity did not escape the space and confines of European thought. Similarly, as in the case of Bengal analysed by Chatterjee, the Straits Chinese leaders continued to accept many of the terms of European reasoning related to issues of racial difference, underdevelopment and government although they also challenged these terms in the name of the future development and modernization of the peoples of the colony.[94] In doing so it can be argued that they were contributing towards the development of a proto-Malayan nationalism that situated the colony as a space for the development of modern society and as a space of political belonging. Nevertheless, in so far as this was true, it was to be mediated by two important factors. On the one hand, there was a belief that the British Empire would itself be a significant agent in the modernization of the colony; and on the other hand, there was also a recognition that racial differences within the colony were fundamental dividing lines, which would structure the colony's future political development.

This juxtaposition of consciousness and reasoning was evident in Tan Teck Soon's essay on educational problems in the colony—an essay in which he would take up a problem central to the issue of social reform amongst the Straits Chinese and which touched also upon the educational challenges faced by the other communities of the Peninsula. Key in his essay was the critique of the supreme position of the Europeans in the colony and in particular their lack of concern for the peoples of the settlement. Echoing his earlier critiques of British governance in the colony,[95] he argued that the Europeans lived in a world separated from the other members of the colony and made only "feeble and spasmodic attempts" to understand and reform the other communities. Criticizing this failure, he stressed that the British Empire had a duty to elevate and modernize the population in the colony whilst acknowledging that the potential for modernization would be determined by the nature of the constituent groups in the colony.

Turning to the Malays, Tan pointed out that they were as a group defined by apathy towards local government—even towards those ordinances "affecting even their highest interests". The only remedy for this situation according to Tan lay in "increasing mutual knowledge" and a "more extended intercourse and exchange of ideas between governors and governed". For him, this necessitated turning Malaya into a political community, in which all groups would participate and discourse. But he also recognized that what was lacking in Malaya was a sense of community itself, made more acute by the reality of the "plural society" in which "except as regards the strenuous pursuit of dollars, each leads a life of his own entirely indifferent to the existence or proximity of the other". Tan's opinion on the plural society in the colony may be seen to anticipate Furnivall's later depiction of the "plural society" of colonial Java and Burma, in which Europeans, Chinese and natives, each contained within their own religion, culture and language, met only in the marketplace.[96] Yet this limited community was also understood by Tan in racialized terms. Echoing European thinking on the Malays, Tan argued that the Malay "want of stamina and character is inherent, and if entirely left to itself the race will in all likelihood degenerate and die away in a not very distant future". For him, what was required for the "child of the soil" was their protection and upliftment by the British.

Hence his advocacy of the education of the Malays, and in particular, of Malay women.

Similar themes would also emerge in a later essay by Lim Boon Keng, "The Chinese in British Malaya" which dealt with the effect of life in Malaya upon the Chinese. One significant factor for Lim was the mixing of Malay with Chinese blood and the belief that life in the tropics was tending towards the degeneration of the resident Chinese race and producing inferior offspring. To him, it was fortunate that "the infusion of Chinese blood from China has frequently checked the degenerative process" and whilst the education of girls could delay degeneration, he argued that "unless young people are removed from the tropics, there seems very little hope of maintaining the stamina and the virile qualities of the race-attributes due principally to the Chinese environment, which itself is the outcome of six millenniums of ceaseless social struggles".

In Malaya, on the other hand, Lim noted that "the pampered lives more of these people lead" ensured that Chinese children were becoming more and more like the Malays. The example of those born in Malaya who were seen to despise manual labour and prefer office work was provided for his broader arguments on the degeneration of the Baba. This concern with degeneration also reflected broader thinking on racial mixing which as in H.N. Ridley's essay to the Society on Eurasians, highlighted the racial weaknesses that mixing was seen to produce. All the same, rejecting the idea of Europeanization, which he argued was "unattainable and undesirable" to halt the degenerative process, he advocated a return to the teaching of Chinese morality and an education system mixing manual labour with an academic curriculum.

Similarly, as with Tan, Lim was equally concerned with the position of the Malays in the colony. Colonial policy, he argued, did not need to interfere with the Chinese because as a race they had the means to uplift themselves if given a system of just and equitable treatment. Drawing attention to mukim regulations in Malacca, he argued that the Malays would require "special care and protection" without which they would lose out to "well-equipped foreigners—Europeans, Indians or Chinese". For him, "Justice requires" therefore "that the Malays should receive more attention from the Government" as well as necessitated differential treatment between the Malays and Chinese to ensure their mutual economic and social development. These important themes emerging from the Society proceedings and developed out of ideas and debates of race, culture and modernity would also assume centre stage in the development of Malayan nationalism later in the 1930s and 1940s.

Conclusion

With the advent of the First World War many European members of the Society were conscripted for war service, whilst others were preoccupied with business, and the Society witnessed dwindling membership. As no records have been kept after 1916 it is not known when precisely the Society was dissolved. It would appear that meetings continued to be recorded between 1916 and 1918 and that the Society continued to meet until at least 1923, but it would seem that by this date meetings were less regular and less well attended.[97] In the post-War years the Society was also deprived of its prominent Straits Chinese members, Lim Boon Keng, the last recorded president of the Society, would be appointed the President of Xiamen University in China in 1921, whilst Tan Teck Soon passed away in 1922. The memory of the Society continued, however, to impact the intellectual life of Singapore. Colonial Secretary Sir Andrew Caldecott would suggest in 1935 for the Raffles College Union to become "an essay club and dialectical society on the lines of the Singapore Philosophical Society", directing members to the papers of *Noctes Orientales*.[98]

Nevertheless, beyond the model of the philosophical society the Society represented, the ideas propounded in the Society can also be said to have had far-reaching consequences beyond its life. The mixture of ideas around liberalism, Darwinism, colonial modernity, and race, constituted the basis for a dominant ideology in colonial Malaya, centred on the necessity of European modernization, a critique of liberal ideas of empire, the protection of native races, and the racial distinction between Europeans and Asians. Yet as the Society also evidenced, this schema also contained its own tensions—tensions which were played out in the presentations and critiques of the Society. More importantly, in opening a space for non-Europeans to engage with colonial thought, the Society also made possible its appropriation and modification and, as in other colonial learned societies, contributed towards the development of an independent intellectual culture in British Malaya, developing around ideas of nationalism and national modernity. This engaged not only with transnational flows of nationalist and modernist thought in the colonial world but also formed the basis for early nationalist thought and development in the Malayan Peninsula. In this process the categories of race and identity remained open to modification, appropriation, and debate. At the same time, they remained an anchoring point around which the intellectual culture of the early twentieth century through to the post-colonial period contested and collided.

Notes

1. See *The Rules of the Straits Philosophical Society* (Singapore: Straits Philosophical Society, 1893), British Library: 003395413.
2. Ibid.
3. Peter Clark, *British Clubs and Societies 1580–1800: The Origins of an Associational World* (Oxford: Oxford University Press, 2000), chap. 11; Benjamin Cohen, *In the Club: Associational Life in Colonial South Asia* (Manchester: Manchester University Press, 2015).
4. T.N. Harper, "Globalism and the Pursuit of Authenticity: The Making of a Diasporic Public Sphere in Singapore", *Sojourn* 12, no. 2 (1997): 272.
5. Ibid., p. 263; Lynn Hollen Lees, *Planting Empire, Cultivating Subjects* (Cambridge: Cambridge University Press, 2017), pp. 150–55.
6. See Su Lin Lewis, "Between Orientalism and Nationalism: The Learned Society at the Making of Southeast Asia", *Modern Intellectual History* 10: 353–74.
7. Ibid., p. 1.
8. Carol Ann Boshier, *Mapping Cultural Nationalism: The Scholars of the Burma Research Society, 1910–1935* (Copenhagen: NIAS Press, 2018).
9. See Partha Chatterjee, *The Black Hole of Empire: History of a Global Practice of Power* (Princeton: Princeton University Press, 2012), pp. 126–33.
10. Jim Jose, "Imperial Rule and the Ordering of Intellectual Space: The Formation of the Straits Philosophical Society", *Crossroads* 12, no. 2 (1998): 28–34.
11. *First Annual Report of the Straits Philosophical Society*, 1893–4, British Library.
12. Gilbert Edward Brooke, Roland St. John Braddell, and Walter Makepeace, *One Hundred Years of Singapore*, vol. 2 (London: John Murray, 1921),

p. 302. *Eighth Annual Report of the Straits Philosophical Society*, 1900–1, British Library; *Twenty-First Annual Report of the Straits Philosophical Society*, 1913–14, British Library.
13. "Letters to the Editor", *The Singapore Free Press and Mercantile Advertiser*, 15 November 1935, p. 2.
14. "How to Bring Culture to Singapore", *The Straits Times*, 4 November 1935.
15. "Letters to the Editor", *The Singapore Free Press and Mercantile Advertiser*, 15 November 1935.
16. Ibid.
17. H.N. Ridley, ed., *Noctes Orientales* (Singapore: Kelly and Walsh, 1913).
18. Ibid., p. ii.
19. "Letters to the Editor", *The Singapore Free Press and Mercantile Advertiser*, 15 November 1935.
20. Ibid.
21. Ridley, *Noctes Orientales*, "Our Philosophers", *The Straits Times*, 21 May 1913.
22. Harper, "Globalism and the Pursuit of Authenticity".
23. Frederick Cooper and Laura Ann Stoler, "Between Metropole and Colony: Rethinking a Research Agenda", in *Tensions of Empire: Colonial Cultures in a Bourgeois World*, edited by Stoler Ann Laura and Cooper Frederick (California, USA: University of California Press, 1997), p. 31.
24. Ibid.
25. Eric Hobsbawm, *The Age of Empire 1875–1915* (New York: Vintage Books, 1989), pp. 187–91.
26. Francisco Bettencourt, *Racisms: From the Crusades to the Twentieth Century* (Princeton: Princeton University Press, 2014), pp. 271–306.
27. Partha Chatterjee, *The Nation and Its Fragments: Colonial and Postcolonial Histories* (Princeton: Princeton University Press, 1994), pp. 16–22.
28. On the colonial construction of primordialist and culturalist notions of community, see Arjun Appadurai, *Modernity At Large: Cultural Dimensions of Globalization* (Minnesota: University of Minnesota Press, 1996).
29. Sudipta Kaviraj, *The Unhappy Consciousness: Bankimchandra Chattopadhyay and the Formation of Nationalist Discourse in India* (Oxford: Oxford University Press, 1995), p. 113.
30. Benedict Anderson, *Imagined Communities: Reflections on the Origin and Spread of Nationalism*, revised ed. (Verso: London and New York, 2006), chap. 10.
31. Bernard Cohn, "The Census, Social Structure and Objectification in South Asia", in *An Anthropologist among the Historians and Other Essays* (New Delhi: Oxford University Press, 1987); Charles Hirschman, "The Meaning and Measurement of Ethnicity in Malaysia: An Analysis of Census Classifications", *The Journal of Asian Studies* 46, no. 3 (1987): 555–82.

32. Karuna Mantena, *Alibis of Empire: Henry Maine and the Ends of Liberal Imperialism* (New Jersey: Princeton University Press, 2010).
33. Mahmood Mamdani, *Define and Rule: Native as Political Identity* (Cambridge, Massachusetts: Harvard University Press, 2012).
34. John Stuart Mill, *Considerations on Representative Government* (London: Longman Green, 1865), p. 86.
35. C.A. Bayly, *Recovering Liberties: Indian Thought in the Age of Liberalism and Empire* (Cambridge: Cambridge University Press, 2011).
36. M.R. Frost, "Asia's Maritime Networks and the Colonial Public Sphere, 1840–1920", *New Zealand Journal of Asian Studies* 6, no. 2 (2004): 81.
37. Harper, "Globalism and the Pursuit of Authenticity".
38. Emily Sadka, "The Journal of Sir Hugh Low, Perak, 1877", *Journal of the Malayan Branch of the Royal Asiatic Society* 27, no. 4 (168) (1954): 25–26.
39. Daniel P.S. Goh, "Imperialism and 'Medieval' Natives: The Malay Image in Anglo-American Travelogues and Colonialism in Malaya and the Philippines", *International Journal of Cultural Studies* 10, no. 3 (2007): 323–41.
40. C.A. Bayly, "Maine and Change in Nineteenth-century India", in *The Victorian Achievement of Sir Henry Maine: A Centennial Reappraisal*, edited by Alan Diamond (Cambridge: Cambridge University Press, 1991), p. 391.
41. See Farish Noor, *A Deconstructive History of Pahang: From Inderapura to Darul Makmur*, 2nd ed. (Kuala Lumpur: Silverfish Books, 2011), pp. 51–62.
42. See Charles Hirschman, "The Making of Race in Colonial Malaya: Political Economy and Racial Ideology", *Sociological Forum* 1, no. 2 (1986): 330–61; Charles Hirschman, "The Meaning and Measurement of Ethnicity in Malaysia: An Analysis of Census Classifications", *The Journal of Asian Studies* 46, no. 3 (1987): 555–82; Timo Kortteinen, "Embedded Ethnicity: On the Narratives of Ethnic Identity in Malaysia and Sri Lanka", *Suomen Antropologi: Journal of the Finnish Anthropological Society* 32 (2007).
43. Lim Teck Ghee, *Origins of a Colonial Economy: Land and Agriculture in Perak 1874-1897* (Penang: Penerbit Universiti Sains Malaysia, 1976).
44. Gareth Knapman, *Race and British Colonialism in Southeast Asia, 1770–1870: John Crawfurd and the Politics of Equality* (London: Routledge, 2017); Syed Muhd. Khairudin Aljunied, *Rethinking Raffles: A Study of Sir Thomas Stamford Raffles' Discourse on Religions amongst Malays* (Singapore: Marshall Cavendish, 2005).
45. Sandra Khor Manickam, *Taming the Wild: Aborigines and Racial Knowledge in Colonial Malaya* (Singapore: NUS Press, 2015).
46. The study of the relationship between colonialism and the problem of "character" is central to Syed Hussein Alatas' *Myth of the Lazy Native*. See chap. 8. See also Hans Pols, "The Nature of the Native Mind: Contested Views of Dutch Colonial Psychiatrists in the former Dutch East Indies", in *Psychiatry and Empire*, edited by Sloan Mahone and Megan Vaughan (London: Palgrave Macmillan, 2007).

47. Daniel P.S. Goh, "States of Ethnography: Colonialism, Resistance, and Cultural Transcription in Malaya and the Philippines, 1890s–1930s", *Comparative Studies in Society and History* 49, no. 1 (2007): 114–16; Goh, "Imperialism and 'Medieval' Natives".
48. Ibid.
49. Hugh Clifford, *In Court and Kampong: Being Tales and Sketches of Native Life in the Malay Peninsula* (G. Richards, 1897), p. 3.
50. Syed Hussein Alatas, *The Myth of the Lazy Native: A Study of the Image of the Malays, Filipinos and Javanese from the 16th to the 20th Century and its Function in the Ideology of Colonial Capitalism* (London: Frank Cass, 1977). For the debate between Paul Kratoska and Lim Teck Ghee, see Paul Kratoska, "Rice Cultivation and the Ethnic Division of Labor in British Malaya", *Comparative Studies in Society and History* 24, no. 2 (April 1982): 280–314; Lim Teck Ghee, "British Colonial Administration and the 'Ethnic Division of Labour' in Malaya", *Kajian Malaysia* 2 (1984): 28–66.
51. Donna Amoroso, *Traditionalism and the Ascendancy of the Malay Ruling Class in Malaya* (Petaling Jaya: SIRD, 2014).
52. On the orientalization of the Islam of the Malays, see Azhar Ibrahim, *Historical Imagination and Cultural Responses to Colonialism and Nationalism: A Critical Malay(sian) Perspective* (Malaysia: SIRD, 2017), pp. 59–63; William Roff, "Islam Obscured? Some Reflections on Studies of Islam & Society in Southeast Asia", *Archipel* 21, no. 1 (1985): 7–34.
53. Sumit K. Mandal, *Becoming Arab: Creole Histories and Modern Identity in the Malay World* (Cambridge: Cambridge University Press, 2017).
54. Azhar Ibrahim, *Historical Imagination*, pp. 59–63.
55. See for example Alatas's concept of the captive mind.
56. Robert Hunt, "The Legacy of William Shellabear", *International Bulletin of Missionary Research* (January 2002): 28–31.
57. See, for example, Hare's essay published in *Noctes Orientales*, "Missionaries in China".
58. Ibid., pp. 28–31.
59. Edward Said, *Orientalism* (New York, USA: Vintage Books, 1994), p. 321.
60. Anthony Milner, *The Invention of Politics in Colonial Malaya* (Cambridge: Cambridge University Press, 2002), chap. 6 and 7.
61. Robert Home, *Of Planting and Planning: The Making of British Colonial Cities* (London: Routledge, 2013).
62. See Brenda S.A. Yeoh, *Contesting Space in Colonial Singapore: Power Relations and the Urban Built Environment* (Singapore: Singapore University Press, 2003); James Francis Warren, *Rickshaw Coolie: A People's History of Singapore, 1880–1940* (Singapore: Singapore University Press, 2003).
63. Saw Swee-Hock, "Population Trends in Singapore, 1819–1967", *Journal of Southeast Asian History* 10, no. 1 (1969): 41.
64. James Francis Warren, *Ah Ku and Karayuki-San: Prostitution in Singapore 1870–1940* (Singapore: NUS Press, 2003), p. 33.

65. Warren, *Rickshaw Coolie*, p. 19.
66. In the same period the gender ratio of the Malay population maintained itself around 1.2–1.6 men to women. Saw, "Population Trends in Singapore, 1819–1967", p. 42.
67. Ibid., p. 43.
68. See Constance M. Turnbull, "Communal Disturbances in the Straits Settlements in 1857", *Journal of the Malayan Branch of the Royal Asiatic Society* 31, no. 1 (May 1958): 94–144.
69. Ibid., p. 96. See also Rachael Leow, *Taming Babel: Language in the Making of Malaysia* (Cambridge: Cambridge University Press, 2018).
70. Ng Siew Yoong, "The Chinese Protectorate in Singapore, 1877–1900", *Journal of Southeast Asian History* 2, no. 1 (March 1961): 76–99.
71. "William Pickering", *Singapore Infopedia*, at https://eresources.nlb.gov.sg/infopedia/articles/SIP_1345_2008-12-03.html.
72. The differing perspectives on the Chinese problem can be found in C.M. Turnbull, *A History of Modern Singapore, 1819–2005* (Singapore: NUS Press, 2009), chap. 3. Some argued for the complete suppression of secret societies, others for restrictions on Chinese immigration into the colony.
73. On the broader contestation of the rule of colonial difference by the Straits Chinese, see Daniel P.S. Goh, "Unofficial Contentions: The Postcoloniality of Straits Chinese Political Discourse in the Straits Settlements Legislative Council", *Journal of Southeast Asian Studies* 41, no. 3 (2010): 483–507.
74. Lim Boon Keng, "Race and Empire with Special Reference to British Malaya", in *The Great War from a Confucian Point of View, and Kindred Topics, Being Lectures Delivered during 1914–1917* (Singapore: Straits Albion Press, 1917), pp. 98–115; Lim Boon Keng, "The Race Question in Colonial Administration", *The Straits Chinese Magazine* 9, no. 1 (March 1905).
75. See the pamphlet co-written by Lim Boon Keng, Straits Chinese British Association, *Duty to the British Empire: Being an Elementary Guide for Straits Chinese during the Great War* (Singapore: Straits Albion Press, 1915).
76. On the role played by the *Straits Chinese Magazine*, see Neil Khor, "Imperial Cosmopolitan Malaya: A Study of Realist Fiction in the 'Straits Chinese Magazine'", *Journal of the Malaysian Branch of the Royal Asiatic Society* 81, no. 1 (June 2008): 27–47.
77. See Chatterjee, *The Nation and Its Fragments*, chap. 3; Ulbe Bosma, "Citizens of Empire: Some Comparative Observations on the Evolution of Creole Nationalism in Colonial Indonesia", *Comparative Studies in Society and History* 46, no. 4 (2004): 656–81; Cemil Aydin, *The Politics of Anti-Westernism in Asia: Visions of World Order in Pan-Islamic and Pan-Asian Thought* (New York: Columbia University Press, 2007).
78. For a later account of the emerging post-colonial identity of the Straits Chinese, see Goh, "Unofficial Contentions".
79. Lim Boon Keng, "Our Enemies", *The Straits Chinese Magazine* 1 (March 1894): 52–58.

80. Goh, "Unofficial Contentions".
81. Lim Boon Keng, "The Great War from a Confucian Point of View", in *Essays of Lim Boon Keng on Confucianism*, edited and translated by Yan Chunbao (Singapore: World Scientific, 2015), pp. 216–17.
82. Lim's role as a doctor and his mobilization of medical and biological concepts to criticize colonial society can be seen to mirror other nationalist figures. See Hans Pols, *Nurturing Indonesia: Medicine and Decolonisation in the Dutch East Indies* (Cambridge: Cambridge University Press, 2018).
83. Christine Doran, "Historicism and Anti-Colonialism in Singapore", *International Journal of Interdisciplinary Social Sciences* 1, no. 2 (2006): 93–99.
84. Lim Boon Keng, *Essays of Lim Boon Keng on Confucianism*.
85. Lim Boon Keng, "The Confucian Cult", in ibid.
86. Lim Boon Keng, "Race and Empire with Special Reference to British Malaya"; Lim Boon Keng, "The Race Question in Colonial Administration", *The Straits Chinese Magazine* 9, no. 1 (March 1905).
87. Universal Races Congress London, *Record of the Proceedings of the First Universal Races Congress Held at the University of London, July 26–29, 1911* (London: P.S. King & Son, 1911), p. 35.
88. "Has the Baba Fallen or Risen?", *The Straits Times*, 31 March 1894.
89. Andrew Sartori, *Bengal in Global Concept History: Culturalism in the Age of Capital* (Chicago, IL: Chicago University Press, 2008), chap. 4.
90. Wang Gungwu, "Lu Xun, Lim Boon Keng and Confucianism", in *China and the Chinese Overseas* (Singapore: Times Academic Press, 2003).
91. See Prasenjit Duara, "Nationalists Among Transnationals: Overseas Chinese and the Idea of China, 1900–1911", in *Ungrounded Empires: The Cultural Politics of Modern Chinese Transnationalism*, edited by Aihwa Ong and Donald M. Nonini (London: Routledge, 1997), p. 40.
92. Harper, "Globalism and the Pursuit of Authenticity". On the dynamics of Straits Chinese identity, see Shin Mun Ng, "Peranakan Identity at the Crossroads of Empire, the Malay World and the Sinophone World, c. 1900-1930", Unpublished Master's Thesis, University of Cambridge, 30 May 2016.
93. William Roff, *The Origins of Malay Nationalism* (Kuala Lumpur: Penerbit Universiti Malaya, 1980), p. 54.
94. Chatterjee, *The Nation and its Fragments*.
95. See Tan's Critique of Gilbert E. Brooke's "The Disadvantages of Education for the Lower Classes".
96. J.S. Furnivall, *Colonial Policy and Practice* (Cambridge: Cambridge University Press, 1939).
97. "Letters to the Editor", *The Singapore Free Press and Mercantile Advertiser*, 15 November 1935; Brooke et al., *One Hundred Years of Singapore*, vol. 2, p. 302.
98. "How to Bring Culture to Singapore", *The Straits Times*, 4 November 1935.

I

The Ideological Basis of Colonial Rule

2

DUTCH AND ENGLISH ADMINISTRATION IN THE EAST

Essay

13 January 1894

by *Walter J. Napier*

Editors' Note

Napier's paper, presented in the early years of the Society, is significant for its comparison of Dutch and English colonial systems at a time when the subject of land policy was being debated in the colony.[1] In comparing the two systems, Napier joined a tradition of contrasting the Dutch Cultivation System with Britain's liberal colonial policy. This was prominent in the writings of Stamford Raffles and John Crawfurd in the early nineteenth century. So too was it prominent in J.W.B. Money's journey to Java in the aftermath of the Indian Mutiny of 1857,[2] as well as later in Alfred Russel Wallace's support in *The Malay Archipelago* (1869) for the Dutch protectionist system, which he saw as superior to the exposure of native populations to free competition.[3]

The paper compares the British and Dutch systems by focusing upon the divergent principles which underlay their approaches to land policy. British liberalism, with its aim to produce a market in land, was criticized by Napier for its tendency to lead to the displacement and indebtedness of native populations. This was contrasted with the "picture of prosperity and order" he had witnessed in the Dutch Indies, based upon their protection of customary land law. These positions reflected earlier debates between Swettenham and Maxwell in Malaya.[4] On Napier's part, whilst he was not uncritical of the Dutch, his experience led him to call for a more protectionist ethos and he would go on to provide justifications for Malay land reservations: "where a race is found by a conquering European power to be in possession of the land of the country, it is permissible—nay, it is the duty of that power by its legislation to prevent that race being ousted".

Ridley, in his response, also criticized Britain's liberal approach. He argued that the "natives" did not appreciate the "high technicalities" of English law, and suggested that in other areas the British could learn from the Dutch. They could follow the Dutch regulations on the movement of natives and their curfew system. The imposition of forced cultivation would encourage the "lazy Malay", who "will not do any more work than he is actually compelled to", to produce more.

What is also interesting about the paper and its commentary is the way in which they anticipate the acclaimed comparative work on British and Dutch colonialism and its impact on the colonized subjects by the noted American scholar Rupert Emerson by several decades.[5]

More than two years ago I paid a short visit to Java, and, like most who have travelled there, became interested in the country and its inhabitants. It is not of my personal observation that I can speak this evening; a mere sightseer, anxious to find cool spots where he can sleep under blankets, without knowledge of the Dutch language, has but few opportunities of really judging of the institutions of a country, and accordingly my paper is chiefly derived from books.

My object is to examine the principles of government which the Dutch have exercised in dealing with their subjects in the East, comparing them with those employed by ourselves. I shall first give you a brief sketch of the history of Dutch rule in Java since Raffles landed in 1811 (for it is to Java that I intend to confine my attention), and shall then point out what appear to be the chief differences between the Dutch system of administration and our own.

The condition of Java at that time I will summarize as follows: the Dutch only held under their direct administration a small part of the country in the North between Batavia and Cheribon, whilst the rest of the island was left to the native chiefs. From these chiefs they required the delivery of produce either gratis or at inadequate prices, and in addition required labour to be given free for any public works they might deem desirable. They had no dealings with the cultivators themselves; everything was done through the chiefs, consequently the wretched *ryots* had not only to satisfy the demands of the Dutch, but in addition those of the chiefs themselves. No private property in land was recognized by the chiefs as belonging to the cultivators. The land was occupied, not by individuals, but by village communities, which still bore unmistakeable signs of a primitive communism. The village was kept in order by the headman elected by the villagers. Each year the paddy-fields were allotted among them, each of them paying his share of the land revenue to the village fund. The land revenue was nominally one-fifth of the produce of the lands, but under unscrupulous officials this was often increased to as much as two-fifths, and Raffles found this rate not an uncommon one. Besides land revenue, the *ryots* had to contribute on births or marriages taking place in the chief's family, and besides there were charitable and religious funds to be subscribed to. Officials, high and low, passing through villages, considered themselves entitled to free supplies; and, to crown all, each cultivator had to work one day out of every five for his chief without remuneration.

So much for the cultivators of the soil; the people on the coast had also been ruined through the restrictions placed on their commerce, and this had driven them into smuggling and piracy.

Nor had the Dutch gained by their system of monopoly. From 1613 to 1693 the nett profits of the Dutch East India Company were 48 million guilders, or on an average about 600,000 guilders per annum, but from 1697 to 1779 the losses were so enormous as to overbalance the preceding profits, and taking the whole period from 1613 to 1779 their total loss amounted to 85 million guilders. When the British landed in Java, paper money nominally worth $6.50 was only worth $1.00.

Raffles set to work in earnest to free agriculture and trade from the heavy manacles with which it was loaded; to free the cultivators from forced labour, delivery of produce at inadequate prices; to abolish as far as possible duties on internal and external trade, and to encourage shipping.

But he did not set to work except after due inquiry and deliberation. The province of Bantam first claimed his attention; it was in a state of anarchy when he landed in Java, but he promptly abolished the pepper monopoly and forced labour, imposing in their stead a land tax levied on equitable principles. So successful was this policy that the revenue in one year amounted to 100,000 rupees. One of Raffles' first measures was to appoint a committee of investigation under Colonel Colin Mackenzie, and in the result the system of land revenue first introduced into Bantam was extended to the whole island.

The Dutch, as we have seen, had no direct relations with the cultivators of the soil, but Raffles was determined to establish such relations, and to recognize no one between the English authority and the cultivator. The work of surveying the island and arranging the amount which was to be paid by the cultivator as land tax was enormous. The result of Raffles' labours I will summarize as follows:

(1) The powers of the native chiefs to be restricted to police work, the whole of that work being entrusted to them, payment being made for their labour in land or money.

(2) The Dutch monopolies were abolished and freedom of cultivation established; forced delivery of produce and all tolls on inland trade were abandoned, and the port dues were equalized. Last, but by no means least, forced labour was abolished.

(3) In order to provide revenue wherewith to administer the country, Raffles commuted all the imposts on the cultivators into one fixed tax, being about two-fifths instead of one-fifth of the produce as formerly. The lands were let out by the Government to the heads of the villages at fixed rates, provision being made that the lands would be relet to the cultivator. It was clearly Raffles' intention to introduce the *ryotwari* system into Java, and to make the cultivator practically proprietor of the soil. This attempt to introduce into Java the *ryotwari* system is in Dutch eyes the forefront of Raffles' offending, and it may be that

it would have been better to have recognized the village community instead of the individual as the unit, as was done in some of the later land settlements in India. Absolute property, according to English law, gives a right to sell and to mortgage, together with a liability to be sold up, and these rights and liabilities Raffles intended to introduce, as we have introduced it here and in India.

The Dutch, when they reoccupied Java, found their old possession swept and garnished, the revenue having more than doubled. They commenced by announcing that they would abolish monopolies of production and allow freedom of cultivation. Further, finding that Singapore—a free port at their very gates—was taking away even such little trade as they already enjoyed, they made a virtue of necessity and largely modified their different duties. But the greatest permanent gains which the Javans obtained from Raffles' rule were the police system and the establishment of Courts of Justice, both of which reforms were maintained. They swept away the *ryotwari* system with decision, with its right to sell and to be sold up, and reverted to the old village system. They reduced the land revenue, which Raffles had fixed at two-fifths of the produce, to one-fifth, and, to compensate themselves for this, reimposed the old forced labour, reducing it from one day in five to one day in seven.

The next landmark in Dutch rule in Java is the culture system introduced by General Van Den Bosch in 1832, and it is necessary to state shortly what this system, for which such great results have been claimed, was. Under it the Government became a partner in a huge industrial and commercial enterprise.

Suppose any district was considered to be suitable for the production of sugar, the system would be set to work as follows: a Dutch contractor, with or without the knowledge of the mode of manufacturing sugar, would be selected, and he would then, under the supervision of a Dutch official called a "Controleur", proceed to erect and furnish with machinery a sugar-mill, the capital being advanced by the Government without interest, repayable by instalments, the first of which was not to become due until after the first lot of sugar had been manufactured. The wood to be used in the mill was got from Government forests, and the labour required was furnished by the natives without payment. The villagers round the mill were ordered to cultivate a certain area of land with sugar-cane by the time the mill was ready, and these canes they were compelled to sell to the contractor at a fixed price; there was also a scale fixed at which they were compelled to cut and deliver the cane at the mill, the money to pay the villagers being likewise advanced by the Government. In return for its help the contractor had to deliver to the Government sufficient sugar to cover the advance for labour and, for the instalment of capital at a fixed price considerably below the market price. This produce, which was exported to Europe through the Netherlands Trading Society, constituted the Government share of the profit. In order to encourage the Dutch and native officials to see that the peasants and contractor performed their share in the national enterprise, they were provided with a percentage on the amount produced.

This culture system was applied to the cultivation of tea, sugar, tobacco, coffee, cinnamon, pepper, indigo, and cochineal. The profits of the system were so great that the revenue rose in twenty-five years from 2 million to 9 1/2 million sterling.

During this period imports jumped from 2 to 5 million and exports from 2 to 8 1/2. Population rose from 6 to 12 million, and it is calculated that at the present time it touches 20 million. There can be but little doubt that the success of the system was due to the low price given to the cultivator for his raw material. In effect it constituted one of those "covert and concealed taxes" which, according to Sir William Harcourt, all Chancellors of the Exchequer love. The author of *Max Havelaar*, a Dutchman with a large experience of official life, says:

> The Javan is by nature a husbandman; the ground whereon he is born, which gives much for little labour, allures him to agricultural work, and above all things he devotes his whole heart to the cultivating of his rice-fields. But there came foreigners from the West who made themselves masters of the country. They wished to profit by the fertility of the soil, and ordered the native to devote a part of his time and labour to the cultivation of other things which should produce higher profits in the markets of Europe. To persuade the lower order to do so they had only to follow a very simple policy. The Javan obeys his chief; to win the chiefs it was only necessary to give them a part of the gains, and success was complete. To be convinced of the success of that policy we need only consider the immense quantity of Javanese products

sold in Holland, and we should also be convinced of its injustice, for if anybody should ask if the husbandman gets a reward in proportion to that quantity, then I must give a negative answer. The Government compels him to cultivate certain products on his ground; it punishes him if he sells what he has produced to any purchaser but itself, and it fixes the price actually paid. The expenses of transport to Europe through a privileged trading company are high; the money paid to the chiefs for encouragement increases the prime cost, and because the entire trade must produce profit, that profit cannot be got in any other way than by paying the Javan just enough to keep him from starving.

The culture system, it will be seen, excluded European merchants from a large amount of trade; it has from time to time been diminished, and will in a few years have died out altogether.

I now come to discuss the system of government in the Dutch Indies as I believe it exists at present; and here I propose to select a few different heads and compare the Dutch and English systems in those respects.

"The Dutch", as Mr. Money says,—and he is their official mouthpiece in the English language,—"do not pretend to take a high view of their mission in India. They consider that Java is given them as an assistance and support to their small mother-country, and as a pleasant home for themselves, considering their duties towards her fulfilled when they have gained the contentment and goodwill of her people."

They accordingly did not hesitate, before Achinese troubles ate up all surpluses, to devote any surplus to the relief of themselves at home. It is needless to say that England does not look upon her dependencies as a source of income, and it is much truer to say that, whatever the indirect benefits she may derive from them, she loses in direct expenditure.

To turn to internal administration. The Dutch Indies are subdivided into a number of residencies, large tracts of country at the head of each of which is placed a Dutch official—the Resident. Each of these districts is divided into several regencies, at the head of each of which is an Assistant Resident. Associated with him is a native official of high rank with the title of Regent; such Regent, who is a paid official, always belongs to the high aristocracy of his country, and often to the family of the princes who formerly governed as independent sovereigns.

The work of administration is done by the Regent supervised by the Assistant Resident. The latter does not come into direct contact with the natives, and all orders are given to them through the Regent. The relations between the Dutch officials and the Regents are very delicate, and—"The European functionary", according to the official instructions, "has to treat the native functionary who aids him as his 'younger brother'". But very often this younger brother is difficult to keep in order. He lives in a palace, surrounded by a number of women and their attendants, and governs through lower officials, generally his relatives. The Assistant Resident, on the other hand, lives simply as a European gentleman. The Regent's power over the natives gives him great opportunities for oppression, of which it is only too likely that he will avail himself. The labour tax is under his control, and can we be surprised if he uses it to order the peasants to work on his paddy-fields, and for more than the number of days prescribed by law? The Assistant Resident is responsible for all this, but he is tempted not to be too strict, whilst those above the Assistant Resident are tempted to disregard his complaints. A Regent, as representing the Javanese element, is in the eyes of the Government a much more important personage than the simple European officer, whose discontent would not be feared, because they can get many more in his place, whilst the displeasure of a Regent would become perhaps the germ of disturbance and revolt.

The Government of Dutch India likes to write home to its masters in the Mother Country that all goes on satisfactorily. The Residents like to announce this to the Government. The Assistant Residents, who receive themselves from their Controleurs nothing but favourable accounts, send again in their turn no disagreeable tidings to the Resident. These are the criticisms of the author of *Max Havelaar*, almost in his own words. That book is the story of an official who tried to do his duty and was crushed by the system. It may be that most of you have read it; if not, I advise you to do so, if you would like to get a vivid idea of the abuses to which the Dutch system may be carried. It seems to me that no more powerful indictment of a system of government could have been written; and it is to be noticed that, whilst it was written in 1860 by one who had been for a number of years in the Dutch colonial service, no reply has ever been made to it. Mr. Money, whose book, *Java, or How to Manage a Colony*, appeared in 1861, and who reproduced in it a eulogistic account of the culture system as explained by Dutch officials, only sees the prosperous surface of the country, and is apparently unaware of the undercurrent of native misery and discontent. It may be said that all this has now been changed. Of this I am unable to get any precise information, but I find a statement in a little book by Mr. Boys, late of the Bengal Civil Service published in 1892, that in April 1889 no less than a hundred natives of Bantam (Max Havelaar's district) were lying under sentence of death for insurrection. This dual system—an attempt to govern through native officials—we discarded as early as the time of Lord Clive in India, and we have since governed directly, all but the pettiest posts being held by Englishmen. Of late years we have encouraged the natives to enter the public service, and have permitted them to fill posts which formerly could have been held by Englishmen alone, but it is to be observed that they do not gain these posts through their positions as landlords or local grandees, and they are often employed in districts in which they are regarded as alien as ourselves.

Another common point of comparison is the relative positions of natives in India and in Java. We take with us wherever we go the modern theory of the equality of man whatever be the colour of his skin, whilst the Dutch have erected an impassable barrier between the "European" and the "native". The offices that can be held by each are distinct, and it is impossible for a native to obtain the appointment of an Assistant Resident or even Controleur. The Courts for the trial of each are kept apart, and a European can only be tried by a Dutch tribunal. So far is the barrier kept up that the natives are discouraged from learning Dutch, and no European would think of speaking to a native in that language. The different treatment by the Dutch and ourselves of the land question merits some attention, and to the lawyer is one of great interest. Western ideas consider as indispensable to progress private property in land, and we have always, even where such private property did not exist, speedily recognized it. The Dutch, on the other hand, have, according to what appear to be Eastern ideas, though similar enough to feudal ideas also, considered the land to be vested in the State, subject to the rights on the part of the cultivators to occupy it on paying a share of the produce as land-tax and giving a portion of their labour free. The interest of the cultivator cannot be seized for his private debts, neither can he sell or mortgage it. Whatever may be the suffering of the natives under the system which still perpetuates forced labour, no one who has travelled in Java can fail to have been struck by the prosperous appearance of the people. A group of homesteads built of wood, each in its own compound encircled by its bamboo fence, surrounded by paddy-fields irrigated so as to be constantly supplied with water, furnish the traveller with a pleasing picture of prosperity and order.

Under their system of land tenure the people, then, appear to be prosperous, and the State has not deprived itself of a great national source of wealth, the unearned increment of the soil. Our earlier dealings in India with the land question cannot be said to have been successful. The permanent settlement of Lord Cornwallis is, I suppose, universally condemned in modern times, except by the landowners themselves. Of course, it is not fair to judge of a measure by the standards of a later day, and without reference to the needs it was intended to meet. It had its merits; it gave confidence in our rule and administration at a time it was sore needed. But we now recognize that its result was bad, for two reasons. Firstly, it converted the zemindars of Bengal, a body of men more like tax-collectors than landowners, into landlords of the Western type, at a rent fixed for ever, and, as this rent is now considerably below what could be obtained by a settlement effected at the present time, we have, by thus denationalizing the land, deprived ourselves of a most valuable source of revenue. Secondly, although it was undoubtedly Lord Cornwallis' intention to recognize and protect the rights of the occupiers, yet this class has endured wrongs which we can only look to the Bengal Tenancy Act 1886 and the Cadastral survey now in progress to remedy. But we have in our later land settlements escaped both these evils, and have, whilst protecting the interests of the occupiers, retained a right to share in the increased value of the land.

As to whether the interest of the occupier, whatever it is, should be recognized as one capable of being sold and mortgaged and of being seized by his creditors, or whether it should be treated as inalienable, there is sure to be much diversity of opinion. It is the old question of competition against protection, the strong against the weak. Mr. Boys, in his little book from which I have already quoted, says:

> By the return of the island to Dutch rule the Javans have escaped that fatal gift of absolute proprietary right which has been the ruin of so many tens of thousands of our peasantry in India, and with which, while striving to bless, we have so effectually cursed the soil of India. It is not too much to say that the loss of all the many benefits which undoubtedly would have been conferred on Java by the substitution of English for Dutch rule is not too high a price to have paid for escape from the many evils of unrestrained power to alienate private property. Under their present Government the Javanese, according to all English ideas, ought to be the most miserable people. That they are not so, but that on the contrary they are the most prosperous of oriental peasantry, is mainly due to one cause, the inability of the Javan to raise one single florin on the security of his fields, and the protection thus enjoyed by him against the money-lender and against himself.

In a country like Java, the Dutch system is probably the only one which would have kept the land out of the grip of the European or Chinese outsider and in the hands of the Javanese. In this colony our position is different; we had to commence with a country which, with the exception of Malacca, was practically unoccupied, and our object has been to get it occupied by the race most fitted physically and morally to survive. But it seems to me that where a race is found by a conquering European power to be in possession of the land of the country, it is permissible—nay, it is the duty of that power by its legislation to prevent that race being ousted. Such a problem we have to meet in Malacca, and I believe it was the opinion of our late member Sir John Bonser—whom, I am sure, we all congratulate on the honour conferred upon him—that steps should be taken to restrict the rights of the customary landowners of Malacca, so as to prevent their lands falling into the hands of Chitty mortgagees or creditors.

The space of time allotted me (which I am afraid I may have already exceeded) and the width of my subject has prevented my doing more than touching on a few of the points of difference between the Dutch and our systems of administration. In the result, although I do not consider the general principles of Dutch administration deserving of the eulogy that has been bestowed upon them in some quarters, yet in their dealing with the land question the Dutch have in my view set us an example worthy of being followed.

CRITICISM
by Henry N. Ridley

In the paper we have just heard, the author has chiefly confined himself to certain methods of procedure on the part of the Dutch with reference to the land question, and these indeed illustrate well the Dutch system of colonial government. For most of us at least, there are considerable difficulties in comparing our system of administration with theirs, as it would probably require some years of study in Java, as well as in India and the Malay Peninsula, to understand the two systems clearly enough to be able to contrast and compare them. But one or two fundamental ideas in Dutch administration which are quite opposed to those of the English one are easily recognized. In the Dutch system the native is compelled to take and keep a much lower position than the European, while under the English system attempts are made to elevate the native population to something like a European standard. All who have been in Java will have noticed how it is impressed upon the native that he is the white man's inferior. The boy who brings your food stoops as he approaches, so as not to stand taller than you who are seated. He may not use a European language, that is the language of the superior. The Dutch say that they are but continuing the old customs of the natives, for the Rajah's language was forbidden to the lower class of native, and nearly all, if not all, these small pieces of subserviency were and still are practised by the low-class native to the superior Rajah. This principle, though it has its good side, is liable to the greatest abuse, and would certainly be an utter failure in the case of a high-spirited nation who had enough pride in themselves not to submit to it.

Some of these abuses have been alluded to by the author of the paper.

Another great objection to this principle is that the white race must be always looked on as conquerors in a subdued country, rather than as friends, by the natives.

Thus force, and not sympathy, is the controlling power in the country. This, I think, is the reason why so little progress has been made with the natives in the outlying Dutch settlements. Many of the smaller islands have Dutch Controleurs, who practically merely reside there and collect the taxes. They seldom travel through their districts, and in many cases it would not be safe for them to do so. The English, on the other hand, treat the native more or less as an European, according to his station. In many cases this is certainly overdone. The oriental is morally inferior, and incapable of looking at things from a European point of view. It seems impossible to Europeanize him. The virtue of honesty and straightforwardness, by no means undervalued by the negro, is utterly incomprehensible to an oriental. Some oriental races are so ingrained with slavishness, that to impress on their minds that all men are equal merely induces them to adopt all the defects of the low-class European, and to combine these with their own ineradicable defects, and, with a ridiculous conceit of themselves, into a character worse than that that they originally possessed.

Still, in spite of repeated failures, the English continue, and I am sure will always continue this system, and I think wisely. We govern more by respect than fear, and I think this is understood by the natives. The Englishman is welcome wherever he goes in the countries under English control.

But this system has been carried too far in many minor points, which makes our governing often a matter of difficulty. Take, for instance, the introduction of English legal methods into the courts where native cases are heard. The natives do not appreciate the high merits of English legal technicalities, and the uncertainty of the result of a trial under the English system, where more rough-and-ready justice would perhaps result in a very different verdict, does not suit the native's idea. It is quite unintelligible to him. He sees criminals escape punishment on a legal technicality, when he and all the spectators know that the man is guilty, and naturally concludes that there has been bribery at work.

Some of the Dutch regulations with respect to natives might well be introduced here, although at first sight they seem a little hard. Natives in the towns after a certain hour in the evening must carry a light. Thus the police can see who are prowling about. A man without a light is presumed to be trying to conceal himself for illegal motives. Every man returning to Java must bring a letter or certificate to show that he is respectable; if not, he is immediately put in jail. This must assist the police a good deal in preventing the incursion of many of the criminal class, and there are many more such regulations. There can be no doubt, I think, that the natives prefer English rule to Dutch. They obtain much greater freedom from that nation, and can do more as they like. But whether this is good for them may very well be doubted. The Javanese is a good and patient cultivator, the Malay is not. He will not do any more work than he is actually compelled to, and consequently many products which might bring wealth to the Peninsula are neglected, and the ground is left untilled. More paddy was cultivated before we took over the country than is cultivated now, because the natives had to pay a heavy tax in paddy to the chiefs. Possibly, were some form of compulsory cultivation put in force, the Malay would develop from the careless, indolent husbandman into a more active, persevering cultivator.

The Dutch idea of the use of colonization seems to be to extract from the natives under their rule as much wealth as possible, for the benefit of their fatherland. The English idea is rather to foster and increase their commerce; so that the systems of administration must necessarily differ to a certain extent.

The Dutch are not much troubled by sentimentalists at home, who ignorantly interfere in cases where they think the native is being ill-used, which gives them a decided advantage over us. At the same time they have apparently no check on their actions towards the natives, except the fear of trouble caused by the natives themselves revolting against their actions. We, on the other hand, are restrained by the sentimentalists from many actions which would be beneficial to the natives, but would appear to those at home to be harsh and un-English.

I will conclude this criticism by saying that I think we might with advantage adopt many of the methods of Dutch administration without necessarily treating the natives under our control with the harshness used by the Dutch, but that it appears to me that though there can be no doubt that the well-known works *Max Havelaar* and *The Prison of Weltevrede*, and other such publications do not really exaggerate the state of affairs in Java at the time that they were written, yet that many of the abuses described therein have ceased to exist, and things are a little better, at least in Java, than they were but a short time ago.

Notes

1. Lim Teck Ghee, *Origins of a Colonial Economy: Land and Agriculture in Perak, 1874–1897* (Penang: Penerbit Universiti Sains Malaysia, 1976), pp. 14–25.
2. J.W.B. Money, *Java, Or, How to Manage a Colony* (London: Hurst & Blackett, 1861).
3. Alfred Russell Wallace, *The Malay Archipelago* (Singapore: NUS Press, 2014).
4. Lim, *Origins of a Colonial Economy*, pp. 14–25.
5. Rupert Emerson, *Malaysia: A Study in Direct and Indirect Rule* (New York: The Macmillan Company, 1937).

3

THE INFLUENCE OF EUROPEANS ABROAD UPON NATIVE RACES

President's Introductory Address

16 April 1898

by *W.R. Collyer*

Editors' Note

W.R. Collyer was a prominent lawyer in the colony who had earlier served in Sierra Leone and the Gold Coast before arriving in Singapore in 1892.[1] His 1898 Presidential Address is notable for expressing a growing scepticism about the liberal aims of empire and its potential for civilizing and reforming colonized societies. In particular, Collyer highlighted a lack of faith in the "universal mission of our race" and the "missionary force and its power of assimilating other races". For Collyer this was rooted in the reality of racial difference. Racial characteristics determined for him the "natural receptivity" of races to different cultures, and whilst the British had been able to spread European ideas to non-European societies, this spread remained limited. Drawing on the British experience in India where the Bramo-Samaj had emerged as a comparable culture to the English, Collyer noted that this had not passed down to the masses and therefore highlighted the unsuitability of Indians for self-government. Yet if liberal reform had failed, he did not believe that this should entail a wholesale abandonment of the civilizing mission. For him, emphasis should move from impressing the "natives with trumpets and drums and gunpowder" or hastening "to get rich with fraudulent goods and short measures" to a gradual process of persuasion and honest and considerate dealings with colonial peoples. This he saw as the more important mission for empire builders.

The subject I have chosen for my address tonight is "The Influence of Europeans Abroad upon Native Races". It is a subject which must frequently suggest itself to all thinking Europeans in a place like this, and may, I think, be considered to a certain extent appropriate in a meeting of Western philosophers in an Eastern city, where, if anywhere, that influence should be exemplified in all its present features, and its strength and weakness, its success and failures, should be manifest to the ordinary observer. The ordinary observer, however, is apt to be very much taken in. Most of us know the feeling of pride in our race and its achievements which rises at the first sight of European life and European commerce at a great commercial centre in a far-off region: it has been a thousand times described in popular books and papers, but what the exact cause of triumph is, depends on the individuality of the particular observer. Triumph of science—triumph of education—triumph of energy—triumph of race—all these names may be given it. And even to the more humane and least vainglorious there comes a feeling that we are trustees, for what we and our fathers have called the less favoured races, of the collected wisdom of the ages. How far is all this justified? Whence do these feelings arise, and when were the first beginnings of a frame of mind which is to humanity and progress what the missionary spirit is to religion? How far is it based on truth, and how far is it a vanity and delusion?

There is no doubt that for a long time, for many generations at least, the Western nations have regarded themselves as the natural leaders and civilizers of mankind; but that such an idea is a comparatively recent one will be evident to any reader of history. Neither in antiquity nor in the Middle Ages does it clearly appear. To conquer an alien race;

to destroy it and take its place—that, indeed, was an object of man's instinctive desire; but the civilization and improvement of a possible rival was not an end worth seeking. Ancient Rome indeed, where many modern ideas seem to have had their earliest manifestation, had more of the missionary spirit than most ages or countries. The splendid outpouring of Roman aspirations in which Virgil relegates supremacy in the arts and sciences to other races, but claims as the birth right of Rome the ruling of mankind under the law of peace, perhaps shows something of the spirit to which I refer; and so does the extending of the potentiality of Roman citizenship to the limits of the civilized world. The Anglo-Saxon race has shown the same spirit in a greater degree than ancient Rome; and the reason of this analogy is not far to seek. The Roman had no rival, and did not dream in the day of his power that any rival was possible; and, in its heart of hearts, our own race has indulged the same day-dream, from which it is to be hoped we may not have too rude an awakening.

Rome fell, and the dream of universal peace, bringing civilization and refinement to the ends of the earth, was dissolved as if it had never been. But a greater power had arisen—the Spiritual Empire of the Church, in which men loved to trace the lineaments of the ancient earthly power. The analogy of universal sovereignty and universal citizenship pleased the Christian enthusiasts, and gave an impetus to the proselytizing spirit of the faith. A new Pax Romana was conceived, more enduring than the old, as spirit is more enduring than flesh, more righteous, more beneficent—eternal.

This vision has also passed away—at least, there are but few eyes to which it is clear; but from the time when Christianity (the oldest proselytizing faith in the world, I believe) ruled in Europe, there has always been the conceit in the Western mind that in our dealings with barbarous peoples we had something to bring them of inestimable value—call it religion, civilization, manners, progress, as it pleases you—but that in any case ours was the benign influence to be carried to the ends of the earth, by every means, even, if need were, by fire and sword. Like all great ideas which become familiarized and then vulgarized, this idea has assumed the form of cant. Nonetheless, it may be traced in many forms of utterance—in the preachings of the Crusades, in "Greenland's icy mountains", at the country church, in the speech of the Methodist bagman, and in the writings of H.M. Stanley. Certainly in England it has been till quite lately the general belief that, in spite of all failures and mistakes, the influence of the white races in the world, by a kind of natural law, must be for the ultimate good of the rest and that the ideals of the West are in some way destined to become the ideals of the world.

This faith, if it had not its origin in the Christian idea, at all events was much favoured by the Christian conception of man's duties and destiny; but its development was gradual. In the middle ages its existence is somewhat doubtful. It is interesting to see the view taken of their relations to the heathen by the warriors of Spain in America, or by the discoverers of the coast of Africa under the auspices of Prince Henry of Portugal. Ordinary desire of conquest and greed of gold was the mainspring of the energy of most of those personally engaged; but there was an underlying feeling of something else, which they symbolized by calling it the glory of God or the advancement of the Church. It is easy to dispose of this in "common form" phrase by calling it hypocrisy; but I do not think that the most subtle hypocrisy ever stood alone, and doubtless the prince who sent the Portuguese expeditions along the coast of Barbary to Sierra Leone really believed that he was doing something not merely for the benefit of his own people, but also for the good of mankind at large. As science gained ground, and the intrinsic superiority of the European peoples became, to them, more and more assured, the notion of a mission to the unenlightened races took a wider range, leaving behind the simple view of religious propagandism, and the Western peoples, in their well-ordered homes, secure from all mischief at the hands of Turk or heathen, came to believe in an universal beneficence, practical and practicable, which would regenerate the world in accordance with Western ideas, giving it a life of energy, progress, and philanthropy, with, I suppose, their attendant self-complacence. I should think that such ideas reached their zenith among good people in England about the time of Sir Stamford Raffles.

We, however, who have had some opportunities of observation, as well as many of the travellers of days gone by, have become sceptical as to the universal mission of our race. Of its steady progress and vitality we may have no doubt, but as to its missionary force and its power of assimilating other races, we feel that there is a good deal to be said on both sides. We perceive the great diversity of the aspirations of mankind, and that Western ideals only satisfy perhaps one-half of them. We must be content to give and take. We feel, too, that when the balance is struck between the good and evil that civilized man effects in his dealings with uncivilized man, the balance is not always one way; that we are constantly working in more ways than one at the same time, and that the aims we put before us, no less than the results which we achieve, are far from homogeneous. And occasionally we perceive a reaction on ourselves, which shakes our self-confidence.

But there is no doubt whatever that for some centuries Europe, especially Northern and Western Europe, has influenced the thought and action of other races in an extraordinary degree, which has led to the popular idea of some intrinsic superiority of the race. The pessimist, on the other hand, sees only the accident that the period when the Western races attained their full manhood, and developed their full power of thought and expression, happened to be coincident with the time when, from natural causes, the great secrets of science become open to human thought and available for the development of human power. Knowledge is power of some sort in all cases; but superior knowledge did not give the ancient Greeks the power to rule the destinies of the Scythians, nor even to claim a "sphere of influence" among them. For some time past, power has been on the side of the Western nations—partly the power of knowledge, partly the power of hard training; but it may be lost when conditions change.

When we come to look into the facts of our time, and try to construct a theory as to the nature and limitations of European influence, the variety of the phenomena seems to make any general theory impossible. Every race seems to receive impressions in a way peculiar to itself, according to its natural receptivity. Prima facie those that have least native cultivation would most readily receive impressions from abroad. The African races, for example, always appear to me to be more susceptible of European influence than any other. Anyone who goes to Sierra Leone will be struck with the extent to which English customs and ideas have got hold of the people. It is ludicrous enough at first, its comic side being the strange caricature of the external manners and ordinary modes of speech of Englishmen, used, evidently with some pride, by the blackest and woolliest of Africans; but in reality I think there underlies all this a real and very general modification of the African character. It is not all good, and the best side of it is a singular adoption of and adherence to the English belief in the importance of abstract justice, and even of honesty in public matters. The Sierra Leone jury, twelve men in white collars, with skins nearly all as black as a well-cleaned stove, was one of the best juries I ever had to deal with. They were Methodistical, and their ways would have excited great astonishment and contempt in this country.

When I had summed up in my first murder case at Sierra Leone, the Jury retired; and I also (for there are no punkahs in that country, and I desired to take my coat off). The Judge's room and the Jury room were adjacent, and a lattice near the roof, for ventilation, permitted me to hear what was going on—an arrangement, by the way, which might sometimes be inconvenient. To my surprise, on the Jury assembling in their room, there was an absolute silence for some seconds. Then the foreman offered up an extempore prayer for the guidance of the Almighty on so solemn and momentous an occasion, and after another short silence the Jury proceeded to discuss the case. Now, this, though a good way removed from our present manners, was evidently perfectly natural to them; and it is most distinctly European. I only mention it as an instance of an almost complete assimilation by the Negro of European thoughts and ways. But Sierra Leone is a very peculiar case. In the earlier stages of its existence it was a sort of hot-house of exotic morals, planted on the coast of Africa in favourable circumstances, and under powerful influence. It was a sort of Sunday-school for liberated Africans, organized and controlled by men of high education and intense humanity, like William Wilberforce and Zachary Macaulay. The materials to be worked upon were liberated

Africans, generally of the humblest and weakest African races, unlike the Mandingoes, with their pride of Islam, or the other warlike tribes. They were generally caught young out of captured slaves, and were easily moulded to the form that pleased the higher race; while the leading principle of those who ruled was not commerce or wealth, but simply the cause of humanity.

So it came to pass that Sierra Leone, in spite of all that can fairly be said against its inhabitants, was a philanthropic success. And even now, in spite of much that is grotesque and low, the good influence has not altogether died out; and in Sierra Leone we see an instance—an unique instance, I should think—of a community whose history appears to support the conventional idea, now exploded, that the universal brotherhood of man will eventually be realized by the simple process of placing before the black man the white man's ideas and aspirations, which he will eventually recognize as all-sufficient, and assimilate in their entirety.

I thought I perceived the same aptitude for receiving Western ideas existent also on the Gold Coast, where I found our law courts exceedingly popular, and the principle of deciding questions in accordance with actual evidence perfectly understood, and much better respected than it is among many more civilized Eastern peoples. I remember two old Chiefs coming down to the Court from the highlands of Akim, a region very seldom traversed by white men. Each brought his courtiers, his throne, his umbrella and gold ornaments; but what was more, each of these men, who had never seen a lawyer, brought the best evidence procurable for his case, and perfectly understood its logical consequences. The case was a rather delicate boundary question, which in former days they would have fought out with spears and clubs. I can quite conceive such men, under European influence, becoming much more European in mind than many races that stand higher in the scale of humanity. I do not think that it is merely their rudimentary condition that makes them ready to fall in with the ideas of a superior power. The Red Indian perceived the power of the white man, mistrusted it and disliked it, and I doubt whether he has ever been influenced by it in any great degree. It may be that the race that can serve is ready to profit by the teaching of its masters, while they who cannot serve cannot so profit. But if that were the rule, should not the blacks of Australia have had a future?

The Maoris, on the other hand, a far superior race, have been influenced to a large extent by British civilization. It went near to exterminating them at one time, no doubt; but there seems to be a better time in store for the remnant. The half-breeds are said to make good men, and I believe that many a native farmer would make quite as good a County Councillor as his English neighbour. In time, perhaps, they may be lost in the mass of population, and then the question will be, what has been the influence of the Maori race upon the British of New Zealand? It must be remembered, however, with regard to New Zealand, that for many years a contest was waged there in favour of the native races, more arduous than that which I have described in Sierra Leone, and by men no less gifted and earnest, and that to their teaching and example much is due.

It is in the East, however, that the question becomes more complicated and more difficult. What has been the influence of Modern Europe upon India? And what upon China? To write in any exhaustive manner of its effect on India would be in itself a great undertaking. Whether we look into history or contemporary romance, we shall find that in politics, in art, and I suppose in religion also, many races in India have been largely influenced by Europe; but the races are so numerous and so little homogeneous that the question becomes too complicated for a "Preliminary Address". The superficial and grotesque side of the matter is that which seems to strike the British public most. Possibly the instinct of the public is right, and the results of British influence in India may be chiefly superficial and grotesque, but I can hardly believe it. I am inclined to believe that a great deal has been done to inspire the people generally with self-confidence and the power of self-help; not altogether, perhaps, to the advantage or convenience of their rulers; but, as an English officer said to a Russian who was lamenting the independence and "cheek" of the nations under British rule, anyone who comes after us will find them harder to govern than we did. One thing seems clear, that from the nature of our rule in India there can be no fusion of Eastern and Western races. No Anglo-Indian race seems possible, though the Eurasians are so numerous, and the influence of the West seems destined to remain an external influence, dependent on prestige, fashion, and material interests, and opposed by the various conflicting religious forces.

There can be little doubt, however, that on the educated Hindoos a great and probably a lasting impression has been made. The Brahmo-Somaj, instituted for the purpose of influencing European thinkers, has its origin in European thought; and its *raison d'etre* is the European, or perhaps one should say the Christian principle, that it is a duty to enlighten your neighbours. I read in a contemporary journal (reviewing Eraser's *Literary History of India*) that the poems and writings of the Indian writers of today show a remarkable capacity for appreciating and reproducing the style, sentiments, and metrical uses of England, with some application to the feelings and circumstances of India. How much or how little this signifies it is not easy to say, and doubtless there would be conflicting answers to the question from those who have had Indian experience. How little European precept and example has influenced the life of the masses in India is shown by the present position of Bombay, the main lesson of which seems to be how unfit the people of India are for any kind of self-government, and how necessary it is, for the preservation of order and peace, that some white race should rule them.

The influence of Europe upon China from a social and political point of view may be considered as nil, and might be dismissed in as brief a chapter as that on the snakes of Iceland. Much might be written on the causes of this impenetrability, but we can only say that in our ethics they see nothing to be admired. They prefer their own social rules to ours; and even our vulgarity, which to more receptive races has proved so attractive, has no charms for them; they have a vulgarity of their own, based upon their own ancient civilization. For vulgarity would seem always to be the crude, untimely fruit of a progressive civilization. It is an accompaniment of civilization, but not of all civilization. It was found in ancient Rome and in Greece; it is found in England and in China; but I should think it found no place in the realms of Montezuma, of Akbar, or of Prester John.

Hitherto I have considered mainly moral and political influence, in which the stronger must as a rule influence the weaker, and the advantage gained by the latter depends on the relative excellence of the system of ethics imported. There is, however, another important branch of the question—the influence of Europe on other countries from the point of view of science and art. The two, however, though the two words go so naturally together, are for the present purpose quite apart. Science now plays such a part in modern politics and morals, that where European influence is felt, it is generally science that either leads the way or comes immediately in support of the movement. So closely are they connected that European science at times forces an entrance for European politics and ethics, even where they are most unwelcome. But art stands on a different footing. The influence of a nation in art does not depend on political power, or even on ethical enlightenment. The art of Greece was a ruling power in Rome, and saturated her educated classes, when politically Greece was nothing, and the brawny centurion valued a hundred Greeks at a bent sixpence. I do not think that modern Europe has come into contact with any non-European nation in which either the fine arts or the industrial arts could be said to be at their zenith—except perhaps in the peculiar case of Japan; but wherever those small arts have been found which show that man, wherever he exists and however humble are his surroundings, will endeavour to refine his mind by some effort of imagination, the influence of Europe has been to destroy these arts, by the necessary pushing of machine-made goods, aniline dyes, and all the other advertised forms of European civilization. If all the inferior races were on their way to become European in thought and character, there would be little to regret in this; as it is, it has the appearance of checking native forms of art without substituting anything better. This, again, is a large subject, worthy of being separately treated. How far, for instance, the introduction of cheap Manchester cottons into Africa has been beneficial to the inhabitants by clothing them cheaply, and how far it has been injurious by injuring the far more interesting and beautiful manufacture of the natives.

The influence of European art in the East is most conspicuous in decorative art, in which the influence seems, sometimes conspicuously bad, the result being monotony and vulgarization. It may be hoped, however, that the rapid interchange of ideas, now possible between East and West, is even now furnishing a remedy, and that Eastern art may be reviled by Western effort. I think there is an instance of this in the dyeing trade. When the aniline dyes first invaded the East, it seemed as if the end had come to all the grand colouring which lends its magic to Oriental scenes. One fatal market at Nijni Novogorod ruined the sellers and growers of madder: good madder lands went out of cultivation and the Smyrna carpets became monstrosities which, in the words of the poet, "bid the rash gazer wipe his eye". Enterprising British collectors, on the principle of "new lamps for old", got what old carpets they could find in the Turkish mosques by munificent presents of new, gorgeous with discordant aniline pinks and mauves, believing that they had obtained priceless treasures by their fraud. But of late a reaction has set in: the Eastern traders, who thought the aniline dyes was such an improvement, have found that the better European taste prefers the old-fashioned colours. Madder lands, I have heard, are beginning to be replanted, and the carpets are beginning to resume a more decorous tone.

Another amusing instance of what was considered a debasement of Eastern art by European influence was the arrival in London of a consignment of Japanese fans on which all the male figures carried on the head or in the hand the black hat symbolical of European respectability. But that, as Rudyard Kipling would say, is another story. In these things Japan can take care of herself, and in decorative art Japan has influenced Europe in a way in which Europe can never influence her. It would require special acquaintance with the subject to decide whether her influence has been altogether good, but at present it would seem that the debt, if there is one, is owed by Europe to her. When, however, we come to the colours in a carpet or the design of a fan, we have come down to trifles, and we may leave the decorative arts.

Music is an art which in all ages and among all nations has had an inexplicable power—a power which is said to be the same at every stage of cultivation. The natural man does not crave for music in advance of that of his time or nation. Foreign influence is therefore less likely to be readily felt in this than in any other art, and I doubt whether European example has modified to any appreciable extent any native music. The rudimentary sources of our music were probably the same as theirs, and a great change must be accomplished in the mental and physical condition of the less civilized races before they can be one with us in musical expression. The European bands of Native Princes seem to me to be merely exotic luxuries, having no relation to the feelings and aspirations of their people. Till the world has approximately attained unity of feeling and aspirations, the music of various races probably must remain distinct.

After all, to speak generally, the influence which one race possesses over another depends on the respect and affection, if such a thing is possible, with which the one is regarded by the other. We may divide the whole world into "spheres of influence", but we cannot, simply by doing this, give ourselves, or our neighbours, any influence except such as the hunter has over the wild beasts. Where moral influence has been exercised on a race of men, it has generally been, in its inception, the work of a few individuals, raised to the level of heroes in the imagination of those among whom their work has been done. Subsequent intercourse almost always brings disillusion, but the seeds sown will by degrees grow—more or less distorted perhaps, but in the end capable of bearing useful fruit. In many cases the harm done, at all events in the transitional phases of imported civilization, appears to outweigh the good, and we all acknowledge the germ of truth in the "common-form" sarcasms about "brandy and the Bible" with which the cynic endeavours to check the ardour of the optimist; but I hope that the northern nations of Europe will never quite abandon the idea that so far as our power extends, its natural consequence should be the spread of "nobler habits, purer laws". We have had the best training for the purpose that ever was given to man. Our race has passed through the two great educational phases of chivalry and puritanism, which should temper the spirit of adventure with that "self-reverence, self-knowledge, and self-control", which "three alone lead life to sovereign power". But it must be remembered that the effect we desire "comes not with observation". A fussy desire to impress the natives will always fail;

and when Europeans are ridiculous. in the eyes of the barbarian, this will generally be found to be the cause.

We who are neither missionaries nor adventurers, who sit as it were on the fence between European and Eastern life see a good deal of the game, like all onlookers; and I think the moral is that those who attend simply to their own business, be it commerce or administration or research, dealing honestly, openly, and considerately with those natives among whom their lot is cast, have the best chance of obtaining an enduring influence. In the partition of Africa, the nation which on the whole adheres to this principle to the fullest extent, neither endeavouring to impress the natives with trumpets and drums and gunpowder, nor making undue haste to get rich with fraudulent goods and short measures, will be the nation which in the end will shape the destinies of the Dark Continent; and the same will be the case even with the ancient and stubborn civilization of China if the world lasts long enough.

Note

1. "Death of Mr. W.R. Collyer", *The Singapore Free Press and Mercantile Advertiser*, 30 October 1928.

4

THE DOCTRINE OF THE SURVIVAL OF THE FITTEST AS APPLIED TO MAN

Essay

15 December 1900
by *Henry N. Ridley*

Editors' Note

Henry N. Ridley was a prominent botanist who played a central role in the cultivation of rubber in colonial Malaya. He was also a prolific scholar with a wide range of interests. According to Edward Salisbury, Ridley's botanical publications numbered more than 350, apart from his books and numerous notes on medicine, zoology, ethnography, mineralogy and geology.[1] As Sandra Khor Manickam has highlighted, Ridley was also important to colonial thinking about race in Malaya at the turn of the twentieth century.[2] This is particularly evident in Ridley's numerous contributions to the Society, many of which were concerned with questions of race and ideas of social Darwinism. In line with his scientific training, Ridley's contributions are also notable for their particularly biological perspectives. In his 1900 paper he emphasized the role of the survival of the fittest in developing higher civilizations. He gave particular emphasis to the role of climate and environment in producing the conditions for civilization in Europe, and a corresponding lack of civilization in tropical regions. Yet, if Ridley saw race in particularly biological and environmental terms, he was also aware that societies could intervene to limit the process of the survival of the fittest through, for example, modern sanitation and medicine. Such developments according to Ridley resulted in a racial "weakness" which pitted the rights of the individual against the health of the race. As with many other of the Society's papers, Ridley's contributions were a critique of liberal individualism, and an argument for race-based thinking to become central to political life and colonial policy. "To improve the position of both at the same time", he would argue, "is the future task of our legislators."

Although the phrase "survival of the fittest" is now familiar to most persons, its meaning appears to have been often much misunderstood, and it is advisable to give some explanation of it before discussing it. The difficulty has lain in the word "fittest", which does not signify the best of all possible forms of the organism, but merely the most suitable or best adapted for the conditions of existence in which the organism finds itself. For most organisms the conditions of existence are constantly altering, and this entails corresponding modifications in the species, or, failing that, disappearance of the race. It is by no means necessary for the fittest to be superior to its ancestors in elaboration of structure, or development upon any one line. Thus, in the case of parasites, the structure and physiology may become simpler and, as we should say, more degraded and degenerate, losing perhaps their limbs or sense organs, yet for their conditions of existence they are fitter than their ancestry.

It is change in the conditions of existence that brings about, to a very large extent at least, the modification of a species, and the factors in the conditions of existence are all things which in any way affect the life, or rather the reproduction of the species; for anything which destroys or modifies life only, without affecting the reproduction of the species, cannot bring about any modification in the species. Having premised so far, we will turn our attention to the species to be studied—that is to say, man.

In the history of man we have three great phases: first, the evolution from the ape into something that we can call man; then, from the savage phase, in which the history of the race is the history of individuals, to the evolution of society, in which, by cooperation and division of labour among the individuals, we arrive at the history of nations.

The story of the first phase is at present only conjectural; we have little or no evidence of the factors which brought it about. The anthropoid apes, from which the human race is descended, were, however, denizens of the tropics of the old world, arboreal in their habits, and feeding chiefly on a vegetable diet, but also, to some extent at least, using animal food as well. All living species, we know, frequently descend to the ground from the trees to search for food, and it is easily intelligible that certain species, whether one or more is not certain, finding food more plentiful on the ground than in the trees, became, to a very large extent, terrestrial, only resorting to the trees for protection from terrestrial enemies. Those who were most active on their legs would most readily escape their enemies, and those whose legs were longest could see the approach of an enemy most clearly by standing erect. Even among the lower apes, such as the K'ra, one often sees individuals who, when suspecting danger, stand erect on their hind legs to look out, and some can even walk for some distance in this way. Having become mainly terrestrial, the whole circumstances of life are altered; the number of enemies is greatly increased, and the more intelligent members of the new race only will survive in the struggle with the terrestrial enemies. The development of the brain commences, and with this, and the modifications of the rest of the body for the permanent erect posture, we have the close of the first phase—the development of the ape into man. Thenceforward the line of development is through the brain. The cleverest hunter will catch the more game, and will find the most eatable plants, will defend himself best against enemies, and will travel further into districts where food is more readily procurable. Formerly the fittest was the best climber, now it is the best walker; defence was then effected by the powerful arms and the canine teeth, now by cunningly-contrived weapons of wood or stone. The most important factor in evolution, whether of plants or animals, has always been adaptability. A plant or animal which can exist and thrive under the largest variety of conditions soon spreads itself over the world. The more specialized an organism the more circumscribed its area. The development of the mental powers produced the greatest amount of adaptability, because by their use the surroundings could be adapted to human needs, and in this way a larger food-producing area was thrown open to man. Thus, the invention of fire threw open the enormous temperate and cold climates to the use of the race.

It appears, from what we know of fossil man, that the race spread over the world when the brain was still in a lower state of development than is now found in any branch of it, and as it did so, the struggle for existence took on another form.

The struggle was now between man and man, and no longer between man and beast.

The human race naturally condensed itself from scattered families into tribes and from tribes into nations, partly from the flocking together of individuals to spots most productive in food, and partly for protection. To this must be added the necessity of cross-breeding, for inbreeding would doubtless exist in places where but few individuals were collected together. As, by the increase of population, game and uncultivated vegetable food would soon disappear, races which did not develop agriculture would soon be eliminated, except in a few spots where the natural food-supply was in excess of the requirements of a slowly increasing race. Such races still persist,—as for example the Papuans, the Australian blacks, and a few other, chiefly tropical races,—but the greater number have died out with the fall of the forest and death of the game from which they drew their food-supply. With the development of village and town life, again, the form of the struggle alters. The enemies now are men of other races, who, driven out of their country by over-population, invade the countries inhabited by weaker races, and either destroy them altogether or, more usually, amalgamate with them to a greater or less extent. The fittest now are the strongest, most intelligent, and most energetic race.

But with the condensation of the population another class of enemy appears, in the form of infectious and contagious disease. It is well known to all cultivators of plants or animals, that when these are kept together in any number, diseases of some kind are sure to appear. Now, though these diseases or pests are in many cases to be found among the isolated and wild plants or animals, yet their isolation prevents the disease becoming epidemic or inflicting any great injury on the race as a whole. When, however, the animals or plants are brought together in large numbers, the disease becomes virulent, and may almost exterminate the race. In some cases, even organisms which were originally quite harmless to isolated plants or animals have so far modified their modes of life as to become dangerous pests. The most notorious case of this is that of the Kei-island parrot, which, on the introduction of sheep, became, from a harmless fruit-eater, to a carnivorous bird, attacking and destroying the sheep. It was probably in some similar way that the bacteria, now producing many of the infectious diseases, evolved from harmless or almost harmless organisms into the deadly pests we know them as now.

The struggle for existence in crowded districts became very severe, both on account of the insufficient supply of food, and also from the attacks of the diseases of civilization. The fittest who survived the latter were, in the case of the tribe as a whole, those who studied and applied the sciences of medicine and sanitation; in the case of the individual, those who were by some chance immune, or partly so, from the disease attacking the community, and those who were sufficiently strong and well-fed to recover. In the days when in Europe the plague, cholera, small-pox, sweating-sickness swept over the country-side, the extermination of the dirty, ignorant folk was enormous, while the clean, intelligent, and immune individuals survived and were the reproducers of the next generation.

Now, as the study of medicine and sanitation progressed, a new phase appears; for whereas previously the mortality among ill-nourished, sickly persons was so great that only strong and healthy individuals survived their youth to propagate the species, now the weakly ones are patched up by medical aid sufficiently to propagate an equally sickly progeny; and as it happens often that the half-starved and diseased propagate more rapidly than others, there is a tendency for the survival of the fittest to become the survival of the unfittest. This is especially the case among the inhabitants of European towns at the present day. The criminal classes marry young and produce rapidly, while the upper, well-to-do classes usually marry late and produce but few children. Criminality, as is well known, is hereditary, and consequently the largest proportion of children produced belong to the class of degenerates. A considerable check, however, is maintained on this by the early death of many in spite of our well-meant but anti-natural effects to save and bring up these degenerates.

Let anyone compare the children of a Malay village with those of a small English town or village. In the first case a deformed or weakly child over, say, three years old is a great rarity; in the latter there can always be found some. The mortality, however, of Malay children of the first year is very great, and the survivors are literally the fittest and strongest children. To attenuate the struggle for existence has been for many centuries the object of the State, and by so doing we have improved the position of the individual to the detriment of the race. To improve the position of both at the same time is the future task of our legislators.

The bearing of war on the struggle for existence has not yet been touched on. With very few exceptions, war has always been waged for markets, as it has been expressed—that is, directly or indirectly, for food. In early days plunder was its object, in later days additional land for the extension of the race. The effect was the extermination of a large number of breeding males, and those usually the strongest and finest of the race. It is true that in the contending parties the weakest were usually destroyed first, and in some cases whole nations were so decimated as to practically cease to exist. Such was the case of the natives of North and Eastern Brazil, who before the arrival of the Spaniards thickly populated the coast-line, and were practically exterminated by the European invasion in a few years. It is difficult to say, however, how much of this was due to the introduction of new diseases from the Old World. But, though in war the weaker individuals were killed first, the mortality among the stronger and bolder was formerly excessive, on account of their aptitude for exposing themselves to greater danger. In these later days, when arms of precision have entirely changed the methods of fighting, the most active, cleverest, and best armed individuals are more likely to survive than the boldest and strongest. In bygone days wars played a considerable part in the struggle for existence, and the ultimate fate of a nation depended on them to a large extent, but for a long time in most cases they have acted neither for good nor evil on the race, except in the way of directly or indirectly interfering to a certain extent with its progress.

But now comes the very interesting question of the struggle for existence among the greater nations of the world. The northern temperate regions are getting over-populated to a large extent, and their inhabitants are pushing their way into countries either thinly populated or populated by weak races. It has often been noticed that the great centres of civilization have always been in the temperate regions. The reason for this is obvious; the struggle for existence in a temperate region is much more severe than in a tropical one, and there has been a constant survival of the fittest in the form of the most energetic individuals, which has been wanting in countries where food and raiment hang on every tree. The white races of Europe have now occupied almost all the temperate climates of the Southern Hemisphere, and the north of the Old World, and are colonizing the tropics. The struggle for the unoccupied portions of the world shows to a large extent the different values of the different European races in the competition, which is destined to be the greatest competition of the future. The Latin races, from the shores of the Mediterranean, are almost beaten out of the competition already. They do not possess the adaptability of the Saxon races. Now, as before said, adaptability to different conditions of existence is, and always has been, the most important weapon in the combat. The Latin race, in colonizing the tropics, has attempted to adapt the surroundings to itself; the Saxon has also adapted himself to a certain extent to the surroundings. The want of adaptability of the French, for instance, is well illustrated in Daudet's delightful skit *Port Tarascon*. Zola, on the other hand, with his optimistic dreams for the regeneration of France, finishes his work *Fécondité* with a vision of a new French empire in Dahomey. If any of the Latin tropical colonies be studied, such as those of Saigon or Rio de Janeiro, it will be seen that the Latin races make no progress, and are gradually swamped by the invasion of the more energetic and adaptable Saxon races. The history of Spanish and

Portuguese colonization tells the same tale; when these races had but savages to deal with, they proved themselves the fittest, and drove the aborigines out, but the more adaptable, energetic Saxon race, wherever it invaded, drove the previous invaders before them, or is at present doing so.

The only other really powerful races in the matter of adaptability are those of China and Japan, and it is quite unnecessary to point out how the former nation is pushing through the world, driving such races as the Malays before them. The potentiality of China is alarming, though their mental state of development at present is so low that they cannot compete yet seriously with the Saxon race, and it is probable that they will never be able to do so.

As the greater part of the temperate portions of the globe are becoming over-populated, the struggle will next centre in the tropics. At present the Saxon races have proved unable to reproduce in hot climates; whether they ever will, or will so adapt the conditions of existence that they will be able to utilize them for the further development of their race, remains quite conjectural.

The inordinate size of the subject tonight has prevented me from doing more than roughly sketch the general outlines of the past and present history of the struggle, and its resultant—the survival of the fittest. The history is really the complete history of man of every race, from every point of view, and if adequately worked out would form not an essay merely, but a cyclopaedia. Many points I have been unable to refer to. The future of the struggle, which, in spite of all attempts to attenuate it, must persist as long as the human race does; the lines on which the fittest will be selected, and the resultant modifications are all branches of the subject on which one could speculate with a considerable amount of probability by judging from the past; but time does not permit of entering into these.

Notes

1. Edward J. Salisbury, "Henry Nicholas Ridley, 1855–1956", *Biographical Memoirs of Fellows of the Royal Society* 3 (1957): 149.
2. Sandra Khor Manickam, *Taming the Wild: Aborigines and Racial Knowledge in Colonial Malaya* (Singapore: NUS Press, 2015).

5

THE DISADVANTAGES OF EDUCATION FOR THE LOWER CLASSES

Essay

11 November 1904
by *Gilbert E. Brooke*

Editors' Note

Similarly to Ridley's contribution of 1900, Gilbert E. Brooke's paper of 1904 gave emphasis to social Darwinism and the problem of race in Europe and the colonies. Brooke, a doctor and medical officer,[1] referenced the ideas of Herbert Spencer to reject the argument that the lower classes, including the native lower classes in Malaya, should have access to an education which would be beyond their needs. The paper is notable for appearing at a time when discussions on educational reform in the colony were developing, particularly in the Malay States where education had been made compulsory in 1895. And whilst these discussions largely favoured the extension of education to all groups, important debates had emerged around the kind of education that should be provided to rural Malays. Brooke's paper is notable for its advocacy of social hierarchy and order, as against educational reform, as well as for its comparative discussion of the European and Malayan cases. For Brooke the education of people beyond their station would induce migration to overcrowded cities, lead the lower classes into crime and women into "bad habits", and produce "neurotic degeneration" in society. So too would it raise people not suited into the station of the middle-class. What was needed then was to move beyond the anarchy of liberal theories of free trade towards an ordered society which he saw as endorsed by "modern social and political economy".

Tan Teck Soon's criticism is notable for its support of education as a societal good and his support for the Chinese system of education in the colony. For Tan this was not an abstract debate, but an important matter of social reform. From 1890 to 1894, Tan was the editor and proprietor of the newspaper, *Daily Advertiser* which kept the Chinese community in Singapore informed of developments in mainland China. He also ran the Singapore Chinese Educational Institute, a night school for working Chinese adults.[2]

Mr President and Gentlemen,

The subject of this essay touches on debatable ground. One member, at least, of this Society will, I know, require immediate definitions so I will proceed to define "Education" as the "heterogeneous mass of subjects usually classed as 'secondary'"; and "the Lower Classes" those (whether European or native) who are engaged in what is commonly termed menial labour, manual labour, or whose occupation is that of a petty shopkeeper or kindred status in life.

It is the object of this paper to show that for these classes anything beyond reading and writing of the mother-tongue and the simplest rules of arithmetic is not only superfluous for the individual, but detrimental to the nation.

The idea of Spencer is that the function which education has to discharge is to prepare us for complete living;—the method of treating body and mind, how to manage affairs, to bring up a family, to behave as a citizen, to utilize natural sources of happiness. This idea, if carried to its logical conclusion, would not result in the modern idea of two comparatively uniform standards of education, but would take into account that as there are well-defined classes in the social cosmos, so the preparation for "complete living" must necessarily vary with each class.

In the somewhat quaint, but in many ways admirable, article on Education which is found in the edition of the *Encyclopaedia Britannica* of 1793, the various social aspects are touched upon. The following is a short quotation which deals with "Persons in the Lowest Rank":

> A considerable part of the members of society are placed in such circumstances that it is impossible for them, to receive the advantages of a liberal education. The mechanic and husbandman, who earn a subsistence by their daily labour, can seldom afford, whatever their parental fondness may suggest, to favour their children with many opportunities of literary instruction. Content if they can provide them with food and raiment till such time as they acquire sufficient strength to labour for their own support, parents in those humble circumstances seldom think it necessary that they should concern themselves about giving their children learning. Happily it is not requisite that those who are destined to spend their days in this low sphere should be furnished with much literary or scientific knowledge. They may be taught to read their mother-tongue, to write, and to perform some of the most common and most generally useful operations of arithmetic... It would be hard if even the lowest and poorest were denied these simple and easily acquired branches of "education."

Practical indeed this old-time philosophy, but how opposed to modern ideas!

The course of European education is most instructive as bearing on this subject; and, at the risk of being wearisome, I should like briefly to review it.

When man had emerged from barbarism into civilization in the Western world, an educated priesthood took the place of the "diviners" and "jugglers" of the olden times. The training which was necessary for this priesthood formed a nucleus for the origin of culture; convenience and gratitude on the part of those benefitted confirmed this priestly monopoly of education. As an example, the schools both of Judea and Egypt were ecclesiastical. Those of the Jews, however, had but little effect on progressive science; not so those of the Nile Valley—their patient work and careful record of observations resulted in stimulating the nascent energies of the Hellenics, and long the dawn of Greek influence revolutionized the educational ideas of the western world. They were the first to develop a scientific education apart from ecclesiastical training; their idea of education consisted of two divisions—the development of the mind and body. To these endeavours the works of Socrates gave a new stimulus; but it was not until Plato wrote his *Republic* and *Laws* that a systematic treatise on education had appeared. In this he proposes to entrust education to the State. He lays great stress on the influence of race and blood, and thinks that science should precede other subjects. When we come to Roman times, however, we have a different view of education. Here we have no abstract aesthetics, but such subjects as would tend to fit a man for the strenuous battle of life. Quintilian's works, although mainly on oratory, give a complete sketch of theoretical education—written essentially for a race of rulers, trained to spare neither themselves nor others. As the dominant note of Greek education had been "Self-Culture", so that of Rome might be called "Self-Sacrifice".

Passing from these to the later European education of the Middle Ages, we find that the only two kinds were of the "cloister" and the "castle"—the education of embryo monks and of budding knights—the former literary, and the latter physical.

The monastic education was spread over a period of seven years, and consisted of the seven subjects;—Grammar, Dialectics, Rhetoric, Music, Arithmetic, Geometry, and Astronomy. In the castle, however, the youthful aspirant to the knightly spurs had also to learn seven things;—to ride, shoot with the bow, swim, box, hawk, play chess, and make verses. The latter were not stately Latin odes, but generally sonnets or canzonets in praise of my lady's face or the prowess of a pet hawk, and were written in soft Provencal or softer Italian.

Gradually, between the twelfth and fourteenth centuries, these forms of education disappeared. Universities and academies rose all over Europe; Arts, the Classics, Law, Medicine, and Theology were all gradually included in the curricula.

One broad fact, however, must here be specially emphasized, and that is—that, from the time man emerged from primitive savagery, all the education which has been so far discussed in this paper had tended more and more to be confined to one class—that is, essentially patrician. This was fostered by the feudal system—that excellent system evolved by the exigencies of the social chaos which existed in the early Middle Ages—a system which is perhaps the *causa causans* of our greatness as a modern nation—the foundation of our constitution, of our social economy; this system, I say, was essentially one which fostered the education of the classes and discouraged that of the masses. What part should the swineherd and the goatherd, the hewer of wood and drawer of water, have in a scheme of erudition that neither befitted his station nor improved his labour? Far be it from me, however, to discourage genius: genius did then, as it probably always will, rise superior to its surroundings. But is it logical, on account of a few isolated cases, to advocate uniformity of education? Our Norman ancestors thought otherwise, and the proof of the pudding was found in the eating.

But now a change comes over the scene. We have reached the time of the Reformation, and behold the Socialist Reformer, Luther—the miner's son—great and true in courage, in integrity, and in intellect though he was, yet mistook the shadow for the substance; and, from a mistaken aim, has mixed the leaven which must surely eventually cause the ruin of Europe. Forgetting the lessons of the years that were behind him, neglecting the factor of "heredity" in the intellectual capacity, outlook, and circumstances of the world around him, he introduced the schoolmaster into the cottage.

What has been the result during the intervening 400 odd years? The lower classes in Europe have gradually obtained more and more access to what may be called higher education, with a consequent forsaking of the walk of life to which they were born. In England at the present day the agricultural dislocation has reached such a pitch that it is doubtful if it can ever recover itself. In its train, the value of rural holdings has so seriously depreciated that the many institutions whose incomes depend on their endowed estates are in a lamentable state of financial difficulty. The "educated" sons of the soil, who, in their intellectual superiority, have forsaken their ancient patrimony, crowd into the vitiated atmosphere of the already over-crowded towns. This competition leads to the unnatural nervous strain, which results either in such undignified hysteria, as was manifested after the relief of Ladysmith, or else helps to crowd the asylums of our country. Not a few of these urban immigrants prove incapable of holding their own in the race, and go under, only to be a tax on the pockets of their more sensible fellows. Others, whose education is superior to their moral instinct, become that very dangerous member of society—"the educated criminal". In the good old days of the old regime, the usual method of crime was to hit your victim on the head (or shoot him, as the case may be) if he refused to surrender his shekels—a very sensible proceeding, because one could be guarded against by any reasonable show of circumspection. Now, however, education has opened up to the lower classes possibilities of stealing amongst the sheep in sheep's clothing; vistas of crime so elusive, so insidious, that every endeavour often fails to discover the perpetrator.

Turn again to the domestic servant question—that bugbear of the modern British matron: where is the excellent, the rubicund Abigail who ministered to our forebears, who spent a lifetime with the family? Echo answers "Swallowed, engulfed, in the stream of education". Education produces contempt for their surroundings—a perfectly comprehensible result, since intellectual superiority in an inferior social environment can tend in no other direction. Thus does the peasant's daughter migrate to the cities to follow the fortunes of the typewriter, of the Lady secretary, etc., while those of her kind who still follow the old calling are so transformed that they can scarcely be recognized. Arrayed in the same style and taste as her mistress, she issues forth, head in air, wheeling her bicycle, her household work half done, filled with a proper pride of her high intellectual attainments.

Not even the domain of physiology is sacred from this weird by-product of the age. A venerable ecclesiastical friend of mine was one day informed by one of his domestics that so much alcohol was not good for the system! *Sic vita est!* One learns to shudder at the very mention of the "Education Act", which has raised such a storm of sectarian feeling throughout the country. With sincere self-sympathy I must admit that its undulations have reached even the shores of Singapore! No fewer than three of my personal clerical friends have, in their epistles to me during the present year, incorporated plaintive pleadings for aid towards their parish "Voluntary Schools", which, under the new Act, must now keep themselves in repair!

It will be noticed that this paper has only dealt with the English side of the question. The time limit precludes the inclusion of other European aspects, and also the very large question of lower-class native education, of which I had some five years experience in the West Indies. I cannot, however, close the paper without a reference to education amongst that remarkable nation with which we have such close dealings. I refer to China. A nation of such hoary antiquity must have many lessons for the Occidental—good points which we should do well to copy—and perchance accumulated mistakes it were better to avoid. I think it may be said that in China there are only five sections or grades of society:

1. Gentlemen
2. Professional men
3. Merchants
4. Agriculturalists
5. The Riffraff

It will be noticed that professional men are not *ipso facto* gentlemen—whatever their employment or wealth.

The gentlemen of China are the governing class—the Civil Service; and no profession except that of serving the state entitles the use of the term "gentleman". This admission to the Civil Service is (with rare exceptions) only obtained by literary culture and the subsequent obtaining of degrees, and thus education is in China the path to aristocracy. Titles of nobility also exist; such as the equivalents of Duke, Marquis, Count, Viscount, and Baron, but these are only an incident of the system, and, with two exceptions, are not hereditary. The exceptions are the families of Confucius and of the famous pirate Koxinga, the sea-quelling Duke who was "thus rewarded for expelling the Dutch from Formosa, by a country forgetful of his crimes". Amongst the Hanchus there are twelve hereditary orders, solely for members of the imperial blood; and further titles exist in the eight families who formerly helped the Manchus to the imperial throne.

Not only are the Civil Servants considered as the only gentlemen, but as a general rule high offices of state carry a title of nobility, and, when it is considered that these prizes and this greatness are open to talent and are quite irrespective of birth, it will be seen how truly democratic China is.

The actual scheme of education is much as follows: it begins at about eight, and usually lasts about four years. Some six elementary books are used—these are mostly on the principles of ethics: no geography, mathematics, natural philosophy, modern languages, nor supernatural religion are taught. The whole constitutes the system of ordinary education. There is a second advanced stage, by which the portals of the Civil Service are entered. The aspirant must matriculate at one of the Government High Schools—first in a district, then in a department school. Nothing disqualifies a candidate for the examination except being a son of parents engaged in one of the disreputable employments, viz: menial service, barber's work, play-acting, and brothel-keeping. About 1,300 candidates per annum pass the final degrees, and as this number is in excess of the vacancies for state appointments, some may have to wait for years.

Chinese education appears to me to have two chief faults: (1) that it is too exclusively ethical, and (2) that it tends to exercise the memory more than the intelligence. With regard to the first, the Chinese claim that their idol "ethical literature" is nobler than the god of the occidental ambition, "material progress". They thus get out of touch with the spirit of the age—they are "too much educated, too little instructed". Enough has been said on this subject to shew that in their own country, at all events, the people of China have not to solve the same problems of education as those which confront the European economist. Perhaps the time is not far distant when that great empire will begin to spin "down the ringing grooves of change". Let us hope in that case that, with many of the accompanying advantages of modern thought and action, they may at least be spared many appalling calamities, of which the subject of tonight's paper is but a solitary example.

A brief resume and I have finished. Savage man came on the earth. The necessities of his structure gradually taught him the use of fire and water, of weapons, of articulate speech: this was primitive education. As his religious systems were gradually evolved, priest-craft became indispensable. As a matter of convenience to those whose time was fully occupied in the necessities of peace or pursuits of war, this priestly body became the natural repository of tribal education. The tribal chiefs and sub-chiefs had also to be persons of importance, and social distinctions had their birth. The social gulfs widened as the centuries passed, until from the autocracy of the Romans was evolved the feudal system of middle Europe. Throughout the Middle Ages, swept though they were with many storms of religious bigotry and misguided intolerance, education grew space, but always, be it noted, more essentially as an upper-class monopoly. With the time of the Reformation began the fatal mistake of education for the lower classes.

Side by side with this education grew a progressive discontent for their worldly circumstances. The continued influx into the towns at the expense of rural districts has led to serious agricultural depression, as well as overcrowding of the trades. In the train of this has followed neurotic degeneration, the increase of pauperism and crime. Domestic service of today can be viewed with nothing less than abject terror by the householder.

The social system of the day is being complicated by the immense growth of a middle class—a by-product of lower-class fermentation—devoid alike of a hereditary intellectual susceptibility as of the polish which they so vainly endeavour to assume. Let us hope that the time is not far distant when this matter, as well as such subjects as Free Trade (however sound they may be in theory), shall be relegated to that oblivion which is dictated by the necessities of modern social and political economy.

CRITICISM
by Tan Teck Soon

In the essay before us, the writer has attempted the meritorious task of widening the scope of enquiry, so as to include both Oriental and Occidental fields of observation. The tendency of modern international politics and commerce being towards cosmopolitan comprehensiveness, the Essayist deserves to be congratulated for having realized the "spirit of the age" in his present literary endeavour. It is in itself a new process of education; to which, it is to be feared, but few of the more enthusiastic and thoughtful moulders of the world's intelligence would voluntarily submit. And yet its advantages are so patent, and its adoption by, and application to, all classes of the community so palpably beneficial, as to preclude the necessity of denial or controversy.

Spite, however, of its wider scope, it is to be regretted that the Essayist has not entered, a little more fully and deeply, into the aims and objects of education. In the preliminary introduction he has given us a concrete definition of the education discussed in his paper, but this is strictly speaking a mere illustration of the term, not its proper definition. It is therefore to be presumed that the education referred to is intellectual, rather than physical, aesthetic, or moral. To pass judgement, therefore, upon the advantages or disadvantages of intellectual education, without enquiring into its definite aims and objectives, appears to me premature and questionable, if not entirely illegitimate; and the judgement itself inconclusive and misleading. Education being more than mere instruction, would its acquisition be, as contended by the Essayist, superfluous to the individual and disadvantageous or detrimental to the nation? If by individual is meant the recipient of the education himself, then I take leave to differ from the Essayist in his sweeping assertion. Education, in the West, having for its object the furnishing of the educated with a weapon with which to fight and win his way in the battle of life, it is evident that it would not be superfluous to its possessor, though I admit that at times its possession would be *injurious*. Could it, however, be detrimental or disadvantageous to the State or the community, of which the lower classes must necessarily form the numerically larger proportion? Leaving out of the discussion all considerations of morality, I am unable to conceive how any State or community could be benefitted by the presence and existence among its population of large sections of the uneducated, the uncultured and the uncivilized. In the struggle for national existence which each State or community has to continually wage against each other, it is not always the fortunate possession of a few master-intelligences that would ensure victory or even safety. In his historical sketch of the military education of the Middle Ages, the Essayist has rightly emphasized the merits of the educated knights of chivalry, the patrician higher classes; but even then campaigns were fought and won by the plebeian rank and file, and the services of the lower orders of men-at-arms, archers, halberdiers, and pikemen should not be overlooked or underestimated. In these days of modern arms of precision, however, greater dependence has to be placed upon the collective intelligence and training of the rank and file than upon the individual skill and strategy of the higher officers; and the State or nation which neglects the education of the lower classes must inevitably suffer. This is true even in social economics.

If the education of the lower classes is not detrimental to the recipients themselves, nor to the nation, we must assume that it is so to the higher classes against whom they are competing. The Essayist has given us harrowing pictures of some of the consequences of this spread of education—serious agricultural depression, over-crowding of the trades, increase of pauperism and crime, tyranny of domestic service. Granting the correctness of these details, I am, however, far from being convinced that he has attributed the effects to the right causes. Increase of population, spread of empire, growth of international trade, and migrations naturally produce dislocations and disorders in the economic systems, even among the most illiterate races. Restriction of the lower classes to the manual labours and menial services of their peasant forefathers would aggravate rather than remedy these evils. The smattering of instruction which the practical old-time philosophy of the Essayist would generously impart to the lowest and meanest of these struggling masses would inevitably result in social upheavals and explosions far more startling than those he enumerates, and perhaps not infrequently even toppling over their heads the whole structure of the civilization for which he evinces so much solicitude. For he has apparently forgotten that the danger to be apprehended from the discontent of the lower classes is not due to the abstruseness of any scheme of erudition propounded to swineherds or goatherds, but to the activity of the living human brain.

But is the Essayist correct in his assertion that the educated sons of the soil and the transformed daughters of the peasantry largely contribute to the "educated criminal" classes, the cycling lady-secretaries, and the athletic typewritters—that the "middle class" is a by-product of lower-class fermentation? Are we to assume that the higher classes seldom forsake their ancient patrimony, and do not as a rule crowd the professions in the vitiated atmosphere of the towns? What becomes of the disinherited, the ruined, the failures, and the disowned of the higher classes? Perhaps their number is insignificant, and doubtless their education saves them from neurotic degeneration and exempts them from the evil effects of dissatisfaction with their environment. As to the middle-class, I was under the impression that it constitutes an intermediate stage to which both the higher and lower classes of society alike contribute. But what is difficult to understand is the suggestion that though the forces of education are strong enough to overcome and modify the factor of "heredity" in the mental faculty of the lower classes, they are yet impotent to influence the intellectual susceptibility and the polished manners, apparently monopolized by those of gentle blood alone.

As to his historical survey of the progress of education in the West, I am afraid the Essayist is somewhat inconsistent in his denunciation of Martin Luther for having introduced the schoolmaster into the cottage. Macaulay had already pointed out how greater intellectual and material progress had been achieved by the Protestant countries of Europe since the time of the Reformer of the period. I am of opinion that he was only instrumental in introducing the Bible, rather than the schoolmaster, to the cottages. It was the leaders of the current opinion of the day, men already trained in universities and seminaries, who actually achieved the Reformation; and although this ultimately did lead to a quickening of the minds of the masses in all directions, we may as well blame Luther for having awakened the human mind to a consciousness of its inherent capabilities, as censure him for the spread of secular education and knowledge. As for the lower classes especially, I do not think that Luther and his contemporaries did ever go beyond the limits fixed by the Essayist himself—viz. instructing them in reading and writing their mother-tongue and the simplest rules of arithmetic. It was rather the subsequent rise of material prosperity, the increase of manufacture and commerce, the establishment of trade guilds and corporations, the extension of navigation, the introduction of gunpowder, etc., that at last compelled the abolition of the feudal system and ushered in the education of the masses.

As to the Chinese system of education, I think it must be admitted that the Essayist has succeeded much better in this portion of his essay, in arriving at a completer and perhaps juster estimate as to national aims and achievements. For he has apparently forgotten that the danger to be apprehended from the discontent of the lower classes is not due to the abstruseness of any scheme of erudition propounded to swineherds or goatherds, but to the activity of the living human brain. I regret, however, that the time available does not allow me to go thoroughly into the matter, although there are many points that deserve attention. But one particular point should not be overlooked, viz., that it is an ethical system of education, designed for the purpose of establishing a virtuous commonwealth, and therefore there can be no disadvantage in its extension to all classes of the community. Chinese culture is a process of evolution, whose germs are in the town and village schools and expand into detailed adaptations to public wants through a graded series of competitive examinations; the ultimate point being the supply of civil and political administrative force. Whatever its defects, it is a singularly original and profound conception of the Chinese mind, and one of the greatest contributions to the philosophy of education in human history. It elevates the school to the place of chief cornerstone in civilization, makes popular culture the basis of government, and carefully tested fitness the ground of official position. No pains have been spared to make this process of selection thorough, and even to utilize the failure of individuals to meet its tests. It is thus a spectacle for the nations. A political system founded on competitive disciplines in the best historical and literary resources attainable—this material substantially moral, and this culture in theory, and to a good degree in practice, peaceful, philanthropic, democratic—a political system like this taking precedence of war, policy, trade, subsisting at the very least for 2,500 years, through all changes natural and civil, controlling wild nomads and bringing hundreds of millions into a single whole, as uniform and orderly as it is complex and refined.

Where else in the history of States do we find a permanent national endeavour to give practical effect to the theory that government properly belongs to the wisest and best persons? Plato theorized: "Not for a child only, but for a man also, it is better to be ruled by his better than to rule." (First Alcibiades). His affirmation—though capable of being misconceived, to the disparagement of self-government, or of government by principles independently of persons—really gives the corner-stone of political ethics. But the Platonic wisdom provided no practical method for accomplishing its ends, and no Grecian State ever made serious attempt to adopt it in the form of disciplines or institutions. St. Paul predicts that the saints shall rule the earth; but Paul's "saints" were worshipers of Jesus, a body of spiritually "elect" persons in the first century of the Christian faith, as far as possible removed from practical or political wisdom, or even from belief in the capabilities of the natural world for continued existence as a political sphere, even for a generation. In classical heathenism the grand abstract truth of the right of the wisest and best to rule was held to be utopian: in Christianity it held itself to be supernatural only. Men shrank from the hopeless task of determining its positive conditions, of marshalling the social elements to its control, of applying its tests and instituting its disciplines. It was for the plodding matter-of-fact Chinese, obeying their instinct of bringing the ideal at once into concrete and permanent form, to put that truth straightway into governmental administration, with a heartiness of faith that has seemed imperishable. All great religions have ideally announced it. The human conscience affirms its "Higher Law". But only the beardless Mongolian ever set steadfastly about making it the *real and positive* law. The civilizations have said "Politics and morality are distinct spheres". "Not so", say the far-descended state-builders of the tribes of Han; "politics *are* morality, or they are nothing". The difficulties do not appeal them; the fearful failures in practice do not quench their faith in that eternal principle; and they even stake their political existence on the possibility of its attainment.

Notes

1. "Brooke, Gilbert E. (1873–1936)", *Representative Poetry Online*, University of Toronto Library, https://rpo.library.utoronto.ca/poets/brooke-gilbert-e.
2. "Tan Teck Soon", *Singapore Infopedia*, https://eresources.nlb.gov.sg/infopedia/articles/SIP_2017-05-17_083013.html.

6

EAST AND WEST

President's Introductory Address
12 April 1907
by *Henry N. Ridley*

Editors' Note

Henry N. Ridley's 1907 Presidential Address to the Society focused on a common topic of discussion in colonial circles: the differences between East and West. The paper is notable for its reflections of Ridley's biological concerns around race. Beginning with the different histories of the races and civilizations of East and West his piece would then turn to the problem that W.R. Collyer's paper had earlier discussed—the possibility of Western culture influencing the East. Although Collyer's paper saw some future possibility of European societies reforming Eastern ones, Ridley's paper suggests the division between East and West to be far more static and emphasized the permanent plurality of races. Using biological metaphors he suggested that whilst cultivation could improve "thorns and thistles", you could not "gather grapes off thorns or figs off thistles... The inherent qualities of the species remain the same to the end of time". And whilst he would see in the early twentieth century the growing adoption of Western science and culture, this adoption would remain superficial for him. The East could adopt Western culture, dress and technology, but this did not entail convergence between East and West as they would continue to remain racially distinct.

It is usual in a Presidential Address to select a subject for consideration which is of a general nature, and it is not, I have found, an easy matter to select one which is suitable for this occasion. I have considered, however, that some reflections on the relations and differences in the life-philosophy of the nations of East and West may prove of some interest, and this the more in that we have had of late in our discussions comparatively few of the studies of Eastern nations which we formerly so frequently listened to. Perhaps this is due to our having, as it might appear, rather exhausted the studies of the nations surrounding us; and thus I have selected the present subject, as suggestive of lines of research and thought on the life and thought of the Orientals. Kipling's well-known lines—

"East is East, and West is West,
And never the twain shall meet"

—occur at once to the mind as a text for consideration.

Is there any such great difference between the two divisions of the world? In what does it consist, and what is its cause and origin?

The East and West are meeting physically at least. What is the effect of the one on the other, and what will be the future outcome of the intermingling?

Let us look back as far as we can into the earliest history we have of the human race. We first find in Southern Europe the remains of a very primitive race with a distinctly ape-like skull, possessing a certain amount of skill in drawing figures of animals on the walls of the caves they dwelt in, and also making rough carvings on bone and ivory, enough to show that they were well developed in a kind of primitive civilization about equal to that of the wild tribes of the Peninsula.

We pass on from them through a stone age with two periods—the period of the rough-hewn stone weapon, and that of the better-finished workmanship, with concomitant improvements in agriculture, and development of more artistic nature.

There seems, however, to have been little real progress for a very long period.

It was from the East that the wave of civilization was to spread, and that, at first, but slowly.

The invasion of the Aryan peoples from the further side of the Caucasus was doubtless the first advance in civilization; and with them came the art of agriculture, and probably the first use of any metal, namely copper. The flow of this race across Europe probably continued for a very long period.

The people mingled with the original tribes they found scattered over Europe, and eventually swamped them. Meanwhile the Aryan races spread downwards also into India, and here was the first development of what may be classed as literature—the Sanskrit Vedas. The two branches of this wandering race spread in two opposite directions—the mainstream pushing into Europe, the rest crossing the Himalayas to the Punjab. Here was evolved perhaps the first distinctive religion, that of Brahmanism, the earliest philosophy, the earliest poetry. The dates of the Vedic hymns seem to be rather doubtful, but it would appear that much of the philosophy of Brahmanism dates from 1000 to 1200 B.C. There is a close resemblance between the Brahman conception of the beginning of things and that of the unknown writer of Genesis. I quote a portion of the Brahmanic hymn from Max Müller:

> Nor aught nor naught existed; yon bright sky
> Was not, nor Heaven's broad woof outstretched above.
> What covered all, what sheltered, what concealed?
> Was it the waters' fathomless abyss?
> There was not death, hence was there naught immortal;
> There was no confine between day and night;
> Darkness there was, and all at first was veiled.
> In gloom profound, and ocean without light.

As Max Müller says, many thoughts in this hymn appear to proceed rather from a school of mystic philosophers than from a simple clan of shepherds and colonists. It is in the Hindus that we first find the beginning of philosophy. They seem to be remarkably gifted for philosophical abstraction. Long before they began to care for the laws of nature or any scientific or practical question, the great question of "What am I?" was the one on which their thoughts were fixed.

A philosophical school can only rise where civilization has developed, and where the circumstances of life are easy for many. A man struggling from morning to night to feed himself has no time to philosophize.

It is probable that the philosophy of the Old Testament was based on some of the old Vedic writings, but pure philosophy is not conspicuous in any part of the Bible. The question of the origin of things is summed up in "In the beginning God created the heavens and the earth". No further inquiry is needed. The Jews, though historians and poets, were of a less inquiring mind. Still, in various parts of the Old Testament one occasionally gets traces of philosophy independent of the axioms of religion. There were great thinkers in all ages and in all the highly civilized nations, but their ideas were bounded by their religious theories, and these constantly restrain the inquiring mind till much later. The Further East was ever the source of wisdom to the Jews, and one does not wonder at the Magi coming from the East in search of the Prophet of Palestine.

Besides the origin of philosophy in the East, we see that all the elaborate religions of the world have developed in Asia. Brahmanism, Buddhism, Christianity, and Mohammedanism have here taken their rise. Compare the endemic religions of Europe, Africa, America, Australia with those of the East. What a primitive class they are! Mostly customs suited for tribal organization, their original meanings often lost, crystallized into a system of ceremonies, with a background of demon-worship.

The Egyptians might be cited as an example of an African race which evolved a high civilization and religion with a more or less distinct philosophy. But who were the Egyptians, the oldest historic race of which we have any definite record, who built temples as early as 6400 B.C.?

The Egyptians were Semites of the same large group as the Jews and Arabs, a branch of the Caucasic race. Their origin is variously conjectured to have been in the region of the Atlas Mountains and in Asia Minor. The great mental and philosophical development of the race of Semites lay in Egypt and the surrounding countries to the East.

As Keane says—concentration and immutability are characteristics of the Semitic intellect, expansion and progress of the dominant characters of the Aryan branch. However, the Semitic civilization all through its development seems to have made a steady progress. Like the Indian early civilization, it seems to have had to a certain extent that dreamy character which suggests an easy, lazy life in a tropical country; and how far the more matter-of-fact and solid nature of the European philosophy, when it was carried into colder climates, with a more severe struggle for existence, is due to the climate, is a subject worthy of consideration.

Another very distinct race appears very early as bringing a strong influence to bear on religion and its philosophy. This race was the Akkads of Babylon, a Mongolian race, whose civilization dates from before 4000 B.C. They appear to have evolved the seasonal form of religion, the death of the God of Fertility in the winter and his reappearance in the spring—a form traces of which were long preserved even to Roman times, all over Western Asia, and which drifted even to Western Europe.

While all these high civilizations were flourishing, Europe remained in a very primitive state of culture, with few arts and no literature, till the wave of the Christian religion spread from the East. With it came art and literature, and a gradually developing higher civilization. But, as Europe developed, Asia degenerated. The old civilizations disappeared; Egypt, Israel, Phoenicia, Babylonia, and India drifted away into insignificance among leaders of thought. Only a few of the Semites, mixed with the people of Europe, have thought and written for many centuries, and their thoughts and philosophies have been those of the Western world.

The civilization developed in Western Europe was quite of a different type from that of the East. It is of course obvious that a civilization arising in a cold climate, with a severe struggle for existence, must be different from one in a warmer climate, with an easier, simpler life. But climate seems hardly sufficient a cause for the difference. The common facts of existence, birth, development, reproduction, death, and all the concomitants of them are the same in every nation, yet the sentiments they inspire are markedly different in different races. Compare the ideas of Western art with those of Eastern art. A fine and suggestive picture of European work suggests nothing particular to an Oriental, who would not at all appreciate English poetry. The idea of religion in Western Europe is very different from that of the Oriental. With the latter, religion seems to be rather a matter of custom and caste. It has no real bearing on the inner life of the religionist, whatever religion he may accept. Such-and-such things must be done, and such-and-such may not be done. Why? No one knows. It is part of the religion, and has always been so. One notices this, not only in Hindu and Mohammedan religions, but also distinctly in the Christianity of Orientals. Though, curiously, all religions of importance, including the Christian religion, are distinctly of Oriental origin, yet they seem to have remained in a rudimentary state all over the East. It is only in the West that we find them developing on an entirely different and higher plane.

Philosophy, and natural science too, first became the study of thoughtful men in India and Arabia, then lapsed into oblivion, and, in the Orient, have never taken root again till the backward wave of Western civilization has commenced to roll back again from West to East. In Europe the autocracy of the Church blotted out much of what had been done in philosophy and science, till the inevitable reaction against ecclesiasticism set men free to think and judge for themselves. But this slavery did not affect the original birthplaces of philosophy and science to any great extent. Where are now the sages of the East? Many centuries have rolled by since an original thinker came Westwards from India or Asia Minor.

It is perhaps proper to point out that philosophers have a habit of flocking together. The proportion of thinking people, even in Europe, at the present day, is very small compared to the population. It is so much easier to just believe what you are told, and not to use your brain in thinking out the "why and wherefore" of things, that a lazy brain-life is more popular than a strenuous one. The philosopher, however bored by the dullness of the non-thinking part of the populace, naturally seeks congenial spirits, with whose brains he can put his own in competition. And this has been the case in all ages, so that we are not compelled to think that all the sages of any given centre of thought belonged to that locality, or to the same race.

When we talk of Eastern nations, we generally include the Mongolian races as well as the Indian, and it may be observed that I have made no allusion to them, but only to the Caucasic race. The Mongols, though occupying a much larger area than the Caucasic races, have produced but few philosophers or original thinkers of any kind, and no religion of any importance has been produced by any branch of the race. Yet some of them, such as the Akkads of Babylonia, and some of the tribes of Central Asia, had in early days a fairly high standard of civilization; some, such as the Turks, Finns, and Magyars, have lived among the Caucasic races for many centuries, but have made no great progress; and even where, as in Japan, they have adopted largely the European ideas, and studied European philosophy, they seem to remain Mongols still. Perhaps we should not wonder much at this Eastern family being and keeping quite distinct in mental characteristics from the Caucasic races, so different are they in all other characteristics, and so distinct do they appear to be in origin.

What a difference there is between the taciturn Malay, a Mongol race, and the talkative Dyak, a branch of the Caucasics! If you invade a native house here, and find conversation slow and difficult to keep up, you will at once recognize your host as a Malay. If he talks fast, tells you in a few minutes all about his family, the local fauna, and all kinds of other subjects, and asks all manner of questions, you say at once that this man is a Dyak settler, and are not mistaken. A Mongol child seems hardly ever to play. Toys are not, so to say, natural to it. It is perfectly happy in loafing about and doing nothing. The Caucasic child invents games for itself, and invests bundles of rags, or anything else, with an imagination which renders the object almost a deity. Dolls are found in the tombs of Roman and Egyptian children, showing that the babies of many thousand years ago possessed the true Caucasic imagination, characteristic of the race in present times. I know no children more difficult to play with than the Mongolian ones. Joke with a Malay or Chinese child, and it seems to take the whole thing as something very solemn, and not at all funny. The Caucasic child, of almost any branch, is quite prepared to romp, and even the African race is equally playful. One is quite at home in a Sakei house, where the little Negritos are quite ready to roar with laughter at the simplest joke, which a Mongol child would take quite seriously.

While I was still writing this paper, I saw a sample of this contrast which delighted me much. The King of Siam's suite included a number of little Siamese boys—typical Mongols, very quiet and dignified, with a shy air as if they were afraid to romp for fear of spoiling their clothes. With them was a little Negrito from the interior of Siam, who had been brought down some time before as a pet for the King. This little animal was very different. At one minute he had seized a ricksha and run off with it; at another he was hanging on to the back of one, and playing as many tricks as a monkey, never still for a minute.

The Southern Indian tribes possess, too, much of the character of the Mongol, as contrasted with the European and Negrito. It is suggested that in these races there is a considerable mixture of a Mongol race. How far this is the cause of the great mental differences between the European and the Indian races, or how far climate has affected them, would be an interesting subject for study.

Certainly it seems, as Kipling sings, the East and West will never meet; they will remain distinct to the end of time, as far as the Caucasian and Mongolian are concerned. But the great wave of migration from East to West, perhaps ten thousand years ago, has ebbed, and the tide is now setting in the opposite direction. The Western nations of Europe are spreading over the East, and bringing with them the ideals and philosophy of the West. As the old order of the West changed with the influx of Oriental philosophy and the Christian religion, so all through the East the efflux of Western ideas is altering the creeds and conceptions of life in the Oriental.

East and West are meeting on physical grounds; can they mingle on intellectual grounds?

When the Aryan wave of immigrants spread over Europe, it is probable that the whole area was thinly populated, and that by a poor and weak race, which faded out before the advancing tribes of more civilized and stronger people. Nor had the invaders any difference in climate, from what they were accustomed to, to contend with. The tide of European civilization towards the East has a very different state of affairs to meet. Many parts of the East are already over-crowded. The climate of a great portion is tropical, and we have not so far effected the conquest of the tropics as to allow our race to become permanently resident in the hot regions. It was five centuries ago that the white Caucasic races of the West commenced the task of subjugating the tropics, but it is only within the last fifty years that science has been able to supply the weapons to fight the diseases and climatic influences of the tropics. Forest, plain, and sea are studded with the graves of the Anglo-Saxon invader, who fell in the war with the invisible army of the torrid zone. Now every year brings improvements in the weapons of attack and defence, and, though the final triumph may be yet delayed for some centuries, the resulting victory is certain.

Meanwhile Eastern races, Caucasic and Mongol, are becoming acquainted with the philosophy and science evolved in the little area of Western Europe. To what extent will they assimilate these ideas? Will only a varnish of Occidental thought overlie the mental blindness of the Oriental? Or will the Eastern races become modified so as to think and act like the nations of the West?

By cultivation you may improve or modify thorns and thistles, but you will never be able to gather grapes off thorns or figs off thistles. The inherent qualities of the species remain the same to the end of time.

Races have disappeared or have been amalgamated with a conquering race when small in numbers, but no one race, so far as is known, has altered its characteristics so as to adopt entirely those of another. The Lapps, living in contact with the Norwegians for more than a thousand years, still keep the characteristics of their Mongol origin; the Turks have shown no signs of being modified mentally into Europeans; the American Negro, in spite of his imitation of the white man, remains in reality in the same state of barbarism as when he left the African coast. His savage characteristics are thinly veiled with a web of civilization, it is true, but he is ready to throw it aside whenever the time and place suit him.

A flood of Western science is spreading all over the East and West of the world, and is eagerly received by the thinking men of the East. Its greatest effects are seen among the Mongols of the colder regions, the Japanese and the Chinese. How far will Western philosophy and civilization pass into the minds of the Orientals as a whole? They may accept the motorcar, the gramophone, the maxim gun, and the theory of the origin of species; they may ape the fashionable civilization, like the Indian Babus, and become merely ridiculous; or they may graft the best parts of the Western civilization on the best of the Eastern, and so further the development of the human race; but Oriental and Occidental will remain distinct to the end of time.

7

UTILITARIANISM

Essay
9 October 1908
by *Henry N. Ridley*

Editors' Note

More direct philosophical reflection was evident in Ridley's 1908 paper on Utilitarianism, which reflects earlier concerns expressed in the Society about liberal reform and theories of equality. Utilitarianism had been central to earlier liberal theories of empire and whilst it had long fallen out of fashion, it was through a discussion of its main tenets that Ridley sought to criticize contemporary liberalism.

In the paper Ridley rejects the idea that the doctrine of the greatest good for the greatest number necessitated the rule of the majority or the rule of the mob. He depicted the mob not as a font of wisdom but as one easily swayed by "catch-cries of loud-voiced orators". Nor was happiness so easy to measure as, according to him, the Malay peasantry of his day was contented in the same way that the English peasantry had been generations before. Moral good, he argued, could then coincide with hierarchy, tradition and order—all of these issues echoed Brooke's earlier essay on education. It was the "Suffragettes,

Socialists, Home-rulers, and other such mono-maniacs" that sought to induce unhappiness in the masses who were the chief problem for Ridley. Whilst the increase in the general happiness of mankind remained important, he argued for gradual reform and improvement rather than radical political upheaval. Venning Thomas, in his response, sought to defend Utilitarianism from some of Ridley's attacks, but he too expressed a similar opinion by attacking "government by public opinion" and socialist politics which, according to him, required a dose of paternalism. "Our action in taking away the 'Keris' of the Malay was not a mere matter of expediency, but one thoroughly in accord with the principle of utility; how much more necessary is it to remove the vote, that weapon of proved danger with which we have armed the mob!"

In dealing with a concrete subject like that of Utilitarianism, it is advisable (as indeed has been the usual custom lately in papers read before this Society) to commence by laying down a definition of the word; and this is the more necessary in the present case, as the subject of the creed or theory is not clearly indicated by the name.

Utilitarianism, a word which seems to have been invented by John Stuart Mill, is defined by him as a creed which accepts, as a foundation of morals, the greatest-happiness principle—that is to say, that actions are right in proportion as they tend to promote happiness, and wrong when they promote unhappiness.

While this theory as a satisfactory basis of a code of morals may be accepted, though open to criticism, it is clear that a very common perversion of it—namely, that what is to be aimed at is the "greatest good of the greatest number"—is a false and pernicious creed, and much opposed to that of Utilitarianism.

The phrase, a very popular one, has on the surface two very prominent defects.

In the first place, one would ask who is to decide the meaning of the word "good" in the phrase. One recommends as a panacea some political fad; another a religious one; a third a moral theory, temporarily popular perhaps among the thoughtless, but none the less opposed to their real interests.

It is by no means easy to decide always what is the best system for the moral welfare of a people in any particular state of affairs or under any local or general conditions, and the usual way of settling this is to decide that what the mob agrees is good is good.

This theory has over and over again proved fallacious. The vulgar mob is by no means the best judge. It is swayed about by catch-cries of loud-voiced orators. The proportion of thinkers is too small to influence the unleavened mass, so that progress becomes either impossible or at least is very slow.

The history of the Church's control of the European nations from about the tenth century to the time of the Reformation is an excellent example of the difference between the theories of Be good and you will be happy, and Be happy and you will be good. The Church robbed, tortured, and murdered people for their good; or at least that was the theory accepted at the time; but one could hardly say that their victims were happy under their beneficent control.

Another serious defect in the greatest-good-of-the-greatest number theory lies in the fact that there is no consideration of the minority, who must suffer for the good of the majority. The minority must naturally include all Progressives—all who are not satisfied with the state of affairs, and who see the direction to improvement. They are the people who should not be made subservient to the morally-stationary majority. Again, the minority have rights individually, of equal value with those of the majority.

The Utilitarian scheme insists on the greatest happiness for all. An action that produces unhappiness to one, though it may produce happiness to two, is immoral.

By happiness is intended pleasure and the absence of pain; by unhappiness, pain and the privation of pleasure. These definitions by Mill seem as nearly adequate as possible, and the theory as thus laid down can, I think, hardly be objected to by any sane person nowadays.

The days of asceticism are pretty well over now, one may hope, and the ascetic theory, by no means uncommon a century ago and even later, that whatever is pleasant is necessarily wrong, finds but few sympathizers now.

Everyone knows the tale of the little Scotch boy who imprudently stated one day that the soup was delicious, which fault was corrected promptly by his father, who filled his plate with cold water to make it disgusting. This was a type of the opposition to Utilitarianism very common some fifty or more years ago. Of course people play at asceticism for themselves still, but there is much less tendency to enforce it on others. The young lady of Society who in the spring retires into a Retreat, and mortifies the spirit by depriving herself of the pleasures in which she revels for the rest of the year, or the jaded voluptuary who takes a spell of the simple life, really derive pleasure from such hardships as they undergo.

Indeed it may be said that a good deal of happiness may be derived, indirectly at least, from unhappiness. A permanently cloudless sky is not appreciated as much as one with occasionally cloudy days. This sentiment is well understood by many people. The hypochondriac would be miserable if he was permanently cured of his ailment, real or imaginary. The man with a grievance would be sadly put to it if so; grievance was removed.

"Oh! isn't your life remarkably flat
If you've nothing whatever to grumble at?"

The great difficulty really seems to be to decide as to what constitutes pleasure, and how A's pleasure can be increased without interfering with that of B. Different classes of mind have very different ideas of pleasure, and what is delightful to A may bore or annoy B.

Pleasures may be divided into the animal pleasures and the mental ones. No honest person can deny that the animal pleasures are very enjoyable. They are appreciated in various degrees by all, except perhaps the ascetic who lays it down as an axiom that all animal pleasures are wrong, and the man who has exhausted them and been exhausted by them, and whose feelings on the subject are those of the reaction after a night of merrymaking. "Mother", says a young girl, "may not I go to the ball?" "No, my dear". "But you went to balls when you were young". "Yes, and I saw the folly of all". "Well, may not I see the folly o-one?"

It was always thrown against the Epicureans that their theory of life levelled them with the beasts, and this idea was based upon the notion that there were no other pleasures than the sensual or animal pleasures. This is not surprising when we notice the vast number, perhaps the largest number of people, who have no power to appreciate any other kind of pleasure; and these people are by no means to be found only in the lowest ranks of life, but form a considerable portion of the higher classes of society. They are certainly much to be pitied. Their ideas of pleasure are limited to but one or two kinds of pleasure, and if by any accident they are debarred from obtaining these, they break down and become physically or mentally hypochondriac.

Study a man of this type late in life. His pleasures consisted of those common to animals, with perhaps the addition of those derived from sports, and perhaps money-making. The sensual pleasures can no longer be enjoyed, even if health permits. Increasing age prevents his enjoying field-sports. He has made as much money as he wants, or is struggling to make more without the interest in it he had when young. It is a slavery now, not a pleasure. He attempts perhaps to seek intellectual pleasure, but it is too late—his adaptability and energy are gone. Imagination, which he possessed probably when a boy, has long been eliminated from his character, and its pleasures, with their variants—those of literature and the arts, those of the study of the superb world and its contents, with its endless interest—are barred to him. He must fall back on hypochondria, or on mental loafing. Without imagination he cannot even fall back on lotus-eating:

> "With half-shut eyes even to seem,
> Falling asleep in a half-dream,
> And dream and dream like yonder amber light,
> Which will not leave the myrrh-bush on the height,
> To muse, and brood, and live again in memory.
> With those old faces of our infancy."

The mental pleasures have great advantages over the animal pleasures, being more lasting, and more easily obtained at any time they are required. If the man has throughout his life learnt to understand and consequently to appreciate them, and to prevent their dying for want of use, they will last as long as his brain, and replace the shorter-lived animal pleasures. Every one possesses a certain amount of appreciation of mental pleasures, but to value them and utilize them to any extent requires a certain amount of education, and perhaps a definite stage of brain-development. But even in the lowest of the human race there seems to be a potentiality for enjoying them.

Mill, I think, labours rather too much in trying to distinguish the merits of pleasures, the causes of the different values of the kinds of pleasure. To be capable of enjoying all kinds of pleasures in turn, so as to have a constant variation (instead of occupying oneself with one pleasure till it ceases to be one, and then looking about for another), is an ideal state of happiness, and is also the foundation of optimism. To effect this in oneself, and to promote it at least in others, is practical Utilitarianism.

It is natural, perhaps, that opponents should affirm that the pursuit of pleasure and schemes for increasing the pleasure of the individual is a doctrine of selfishness, but this error is really due to the opponent not understanding what pleasures, carried as far as may be, entail; for the greatest pleasure, perhaps, that an Utilitarian can possess lies in causing pleasure to others, and especially to those whose share of pleasures is small, and it is easier for one who appreciates all kinds of pleasures to do this than for the man whose knowledge of pleasures is limited. This form of pleasure, indeed, has become so popular that it has perhaps done some amount of harm, for as children are spoilt by the innumerable treats and presents showered upon them by relations and friends, and cease to value too frequent pleasures, so the poorer classes have been largely spoilt by the kindnesses, first showered on them out of pity, but now looked upon as their own rights. The poor man who used to work hard for his pleasures, and enjoy them all the more for the difficulty of attaining them, is now a Socialist, who demands as a right, from those who have earned them, the pleasures which he does not take the trouble to earn, and which consequently he hardly enjoys. These pleasures are, of course, animal pleasures only, as anyone can obtain most of the mental pleasures by taking the trouble to seek them, and they cost little or nothing.

Animal pleasures constantly and regularly repeated cease very soon to be pleasures at all. To a man who can seldom afford it a glass of beer is a treat; to one who can afford as many as he likes, and drinks it as a matter of course constantly, it is no more a treat than the glass of water the poor man drinks.

The really poor man, then, has a greater potentiality for animal pleasures than the rich, and though he is usually under the impression that if he could gratify all such animal passions always he would be happy, this deduction does not by any means necessarily follow. There are many who under any circumstances would never be really happy, but I cannot at all agree with Mill's pessimistic statement that nineteen-twentieths of mankind, even in those parts of our world which are least deep in barbarism, do without happiness. Some of the happiest people I have met have been for a long period slowly dying or crippled, and it may be doubted if one per cent of the lowest savages is ever very long unhappy.

Still there is a great deal of unhappiness in the world—privation of pleasure, and pain, mental or physical—and most strenuous attempts are made to remove this misery. The cause of this lies chiefly in the struggle for existence, and though this is by no means as severe as was the case some centuries ago, still it calls for amelioration. The actual competition is naturally greater, of course, on account of the increase of population, and also on account of the diminution of hardships caused by the struggle for existence, which in old times increased the proportionate mortality. The hard-ships, however, are much less severe than formerly. Let anyone read the account of the happy peasantry in Queen Elizabeth's time and compare it with the luxuries of the poor in this century. There were not above two or three chimneys, if so many, in most towns, except in religious houses and those of the lords. The poor slept on straw pallets, on rough mats, covered only with a sheet, under coverlets made of dagswain or hop-harlots, and a good round log instead of a pillow. As for servants, if they had any sheet above them it was well, for seldom had they any under their bodies to keep them from "the pricking straws that ran oft through the canvas of the pallet and rased their hardened hides"; and their sanitary arrangements were of the worst style. There would be an outcry of horror if the English peasantry lived in such style, yet it does not at all appear that there was an absence of happiness among them, or that they were much more unhappy as a whole than people of the present day. I have known Socialists at home quite horrified at an account of the life of the poor Malay, with his simple fare and clothing, and small wages, and absence of the luxuries of the English working-man. Nor could they understand how the village Malay as we know him, a much happier person than the English poor-man, could be anything but hopelessly miserable.

The fact is that contentment is one of the essentials of happiness, and is possessed by the Malay, as it seems to have been by the old English peasantry, and was as late as a century ago considered a virtue. It is nowadays treated as a vice of the worst kind.

It is very easy to persuade the larger portion of the uneducated classes that they have a serious grievance in not possessing a vote, or a position, or some kind of luxury that they do not want at all, and are happier without, as the Suffragettes, Socialists, Home-rulers, and other such mono-maniacs have long discovered, and Societies for increasing unhappiness by stimulating discontent are very abundant at present.

Discontent, being one of the most fruitful causes of unhappiness, is naturally distasteful to the Utilitarian. Of course it will be said that abuses must be reformed by stirring up discontent, and such words as slavery, liberty, rights, and other popular cant-words will be freely scattered about by the opponents of contentment. But abuses and real grievances get scarcer and scarcer, and there really are nowadays not nearly enough to supply all the monomaniacs who are eagerly hunting for them, who are reduced to inventing imaginary ones.

I have not attempted to criticize Mill's Utilitarianism in all its aspects, or to discuss every point he raises. Though only written in 1861, much of the work has already a truly archaic flavour, so much has opinion developed since that date. Thus, in admitting that people desire things which are distinct from happiness, he cites the desire for virtue and the absence of vice as an example, and labouriously tries to show how virtue is desired as a part of happiness. But does anyone now talk of virtue in the abstract, or of a person as virtuous, except on a tombstone? We say that A is generous, B good-natured, C is honest, and so on, or that D possesses all these qualifications. But a careful analysis of all these virtues will show that those who possess them do so because these qualifications make their possessor happy when he acts upon them or unhappy when he does not. To A the pleasure of seeing a poor man suddenly made happy by his generosity is the greatest he can feel. It appeals to his emotions, and there is a feeling of superiority in his mind. To C the idea of shady conduct is repulsive. He prides himself on being more honest than E, whose transactions are not above suspicion. This may appear a cynical way of looking at good actions, but it is undeniable that when the motives of these actions are carefully analysed there is almost invariably an element of the feeling of superiority somewhere hidden in the background. That this is so is, I think, proved by the fact that when a vice becomes popular no one is ashamed of being accused of it, but, on the contrary, is rather proud of it.

When Mill gets to the relations of Utilitarianism and Justice, he seems to me to get unnecessarily foggy. The matter seems briefly to be this. The object of laws is to permit of everybody being happy, by preventing persons from obtaining their own pleasures at the expense of other people's happiness. The pleasures (animal, of course) of A, a burglar, destroy those of B, a householder; A is deprived of his pleasures and made unhappy by being put into prison, with a view of constraining him on his release to devote himself to pleasures which do not destroy those of anyone else. Now, A is a chronic criminal—that is to say, he cannot be induced to modify his ideas of his own amusement: and it is further clear that the unhappiness of the prison life has not induced him to amend. What is to be done with him? According to the Utilitarian theory we should not interfere with his happiness, any more than he should interfere with that of B. Theoretically we should put him in such a position that he can enjoy happiness of a different and harmless kind. Practically we cannot do this because of the expense. We have, therefore, to make use of an expedient opposed to the Utilitarian ideal, and simply continuing to make him as unhappy as we can, in order to ensure the happiness of B and all the other people he victimizes, justifying our action on the ground that if there is only the choice between the unhappiness of one man and that of a large number, it is preferable to make one man unhappy than many.

In fact, the ideal Utilitarianism cannot at present be carried out completely in the present state of civilization. The only thing that can be done is to carry it out as far as possible, pushing it farther in every direction possible, as real civilization progresses; and that, in spite of obstacles thrown up by certain classes of monomaniacs, is what is being gradually done.

CRITICISM
by G.E. Venning Thomas

The subject, as treated by the Essayist, is an extremely difficult one to criticize. It is practically non-controversial, save perhaps to a mind which has drawn its sustenance from *Coke upon Littleton* and similar textbooks of the science of law; that amenable type of mind, trained to argue, with every semblance of conviction, upon any side.

We may anticipate, then, that the discussion of this essay will reveal a unanimous acquiescence in its general theories. The soup, in fact, is good, and we do not propose to add cold water, though, having a fondness for such extraneous and really unnecessary additions, some of us may contribute a little Worcester sauce. In so doing we shall be but applying the moral which, as the Essayist would no doubt allow, may be deduced from a study of his paper.

Having no fault to find with the food, the critic must perforce attempt some comment upon the manner of its serving, and, in a paper treating of the virtue of happiness, we are sorry to find illustrations unhappily placed before us. The chimney is, for Singapore, a singularly inapplicable symbol of a contented mind, and a coverlet of dagswain—whatever that may be—does not seem to us an appropriate sign of joy and happiness in 80 deg. F.

The view taken by the Essayist of the mental attitude in which certain virtues, such as morality, good-nature, and honesty, are exercised is, as he justly admits, cynical. But it is justified by the perfectly true statement that, in exercising such virtues as some of us possess, we are merely gratifying that sense of superiority which is enjoyed by all of us. This is recognized, and discounted, by Mill, who says: "Utilitarian moralists have gone beyond almost all others in affirming that the motive has nothing to do with the morality of the action, though much with the worth of the agent. He who saves a fellow-creature from drowning does what is morally right, whether his motive be duty or the hope of being paid for his trouble." In reply to a critic who failed to discriminate between motive and intention, Mill defines the theory quite clearly in the following passage:

> The morality of the action depends entirely upon the intention—that is, upon what the agent wills to do. But the motive—that is, the feeling which makes him will so to do—when it makes no difference in the act makes none in the morality.

This pronouncement affects the Essayist's illustration regarding the Church's methods of exercising its temporal-control from the tenth century to the Reformation—robbery, torture, and murder. As it was claimed by the Church that the intention in applying these apparently severe methods was a moral intention, the result aimed at being the immediate or eventual good of the Church, and not necessarily that of the individual, it cannot be argued that the Church's methods were opposed to Utilitarianism. I would explain that there is no intention of flippancy in describing the measures taken by the Church for her advancement, and often for her very safety, as being apparently severe. One is inclined to forget the difference in point of view from century to century, though the change is strikingly dwelt upon by the Essayist in discussing the relative condition of the English peasantry in the sixteenth century and today.

There is this very real difficulty in judging the doings of one age by the standard of another, and an attempt to illustrate the truth or the fallacy of a theory or creed by comparison between past and present applications is equally perilous. I suggest, therefore, that we pursue the inquiry as to the philosophy of Utilitarianism, as explained in the Essay, rather on the aspect it bears upon current conditions than upon the happenings of the past.

The question whether the principle of utility is being followed by present-day nations in their legislation is one which affords immense scope for inquiry and discussion. It may be argued, for instance, that compulsory education has resulted, in England, in unhappiness and discontent. Bentham states "that which is conformable to the utility, or the interest, of a community is that which tends to augment the total sum of the happiness of the individuals that compose it", and it is not easy to reconcile with this principle an action resulting in general discontent. The essay touches upon the question in suggesting that the happiness of conferring happiness may be carried too far, and that it may not be utilitarian to so raise the standard of happiness as to make it a luxury.

In Kipling's lines—

"The toad beneath the harrow knows
Exactly where each tooth-point goes;
The butterfly upon the road
Preaches contentment to that toad,—"

there is an indication of failure to properly apply the principle of utility. The toad is not content to remain within the safe limits of its cosy ditch, and there enjoy that sufficient measure of happiness afforded by successful search for the succulent snail. He is, instead, lured to unaccustomed sunshine, where, blinking, and anything but happy, he not only encounters a harrow, but is obliged to listen to a philosophic address from the very butterfly on which he had designs.

The Essayist remarks on the difficulty in deciding upon the proper or improper application of the principle of utility, and is severe—reasonably so—in his comments on the usual way of settling this. Popular government, that is government by public opinion, is the latest, though it is unlikely to be the last, of a series of systems. The judgment of the mob, as exemplified by the election of such representatives as Mr. Keir Hardie to the present English Parliament, is very evidently an unsound and perilous means of providing for the government of a state, and the various causes—among which compulsory education certainly ranks—which contribute to the possibility of such judgment are instances of the misapplication of the principle of utility, and not of any fault in the principle itself.

But one cannot blame the mob for any use it makes of the weapon with which we arm it, any more than one may blame the child for cutting himself with a knife. The culpable party is, in either case, the nurse. Our action in taking away the *"keris"* of the Malay was not a mere matter of expediency, but one thoroughly in accord with the principle of utility; how much more necessary is it to remove the vote, that weapon of proved danger with which we have armed the mob!

It is a question for grave consideration whether utilitarianism as a guiding principle has even a remote influence upon the policy which has placed in such hands the control of the domestic, no less than the wider imperial and foreign, affairs of any nation. The recent experiences of Russia in the possibly sincere attempt to set up some form of representative government seem to show that the making of a Duma, like that of our own representative assembly, should be the work of skilled and capable men, and not that of a mob "swayed about by catch-cries of loud-voiced orators".

An interesting case is furnished by Japan. There, too, a popular constitution, universal education, and some indications of a coming democracy are now to be found. One may grant that Japan is to all appearance destined to reach, has in fact already taken, high rank among nations. Her position may be cited in illustration of the results attained by the combined efforts of a people, rather than those of her rulers, and, in common with other civilized peoples, Japan will doubtless contribute to what we are pleased to call the general prosperity of the world at large.

But it may be argued that the advance of Japan, and that of some other nations we may mention, has been made at the expense of the real individual happiness of her people, and is therefore opposed to the principle of utility. This is an interesting line of thought, but being in equal danger of exceeding, in time as in matter, the limits of criticism, I must leave it to be dealt with in discussion.

8

THE INFLUENCE OF CLIMATE ON CHARACTER

11 May 1915
by *Rev. W.M. Runciman*

Editors' Note

Rev. W.M. Runciman's essay of 1915 highlights the continued importance of social Darwinist and environmental determinism in the Society's papers. Runciman was a Presbyterian minister and associated with other ministers like W. Murray, who was also a member of the Society.[1] Runciman's essay took up the theme of environmental influence on character and race which had been the focus of Ridley's earlier contributions. Whereas Ridley saw racial difference in far starker terms, and government attempts to intervene in processes of natural selection as harmful, Runciman would differ. Runciman saw climate as playing a determining role in racial characteristics, preventing permanent European settlement of the tropics and modifying settled races elsewhere. Yet this was not to assume that racial differences were solely subjected to the environment. He surmised that the development of human society, science and religion "of the right type", could counteract the negative effects of climate on societies, thus making their reform and "improvement" possible.

To those who live among or have travelled among peoples differing widely from their own nation, there must always be a great interest attached to the study of the differences and the reasons for them. There are perhaps few places in the world so favourably placed as Singapore as a meeting place for various types of humanity, representing several races. Under our tropic sun we have men from the Land of the Midnight Sun, as well as those whose home is anywhere on that imaginary line that from time immemorial has been running round the earth. From many spots between the Arctic Circle and the Equator men have congregated in this land of sunshine and shower.

It is surely a useful question to ask if the change of climate has an influence, beneficial or disadvantageous, upon those who immigrate here, for short or long periods. It has been asserted that to man belongs the exclusive privilege of being a denizen of every region of the earth. While plants and animals have their particular habitats, man can make his abode anywhere, from the Torrid to the Arctic zone, from sea-level to mountain-top, from the depths of the sea to the heights of the atmosphere. It would seem that man has the advantages not enjoyed by the animal and vegetable kingdoms. But some little consideration of the subject at close quarters will convince the student that such a generalization may be too hasty. It is true that man wanders far from the place of his nativity, and takes up his abode in regions differing widely from it in climate as well as social and economical conditions. The enquiry of importance is, whether the change of habitat is accompanied by degenerative changes of a physical, mental and moral kind.

The problem is one of some considerable importance for it investigates what must be the ultimate result of colonization. If carefully worked out, as it has been in certain cases, it would be possible to accumulate such data as would enable general principles to be deduced, principles possibly, of great value. To the British nation, so pan-climatic—if one may invent a word—in its ramifications, it is of great interest. Into East and West, North and South, her sons are thrust out. Can they go without loss, make homes for themselves whither they go?

That question admits more than one answer. On the North American continent, on the greater part of Australia, in New Zealand, in South Africa, the sons of Britain have found a home and a permanent heritage; but in India, in Malaya, in the tropical zone of Africa permanent homemaking has not proved possible. For the white man there seem to be certain climates that are impossible as permanent abodes, consistent with the maintenance of his qualities, physical, mental and moral. There are others for which he adapts himself with no great difficulty.

That certain physical types are most naturally fitted for certain climates is self-evident. Whether we are monogenists or polygenists, we will affirm that the differences of a physical nature distinguishing a Malay from a European are largely accounted for by the age-long influence of climate. It may be asserted also, I think, that time was when the human organism was more plastic than it now is, and responded more readily to the stimuli provided by the environment. The conditions of light, of heat, of humidity, of atmospheric pressure, all have an influence on the human body. The pigmentation of the skin found in the tropics and subtropics has risen through the adjustment of the race to the conditions. Even under favourable conditions such adaptation must have taken ages and must have been at the cost of many individuals who were found wanting. Being a monogenist in theory I think that the physical differences we see between races is largely due to climatic influences secularly applied.

Our problem, however, is one of the present. I have already said that in America, Africa, and Australia the European can make a home. Does the change produce any change of a striking nature—physical, mental or moral? It is not yet possible in some cases to give a final judgment but in the case of America some general conclusions might be drawn. Three centuries of segregation ever modified by new immigration has produced a distinctive type, known by the cut of the trousers if by nothing else; known also by an abundant use of the nose—in its proper function "blowing". The American has a restless energy and initiative characteristic of no European race, save perhaps the French. Yet the main elements in the Euro-American race are Teutonic and Celtic. When comes their nervous temperament. It might be possible to explain it on the ground of the mixture of racial types, but it may also be due to other causes. It must not be forgotten that America has been a continent of pioneers—a new nation with their way to make, and that demands nervous energy. I should certainly trace the peculiar American temperament to the necessities of a people determined at all costs to get their place in the sun.

It has been said that physically the typical American resembles the indigenous Indian, but I do not think that there is any ground for such an opinion. The traditional portrait of Uncle Sam shows the hatchet face and the lanky form, but he is no more a typical American than John Bull is a typical Englishman. To what extent climate has influenced the typical American it is difficult to say. His enterprise is the result of the necessity. Add to that the initiatives upon which Bagshot lays emphasis, and the type is soon established.

The Australian type—of British descent—differs somewhat from the native British. There is generally greater stature I believe and a general breeziness of manner that is characteristic. The climate permits them to lead a much more open air life than in Britain, and that reflects itself in their general bearing. I am also told that the Australian is an inveterate gambler and the reason was given that the climate renders uncertain the results of agriculture and stock-breeding. The Australian takes his risk in these things and learns to take risks in other things. I should imagine that there may be a deal of truth in the contention. On the other hand, the predominant immigrating type has to be considered. In fact, it is very difficult to discriminate what is due to external influences and what is due to the personal equation.

It would be hard to make any prophecy as to what may occur in a few more generations. The general travelling instinct now prevalent, and the ease of travel, and the nature and general diffusion of education make the problem very difficult. But it can be asserted with fair certainty, I venture to think, that the white races in their purity will never settle in the tropics. Centuries, milleniums of separation and artificial conditions make permanent physical accommodation difficult. I am quite aware, of course, that the Indians are of the same race as the Aryan nations of Europe. They likewise have lost the power of accommodation as a race to other climates.

Take the case of the Malay Peninsula. I do not suppose that there is a pure European family here of three generations standing. The climate does not suit them. They lose both in physical and in moral stamina. It is not altogether a conventional opinion that dictates that European children shall be sent home for their education and kept at home as long as possible. They have not the physical strength here that would be their dower in a temperate climate. They acquire a lassitude that puts them at a serious disadvantage when anything requiring application is set them as a task. For capacity in mastering a subject the average boy at home is superior to the average boy of the same nationality here. The climate is largely responsible. I use the qualifying world "largely" because I believe that if much more attention were paid to diet and proper exercise the influence of climate would not seem to be so great. But granting the possibility of modifying the influence of climate favourably by proper diet and exercise, the general loosening effect of climate is considerable. Then again there is the sex factor. Those warm climates have a tendency to accelerate the age of puberty. In the interests of character that age is better retarded than accelerated. The character of a child born and trained in the tropics meets a double danger—from the general enervating influence of the climate and its consequence, deficiency in the power of application, and from the acceleration of instincts that are better retarded.

It is really the children born and reared in a country that give the criteria as to the suitability or unsuitability of a climate for their race. The experience of India is, I understand, that the pure European race does not continue beyond the third generation. It degenerates and becomes infertile in the tropics. The mixed races—the Eurasians are more adapted to tropical conditions, and of these the progeny of miscegenation with southern Europeans are most stable—for example, the local Portuguese. In estimating the influence of climate on character the Eurasian question might be dealt with. But here it is exceedingly difficult to resolve the factors that produce the typical Eurasian character. Social influences bulk largely. There are Eurasian types that compare favourably with European types. The social ostracism that they endure is probably a weightier factor in their character than climate, as it kills ambition.

When we deal with the immigrant European himself the influence of the climate on his character is rather a delicate subject to touch on—we are all in that category. Have we advanced in character or stood still or have we degenerated? Present company is always excepted, so that none of us are included in what I am about to say... Are we not philosophers?

The average European coming to the tropics begins very soon to show the influence of the climate. The physical results produce mental and moral results. He is not so keen a student as he was, nor is he so morally fastidious. He says he has broadened in mind. Unfortunately it is because he has levelled down the former heights. Is it all due to climate? Physical lassitude and the general condition indicated by the phrase *"tidak apa"* are characteristic of Europeans after some time: but I believe and I think Dr. Galloway in a communication to this Society some years ago pointed out, that the influence of climate on those respects could be much modified by a proper system of diet and suitable exercise.

I am certainly of the opinion that we eat too much, imposing tasks upon our digestive organs that deprive us of nervous force for other things. We would gain much by a simplification of our diet—even the *kira-kira* would be more satisfactory. The crop of stomach complaints and "liver" problems would be less in evidence. Simpler fare would have good moral results also. Plain living goes with high thinking. High living is easily accompanied by very degraded thought. There is no real reason why the whole standard of living should not be raised here by habitual abstemiousness and absolutely clean morals. I do not say there would be no residual influence of the climate on character but it would be reduced to its proper proportions. The mental and moral elements should certainly dominate climatic influences. The beauty of the prodigality of nature would cease to be associated with vice and the excuses of the immoral would cease to have even apparent force. The climate would even then be unsuited for the permanent abode of Europeans, but the unsuitability would not be so disastrous physically and morally as it is often supposed to be. Eliminate from these regions malaria and dysentery, which are largely preventable, and our temporary life here would be robbed of most of its real dangers provided that what we have already said is attended to.

In the above essay I have dealt mainly with the influence of climate upon the immigrant population, continuing even that within very narrow limits. The moral results in character are not easily defined. The general question of the influence of climate on character is a very large one. One might, for example, take the Malay race and show how the climate of this part of the world has produced the more prominent features of their mental and moral outlook, modified by ideas from without such as the conversion to Mohammedanism. We call the Malay lazy. He need not be anything else in a climate where his bananas and coconuts grow with minimum assistance from him. The waters around him abound in fish. In such surroundings he cannot be expected to learn the patient perseverance of a European peasant. He learns nothing from the contrast of seasons for he has none to speak of. He learns nothing from the silences of desert or hilltop, for the air is always abuzz with sound. He learns nothing from the thousand and one things that in the temperate and colder zones made necessary a continual provision against the inclemency of nature. The sturdiness of the European character is the result of struggle in which climatic influences are formative. The climatic factor reinforced by moral and religious teaching is responsible for whatever of strength and beauty it may have. But I am prepared to go further and say that given the proper moral and religious influence the tropical peoples are capable of vast improvement. The mental and moral outlook, while themselves contributed to by climatic influences can be modified by the bringing of a higher and better conception of life from races trained in a severer school. The influence may with advantage sometimes be mutual. It is quite possible for us to learn from the religions and philosophies of India, to take an example.

Races in isolation develop characteristics in which climate has been greatly influential. The great amount of mixing that has gone on has, in many cases, obscured the pure climatic influence. I should imagine that a careful study of the characteristics of the Jewish race would yield considerable data of value. They are less mixed than other races, and even more cosmopolitan. Their religious and moral teaching has been shown to have been influenced by the climate and configuration of Syria and Egypt. Have their views been changed elsewhere by similar influences or is their character fixed?

The negro race in America offers another opportunity for study of the problem before us, as they are under very different climatic conditions from those of tropical Africa. There again climatic influences are complicated by great economic and social factors. To eliminate the latter and isolate the climatic influence would be a task of very great difficulty. The proportion of pure negros in America is, I believe, very small. Many reputed negroes have white blood, just as many who passed off as pure white extraction have a touch of the "tar brush". The estimation of climatic influence on character becomes very difficult in such circumstances.

In an age such as ours the subject bristles with difficulty. Other circumstances than climate count for so much. Of the influence of climate upon character in more primitive times there can be no doubt. But in an age when they live less directly in contact with nature, if not wholly, artificially that influence becomes of less importance for it is more under control. For physical reasons there are zones into which we go at a certain amount of risk, but there is little reason now for pleading the excuse of climate in defence of the degeneracy in character, for science and religion of the right type, properly applied, provide the antidote to the moral rot.

Note

1. Robert M. Greer, *A History of the Presbyterian Church in Singapore* (Singapore: Malaya Publishing House, 1956), pp. 105–6.

II

Governing the Colony:
Race, Crime, Opium, and Law

9

ON THE CONTAGIOUS DISEASES ACTS

Essay

9 July 1893
by *David J. Galloway*

Editors' Note

"On the Contagious Diseases Acts" was one of the earliest contributions to the Society. The paper was written by David J. Galloway, a doctor and founder in 1890 of the Straits Medical Association.[1] The paper would be responded to by G.D. Haviland, who, between 1891 and 1893, had served as a medical officer in Sarawak and a Curator of the Sarawak Museum in Kuching before arriving in Singapore as the Raffles Library and Museum Curator.[2]

The background to the discussion was the Contagious Diseases Ordinance (CDO), a public health ordinance which regulated the sex trade in the Straits Settlements through a system of registration and inspection. This gave the police powers to detain sex workers in "lock hospitals" and subjected them to compulsory medical examination.[3] The passage of the CDO had precipitated objections, both in Britain and in the colony from a number of social groups including moral reformers, missionaries, feminists and civil libertarians, who successfully lobbied the Liberal government of Britain to repeal the Ordinances in 1886.

In Singapore the CDO was introduced to protect British sailors and soldiers, not the population of the colony. Through the influence of the Chinese Protector Pickering, the CDO was expanded from its initial focus on "all nationality" women (Europeans, Indians and Japanese sex workers) to also focus on Chinese sex workers, who were to be examined on a monthly basis.[4] Soon after, the CDO was placed under the Chinese Protectorate and contagious disease was conceptualized as a "Chinese problem", defined by the significant demographic disparity between Chinese men and women in the colony.[5] The repeal of the Ordinances in Britain placed the question of repeal on the legislative table in Singapore and led to debates within the colony between moral reformers and the colonial government. The former argued that, due to the prevalence of sexual diseases in Singapore, and the colony's demographic disparity, an exception should be made and the CDO should be retained. Rejecting this, the Colonial Office ordered its repeal in 1887.

By the time that Galloway was addressing the matter to the Society, the Act had already been repealed for six years. However, the debate around the repeal and its effects was still clearly alive. In presenting to the Society, Galloway followed the position of colonial officials in Singapore. He argued against the repeal of the CDO and noted that the repeal had made worse the spread of disease and "immorality among all classes". A central question of his paper was how the retention of the CDO in Singapore could be justified in view of the strong objections from moral reformers in Britain. Galloway's response was two-fold. Firstly, he echoed concerns about the scale of the problem in Singapore, noting that it was worsened by the lack of knowledge amongst the Chinese of sexual diseases. Secondly, he noted that the propositions put forward by moral reformers, feminists and civil libertarians in Britain could not be similarly applied to the Chinese sex workers of Singapore. Rather, he argued, the intervention of the state through the CDO, and the system of detention and inspection did not oppress them but offered them hope of being raised up to the level of European civilization. This argument to justify intervention and coercion against non-European populations was made on the basis of racial difference.

Nevertheless, as Haviland's response shows, there was also opposition to the CDO in the colony. Rejecting Galloway's assertion that opposition to the CDO was a matter of Christian morality, Haviland argued that opposition to the CDO could be justified by secular, social Darwinist morality. Opposition to sex work was, he explained, a sign of the level of civilization of a society, in its distinction between honourable and dishonourable women, whilst sex work was itself the expression of an overpopulated society which through disease would tend towards depopulation. This was being forestalled by modern medical knowledge which made sex work safe. This resonated with Gilbert E. Brooke and H.N. Ridley's fears that modern medicine and government were curtailing natural selection.

The first thought which strikes the comer to Singapore is the variety of the races aggregated together; the second, how such a heterogeneous mass can ever form a society; and yet such an organization has been formed. While each citizen has been pursuing his individual wants and none taking thought of aught else, a complete organization has arisen from the pressure of human wants and activities, not only so, but little by little, by steps so small that year by year the industrial arrangements have seemed to men just what they were before, this social organization has not only become the complex array of workers which we see, but has advanced to a certain degree of specialization. It has become an axiom in sociology that the civilization of a race is to be judged by the amount of specialization which it shows, but this does not apply to any organization composed of an admixture of races. Among us specialization is probably at its highest, due, not to advanced civilization, but to racial peculiarity. This, to the student of sociology, is a most enticing by-study and one in which little work has been done. But the ethical aspects of this industrial mass are what specially concern me in this paper—and it might be well first to attempt to define their ethics or morality. Morality is, and at all times has been, a variable quantity even in civilized nations, varying not only with the development of any nation, but even in the individual at different times and under different circumstances, and yet, although there is no uniform rule of right and wrong in human minds, morality is by no means a matter of prejudice or fancy. It would be a needless waste of your time to trace out the progress from its first stages up through its many phases of the formation of the elaborate producing and distributing organization existing among ourselves here. Political economists have long since described this evolution. But although each nation, each section of a nation, each class of makers or teachers have assumed separate functions in the industrial organization, they have all assumed a common level of business morality, produced partly by the spontaneity of a common benefit, partly by legislative influences, influences whose fitness to the local conditions is in direct proportion to the local prosperity. But here all community of ethics ceases—and gives place in all the other aspects of human life here, to the widest divergence; and this is the chief difficulty in the treatment of our subject tonight, as it is absolutely essential that each race must be judged upon its own merits and from its own moral standpoint.

In discussing this morality, a careful analysis of the masses must first be made, and secondly, to ensure a perfectly unbiased judgement of the principles or lack of these which actuates these masses, we must disabuse our minds of any fixed standard of morality, and even of many of the more tender feelings which have been developed in us, as an essential element in human civilization.

To proceed with the analysis we find that in the indigenous races i.e. Malays, Straits-born Chinese and Eurasians, the proportion of the sexes is, roughly speaking, equal, but in the immigrant races a very different ratio is evident. Thus in the European resident population the ratio of women to men is about 5 per cent, in the floating population 4.3 per cent and in the military 1.7 per cent.

Among the Chinese immigrant tribes there are 11,806 females to 90,769 males, and a division into the respective tribes seems to accentuate this disparity.

Thus among the Cantonese there are 6,593 women and 14,966 men, or 44 per cent—in the Hokkien women from 7.4 per cent of the whole number, in Hylams 1.06 per cent, in the Kehs 62 per cent and in the Teochews 7.05 per cent. In other races a similar disproportion of the sexes exists, thus in the Tamils, women are as 16 per cent to the men. Two notable exceptions are the Siamese and Japanese; in the former the females being 200, in the latter 400 to each hundred males. I have only to mention this fact to enable anyone at all familiar with local conditions to imagine the rest.

So far, I have dealt with proportion only, and now I proceed to discuss the relations of the sexes, and if possible to define in each case a definite moral standard. First then, taking the Malays. From a wide experience of Malays and extended enquiry, it seems that monogamy is the rule among the common class. I am aware that this is contrary to general opinion, but that fact has only tended to make the enquiries more careful and more exact and the results of these three show that not only is the preceding statement correct, but that conjugal fidelity is not the rarity it was supposed to be. Now what is the cause of this? We must at once eliminate any religious element in the course followed by these comparatively unenlightened people as monogamy is not enforced, not even recommended in the Kuran, and we can only conclude that, unenlightened as they are, they have ascertained and it may be through the experience of centuries, that such sacrifice of their own enjoyment is a real good, and, moreover, that such conduct if it became general, would promote the wellbeing of the community at large. Thus their moral standard is a purely social one.

Now let us consider the Straits-born Chinese. Here also is monogamy the rule, practically without exception, and also without any religious element as a factor of this rule. Of all nations the Chinese have a stupendous belief in a stupendous ancestral legendary and literature and to that may be traced the preceding rule of conduct. Doubtless that had its origin primarily in much the same way as among the Malays, viz. that such a course was best and most suitable to the circumstances of the individual, the family, the tribe or whatever the social aggregate may have been. But, unlike the Malays, infidelity to a wife is considered most reprehensible, always, it seems to me, on the ground that it is a slight to the wife, deeply resented by the mother and all the relations of the unfortunate lady. This is undoubtedly a moral veto but the feelings which supervene on such a breach of marital fidelity have no clement of any religious nature in them, but are simply the outcry incident on a breach of an arbitrary rule which has been approved by their society at large. Thus the sin is purely a social sin.

But the unmarried Straits-born Chinaman is at liberty, so far as religious and social grounds go, to do as he pleases in these matters. There seems to be no approbation or disapprobation, no praise or blame attached to promiscuous sexual intercourse, simply because there is no ethical standard by which to judge him.

The last of the indigenous races, the Eurasians, may be dismissed by the statement that they are all Christians, chiefly Romanists.

Now, we may treat of the immigrant races, and of these the Tamils first; the women in this race being 16 to every 100 men. The conditions of life are rarely monogamous, the most common condition being that of polyandry, one woman being related to a number of men.

The non-indigenous Chinese are, however, the crux of this question, forming as they do the vast bulk of the population, and any catch-census represents, very inadequately indeed the enormous wave of Chinese life which flows in a continuous current through this and the other towns in the Peninsula, going, coming, seldom remaining more than a few days or weeks. when we know that in May over 30,000 Chinese passed through Singapore, not only passed through, but landed and intermingled with the inhabitants, you can form some idea of the constant change and interchange which goes on quietly, regularly and in perfect order, so orderly indeed that we residents incline to forget the immense amount of work which has to be gone through by the officials of the Protectorate.

For my purpose these Chinese must be subdivided into four classes,

1) Those from China in search of labour.
2) Those returning to China from mines or plantations or whatever industry they followed.
3) The industrial classes resident in the towns.
4) A small class of traders resident here only for a time.

It must be evident to you that the first class, those in search of labour, are, so far as our subject is concerned, of little moment. They arrive here penniless, are kept closely guarded by the broker to whose interest it is that none go missing, and in a few days, rarely weeks, are shipped off to their ultimate destination. But the second class, those returning to China, usually with a little money at their command, require a fuller consideration. Think of the life they have probably been leading, herding with scores, maybe hundreds, of their fellows in a plantation or at a tin mine, with hard work, very hard work if on piece work, what wonder then that on arriving at a town they proceed to enjoy that relaxation which they have earned, and what wonder that the professional gambler, the opium fiend and the brothel pimp all find in them easy prey? Relieved of much of their hard-earned gains, they sail for China, and, if we could only follow them, we would find that they leave in their wake a trail of disease and suffering. If we consider the extreme disproportion of the sexes in the Hylams (being 1.68 females per centum males) who form the largest part of the industrial class, and never form any relations of a permanent kind here, we can easily imagine the result.

The fourth class, that of the Chinese traders, requires special consideration in so far that they are decidedly polygamous and this may be accounted for by the fact that their financial position permits them to retain a plurality of women in their households, for their personal gratification.

In all the classes mentioned above, it is futile to attempt to fix any ethical standard. Creatures of impulse they follow no law, their only limit being their pecuniary and physical capacity.

We now, in sequence, come to the Europeans, and first let us consider the army. The large amount of incapacity for service and often early invaliding due directly to venereal disease, has been and is a matter of most serious consideration for the military authorities. While in spite of the exciting literature of the day and the looseness of some of the older boys at our public schools and universities, the moral tone of the young man of the present day is better than it was half a century ago, the conservation of the classes from which the soldier is drawn still remains coarse and often lewd, as it was generations ago. It is generally admitted that, leaving out of account the suppression of concomitant vices such as intemperance, there are three chief ways of encouraging continence in men,

1) Physical—by severe muscular work.
2) Mental—by reading of an elevating nature or by hard intellectual work.
3) By deep emotional or religious conviction, or
4) By any combination of these, and to the credit of the military authorities be it said that everything possible on those lines has been done to help the British soldier.

Gymnasia have been erected in every barracks, and every encouragement given to the practice, libraries have been formed, and facilities given to attend religious services of all kinds, and still the result is failure in a large degree, but temptation falls with even a heavier hand upon the mercantile youth of these colonies. Admitted that they from an educational point of view occupy a higher level than the private soldier, that they on that account should have a more stable moral base and higher conceptions, yet the counterbalancing condition, the pressure of their environment is so much the greater. As effectually prohibited from marrying by their position in the social system of which they form a large part as if they were under a celibate law, the leisure time at their disposal, the possession of the wherewithal to satisfy their individual tastes or inclinations, the absolute absence of family ties, combined to give them a freedom of action which is in itself a source of danger. "Everyone has to fight his own Marathon and Thermopylae, everyone meets the Sphinx on the road he has to pass, and to everyone, as to Hercules, is offered choice of vice or virtue, and each may, like Paris, give the apple of life to Venus, Juno or Minerva."

In this relation we may go back to the time when civilization in the Straits was in its infancy—a pioneer society exclusively male, when unions with native women were formed, some of which unions, to the credit of the Europeans be it said, were held to be as inviolable as if consecrated by the Church. Something, though little, may be said in defence of such a state of matters. The complete isolation, the dangers, the effects of daily contact with, and intimate knowledge of the lax laws of sexual union obtaining in the races among which their lot was cast, and, above all, that love of domesticity so deeply imbued in all Europeans, must all be carefully considered before passing a sweeping criticism or condemnation. It cannot be denied that much of that laxity yet remains, but with the growth of colonies, the formation of society, much more has disappeared. There are, and ever will be, societies in which a breach of social etiquette is considered worse than a breach of morality, a vulgarity than an actual sin, but there can be no mistaking the direction in which social sanction tends if we consider the very pronounced social veto, becoming more pronounced year by year, which society passes on any known act of sexual immorality.

As Sir James Paget so eloquently observes "Chastity does no harm to mind or body, discipline is excellent, marriage can be safely waited for." As the Church well describes it continence is a "gift", but a gift not generally possessed.

I have striven in the preceding argument to prove to you that in a mixed population such as we have here, a population with elements from probably every nation under heaven, with every shade of difference of eruditions, from the perfectly savage Bugis or Nubian to the cultured European, it is impossible to fix any standard even a relative standard of sexual morality, neither from a religious or from a social aspect. Deprived of these, it naturally resolves itself into a purely sanitary matter, as purely sanitary and as certainly the duty of the Sanitary authorities as the guarding of the people against concealment of infectious diseases is. We reprobate the jerry builder, who, in his thirst for gain, omits to provide proper drains in waste pipes in his houses, and thus engenders typhoid fever, we can scarcely find language forcible enough to express our opinion of the man who wittingly conceals a case of small-pox or cholera in a crowded locality, and yet, matters are as they are.

The Contagious Diseases Ordinance, itself is purely sanitary. It does not deal with matters moral, and wisely so, it leaves to the moralist the duty of drawing attention to the subject, and of insisting on the responsibility attached to a knowledge of it. As an ordinance it is singularly fair. Every care has been taken that no vexatious pressure consistent with thorough efficiency, should bear upon the unfortunates, they are hedged round by any number of by-laws, each having for its burdensome restriction on the action of the authorities, tending to lessen any feeling of compulsion which other clauses might awaken in the women concerned. It seems as I previously stated, a "fair" act, and this becomes evident on contrast with other acts of a similar nature, such as for instance, the Paris Municipal Ordinance, where, in addition to the laws specially applied to the suppression of disease, the police have issued a series of sumptuary laws, decreeing that the women must dress in a certain way not calculated to be distinctive or attract attention, that they must keep their windows closed and well curtained, that they shall walk only in certain streets and at certain hours, and a host of irritating and superfluous injunctions.

How heavily this falls upon the unfortunates is shown by the fact that in 1888 of 10,355 detentions by the police only 55 per cent were cases of disease. They have overstepped their duty, and the limitations of the act, they are no longer only the guardians of the public safety, but have constituted themselves the guardians of the public morals, their belief in which morality is in inverse ratio to the extreme care they take to guard it from gratuitous temptation.

The Contagious Diseases Ordinance was instituted here in 1864, not with any idea of protecting the general inhabitants but solely because Singapore was a garrison and seaport town, and in accordance with the statement of a Select Committee of the House of Commons "that the prostitution at our naval and military stations was appalling" and urged measures for its amelioration. The result was the Act of 1864. From its institution, constant attempts have been made to repeal it, and so far, they, by pouncing upon the weak clauses, or vexatious elements in the Ordinance, did some good unwittingly, but did not succeed in their purpose. Amendments in 1866, 1863, 1869, followed, and in 1870 a determined attempt to repeal them was defeated by a large majority, and in 1873, 1875, 1876, 1878, 1879 attempts in this direction were followed with a like result. In 1883 the compulsory examinations of women were abandoned in consequence of a resolution of Mr. Stansfeld to that effect having been carried by what is admitted to have been a snatch vote. Shortly afterwards, on 16 March 1886 the same gentleman proposed that the acts of 1866–69 be totally repealed, a proposal which was carried.

By this repeal all control of the lost classes was abandoned, but in this colony by some means or other, the repeal is only partial. There still remains a hospital where any diseased woman may be admitted of her own free will, and obtain treatment and shelter as long as she may care to remain; there is still a system of registration and supervision, quite contrary to the spirit of this repeal.

It is impossible to estimate the benefits conferred on the general mass of the people by the institution of the Contagious Diseases Ordinance, impossible to estimate as there could not possibly be any statistical evidence obtained relative to the amount of disease in existence before its institution, but the gradual diminution of disease among the unfortunates themselves, a diminution accentuated year by year, was proof sufficient that the ordinance was fulfilling its end. But apart from its own inherent beneficial effect, it formed a centre, around which many smaller ordinances resolved, and all together formed probably one of the most thorough and most workable departments in the administration of this colony. Take, for instance, the Girl Slavery, and other ordinances relating to the welfare of women and children in the colony. They, with the CDO, formed a group which by their action and interaction, it was almost impossible to evade, and it is not too much to say that the basis on which they worked was the Contagious Diseases Ordinance. But this is foreign to my subject.

Let us consider a little in detail some of the arguments used by the party to whom are directly traceable, the agitation which eventuated in the repeal of the Contagious Diseases Ordinance. That the agitation had a basis in fact, no one will deny and the Cass case was an occurrence quite as avoidable as it was to be regretted, yet the possibility of avoidance of any recurrence of this mistake was never for a moment considered, in fact, studiously avoided, and, relying on the spirit of chivalry not yet extinct in the breasts of Englishmen, they used this mistake as an example of what any time, a statement which needs only a total ignorance of the clauses of the Act to ensure acceptance. Many of the arguments used by them could only be believed on the same conditions, many more defeated their object by their gross exaggeration, but all were founded on, not a misconception of the Act, that would be excusable, but upon the knowledge that not a tithe of the masses had any idea, however hazy, of its working. And upon this mass of ignorance they worked.

We heard much of State "encouragement" of vice (regulation and encouragement being synonymous in their vocabulary), let us see what the facts are as regards this town. In 1887 the last year of the Ordinance there were 224 registered brothels containing in all 1,796 prostitutes of whom 25 were European. In 1888 the first year after the repeal there were 236 brothels containing 2,124 prostitutes, of whom 25 were European. In 1891 the fourth year after the repeal there were 238 brothels containing over 2,000 prostitutes not including Europeans. It requires simply a common amount of observation to see for yourselves that that latter class has enormously increased in number, in fact, opposite the chief girls' school of the town there two of these cafes planted for months. These were, however, placed under close espionage by the police and literally starved out of the position they had taken. It shows the absolute necessity of a Contagious Diseases Ordinance, that the means used to dislodge these objectionables were distinctly illegal.

In addition to these houses are many Malay and Siamese, (quite a new creation since the repeal) of which it is impossible to give any numerical estimate, so that the conclusion we must arrive at is that if in this as in other matters, demand dominates supply, then vice has increased by great strides since the repeal, and that State encouragement, or regulation, of vice, tended to reduce immorality.

That disease has enormously increased has been so amply proven by statistics and is a statement now never questioned, but the burden of this does not fall equally on all classes. It was supposed that the enhanced risks run by incontinent men would form a sufficient deterrent, and however true that may be in Britain, it has no possible bearing on Europeans in the East. We must accept them as being the race meant, as they certainly are the only class who comprehend the full extents of the risk they run. Most of that class are in such a position that if they do not possess the "gift" of continence they may form a temporary monogamous union. It is upon the very races with whose sexual ethics we have no power and very little right to interfere, that the disastrous results of the repeal fall. Unaware of the effects of the constitutional disease, they are not restrained by a knowledge they do not possess, and thus the evil goes on, and is perpetuated. The more enlightened among them do resort to treatment, but on the disappearance of the primary and secondary symptoms, it is stopped, and probably never resumed. But everyone knows that syphilis cannot be so easily treated, and it is a law in medicine that no one can be considered harmless under two years.

It has been stated as a palliative argument in favour of the repeal that soon matters would equalize themselves and the number of cases of infection become less. That is true, simply because the number of uninfected persons will become less, year by year, and so long as a trace of the venereal poison remains in the system, re-infection is impossible. But surely this cannot be used as an argument in favour of the repeal. Let me remind you of the statement I made about the unmarried Straits-born youth. After some years of laxity he marries. The chances are that he infects his wife, either directly or through the uteroplacental circulation, or though not actually syphilitic, she may undergo some imperfectly understood transformation which renders her for the future insusceptible to actual inoculation. But what of the children of these unions? My experience, and it is somewhat wide, is that time and again the mother aborts, each successive abortion being of a greater age than the last preceding, then a full-term child is born, dead; then a child which, by a merciful disposition of Providence, dies in a few days, and so on, and then probably the succeeding child lives. But what is it, cursed as it is by the malady which has followed it from its birth, or rather its conception. As infants they grow slowly, are difficult to rear, and walk late, and, when growth is accomplished their figures are slight and much below ordinary height, a boy of 14 or 15 years is like a healthy one of 10—a girl may not develop until 18 or 20. If they escape idiocy their mental development is slow, and the whole condition has been aptly named by Fournier "Infantilism". Below par, mentally and physically, they may be deformed; are these likely to form useful members of society? If it were possible to collect the records of every family which has been formed during the last four years, a picture of misery would be shown, sufficient to convince even Exeter-hallests of the irreparable damage done by the ill-advised repeal of the Contagious Diseases Ordinance in the Straits Settlements.

Next comes the well-worn assertion of the demoralizing effect which the operation of the Act has upon the women. Denying this even in Britain, I may pass on to state the fact that only one prostitute in every 85 in this town is European, and probably there are none at all in the other towns of the Settlements. Thus I am left to consider the demoralizing effects the operation of the Act has upon the other races, in fact, I may say, upon the Chinese, who form the bulk of the remainder. Chinese and even then of a low class, physically women, mentally children, morally nothing, who have probably never known any other environment than that of a brothel, is it likely that their feelings would be shocked, their "morals" degraded by anything the Act might require of them?

Is it not more likely that the strict supervision, the enforced cleanliness both of person and house, the probable detention in hospital where they are strictly under European rule, and the opportunity while there of breaking with the life they had led, all might with perfect truth be cited as powerful arguments in favour of the continuance of the Act? I have already, I hope, proved to you that the Repeal of the Contagious Diseases Ordinance has (1) increased immorality among all classes; (2) increased disease among all classes; and (3) had a demoralizing, or to put it more accurately, relapsing effect on the prostitutes themselves, and I may go on to a further statement it has acted as a bar to marriage in Europeans.

First, possibly by contraction of disease. I know of several instances in which men, engaged to be married, have contracted the constitutional disease, and, being prohibited from marrying for at least two years, have either broken off their marriage or postponed it indefinitely.

CRITICISM
by G.D. Haviland

The subject of Dr. Galloway's most interesting essay is so closely connected with matters of far reaching importance that I much regret having to criticize it before we have heard the essay on sociology with which, according to the syllabus, Mr. Reith will someday favour us.

Dr. Galloway's subject in its broadest view may be divided into three portions.

1) The strictly social portion.
2) The medical portion.
3) Local and temporary governmental exigencies and politics.

The first seems to me by far the most important, but to have been much neglected by Dr. Galloway; it is therefore with it that I shall chiefly deal.

The second or medical portion, Dr. Galloway has, I think, rightly assumed, is a matter for medical experts to decide, and I suppose that no one here tonight will question Dr. Galloway's decision, nevertheless I would point out that if it be shown that there are strong social objections to the CDO, the actual evil of venereal disease, especially on a permanent society after many generations would have to be weighed more carefully than Dr. Galloway has been in a position to do tonight.

The third portion, the question of local and temporary governmental advisabilities seems to me a matter of secondary importance to a Philosophical Society, but Dr. Galloway has almost limited his essay in locality to Singapore, and in time to one or at most two generations from the present. Further Dr. Galloway has been constrained to open his essay by trying to show his rights to regard the inhabitants of Singapore as forming a society, and very ably he has argued, yet a society of which non-indigenous Chinese from the vast bulk of the population flowing in a continuous current, going, coming, and seldom remaining, and of which the Governing Class are a small minority holding their own only by the support furnished by a powerful distant nation, to which they still maintain they belong, and to which they intend to return as soon as dollars are sufficient. Calling it indeed with Dr. Galloway a Society, yet is it a fair one to take in considering the social aspects of the Contagious Diseases Ordinances? Dr. Galloway's remarks on the matter are indeed most interesting, I cannot think, however, that he should attribute the increase of prostitution in Singapore, to the repeal of the Contagious Diseases Acts. The increase of prostitutes in Sarawak has also been great though there has been no change in the manner in which the prostitutes are treated, there is and was a nominally compulsory examination but no means of seclusion. I do not think that the Contagious Diseases Acts or their repeal could have so rapid an effect on the amount of prostitution. One of the most plausible reasons advanced for examination of Kuching prostitutes was that it would hinder the importation of Venereal Disease into genuine societies of Dyaks, where Contagious Diseases Ordinances were impossible, and no doubt such sea-port towns as Singapore do spread venereal disease, if there is no supervision.

I now pass on to the important strictly social portion, and here I find myself not so much on opposing ground to Dr. Galloway as in a wholly different country. Dr. Galloway says "the repeal was agitated for on moral grounds alone. This virtually means that the only people considered were those whom we may class under that most elastic term Christian." This statement reminds me that I have heard from a pulpit that without Christianity morality must disappear, the preacher rested his Christianity on the moral instincts of his hearers, then pulled morality from under and says it must rest on Christianity not Christianity on it, but Dr. Galloway has to me the appearance here of confounding morality with Christianity, and then giving the latter a contemptuous shove; although in other places it is true he does distinguish morality from Christianity.

When I hear these doctrines I feel like a person in a strange country, and like such a one I am doubtless mistaken in my interpretation of what I hear.

There is no need to introduce Christianity here, morality if necessary, can stand alone, stand deep rooted in our instincts and stand justified before Chief Justice reason in the Court of Natural History.

And again Dr. Galloway says "whilst each citizen has been pursuing his individual wants, and none taking thought for aught else", of course Dr. Galloway did not imply what these words can be held to mean, but even then they are not pleasing to those accustomed to pride themselves on British fore-sight and instinctive love of working for the common good, and like to attribute it to British success in gaining the confidence, respect, and peace of Asiatics.

One more sentence of Dr. Galloway's sounds strange, stranger than the others, he says "we must disabuse our minds of any fixed standard of morality", perhaps he was only thinking of sexual morality, yet even this surely is not so. Morality I take to be that which concerns one's duty towards one's neighbour; whilst religion is that which concerns one's Duty towards God. There is but one standard of morality, it is to love one's neighbour as one's self, and there is but one standard of selfishness, it is "Every man for himself", and the devil "take the hindermost". Though we all fall short of both these standards in different degrees and in different directions, and that difficult question of who is one's neighbour is always cropping up, the old answer is the best that the Good Samaritan is a better neighbour than an evil relative. Those are our real neighbours who do to us as we should do to them, who recognize social calls for assistance and compacts never even spoken, who do not want the stimuli of public opinion, of free-masonary forms, of legal documents, of law courts, of police, of soldiers or of dynamite.

I have seen this instinct dominant in Europeans who have ceased to profess Christianity. I have seen it in Sea Dyaks, not of that class so easily bribed to hypocrisy by missionary offers of free education, nor to that class which are easily led and easily misled, but amongst those who will not turn Christian, and I have one in particular in my mind who much wanted to learn to read and write, but gave it up rather than pay the required fee of becoming a Christian.

The instincts of good and evil in man are very deeply seated, he loves good first and God after, he hates evil first and the devil after. The origin of these instincts was natural selection. Moral instincts were produced when small tribes united stood but divided fell. The selfish instincts arose when tribes and nations were safe enough for individuals to break faith with and cheat one another. Individual competition though a stimulus productive of much temporary activity and good yet in the long run may, under unguided circumstances, be the selector of selfish people, the destroyer of social life and the origin of evil. Looking then upon good instincts as those leading the individuals to work for the welfare of society, tribe or species, we must extend our idea of neighbour from the present to the future, to future generations yet unborn whom our present actions may affect, and we must not forget that a man's actions may go on bearing fruit many centuries after he is in his grave.

In sexual morality the standard is the same, but the subject is more complex. No doubt the sexual instincts are immeasurably older than the social ones, and are as necessary to the perpetuation of societies and tribes as of species. But even amongst most rudimentary societies of animals, sexual competition followed by jealousy and selfishness has appeared, and produced war-like weapons of offence and defence, and may possibly have been the cause of the extinction in some no longer existing species. There have been two ways in which this sexual jealousy has been partly avoided in different species. Our method is to form permanent monogamous unions recognized, sectioned and upheld by public opinion and by law. Dyaks have the same method, but more readily divorce, and Dr. Galloway's observations on the frequency of monogamy Mohametan Malays suggests that their instincts favour the same action. Of course with men there is a stronger reason for monogamy than this, for the children require the assistance of the father for a great number of years, but even many birds as pigeons are monogamous and here the young develop quickly.

The other method of avoiding selfishness is far more advanced than ours, it is that adopted by ants, bees, and wasps. The majority in each social community are sterile, and these sterile ones are typically unselfish, each one values himself only as of so much use to the colony, each loves its neighbour as itself, but they love their queen better because she is more important to the colony, yet they are colonially selfish and will rob the bees of other hives, for there is colonial competition, the queens or breeding females are the types of selfishness and two can never meet without a fight. The drones or males again are the type of laziness.

Amongst the lower class of Europeans and amongst society in more rudimentary conditions, sexual intercourse amongst unmarried people is generally not held in much disgrace, provided that both men and women are ready to stand by the consequences, the fault in this case is rather thoughtlessness than selfishness.

But amongst races showing a greater amount of specialization and therefore according to Dr. Galloway's sociological axiom more civilized, women have been differentiated into the honourable and the dishonourable, the former are to be always virtuous, ready to supply the male with home and his virtuous pleasures when he wants to wear his best behaviour, and the other always degraded, ready to supply the male with his dissolute pleasures when he wants to wear his loose behaviour and yet we hear of the brutal way savages treat their females. I believe with Dr. Galloway that the spirit of true chivalry is not yet extinct in the breasts of Englishmen, yet let us not confound with this the base selfishness which leads some men to lay great stress on the honour of their sisters and relations whilst they purchase with money the dishonour of their poorer neighbour's sisters.

There is another factor in the question which I am surprised that Dr. Galloway did not mention, that is the too rapid increase of population. A society not increasing in numbers supplies no *raison d'etre* for prostitution, children are in demand both by the state and the individuals and happy is the man who has his quiver full of them. One of the things I noticed in Sarawak was the frequency and readiness with which people in that thinly populated country adopt other children than their own. Amongst Societies steadily increasing something must someday occur to stop the increase, what shall it be? The natural means are starvation, exposure, disease and war, all these we are endeavouring to avoid. The unnatural means are celibacy, prostitution, infanticide and other more modern methods and all these are bad, but of all in my opinion is common prostitution the most objectionable, and I venture to assert, contrary as it is to Europeans that a man who kills an infant for fear of overpopulation does no more harm to the individual and to the state than the man who makes a prostitute. But please do not imagine from this that I am advocating infanticide, I am rather expressing a very strong opinion against public prostitution, and asserting the impossibility of continuing a steady increase of population for an indefinite length of time. Our difficulties in this matter are, however, the result of our increasing knowledge. By its use we have removed the natural means of keeping down the population, but by a further increase of biological knowledge we shall probably be able to overcome our difficulties before they overcome us, and to turn them into future helps. We must not forget that it is this tendency to increase of population which is our most valuable heritage, it is the reserve force by the guidance of which alone, can selection, natural or artificial, improve or liability to disease physical, mental, or moral.

Dr. Galloway has mentioned four legitimate ways of encouraging continence in man, and they are no doubt very useful, but we must not forget that encouraging continence in the virtuous and leaving the incontinent to breed would in the long run be a fatal policy for future generations, that by encouraging prostitution the incontinent leave less children, and that by encouraging infanticide we might in the long run increase parental affection.

Already as we have, I believe, reached an age when breading societies could be formed amongst the better class, in which those tainted with an unusual amount of liability to physical, mental or moral disease, would not be allowed to remain in the society and breed, and the societies might in this way effect a visible improvement in themselves in a few generations, but I trust that Dr. Galloway's test of civilization will never excuse men for dividing women into the professionally honourable and the professionally dishonourable, nor excuse the better class for improving themselves at the expense of the lower, or justify their burdening them with their refuse, or for splitting mankind generally into the improving and the degrading.

In conclusion, I would say that I quite admit Dr. Galloway's medical views of the question, and have learned much from his statement of the special conditions in Singapore, but I differ so entirely from him on what I regard as the truly social aspects of the case, that in criticizing I have had to cover a much larger ground than I thought at first would be necessary, and that the time at my disposal would grant me to properly defend.

Whilst Dr. Galloway undervalues moral sexual instincts, appearing to regard them as whims of Christian minorities, and entirely neglecting the future of the human race, I look on moral instincts like bravery as developed for the good of the society or tribe; immoral instincts like cowardice as the produce of selfish competition, the destroyers of society, the origin of sin.

One of the most unfortunate cases of syphilis I know was contracted by a man travelling on the continent of Europe, at a place where he thought prostitutes were examined and he might safely be incautious. I am sure that venereal disease discredits sexual immorality, and I think that government regulation, even to the examination of prostitutes, lessens the strength of public opinion against prostitution. Public opinion rules the greater half of the world especially that half which most requires assistance against the sexually immoral impulses. I fear that the carrying out of the Contagious Diseases Ordinances will, in greater part than it diminishes contagious disease, increase infectious moral disease for which Iodides and Mercury are in no way specifics.

Notes

1. J.W. Schariff, "The Life and Times of Sir David Galloway", *Singapore Medical Journal* 1, no. 3 (September 1960): 84–86.
2. "Haviland, George Darby (1857–1901)", *Natural History Museum, Plant Collectors* at: https://plants.jstor.org/stable/10.5555/al.ap.person.bm000390277.
3. See James Francis Warren, *Ah Ku and Karayuki-San: Prostitution in Singapore 1870–1940* (Singapore: NUS Press, 2003), chap. 5.
4. Ibid., p. 106.
5. Ibid., p. 109.

10

THE OPIUM PROBLEM IN THE STRAITS SETTLEMENTS

Essay

12 August 1893

by *Rev. George M. Reith*

Editors' Note

As with the sex trade, the opium trade was another contested area of British policy in the Straits and one which was the object of discussion in the Society in 1893 on an evening in which two papers on the topic were presented. At this time the colonial policy of revenue farming was coming under pressure from moral reformers and Liberal politicians in Britain and by 1893, a Commission was appointed by Gladstone to investigate whether the trade should be suppressed across the Empire.[1] In 1893 the Secretary of the Anti-Opium Society would arrive in the Straits to study the situation in the colony,[2] whilst there was also emerging a growing anti-opium movement led by missionaries such as Rev. W.G. Shellabear, Rev. A. Lamont, Rev. J.A.B. Cook and Straits Chinese thinkers like Lim Boon Keng and Tan Teck Soon.[3] As with Galloway's essay, a dominant theme in Reith's essay was how, in the face of liberal criticisms, an exception could be made for the colony, and the opium trade justified. In doing so Reith would follow arguments not dissimilar to those made by Galloway. An exception was firstly justified because the scale of the use of opium in the colony made demand difficult to eradicate. Secondly, suppression of production in British India would only drive traders in the colony to source opium from China, sending the trade underground, increasing smuggling, and harming the tax revenue of the colony. Finally, he argued that suppression of the trade would worsen relations between the Chinese and Europeans, citing recent disturbances in Kulim as proof.[4] In this way Reith resurrected the spectre of the violent and difficult to govern Chinese to justify the continued trade in opium.

Though the object of a Philosophical Society is to dig about the roots of things, to question fact or imagination about the causes of things, and to weave theories about the moral bearing of things, yet the Straits Philosophical Society can hardly discuss the much discussed question about the opium traffic, without having much to say about the opium problem as it presents itself to this colony.

We are threatened with legislation which may seriously affect the financial standing of the colony, and which may establish an altogether new and perhaps unpleasant relation between the ruling nation and the majority of the population. Such legislation, if it comes, will be found to be, for the most part, prompted and passed by men unconversant with the facts and difficulties of the case, by men, who, most likely, are unable to distinguish between opium problems in India, and the opium problem in the Straits Settlements. My contribution to this evening's discussion is, therefore, a statement of the opium problem in the Straits Settlements as it appears to me; and I make it not without a selfish reason. Good people at home expect men of my profession to be against the opium traffic and to agitate for its suppression in season and out of season; they call us traitors to a sacred cause, if we give an uncertain sound on the subject. To them, the Right is always the Possible—a sentiment with which I cordially agree—but they do not appreciate the difficulties of a man, who lives on the spot, in his search for the Right in a problem which is not as simple as those who look at it through a telescope imagine. Further, as I have had before, and may have again, to justify my attitude on this question, to angry total abolitionists who think there is no room for doubt on the matter, I am anxious to know if my view of the problem commends itself to those who have lived longer in the colony than I have, who have given the question more thought, and have opportunities of more intimate knowledge of the subject.

In the first place, I take it as an admitted fact that the opium habit, in all its forms, is injurious, and therefore, to put it mildly, should not be encouraged. Any system that tends, directly or indirectly, to the encouragement of the habit by increasing the supply of opium, cheapening it in the market, or entrusting the control of the traffic to persons whose interest it is to push the sale of the drug, I would regard as unjustifiable, on grounds of wisdom and morality. To encourage the weakening and enervating of the governed to increase the revenues of the Government is a policy both short-sighted and foolish.

But in the Straits Settlements there is a demand for opium—a great demand; and the problem is how is that demand to be met? By an absolute refusal—or how?

The opium monopoly in India—reference to which will probably be made tonight—has very little bearing, it seems to me, on the problem in the Straits Settlements. Suppose the growth and sale of opium in India, under Government auspices, wholly suppressed at once—our problem would remain unchanged. There would be no more opium from India, but China, in a very short time, if not immediately, would be able, and glad to, supply the local demand. Thus our problem remains the same. How shall the Straits Government treat the large local demand for opium? There are four courses open to the Government: first, free trade in opium, allowing the unrestricted importation and sale of the drug. That is a course which none but the confirmed opium smoker would advocate. Second, total suppression; the absolute prohibition of the importation and sale of opium, save for medicinal purposes. Third, the farm system at present in existence; and fourth, a system like that which places the liquor traffic in the United Kingdom under the direct control of a Government department, levies a heavy excise duty on the liquor made, imported or sold, and exacts a large sum for license to carry on the trade. This last is a scheme with several advantages, for it puts a restriction on the traffic by increasing the cost of the drug, strictly limits the number of shops where it is sold, and does not place the control of its importation and sale in the hands of persons whose interest it is to push the traffic.

There are very strong objections to the total suppression of the traffic, all practical objections. No doubt we all admit the desirability of its suppression; it would be a good thing if the opium habit were totally eradicated; but when, as practical men, we are face to face with the question—How is it to be done in this colony?—the difficulties seem insurmountable.

The desire for stimulants and narcotics is almost universal. Alcohol, tobacco, ganja, opium, and twenty other drugs are used by various races, and according to the demand so is the supply. Even the good people who frown on the use of stimulants and narcotics have in the sense of superior virtue which accompanies the criticism of other men's weaknesses that which is as exhilarating as any stimulant and at the same time as soothing as any narcotic. The question opened by this almost universal demand for such things is—How far is a Government entitled to refuse so large and so persistent a demand? The existence and persistence of the demand may be regrettable; but here it is, what are we to do with it? Total suppression of the opium traffic in this colony would entail a large additional expense for the establishment and maintenance of a preventive service. This would be an absolute necessity, for Europeans and natives alike would jump at the chance of fortune given them in smuggling enterprise. The Chinaman will have his opium somehow; if not with the consent of the Government, then without it. Even now, owing to the dearness of opium, large quantities are smuggled into the colony every month, despite the vigilance of the opium farmer's detectives. Total suppression of the traffic would cause an enormous increase of smuggling, and opium would be as plentiful as before, if not more so.

Then, again, total suppression would give rise to unpleasant relations between the Chinese and the Europeans. The recent incident at Kulim has its moral. There was a legend in the colony when I arrived, to the effect that the Straits Government would yield anything on the threat of a Chinese riot. If that be true, between the Colonial Office and the

Chinese the Straits Government would be in very uncomfortable quarters, if an edict for total suppression came from England.

These are some of the practical difficulties that occur to me. There are probably many others.

With regard to the farm system, that, I think, should be abolished, on moral grounds; for the farm being sold to the highest bidder, the lessee has his own profit in view when he bids, and it is his interest to push the sale of opium. The more opium smokers, the merrier for him; it is to his advantage to sell as much as he can to encourage the trade by all means in his power.

But the opium traffic is not a trade to be encouraged; the contraction and satisfaction of the opium habit should be made as difficult as possible; and though the farm system saves the government considerable trouble and expense, its tendency is to directly foster a traffic which right-minded men would most gladly see diminished, and ultimately stopped. In this colony however, its suppression seems beyond our power; the next best thing to do is to regulate and restrict it in every possible way.

Notes

1. See Carl Trocki, *Opium and Empire: Chinese Society in Colonial Singapore, 1800–1910* (Ithaca: Cornell University Press), p. 184.
2. "An Opium Agitator on the way to the Straits", *Straits Times Weekly Issue*, 28 November 1893.
3. Cheng U. Wen, "Opium in the Straits Settlements, 1867–1910", *Journal of Southeast Asian History* 2, no. 1 (1961): 56; "The Anti-Opium Meeting in the Town Hall", *Daily Advertiser*, 7 March 1894.
4. On the disturbances in Kulim, see Wu Xiao An, *Chinese Business in the Making of a Malay State, 1882–1941: Kedah and Penang* (Singapore: NUS Press, 2010), pp. 67–69.

11

THE RELATION OF THE OPIUM TRAFFIC TO LOCAL REVENUE

Essay

12 August 1893

by *Arthur Knight*

Editors' Note

In contrast to Reith's sentiments, his fellow member Arthur Knight, a prominent civil servant and Freemason,[1] represented the voice of moral reform in the colony. He argued for a duty of moral improvement on behalf of the British Empire and challenged the inevitability of the trade. He also highlighted both the opposition amongst the Chinese to opium use, as well as the evident British interest in the continuation of the trade. At the time of this discussion the British trade in opium was considerable and lucrative so a defence of the continuation of the trade was not unexpected. It has been estimated that opium revenue comprised 43 per cent of the total revenue of the Straits Settlements in 1895.[2] It was not until 1907 when China signed a ten years' agreement with India—whereby China agreed to forbid native cultivation and consumption of opium on the understanding that the export of Indian opium would decline in proportion and cease completely in ten years—that the trade began to be suppressed. In the Straits Settlements though, the opium trade continued to be a major contributor to government revenue right until the Second World War.

As I said at our last meeting, there is an important distinction between the Indian opium revenue and the opium revenue of this colony. The Government of India is the great grower and manufacturer of opium for sale. In this colony the revenue raised is very much in the nature of an excise, and differs little in principle from the excise on liquor which contributes so largely to the revenue of the mother-country.

I understand that I am expected to furnish some facts bearing on the question as it affects this colony.

First as to the revenue from this source. I shall give in most cases the actual figures, but as the opium and spirit farms are sometimes combined, I have had then to estimate the proportion attributable to the opium. However, my figures will be sufficiently exact for practical purposes.

The transfer of these Settlements from the Indian to the Colonial Government took place on the 1st of April 1867. The excise farms were an important part of the revenue then taken over, and the opium farms yielded in 1868, the first complete year after the transfer, a total of $432,525. For some years this and the other sources of revenue advanced so slowly that the then Auditor-General, in two successive annual reports, spoke of the revenue as being essentially inelastic. At that time the farms were let by public auction, at first annually and then for periods of three years. For the three years 1874–76 the letting had only risen to $552,000. For the next triennial period it rose to $709,392; but the increase was almost wholly in Penang; so it became evident that the farms at the other Settlements were greatly underlet. This was effected by combination among the Chinese to keep down the biddings, and the result was that the Chinese concerned in the farms grew enormously wealthy at the public expense. The advance secured in Penang on the occasion in question was, in fact, merely the consequence of a split among the Chinese capitalists at that Settlement. It was to counteract the combination referred to, and to secure something like the fair value of the farms, that the plan, still in vogue, was adopted of letting the farms by tender. The prices then rose rapidly, the lettings for the three succeeding periods having been $1,143,000, $1,593,600, and $1,779,600. Then came the greatest rise of all, the opium farms, for the years 1889–91 having been let for the large sum of $2,331,200. But the capitalists had over-reached themselves, there came a check in the prosperity of the colony and diminished Chinese immigration; in 1890 the Penang Farm failed, and the Singapore Farm had to seek relief. The actual amount recovered for that year was $2,312,200 and some of this was not paid till 1892. For 1891 temporary arrangements were made at the reduced revenue of $1,827,558, and for the period 1892–94 the farms were re-let for $1,545,555.

This is still considerably above the period 1886–88, the last letting before the great rise, and is more than half the total revenue of the colony. It is difficult to forecast the future revenue from this source. It depends not only upon the measure of general prosperity, but upon the effect of the Indian currency changes on the cost of procuring the opium. I read that on the announcement by the Government of India of the closing of the mints to silver, the price of opium fell R100 a chest at Calcutta but that fall was not permanent, and the depression of the rate of exchange with India greatly increases the cost of remittances.

There remains also the prospect of the agitation against the opium traffic eventuating in putting an end to the Indian opium trade. We might still get opium from China or elsewhere; but there may even come a demand for prohibition of the import and sale. If this could really be at once prevented, it would only be at the cost of terrible popular commotion; but it would really be impossible to prevent it. The drug would still be imported and used, and things would not be improved, but the revenue would be destroyed.

From one point of view, the raising of revenue from an article which (not to beg the question) I will call an instrument of self-indulgence seems most unobjectionable; but on the other hand, it has the effect of giving the Government a direct interest in increasing the consumption of a substance the excessive use of which is very common and most injurious. Our Government does not by any *direct* action encourage the consumption. It fixes a maximum price for the retail sales of the prepared opiums, and endeavours so to fix it as to limit the consumption by rendering the article expensive, while not rendering it inaccessible to those who have contracted the taste for it. It is to be feared, however, that the farmers or their agents do not refrain from devices to tempt people to indulgence in smoking. And herein lies the objection to the farm system; the old evil connected with farming revenue—that of opening the way to extortion—being avoided by the limiting of the price. But it is certain that by no other method could the government raise the same amount of revenue; and this has, in fact, been shown by the result of an experiment in Hongkong; for it would be impossible for the government to equal the farmers—Chinese themselves—in circumventing the "ways that are dark and tricks that are vain" of Chinese in their endeavours to obtain cheap chandu either for their own consumption or for sale at a profit.

The profit is, of course, enormous, or the revenue would not be secured. A chest of opium costing now $560, will yield besides some other products about 1,070 taels of chandu, which at the present price $2.20, yields, $2,354, and the cost of preparation is comparatively trifling. It is no secret, however, that the attention of this Government has already been called by the Secretary of State to the advisability of re-considering the present mode of collecting the opium revenue.

As regards the number of opium shops, the farmers have given me the following figures: Singapore, 475; Malacca, 90. In Penang and Province Wellesley I am informed the number is 132 of which number 22 are what are called dens. In Singapore I have not ascertained the number of shops which have smoking accommodation but taking the Penang proportion it may be put at about 80. These figures are perhaps worth recording, because I notice that Mr. Henry Varley, with his usual regard for accuracy, made at a meeting at Bombay the preposterous statement that there were "1200 licensed Opium dens in Singapore alone". I cannot give with certainty the amount of chandu consumed, but from various data I estimate it at about 90,000 lbs. per annum in Singapore, Johore, and the neighbouring Dutch islands combined.

It cannot be denied that the question of revenue is a very serious element in the opium question, both in India and here, yet I hope that we here are all prepared to consider the question in the light of what is right and just. It does not come within my province to discuss the moral question at large, but I ask permission briefly to refer to the three facts, or rather classes of facts, from my statement of which you will gather that I regard the opium trade as on its defence.

First, I fear it must be admitted that we practically force our Indian opium upon China; and, although we are not chargeable with the first introduction of the drug into that country, it cannot be doubted that its use has largely increased since the import has been permitted; and that however harmless, and possibly beneficial, it may be to certain hardworking classes using it in moderation, that it has been productive of widespread injury to the people. Further, the growth of the poppy in China itself has increased, and the Chinese urge that it is permitted in self-defence, and that if the importation were prohibited, they could and would in time put down the growth.

Second, I remember that some years ago, before the anti-opium agitation had attained its present strength, its leaders gave prominence to the argument that the "Indian-Government were forcing upon the Chinese a drug of whose injurious qualities they showed themselves conscious by prohibiting its sale among their own people." But now we hear a different story; of late years the Government of India has been pushing the sale in that country, and has even introduced it in Upper Burma, whence it was excluded by the barbarous Government which we displaced.

Thirdly, what is the estimation in which opium and its use for self-indulgence are generally held? First, we have the fact that it is rigidly excluded from Japan. Then, I have often heard here from natives the scornful expression *"dia makan chandu punya orang sahja"* (he is only an opium-smoker) as a sufficient description of a worthless and degraded character. And lastly we have the practically unanimous testimony of Christian Missionaries, Roman Catholic and Protestant, and of Native Christians. It is the fashion with many persons to scout the opinion of missionaries as prejudiced; but they are, of all classes of outer barbarians, in the best position for ascertaining the mind of the Chinese; and it must be admitted that if self-interest comes into this question it is not on *their* side, except indeed, for the hindrance that opium presents to the work in which they are engaged. It is well known that in China the use of opium, nay, even its growing or selling, is universally held to be a sufficient ground for exclusion from a native Christian Church; and I have read of more than one case in which the Native Christians have been more strict in enforcing this rule than the missionaries themselves.

Notes

1. "Obituary: A Singapore Veteran, Mr. Arthur Knight", *Malaya Tribune*, 29 November 1916.
2. Cheng U. Wen, "The Chinese in Malaya", *Journal of Southeast Asian History* 2, no. 1 (March 1961): 52.

12

THE PREVENTION AND REPRESSION OF CRIME

Essay

14 October 1893
by *C.W.S. Kynnersley*

Editors' Note

C.W.S. Kynnersley joined the Straits Settlements Civil Service in 1872, before becoming Superintendent of Prisons in Penang in 1877 and later served as a Magistrate in Penang.[1] According to Ridley in *Noctes Orientales* his paper of 1893 was one of the few contributions to the Society to affect a policy change in the colony.[2] As with earlier essays on sex work and opium, Kynnersley's contribution placed emphasis on the Chinese population of the colony, who formed the bulk of the prison population, and who he saw as vital to study in order to understand the roots of crime in the colony. For Kynnersley, the realities of migration and the lack of traditional authority were central themes. In China the Chinese were "under restraint, like a child reverencing his elders and betters", in Singapore they had no respect for European officials. In such a racialized context Kynnersley would reject liberal opinion in England which saw education as preventative of crime. Instead, he argued that what Singapore required was a better policing and penal system. At the same time he noted that the system's focus on hard labour tended to produce only hardened prisoners and ignored the potential for their reform and improvement through work.

Tan Teck Soon's contribution provided a counterpoint. Drawing on the discourse of moral reform in the colony he argued that a proper channel of communication between the Chinese and the authorities would make possible the use of education as a means to teach people the benefits and advantages of upholding the law. This was more than just a question of moral reform for Tan. For him, the Chinese were no longer just temporary migrants but had increasingly made Malaya their home, and the colonial government had an obligation to develop a civic basis for order in the colony. As one of the two Chinese members in the Society, it has been noted that Tan's notable contribution, as an intellect and writer, was in reconceptualizing Chinese civilization as progressive and open to change, which challenged the prevailing Western idea that Chinese civilization was antiquated and unprogressive.[3]

When, owing to an unavoidable change in our Syllabus, I was asked at a recent meeting of this Society to read an essay, I rashly undertook to address you on the subject of the prevention and repression of crime.

My reason for selecting this subject was that I had been led to consider this important question in connection with the prison, and had formed the conclusion that the system there in force, far from tending to repress crime by exercising a deterrent effect on the criminal classes, had the very opposite result, and was one of the principal factors in the promotion of crime.

Except when they are robbed by their Hailam servants, Europeans out here do not concern themselves with the subject of crime and criminals.

In England the subject in connection with the great social problem is continually forced upon us.

In discussing this question I might have attempted to deal with the various methods which have been suggested or adopted in various countries at different times for the prevention of crime, but I have thought it better to confine my remarks to crime in this colony, and to the measures which might be taken to check and diminish it.

I have further narrowed the scope of my essay by confining my remarks to Chinese criminals, as they form the bulk of our prison population (650 out of 840), and by taking crime in its restricted sense to mean offences against property, such as theft, housebreaking and robbery.

It is commonly thought that when the Government has established a police force, courts of justice, and prisons, it has done all that can be expected of it. This, at least, was the common opinion in England until the beginning of this century. The best way of stamping out crimes like theft was thought to be the hanging of the guilty parties. It is unnecessary to refer to the barbarous treatment of prisoners in those days, suffice it to say that, instead of operating as a deterrent, these punishments, by being so common, had no effect whatever in suppressing crime. Then a more enlightened age dawned, and it was recognized that one of the duties of the State was to see that the people were educated. The death penalty was reserved for the crimes of murder and treason. Transportation for life was abolished. Convict prisons, instead of being perfect hells on earth, were transformed into places where a criminal had a fair chance of amendment. Ardent prison reformers arose, and schemes without end for making criminals into virtuous men were propounded. Reformatories and industrial schools sprung up. Prisoners' aid societies, to assist the criminal on his release, were started; and it must be admitted that a wonderful advance has been made during the last fifty years in this branch of social science.

It may be useful at this point to consider the very different conditions under which crime is propagated here and in England.

It is well known that more than three-fourths of the crime committed in the British Isles is directly traceable to drink. Happily in this colony drink is answerable for a very small percentage of crime, and it will not be necessary to deal with this terrible curse of European lands. It cannot be doubted that much of the crime in England is hereditary. Born and bred in the slums of our great towns, the offspring of drink and destitution, a race of criminals is reared, which goes forth to revenge itself on society.

I do not know who is the oldest inhabitant of the Settlement, but it may well be that there is some ancient mariner still living who saw the British flag hoisted for the first time amid the jungle of Singapore.

The Settlement has indeed barely exceeded the allotted term of a man's life, and we have none of those terrible evils to contend with here which afflict darkest England, and are the outcome of our imperfect civilization and the system of competition. Here we have no land monopoly, game-laws, or poor-law to inveigh against and point to as the cause of poverty and crime. This is indeed a free country, and I contend that, with the exceptional advantages we enjoy, it is our duty as citizens seriously to consider whether the amount of crime which exists among us cannot be greatly diminished.

We do not read in the papers items like the following, which I take from a county paper:

> At the police court on Thursday, Maria Brockway, found asleep under a tree in a meadow, 7 days' hard labour. Walter Shepherd, for sleeping in the open air and having no visible means of subsistence, 7 days. Prisoner said he had nowhere to go, and had been turned out of doors. James Harford, a travelling workman, was charged with sleeping in an outhouse. Prisoner said he had come to lie down, and was discharged on promising to quit the town.

Major Grey, in one of his annual prison reports, remarks that the bulk of the Chinese population is composed of a low order of males in their prime, unrestrained by domestic life or ties of any kind, than whom it would be difficult to find in any portion of H.M. Dominions material better adapted for the production of criminals. I do not entirely agree with this. It is, of course, a fact that there exists a great disproportion between the sexes.

At the last census there were in Singapore 100,446 male Chinese and 21,462 females. Whether the absence of women tends to increase crime—I speak of crimes of violence and crimes relating to property—I am not prepared to say. It is, of course, an evil, but under the circumstances almost a necessary evil. At all events it tends to check the propagation of vicious children, and though we get relays of adult criminals, the number of home-bred youthful offenders is so comparatively small that there should be no difficulty in looking after them.

I do not admit the absence of home ties. With English people it would be different. Say there is a rush to a mining district in Australia. The greed for gold at once attracts several thousand able-bodied males. They, it is true, have no home ties. They give way to drink, crimes of violence and rapacity. With the Chinaman here it is entirely different.

The cause of emigration from China is almost invariably want or political necessity. Hordes of uneducated Chinese flock yearly to this Golden Chersonese, and by their industry in a few years earn sufficient money to return to their homes and families, taking with them their earnings.

They leave their parents, wives, and children in their native land, and come here for the sole purpose of accumulating money. The influence of home is always with them, and family remittances are regularly made even by the poorest coolie. The most abandoned criminal never loses the sense of filial piety, and one of the things which prisoners feel most is that while in jail they cannot earn money to send home.

By nature the Chinese are a hard-working, energetic race. So long as they are physically fit they have no difficulty in earning a livelihood. Thus they have not the temptations that an Englishman has to prefer a dishonest way of gaining a living. Here we have no hereditary pauper class; there is no poverty. There is no drink. The craving for opium may induce theft, but the opium-smoker does not commit crimes as the result of smoking. Gambling is a vice to which the Chinese are greatly addicted, and no doubt in many cases gambling leads to crime. In this city we do not see, as in London, the mansions of the rich and the display of opulence in juxtaposition with the dens of poverty and vice. The only daily want is a few cents to buy rice. Lodging, fires, clothing, and other necessaries of life are not required here.

The Chinaman may land in this free port without money, without friends, but he will find no difficulty in getting employment. Unless he has been too poor to pay his passage from China—in which case he is bound by an agreement for a year to repay the money advanced on his behalf by his employer—he is his own master, and enjoys full equal rights with the Englishman. Now his dangers begin. At home in his native village he was under restraint, like a child reverencing his elders and betters. Here he is monarch of all he surveys. He has no respect for red-haired governors, or for the race of barbarians who perform the dirty work of government for his benefit. For the Tai Jin, who has taken the trouble to learn his language, and dwells in a Chinese house hung with mystic scrolls, he has some regard, especially when later he finds that he carries banishment warrants about him.

When he was at home he was taught to reverence authority. The magistrate of his district was a man to be feared, and he could see the punishment meted out to evil-doers. We have all read descriptions of the forms of punishment in vogue in China. Whether they are found effective in repressing crime I am not prepared to say, but there is certainly no deception about them. The torture is very real and very visible. There he toiled on honestly till, impelled perhaps by the pinches of poverty or by the glowing tales of returning emigrants, he felt it his duty to his family to go forth to a country which, though nominally under barbarian rule, is to him a Chinese colony.

Transplanted here, all is changed. He finds some clumsy kind of machinery which serves as law, but so uncertain and incomprehensible that it may safely be disregarded. The magistrate, instead of being a venerable man surrounded with all the insignia of important office and armed with terrible powers, he finds is a comparatively youthful red-haired official, armed with very limited authority, and kept in check by a useful, though somewhat extortionate, class of barbarians, who, for a consideration, will prove that what to the common eye has a black appearance is in the eye of the law white.

Until by recent legislation the dangerous societies were suppressed, the Chinese immigrant was soon sworn in and became a member of the brotherhood. From that moment he had all the power of his society at his back. If he was unfortunate enough to be arrested, his society bailed him out; if a lawyer was required, his society came forward with the necessary fee. If he required witnesses, they could be procured in any quantity. If he was compelled to be a fugitive from justice, the society would harbour him or get him safe out of the place; if the police demanded a victim, one was found. Thus, and in countless other ways, was justice defeated and our system of government brought into supreme contempt. Happily we have changed all this. I do not mean to say that there are no secret societies existing at present. So long as this colony is peopled by the Chinese race, such societies will be started, and if at any time the watchfulness and energy of the Protectorate fail, then will these societies become dangerous again. But the great point is that all such societies are under a ban, and we no longer recognize an *imperium in imperio*.

Having thus got rid of what was a great blot on our administration, it is worthy of consideration whether something might not be done to utilize, in the interests of government, some of the most prominent and respected Chinese citizens. It cannot be denied that there are among the Chinese inhabitants of Singapore many men of position and worth, who might well be trusted to assist in the work of governing their countrymen.

Something has of late been done in this direction by the institution of an advisory board, which is consulted on questions affecting the Chinese part of the community.

The Po-Leung-Kuk, too, does useful work; but no Chinaman is employed in a position of authority higher than a revenue officer or a detective.

Having now, so to speak, cleared the ground to a certain extent by contrasting the conditions under which crime exists and flourishes at home and in this colony, and landed the potential criminal on these shores, I will discuss the means which might be taken to prevent the increase of crime.

I come before you not as a professional philanthropist, nor as a faddist believing in any nostrum which is guaranteed to cure vice, whether inherited or not, and make the oldest offender virtuous.

The expectation that crime may be cured by education, or the silent system, or the separate system, or any other system invented by man, must be regarded as purely Utopian. I ask you, as men of the world, to consider this question from a practical point of view. It is our duty as the governing power in this land to take measures for the repression of crime, although the criminals are of an alien race. This country—I do not speak of the three Settlements, but of British Malaya—has undoubtedly a great future, and year by year will the tide of Chinese immigrants flow in till they cover the Peninsula. It rests with us, and with those who come after us, to establish a reign of law and order, and to see that we do not breed up in our midst a race of criminals. If the dragon's teeth are sown now, they will come up as an army of robbers.

It is a common opinion in England that education is in itself a preventive of crime, whereas the fact is that ignorance and crime are not cause and effect; they are coincident results of the same cause. Scarcely any connection exists between morality and the discipline of ordinary teaching. Mere culture of the intellect (and education as usually conducted amounts to little more) is hardly at all operative upon conduct. Creeds pasted upon the memory, good principles learnt by rote, lessons in right and wrong, will not eradicate vicious propensities. In the majority of cases precepts do not act at all.

Men cannot be made virtuous by Act of Parliament, neither can they by moral maxims. The Chinese are brought up from their infancy on moral maxims. The influence of the teaching of Confucius is strongly marked in the national character. The sage himself was once Minister of Crime. The result of his work was, we are told, that, as in the days of King Alfred, a thing dropped on the road was not picked up; there was no fraudulent carving of vessels; coffins were made of the ordained thickness; graves were unmarked by mounds raised over them; and no two prices were charged in the markets. Crime is said to have disappeared, and the penal laws remained a dead letter. Crime, he held, is not inherent in human nature, and therefore the father in the family and the Government in the State are responsible for the crimes committed against filial piety and the public laws. He relied on the force of example, and inspired men with a spirit of loyalty and good faith. When someone, distressed about the number of thieves in the State, inquired of Confucius how to do away with them, the reply was: "If you, Sir, were not covetous, although you should reward them to do it, they would not steal." Such was the admiration felt for the sage that for a time his example was copied by those in authority about him, and this no doubt reacted on the common people. Honesty was shown to be the best policy, and the people became honest. Truly great is the force of example. Take an Eastern State like Siam. The king is defrauded of his revenue and deceived by his princes; the troops and police are not paid—judges will do nothing unless they are bribed—the police, not being paid, take it out of the people, and so on. Here we flatter ourselves we are much better, but can we say that the standard of morality is a high one? The competition in trade is becoming keener every year, and it is a case of everyone for himself.

As I have said, I do not in this paper propose to treat of crimes such as fraudulent bankruptcy, cheating, criminal breach of trust, etc., but I cannot ignore them. You may, I think, justly complain that I have treated you to a lecture on crime, but so far have not suggested any remedies. I will now proceed to do so.

In the first place, so long as this colony is looked upon as an asylum for all the bad characters who have either been banished from, or have found it expedient to leave neighbouring countries, the criminal class will be constantly recruited.

Our neighbours the Dutch take the most stringent measures to prevent the importation of criminals.

The general terms of the law in force in Netherlands India are that all foreigners arriving in the country must within three days of their arrival report themselves to the local authorities and give proof of their identity; from where they come, and of their object in coming to Netherlands India.

Transgressions of this law are punished with fines at so much per day. Non-residents travelling without a permit, or found in Netherlands India after the prescribed period without a permit to travel or reside, are sent out of the colony by the head of the local Government. Here we have no enactment of the kind. If it so pleased the Dutch Government, they might, instead of imprisoning their convicts, pay their passages to Singapore, and no questions would be asked. I merely mention this as one factor that must be taken into consideration in regard to this question. The supply of criminals is thus constantly kept up, and any attempt to check this influx of bad characters by special legislation would, I fear, be regarded as contrary to English principles.

Secondly, it is the duty of the State to see that youths are not brought up to be criminals. Here we are on common ground with English social reformers. Owing to the fact that the labouring classes who form the bulk of our prison population leave their wives and families behind them, the number of children is comparatively small.

It would, however, be a fatal mistake to ignore the rising generation on that account, and anyone who has sat as a magistrate, or had anything to do with our prisons, must be aware that there are a very large and increasing number of youthful offenders. Magistrates are very averse to sending them to prison, where they will work in association with adult criminals, and there is no kind of reformatory institution to which they can be sent. We have, it is true, a Reformatories Ordinance (No. II of 1890); but if "stone walls do not a prison make", still less does an Ordinance make a reformatory, and meantime the only alternative is whipping or imprisonment. Numbers of youths who have left their parents, or have no proper guardians, receive an early criminal training, and the prison records show that when once they have been convicted they almost invariably return to jail, and end by becoming the worst characters in the place. I will further deal with the question of youthful offenders when I come to discuss prison discipline. There are no insuperable difficulties in the way of starting a reformatory. There are numbers of wealthy and benevolent Chinese here, who, if they realized how many youths were being trained to become convicts, and what it costs to keep them in jail under the present system, would assist such an undertaking. There would be no difficulty in obtaining sufficient land for cultivation in the country, where the boys would be employed chiefly at outdoor work, growing vegetables, etc., and would be taught carpentering, etc.

Thirdly, crime may be prevented and checked by an efficient police. The chief objects of a police force are to render it difficult to get at property; difficult to convert it and reduce the profits of its conversion; to narrow the chances of escape of the thief, and make a dishonest career not a paying one. It is commonly said that if there were no receivers there would be no thieves, and one of the most important branches of the force is the detective one.

The machinery of Government runs on, but there is no real attempt made to deal with crime and criminals on an organized system. There is no minister of crime or head of a criminal investigation department. The Inspector-General of Police, as head of his department, is responsible that the force is kept in efficient order, but he has little or nothing to do with common criminals. Once a year he writes a report, explaining why murderers are not caught, and giving some statistics to show that on the whole the state of crime is satisfactory.

No one, unless it be the magistrates, knows better than he does how very inefficient that force is, how hopelessly corrupt and worse than useless are a large proportion of the native contingent. The common clumsy thief who is detected in the act, or runs when pursued into the arms of the police, is bagged freely and consigned for a time to jail. On the other hand, robberies are of daily occurrence, and it is rare for the perpetrators to be discovered. Stolen property is often recovered, it is true, by the simple expedient of placing a detective at the door of each pawn-shop, who on the slightest suspicion pounces down on the pawner. It must be admitted that the police labour under great disadvantages. The fact that oriental houses are so open and easily entered naturally facilitates housebreaking, while the practice of keeping cash and gold ornaments in houses imperfectly secured is a strong temptation to the enterprising burglar. Females and children go about the streets wearing gold and diamond ornaments, and fall a constant prey to the professional thief who lurks about the corners of the streets.

It has always appeared to me that the police pay more attention to interfering with the peaceable and honest inhabitants than they do to disturbers of the peace and thieves. The natural inference is that it is more profitable to them. In the first place, by arresting a peripatetic hawker for resting on the road, the constable gets off his beat, and gets credit for a case in the police court, and zeal of this kind is often rewarded. When, before the passing of the Jinrikisha Ordinance, the police could run in any poller for loitering, they reaped a rich harvest, and hordes of these unfortunate men were consigned to jail to herd with criminals. There are 4,500 rikishas in Singapore, and every rikisha has two pullers and many three. Altogether the Registrar estimates that there are 12,000 employed in the rikisha business. Here is a vast amount of raw material ready to be manufactured into criminals. I must ask you to pardon me for a slight digression here, to consider the question of the rikisha traffic in connection with crime. It must be remembered that a large proportion of these men are quite wild, and that many of them speak a dialect hardly understood by their fellow-countrymen here. They are used as beasts of burden, or rather draft, day and night in all weathers, in blazing sun or pelting rain. On their return to their stables at night, they seek relaxation in a mild gamble. Here they fall an easy prey to the officers of the gambling suppression department. It is well known that gambling goes, on to a large extent in the houses of the well-to-do, and that lotteries abound, but as a rule it is only the poorest class who are arrested. Cannot something be done for the unfortunate rikisha coolie? Europeans regard him as an unmitigated nuisance, but there can be no doubt as to the popularity of this form of locomotion among the Asiatics. Their lot is far from being a happy one, and unless something is done for them I fear they will become a regular criminal class.

Fourthly, I now come to what should be the most powerful agency for the repression of crime. I mean the jail. I maintain that the present jail system tends to manufacture criminals. It can hardly be pretended that the discipline is in any way reformatory, and statistics show that it is in no way deterrent. It is very costly—$80,000 a year—and the proceeds of prison labour are insignificant. Prisoners who come in bad certainly go out worse members of society, and those not originally bad are corrupted. Youthful offenders who work in association with hardened offenders become confirmed criminals. There are confined in the same prison convicts undergoing life sentences and men who have been committed in default of being unable to pay small fines for breaches of municipal law or trifling street offences. There is no proper classification. The whole system is brutalizing. If a society were started for the propagation of crime, the first thing they would do would be to establish a jail. As professors would be engaged men who had been guilty of nearly every heinous crime, and classes would be formed containing a proportion of professional thieves and new-comers. All would be subjected to strict military discipline, and treated so far as possible like brute beasts. I can conceive no more refined method of training up a dangerous criminal class than a model institution like the Singapore jail.

Enter the prison for a moment, and watch that gang of able-bodied Chinese coolies sledging stone. They are fond of hard work, and could, if they chose, earn good wages outside. This punishment is supposed to be deterrent to them. How, then, has this man twelve previous convictions against him? You will notice that when he first came to jail he was 18. He is now 35, and if you come and visit the jail in ten years' time you will very likely see him again.

When I speak of criminals, it is to this class I generally refer. Prison authorities would tell you that they are incorrigible thieves—not that their conduct in jail is bad—for in many cases they are excellent workers, and the prison crimes, recorded against them are nothing more serious than "singing in their cells", "loud talking", or having tobacco in their possession. The discipline of our prison is regulated by what is necessary to maintain the most insubordinate prisoner in constant subjection, and not by a standard of what is required to keep in order and measure out a just and reasonable daily punishment to the average type of fairly-conducted prisoners.

This is the weak point of a system which, having grown up in our home convict prisons under military governors, and brought to perfection, as is generally believed, by Sir Edmund Du Cane, has been introduced here, with one serious omission, and that is the reformatory process.

Our criminal prison is thought by many to be a model institution, and visitors remark that it seems to work like a machine. So it does, but if it is proved that it has a tendency to produce criminals, however well it seems to work, it must be pronounced a bad machine.

In modern European and American prisons every effort is made to reform prisoners during their detention. Here scarcely anything of the kind is attempted. From their admission, prisoners are treated as the enemies of society, and subjected one and all to the strictest military discipline till their term expires, when they are turned out to have their revenge on society. The one idea seems to be to make prison life so distasteful and irksome that those who have undergone a course of it will not return, and others will be deterred from crime. Prisoners admitted for the first time, no matter what their offence, equally with habitual criminals toil on the tread-wheel. The strongest of the short-sentenced prisoners are turned into beasts of burden, and marched in chains through the public streets in cart parties, under an armed escort, to carry stone from the municipal yard. The slightest offence is punished with cells or crank, and for grave offences, which happily are of rare occurrence, corporal punishment is inflicted.

There is a tendency, as I have said, for the whole system to become brutalizing. At home it is found that work, education, and moral teaching are the three great forces to be employed in the reformation of criminals. Here there are great difficulties in the way of education, while the opportunities for moral teaching are few. Work, then, remains, and every effort should be made, not to drive the prisoner as if he were a brute, but to encourage him to work with all his might.

It may be said, admitting that the prison discipline is not in any way reformatory, it is deterrent, and the punishment is at least retributive. I deny the statement that it is deterrent. It is not borne out by facts. To what class of criminals is the discipline of the prison deterrent? To the young? Most assuredly not. The records will show that a very large number of the most confirmed criminals have been brought up in prison from their youth.

In July there were 24 prisoners in the gaol under the age of 20. This out of a total of 850 may be thought a small number, but it must be remembered that the magistrates are very averse to sending youths to prison. I present you with photographs of two promising juvenile delinquents—John Bull, aged 17, and Pakiri, aged 14. These are both classed as habitual criminals. It is probable that these youths, before receiving their present sentence, have been frequently whipped by order of a magistrate. Outside the prison there are a very large number of boys qualifying for jail life in company with professional thieves, and it is only a question of time before they are admitted within its walls. Once in, they will probably pass the greater part of their lives there. An adult who has been sent to jail may not again be convicted, but a youth who has been to jail once, say for a petty theft, almost invariably returns within a short time, and continues his career till he eventually gets a long sentence for house-breaking or some other serious crime.

A reformatory, and not the criminal prison, is the place for such youths. The ranks of adult criminals will always be swelled from China and other countries, but at least it behoves us to see that boys are not being trained up as criminals.

There are in the jail at the present time a very large number of prisoners who entered its walls for the first time as youths.

For instance, Yew A Chin, aged 20, with ten previous convictions, was discharged on 11 August. Kweh Tam, age 22, with five previous convictions, and Lin Kim Ling, aged 24, with seven previous convictions, sentenced to three years. Soh Sang, sentenced at the age of 23 to five years for house-breaking, with nine previous convictions. Here is a man named Soh A Weng, sentenced this year to ten years for house-breaking. After six previous convictions in Penang, he was sentenced, at the age of 21, to three years for theft. On his release he was almost immediately convicted of house-breaking, and received a sentence of five years. No sooner was he out of jail than he was, once more convicted of house trespass and theft, for which he was awarded 18 months, and within a month of his discharge he received his present sentence.

Tan Yoh Soon began his prison career at the age of 18. He has nine convictions, and, after a sentence of four years for theft and causing hurt in 1883, he was sentenced in 1888 to nine years for the same offence.

Kow Seng Kwang was 17 when in 1880 he came in for two weeks for theft. He has nine convictions. In 1884 he received five years for house-breaking. Did this sentence deter him? No. On his discharge he was again convicted of the same crime, and was awarded seven years.

Eng Ah Tay, when aged 19, was committed for one month as a vagrant. He has nine convictions. In 1885 he received four years eight months for house-breaking and escaping from legal custody. Since then he has undergone three sentences of one year.

Tan Ah Joo was 16 when in 1880 he was sentenced to two months for theft. He has 11 convictions. Here is a youth, Tan Chin Poh, who is only 18. There are eight convictions recorded against him, and when in 1887 he received six months for theft he must have been a boy of 12.

Tan Tay was 20 when he received two months for theft in 1887. He has 13 convictions. Twice has he had a three years' sentence, and he is now undergoing six years' imprisonment. I might give numerous other cases, but I think the above will be sufficient to show two things—(1) that a very large number of our worst criminals are admitted at an early age, and (2) that the jail discipline, irksome though it may be, has no deterrent effect on this class of criminal.

Besides the able-bodied prisoners, there are a certain number of men who are physically unable to work. When outside they are vagrants, gamblers, opium-smokers, and thieves. To them a sentence of rigorous imprisonment means nothing beyond a private room and regular meals without work. A pauper asylum, and not the criminal prison, is the place for such men. Crimes of violence are rare here compared with England, where drink is the cause of three-fourths of the total amount of crime. For the purposes of our present discussion I may exclude crimes of this nature. It may be said, although the prison system is proved not to be deterrent, it is retributive. "This man", you will say, "has broken the law, and it is only right that he should be made to suffer for it by undergoing a severe course of punishment." It is not necessary here to enter into this phase of the question, for it cannot be argued that any amount of retributive punishment will tend to diminish crime. There is a growing feeling against a vindictive policy with regard to the criminal classes, and of the injustice of disproportionate sentences. Those whose duty it is to administer the law should make themselves acquainted with the effect of the punishment they award. As Mary Carpenter says: "Society ought to realise that when it takes away liberty from a fellow-being it is responsible for the way in which that being is treated." Society suffers if it misuses the prisoner. It will not do to say: "These men are Chinese; you cannot educate them, you cannot teach them religion, therefore punish them." Any system which only aims at mere punishment is equally dangerous to society and to the criminal himself. Such imprisonment produces, as has been proved, from 40 to 45 per cent, of recommitments.

"Make men diligent", said Howard the philanthropist, "and they will be honest", and this is true all the world over.

What is called the revenue grade comprises all prisoners who are committed to rigorous imprisonment in default of payment of fine. During the month of July 1892, 258 prisoners were committed in this way, the majority of them for very short terms. These men work in association, and among them are a number of old gaol-birds—gamblers and the like. In their company are men who have been guilty of no offence of an immoral or disgraceful character, but have perhaps caused an obstruction in the street while selling their wares, or have broken a municipal by-law. The fact that these men are made to herd with the lowest criminals tends to encourage the idea that it is a misfortune, rather than a disgrace, to be sent to jail. The tendency of recent legislation has been to multiply offences, and I can conceive a time when, if the police and municipal officers were given a free hand, the accommodation of the jail would have to be doubled, not because of the increase of crime, but because so many persons were sent to jail because they were unable to pay fines imposed for breaches of the Summary Jurisdiction Ordinance and the Municipal Ordinance.

I now come to a very important point in a prisoner's career, i.e., his discharge.

In England, discharged prisoners' aid societies do excellent work in looking after prisoners on their discharge—getting them work and keeping them till they can obtain employment. Here there is no agency of the kind, and the consequence is that directly a prisoner is discharged from the prison, after undergoing, say, a sentence of three years, he has to shift for himself. It is scarcely to be wondered at that so many men, within a very short time of their release, return to prison. Perhaps the Advisory Board might propose some agency which would to a certain extent act as prisoners' aid society, and either find work for prisoners or send them elsewhere. In England a convict can earn £3, and if he gets in a certain class, as much as £6. Looking at the enormous cost to Government of maintaining these criminals in prison under the present system, it would be true economy to pay over to an agency even as much as $50 if by so doing it could be insured that they would not return to jail. The experience of the metropolitan discharged prisoners' relief committee was that not more than 5 per cent, of those assisted to obtain employment are reconvicted. Here it is far easier for a man of this class to get work than in England, and I feel confident that much good might be done in this direction.

The prison should be divided into a convict prison and a house of correction. Experience at home has shown that in those prisons where the work is productive the proportion of recommitments is far less than in strictly penal establishments, and it is admitted that a convict prison of a certain size should be self-supporting. Each convict requires individual treatment, which is impossible in a mixed prison like ours, where the majority of the prisoners are coming and going perpetually. Section 55 of the Penal Code provides that, in any case where a sentence of not less than seven years has been passed, the Governor may, with the consent of the prisoner, commute the punishment into perpetual or temporary banishment from the colony. On the 20th July there were 153 prisoners undergoing sentences of seven years and upwards, and it would be a benefit to the colony to get rid of a considerable number of these men. Many would be only too glad of the alternative of banishment.

I would also strongly urge the advisability of applying the provisions of the Banishment Ordinance to those aliens whose career of crime, as faithfully recorded in the prison books, and their punishment rolls while in jail prove that their presence in the colony is a source of danger to the community.

In conclusion, I will briefly recapitulate my suggestions for the prevention and repression of crime:

1. We have a law providing against the landing of decrepit beggars—let us provide against the importation of criminals who have no visible means of subsistence, and can give no account of themselves.
2. Establish a reformatory for the reception of youthful offenders.
3. Let not hard-working men who have been guilty of no dishonest or immoral act be sent to a convict prison, where they will herd with bad characters.
4. Do not make prisoners, who go into jail bad, worse by brutalizing them.
5. Banish aliens who are proved to be incorrigible old offenders and a danger to the community.
6. Let each long-sentence prisoner be treated individually in the way best calculated to turn him out well.
7. Make the prisoners work so as to pay for their keep if possible. Reformation should be an extra, chargeable to the State.
8. The police organization is defective, and unable at present to cope with professional thieves. Too much of their time is taken up in harassing honest people.

9. Some agency in the nature of a prisoners' aid society should be started to assist those prisoners who are anxious to go to China or elsewhere, and also to secure work for those who apply for it.

CRITICISM
by Tan Teck Soon

In the treatment of his subject Mr. Kynnersley has wisely limited the discussion to "Crime and its Prevention" with reference to this colony only, and further restricted its definition to offences against property. This not only enables him to narrow the field of research, but also to dispense with deep and comprehensive studies of the ethical, moral, and social conditions of a community, in order to ascertain the origin and to trace the evolutionary stages of crime in its midst. I do not, however, consider that it is entirely safe to ignore these considerations. Mr. Kynnersley has twitted the European community of this place with indifference on the subject of crime and criminals, unless, of course, should their personal interests be threatened thereby. This indifference, though regrettable, is not, in my opinion, so startling, or so characteristically English, as the opposite tendency, to deal with alien criminals without a sufficient insight into their national peculiarities, and without a full knowledge of the different agencies surrounding and influencing them.

But perhaps the data for any such studies are non-existent. British rule over members of the Chinese race has not existed for any sufficient length of time to enable all the data on the subject to be systematically collected, adjusted, and properly applied. On the other hand, the necessities for dealing effectually with crime had arisen simultaneously with the establishment of government. Hence doubtless has arisen the practice of wholesale importation of British legislation, so that lessons learnt after a lengthened experience among one set of people are made to apply and work amidst a civilization entirely alien and new to their requirements and environments. That the prison establishment, notwithstanding its costliness, should be regarded by Mr. Kynnersley ineffectual as a deterrent to crime, would not therefore be surprising—the machinery is too foreign and too complicated to suit native conditions and institutions.

But I hasten to assert that it would be extremely impolitic to form sudden judgments even in regard to dismal failures. An old Chinese philosopher was able to demonstrate the use of the useless, and so I hope I shall be permitted to extract a value even from failures. The opinion that, because a certain measure has failed, it is therefore valueless, has doubt-less arisen from the constant habit of expecting too much and meeting with disappointment. We are apt to regard the establishment of any new governmental department as a final step for special objects. If these objects are obtained, then we pronounce the measure a success; otherwise it is a failure. We very often overlook the educational uses of such failures. If, however, for such special objects as the controlling of aliens, every legal enactment or every executive and administrative action were held to be merely tentative or experimental towards a more comprehensive knowledge of such objects, then their ultimate value as an educational process could not be gainsaid or denied. True knowledge demands not merely conscientious studies, but also systematic experiments in all possible directions; and as there is no royal road to success, each experience has to be purchased at its full price. Even as a check to crime, I would therefore contend that the prison has justified its existence. If only, instead of frittering away their time and attention upon the discipline and treatment of prisoners, our prison authorities had devoted more of their energies to the collection and tabulation of additional particulars concerning their social and moral surroundings, then man's valuable lessons and statistics would by this time have been available towards a progressive solution of the problems connected with the crime and its prevention. If, for example, some such particulars as the following had been collected in the case of each prisoner, we would have by this time most valuable data for learning the causes of crime and for devising proper methods for diminishing and controlling them:

1. Personal particulars: province, department, and district in China; age on leaving China, and on arrival at colony, also on commitment to prison.
2. Family particulars: parents, whether living; wife, children, whether here or in China; relatives or clan connection in the colony.

3. Social and economical particulars: means of livelihood in China and colony; guild or trade association; habitation in colony; average monthly earnings and expenses.
4. Moral particulars: whether educated, and to what extent; whether addicted to drink, gambling, opium, and vice.

Some criminal particulars, or short narratives as to circumstances leading to commission of each offence, might also afford means for a comparative study of the effects from the foregoing causes.

The methods employed by the Chinese and other foreign Governments towards solving the same problems among similar classes of people, and the experiences at their disposal, are also wide fields for our explorations. Hence, at this late date, if the data for a correct comprehension of crime and its prevention are not available, the blame should lie at our own door.

In ascertaining the different causes that directly or indirectly lead or contribute to the commission of the particular crimes selected by him for discussion, Mr. Kynnersley has dwelt but slightly on causes inherent to the colony's situation and trade—he is unwilling to admit the full significance of enforced absence from family ties—denied entirely that social or economical conditions are favourable to its propagation—and has given only a small place to immorality and ignorance. So far as I have been able to examine his arguments, I think he attributed the prevalence of crime in our midst to such extraneous causes as—(1) unrestricted immigration of criminals from abroad; (2) contamination of youthful offenders with confirmed criminals; (3) extent of raw materials ready to be manufactured to criminals, apparently by the police; (4) and lastly, to unsuitability of prison discipline,—the prison, in fact, being, in his own words, "one of the principal factors in the promotion of crime". In regard to re-commitments, Mr. Kynnersley deplored the absences of—(1) a reformatory; (2) a house of correction; (3) a self-supporting convict jail; and (4) a prisoners' aid society.

I hope that I am not doing Mr. Kynnersley any injustice in the preceding enumeration, but if so, I am very pleased to confess that, so far as I am able to judge, his causes are indeed preventable, or could easily be remedied by good governmental measures. I am very glad indeed that Mr. Kynnersley as the responsible authority in this place, endowed with powers to deal with crime and criminals, is so hopeful in ultimately checking or reforming them; but I very much fear that these causes lie deeper, embedded and mystified in inherent and perhaps natural causes, and too subtle or too stupendous to be so easily and effectually dealt with. In the following I shall endeavour to discuss a few of them.

Inherent Causes. The consideration of these is certainly of the first importance. Mr. Kynnersley, as a believer in hereditary transmission of crime, should not neglect causes inherent to human nature and surroundings. They necessitate, of course, an acquaintance with the history of people and their topographical and other environments. The Chinese population of this colony consists of emigrants from the Fukien and Kwang-tung provinces of China, and their descendants born in these Settlements. Fukien emigrants embark from Amoy only; Foo-chow, although a treaty port, does not possess direct communication with Singapore. Those from Kwang-tung proceed from Swatow as regards Khehs, Hai-loh-hongs, and Teochews; from Canton, Hongkong, and Macao, as regards Cantonese; and from Kiungchow as regards Hylams. All these bring with them into this colony their peculiar habits, organizations, and dispositions. Of the two provinces, Kwang-tung will thus be seen to afford better facilities for the transportation of criminals than Fukien. It is also the more turbulent of the two, and a comparison of our criminal records will, I believe, reveal that, of the more violent crimes, the larger proportion is committed by offenders from this province.

In China particular offences will also be found peculiar to particular communities. Thus, owing to their possession of better financing facilities, the Cantonese will be found among the most violent robbers, pirates, kidnappers, and smugglers; the Teochews will be among the most inveterate gamblers, rioters, and highway robbers, owing to the effects produced by their peculiar clan organizations; while the Khehs and the Hokkiens will be among the worst cases of thefts, petty larcenies, and house-trespass, owing to their addiction to the worst form of opium-smoking and to their social condition. I am of opinion that these causes and effects will also be found operative in this colony among similar classes of people. The individual ages of criminals, length of absence from home, and residence in this colony would also furnish clues to the causes and prevalence of peculiar offences, hence their comparative study is also valuable. The imperative demand of Chinese labour for the development of British Malaya forbids the institution of restrictive measures against their indiscriminate admission; and this being a free port renders, the employment of restrictive agencies almost impossible. Criminals are not so apparent to the eye as paupers.

Absence from Family Ties. Mr. Kynnersley has refused to admit that, in the case of the Chinese, there has been any severance of home ties. This is unintelligible, unless, of course, if he meant to refer to complete or absolute severance. There is no doubt that, among a filial people like the Chinese, any temporary, if not permanent severance from all that is implied, by themselves, of ancestral authority, parental influence, and family responsibility, is prejudicial to the healthy growth of their moral nature. If this is admitted in the case of Europeans, I contend that it should also apply to the Chinese, as, with the latter, home ties mean a great deal more than what those nebulous connections usually convey to the minds of others. Another effect of this deprivation is the loss of a sure asylum in moments of adversity, of sickness, of temptation—so that its indirect effect upon the prevalence of crime is at once manifest. Their clans and guild associations do certainly afford temporary and spasmodic reliefs in the above cases, but they possess no influence whatever of a deterrent nature as regards crime—rather the reverse.

Economic Conditions. The social conditions of the Chinese have organized them into huge industrious armies, for the battle of life. It is to their industrious achievement, as it progressed through the ages, that they now owe the commanding position assigned them in the modern world, and it is to their possession of the working faculties and impulses that they are today freely admitted to this colony. But the constant friction of uniform drudgery, the irresistible effects of competition within limited spheres, the stern decrees of natural processes and penalties, demand enormous sacrifices from their weaker and less endowed battalions. Recent vital statistics reveal a higher proportionate waste of life among the Chinese than among others, and, looking the facts squarely in the face, there is no doubt that they suffer disadvantageously from economical laws. The weaker has ever to go to the wall, even among them. The persistency with which they cling to the struggle, their cheerful methods of replacing damages, and the stoical courage with which they face disasters, are of course evidences of a vigorous national life which appeal to everyone, but their pathetic aspects, the attendant disappointments, failures, and despair, should not be overlooked in any critical study of their results. The effects of these upon crime are too apparent to need any elaboration on my part.

Moral Considerations. I regret exceedingly that on this important ground, in which the subject had been philosophically treated by Mr. Kynnersley, I am utterly at variance with his contention that mere culture of the intellect is hardly operative upon conduct. I cannot believe that his remarks could apply to true discipline of the moral faculties. At all events, if his conclusions as to culture are true, I do not think that the same could be equally affirmed of the opposite influence of ignorance over vice. And as a Chinaman, and an exponent of education, I am unable, conscientiously, to admit that there is no connection between knowledge and morality, or between ignorance and vice. Although the one is not positively the other, the Chinese throughout the long course of their national history have systematically associated them together. Not only that—they have also carried their principles into practice, and instituted a method for testing the virtue and knowledge required for political uses; and to this institution, the competitive examination, they have committed themselves without reserve, staking upon its truth all their national ties, traditions, and hopes. Their boundless enthusiasm and their implicit confidence upon its practicability have influenced them to such an extent, that they even firmly believe upon the possibility of establishing, by means of moral education, a virtuous commonwealth. The difficulties of determining its positive conditions do not appal them, neither do the fearful failures in practice quench their faith in the original goodness of human nature, and in the power of culture to discipline and develop it. With them these truths are self-evident ethical laws, and it speaks a great deal for the success of their endeavours that even here, amidst a population consisting of the scum of the population of South China, the percentage of criminals, according to Mr. Kynnersley, is so small, viz., 650, out of a total population of 122,000, or one-half per cent. I admit Mr. Kynnersley's arguments as to the inspiring force of example, but this certainly postulates a sensitive, sympathetic temperament on the part of those influenced. The Chinese affirm that there is a scope for culture to produce this temperament, and that the intellect possesses a positive influence in the sphere of conduct.

The extent to which ignorance and immorality are answerable for crimes, here as well as elsewhere, should not, in my opinion, be under-estimated. I shall in a subsequent paragraph refer to a few minor results produced by ignorance among the Chinese here, but I may as well mention at once that the least objectionable of these appears to me to be the absence of public spirit among them, except perhaps on occasions when they are worked upon by interested persons, for their own egotistical purposes—thus opening the door for one of the worst features in their social organization—the secret societies. As to the effects of such vices as opium-smoking, gambling, and drinking upon crime, they are patent to anyone who has the moral welfare of humanity at heart and who labours for their reformation.

Among the projects for repressing crimes, Mr. Kynnersley has not thought any measures conducted on the principle that "prevention is better than cure" capable of successful accomplishment, and so he has refrained from recommending them. Against aliens he is willing to try such experiments as exclusions, and banishments of bad characters, but as regards the select ones within the colonial ring-fence, the only measures recommended by him, viz., police supervision and prison discipline, are remedial, not preventive. In my opinion, remedies are only applicable when something has gone wrong. Mr. Kynnersley has referred to the lamentable corruptions and untrustworthiness of our police force; but I believe that, if the truth could be fully ascertained, this result will be found largely due to the belief, prevalent among their members, that their personal interests would be better benefitted if they could be credited with a larger number of "cases arrested" irrespective of other qualities. Among them the test for smartness and for efficiency is evidenced by statistics merely. Hence their superior uses when put on detective duties. As to prison discipline, I shall reserve my remarks for the end of this paper.

Mr. Kynnersley has claimed that, in this discussion, he has not come forward as "a professional philanthropist, nor as a faddist believing in any nostrum which is guaranteed to cure vice". I regret exceedingly that he has refused to recognize the utility of education as a preventive factor. I believe he must have overlooked its powerful function for the enforcement of respect for laws and institutions. Materialistic and servile as it may be imagined, Chinese civilization rests on the systematic preference of moral to physical forces. Hence their peaceful, law-abiding characteristics. But they require that these laws and institutions should be first fully explained to them, and when their positive good and application are once admitted, they easily accommodate themselves to their requirements. This I believe is a matter of education. The Chinese in the Straits Settlements labour under the disadvantage of not possessing, or not being provided with, any recognized channel of communication, through which they could learn the intentions of the authorities or make their own wishes fully known. The Protectorate does not secure their confidence, while the Advisory Board and the Po-Leung-Kuk are only useful within their respective spheres. None of these possesses any influence whatever over crime or criminals. The shortcomings of the police force have been pointed out by the Essayist. Such punishment as deportation is fast being regarded by the Chinese as a mere inconvenience only; so that, in everything but name, the Chinese in this colony may be said to govern themselves. They pay just as much or just as little obedience to law as they please, and when they are prosecuted for any offence, or visited with any just penalty, they consider themselves as merely unlucky victims. With them, breaking the law is a matter of speculation. They calculate to a nicety how much they would gain on the one hand, and on the other how much they should risk in bribing the police, feeing lawyers, and paying the penalty imposed by law. We have seen that the prison possesses no terror in their eyes, and there are even prisoners who would volunteer to remain there for money considerations. All these are certainly extremely unsatisfactory, and have arisen and continued to exist from their imperfect comprehension of British legislation and institutions. But in my opinion the only remedy for these lies in educating the people, and in making them feel that their real benefit lies in maintaining the supremacy of laws, that obedience to them confers advantages and not only immunities. The choice of methods for enforcing these principles upon the Chinese is entirely with the Government, but, if I may be permitted to offer a suggestion, I should say, utilize their recognized clans, guilds, and other associations, place them under proper control, and endeavour to work and to reach all classes by their means; make punishment deterrent, and compel the vicious by some system of prison discipline to stick to the path of virtue.

As a deterrent to crime, nothing, in my opinion, exceeds the importance of providing useful occupation for the populace; in other words, utilize the working faculties of the Chinese to their fullest extent. This may be patriarchal in theory, and unsuitable to the independent manly races of the West, but with a people accustomed to be treated, encouraged, and overawed as children, advantage might be taken of their pliant disposition to keep them out of mischief. I do not mean, by this, that provision should be made in every individual case, nor even with regard to traders and handicraftsmen; but as the bulk of our immigrants are land-labourers, some scheme could be devised by the local Government to encourage their settlement in agricultural communities. The food problem of this colony will before very long demand the gravest consideration of the community, and the Government should not allow the time and the opportunity to slip away, until some positive danger should threaten them.

Coming to the last question of prison discipline, I must confess that I am entirely ignorant of its internal arrangement, or of the discipline enforced therein. I shall have, therefore, to accept Mr. Kynnersley's testimony that on the whole it is unsatisfactory as a deterrent to crime. This being so, I hope I shall be permitted to offer a few remedial suggestions. The true end of punishment, according to the Chinese Penal Code, is to make an end of punishing. Viewed in this light, I think Mr. Kynnersley is right in suggesting divisions for correcting and for reformatory purposes. But as regards the present building, I think it is in every respect a model institution, suitable to all possible requirements. As regards discipline, however, I think that the punishments awarded to prisoners should be divided into three grades, viz.: (1) Penal hard labour; (2) Industrial and educational; and (3) Reformatory. For default in payment of fines and minor offences I would recommend public whipping, and public exposure in stocks at the police station nearest to the scene of offence. All prisoners sentenced to imprisonment, whether for first or subsequent offences, should be punished with hard labour at stone-breaking, etc., and solitary confinement for the first period of their imprisonment, with remissions if of good behaviour. For breaches of prison discipline the time in this grade could be extended, or whipping, exposure in stocks, deprivation of privileges, could be resorted to. The experience at this grade should be of such deterrent nature as to render prisoners chary of returning to it. Passing from thence, prisoners should be placed in the 2nd grade, the industrial and educational stage. Here handicraftsmen should each be set to his own work, and those ignorant of any trade should be apprenticed to one. This would render the second grade the first preparatory stage to a prisoner's subsequent reformation, and there is no reason besides why this division of the prison should not be self-supporting. After a certain number of years' confinement, long-sentenced prisoners should be given a chance of reforming, outside the control of strict prison discipline. But they should not at once be given their liberty. They should be transported to some penal district, established at some unopened portion of British Malaya, and there given some means of labour, agricultural or industrial, but placed under the strict surveillance of a police authority stationed in their midst. This supervision could be discontinued at the expiration of their sentence. By some such system, I believe, even old criminals would be constrained, after perhaps frequent repetitions, to admit that after all the path of virtue is the easiest. It possesses, at all events, this recommendation, that it is a faithful imitation of the gradual processes of nature. In this case there would not be the too sudden transition from dependency to liberty, from bondage to absolute freedom, and from adequacy of food and raiment to actual want and deprivation, which I am afraid in many cases have induced released prisoners to seek re-admission by repetition of offence, a practice which, I fully admit, has the most deadening effect upon the moral sense.

In conclusion, I sincerely trust I have not wearied you all beyond endurance with my erratic and immature reasonings, and perhaps rather Utopian projects. I hope I have not been too venturesome in a sphere where angels fear to tread. I must confess that I have never before publicly criticized the actions of public governments, and it is therefore a new sensation to me to make my debut tonight in the somewhat questionable character of a prison-reformer without one qualification. I repeat the hope expressed by the Essayist tonight that our subsequent discussion on this subject will be profitable, and if in any portion of my criticism I should appear to deal but scant justice to the real merits of the essay, I trust I shall be excused if I plead that the time at my disposal has been very limited.

Notes

1. "Death of Mr C.W.S. Kynnersley C.M.G.", *The Singapore Free Press and Mercantile Advertiser (Weekly)*, 21 July 1904.
2. H.N. Ridley, ed., *Noctes Orientales* (Singapore: Kelly and Walsh, 1913), p. iii.
3. Christine Doran, "Bright Celestial: Progress in the Political Thought of Tan Teck Soon", *Sojourn: Journal of Social Issues in Southeast Asia* 21, no. 1 (2006): 46–67.

13

THE APPLICATION OF ENGLISH LAW TO ASIATIC RACES
With Special Reference to the Chinese

Essay

9 September 1899

by *W. J. Napier*

Editors' Note

Debates over the application of English law which took place throughout the British Empire often centred on the relationship between English law and existing customary practices. As Napier's piece highlights British practice was to apply English law, except in cases of personal law where they regularly deferred to Hindu and Islamic legal practices. Yet in spaces like the Straits Settlements which were declared to be unoccupied land, no such recognition of customary law was afforded. The history of this problem was addressed by W.J. Napier in his *Introduction to the Study of the Law Administered in the Colony of the Straits Settlements*. In his 1899 paper to the Society he addressed this problem in reference to the Chinese population. This population, which had grown significantly from the 1870s, brought issues of marriage and inheritance amongst the Chinese in front of English-law courts. Yet the colonial administrators, many of whom had arrived in the Straits via India, had little or no familiarity with Chinese law, language and customs. This was the source of constant dissatisfaction amongst the Chinese community when they turned to British courts for justice.[1] Whilst the British sought to better communicate English legal decisions in Chinese, a figure such as Governor Blundell feared that any attempt to translate English law into Chinese was "utterly hopeless" on account of the nature of the language.[2]

The colony's Arab community, on behalf of the Muslim community, had been able to lobby for the introduction of the Mohammedan Marriage Ordinance in 1880. But it was only until the 1890s in the Malay States that Chinese law began to attain greater recognition and a draft code on Chinese customary law was developed. This legacy of the division between the colonial administration and the Chinese population was one of the factors that laid the groundwork for the Chinese to adopt a system of self-government for the resolution of disputes and the regulation of social life through their clan networks.

This being a legal subject, it is impossible to divest it of its legal aspect, but I shall attempt to deal with it in as general a manner as I can.

According to the principles of English jurisprudence, when a territory having settled institutions is acquired by treaty or conquest, the existing laws and institutions continue until change by competent authority. Thus, the old French law is retained in Lower Canada, the Code Napoleon in Mauritius, and the Roman Dutch law in Ceylon, British Guiana, and the Cape. But where a settlement is made of unoccupied country by British subjects, then, as the law is the birthright of every subject, so wherever they go they carry their laws with them, and therefore such new-found country is to be governed by the law of England. I would note that when I speak, now and elsewhere, of the introduction of English law into a colony, it must be taken with this qualification, that only such parts are imported as are of general and not of merely local policy. It was under this second principle that English law was introduced into North America, and that the rules of the Common Law are the heritage alike of the United States and of ourselves. The Indians gradually retreated before the white men, and, so far from administering their native laws to the Indians, we find that as late as 1756 the New England Government paid money for Indians' heads.

But in the East we had to face another set of facts. Instead of a territory inhabited by a few migratory Indians, we there occupied a cultivated country, teeming with inhabitants, with rules of law and custom more or less defined. At first we claimed no jurisdiction over the natives, but later it was impossible to evade it, and regular Courts had to be introduced. The Courts of Bengal decided that the general law there was the English law as it existed when the Mayor's Court was established in 1726, and that English Statutes passed after that date did not apply, unless extended to it expressly or by necessary implication. But Warren Hastings saw that it was impossible to apply the technicalities of the English law to the domestic relations of races brought up under ideas so alien to it, and the plan which he promulgated in 1772 for the administration of justice recognized the native law in these domestic relations, and provided that Moulavies and Brahmins should attend the Courts for the purpose of expounding the Mohammedan and Hindoo law. This salutary principle was incorporated in the English Statute-book in 1781, when Parliament enacted that "inheritance and succession to lands, rents and goods, and all matters of contract between party and party, shall be determined in the case of Mohammedans by the laws and usages of Mohammedans, and in the case of Gentus" (that is to say, Hindoos) "by the laws and usages of Gentus."

This law, it will be noticed, does not apply to natives generally, but only to Mohammedans and Hindoos. There are, of course, many natives of India who are neither Hindoos nor Mohammedans, such as the Portuguese and Armenian Christians, the Parsees, the Sikhs, the Jains, the Chinese, the Buddhists of Burmah and elsewhere, and the Jews. The tendency of the Courts has been to apply to these classes the spirit of Warren Hastings' rule, and to leave them in the enjoyment of their family law, except so far as they have shewn a disposition to place themselves under English law. At first, as we have seen, native experts attended to prove the customs, but this fell into disuse, the Judges, as their knowledge extended, going themselves to the original sources of the Koran or of the Code of Manu. Sir William Jones, known to lawyers as the author of a standard work on "Bailments"; to men of science and naturalists as the founder of the Bengal Asiatic Society, and as giving his name to the "Jonesia Asoka"; and to the world generally as the first Englishman to explore into the mysteries of the Sanskrit language, must be mentioned in this connection. As a great jurist, Jones understood that the power of England in India must rest on good administration, and that the first requisite was to obtain a thorough mastery of the existing systems of law in India and to have them codified and explained. In short, to use his own words, he "purposed to be the Justinian of India". With this idea he decided to prepare a complete digest of Hindoo and Mohammedan law as observed in India. Needless to say, he did not complete his labour. His views on the application of law to natives, taken from the introduction to his "Institutes of Hindu Law, or The Ordinances of Manu", are worth quoting:

> It is a maxim in the science of legislation and government that "laws are of no avail without manners"; or, to explain the sentence more fully, that the best-intended legislative provisions would have no beneficial effect even at first, and none at all in a short course of time, unless they were congenial to the disposition and habits, to the religious prejudices and approved immemorial usages, of the people for whom they were enacted especially if that people universally and sincerely believed that all their ancient usages and established rules of conduct had the sanction of an actual revelation from Heaven.

The subsequent history of law in India is interesting. Indefinite customs have found it hard to stand when administered by lawyers trained in the traditions of the rigid rules of English law; customs, where repugnant to our Western ideas, had to be modified; and, in the result, codes, embodying for the most part the rules of English law, have trenched upon the provinces in which native laws were to be observed. As an example of this, the law of contract, which by the Statute of 1781 was to be governed by the native law of the defendant, is now included in the Contract Act, which is almost a code of the law of England on the subject.

I now leave India, to come to the familiar soil of the Straits Settlements. The conditions of the Settlements of Singapore and Penang, when occupied by us, were in the main the same, and very different from that of India. The only existing population was Malay, subsisting on fishing and piracy, and the Settlements clearly came within the rule that, being unoccupied, English law was introduced. Nothing is said in the Charters by which the Courts, first of Prince of Wales Island and subsequently of the three Settlements, were constituted as to the law to be administered. Some rather indefinite references are made to the manners and customs of the inhabitants, and the Court is to give and pass judgement and sentence "according to justice and right". Sir Benson Maxwell, who more than any other man has moulded our laws, noted the absence in our charters of the provisions of Warren Hastings' rules, and held that "justice and right" meant the law of England, and, but for some necessary concessions to native customs, pure and unadulterated English law reigns supreme. Some parts of the English law are not in force, as being inapplicable to the local needs of the colony, but the principle of equality in the Courts and of personal liberty, with its appropriate remedy of Habeas Corpus, is as a general rule as much in force here as it is in London.

I do not mean to say that there is not some legislation which startles a lawyer fresh from the Temple or Lincoln's Inn. That a man may, if he be an alien whose presence in the colony is considered undesirable, be summoned before the Executive Council, deprived of the assistance of counsel, and tried by a Court every member of which is sworn to secrecy irresistibly reminds one of the Star Chamber and of Courts Martial in France. The provisions of our Labour Ordinances as to inspection of estates have their counterpart in the Factory Acts, and the ignorance and poverty of the Chinese just down from their native country probably sufficiently justify the special legislation contained in the Immigration Ordinances.

But it is the sphere of law in which, as we have seen, native custom reigns supreme that I wish more particularly to discuss. Sir Benson Maxwell and other Judges following him felt themselves, in the absence of express words in the Charters, unable to lay down the broad rule that in domestic matters, such as succession and inheritance, native law should be recognized and followed. The result has always appeared to me to be unsatisfactory. It was necessary to relax the English law in some respects, or otherwise every native marriage must have been in law an illegal connection, not having been celebrated in accordance with our Canon Law, and we must have been branded as a colony of bastards. The facts of life had to be faced, and accordingly a marriage concluded in accordance with native customs had to be held a valid marriage, although without all the results of a marriage contracted by bands in the Cathedral.

I think I may state the law of intestate succession as applied to the estate of a Chinaman domiciled in the colony as follows: the estate is divided in exactly the same manner as in the case of an Englishman, except that (1) where the deceased left several widows they take between them the share which an English widow would have taken under like circumstances, and (2) children legitimate according to Chinese law are to be treated as legitimate in our Courts. These rules constitute what is known as the *lex loci*—that is, the whole of the estate of a Chinaman domiciled in the colony is distributed by them, as also the landed property of a Chinaman wherever domiciled. There can be little doubt that the moveable property situated in the colony of a Chinaman domiciled in China should be distributed according to the law of China, and it is a strange matter that this has never been done, nor has such a mode of distribution been discussed in our Courts.

The wholesale introduction of English law disappoints Chinese expectations and ideas on three points at least—(1) in its non-recognition of adoption, (2) in its giving the wife and the daughters a large, and in the case of the latter an equal share with that of the sons, and (3) in the impossibility of tying up property for several generations with a view to the due performance of the *"sinchew"* or ancestral worship. All these questions have been fought out in the Courts of the Colony, and in each instance have those Courts refused a recognition of the native custom. I have sometimes wondered that the Chinese have not made an attempt to get these decisions reversed by the Privy Council, but I suspect that in many cases family arrangements are come to, and forced by Chinese opinion on unwilling members, whereby the rules of the English law are evaded.

I will say no more with regard to the last of the three points indicated above, than that the rule which prevents property being tied up for more than a certain time is one founded on considerations of high commercial policy, and could no more be relaxed in a British colony in favour of the Chinese than it could have been at home to keep together the family estates of an old county family.

The Chinese law of domestic relations and succession, as I understand it, is based upon the continuance of the family after the death of its head, and upon the due performance of ancestral worship. A man is allowed only one principal wife, but as many inferior wives as he can maintain properly. The privilege is, as a rule, in China only taken advantage of when the principal wife has no son. A son is necessary to represent the father at the ancestral worship, and in default of a son by the principal wife, inferior wives are taken, and in default of a son by them again, adoption has to be resorted to. Children by inferior wives, or even by concubines if born in the family house, are considered in law as the children of the principal wife and legitimate. Adoption is the last resort, and only takes place where a man leaves no son to perform his *sinchew* rites. The nearest male relative of the "Seh"—or, to use the language of the Roman law, the nearest male agnate of the same generation as the son's, if he had existed—is selected; but in default of such being available, cognates, or even strangers, are adopted. The adopted son, if of another "Seh", becomes a member of his adoptive father's "Seh", and, as in Roman law, an adopted son becomes dead to his own natural family, and for all legal purposes (succession among them) is treated as being a son of his adoptive father. The son, whether natural or adopted, who represents the father at the ancestral worship takes a larger share of the estate than the rest. As a rule he is the eldest son of the principal wife, but the father has a right to select among his sons such one as he desires for the purpose. On the death of a Chinese paterfamilias, females take nothing. The family house is continued under the rule of the principal widow, and there the inferior wives and daughters are entitled to maintenance. Apart from the expenses connected with a suitable marriage being provided, daughters get no share in their father's estate.

The Chinaman who complains of the non-recognition of his ideas and customs by the Courts is told that this may be remedied by making a will. But a man may, from ignorance or from many other causes, omit to make a will, and that is no reason, to my mind, why his property should be distributed on quite a different system to that which he would naturally have intended. Some years ago I came across a case which my clients deemed particularly hard. A Chinaman had adopted a son, and had left him by will a considerable fortune. He died under 21 years. I had no alternative but to advise that according to the decisions of our Courts the whole property left the natural family of the adoptive father and went to the natural family of the adopted son. I went on to say that the question had never been before the Privy Council, and that doubtless much might be said in their favour by eminent counsel there if they should appeal to that body. They preferred to keep their money in their pockets and to forego the satisfaction of having their names immortalized on the pages of the Law Reports.

No legislation has been attempted for the purpose of tempering English law in accordance with Chinese custom. The only class of the community who have been thus favoured have been the Mohammedans. The bill which subsequently became law under the title of the Mohammedan Marriage Ordinance 1880 was prepared by the then Attorney-General at the instance of the Arab community. It provides for the registration of marriage and divorce, and states down generally the law of succession to be applied to Mohammedans in a manner which has, I believe, satisfied the class for whom it was passed.

It is interesting to note that in the Native States, as a general rule, the Indian principle is being followed, questions of succession to a Chinaman being decided according to Chinese law. In Perak the recognition of Chinese laws and customs is provided for in suits where either party is of Chinese nationality, or which relate to the estate of deceased persons of Chinese nationality, by special enactment, but Chinese born or naturalized in any British colony or possession, or born in the Federated Malay States, as also Christian Chinese, are excluded from its operation. With regard to the recognition of Chinese customs in the other Native States, I feel a personal interest, as I argued in favour of their recognition with success before the Chief Magistrate in Selangor, and this decision, which was afterwards affirmed by the Judicial Commissioner, caused considerable satisfaction among the Chinese community in the Native States.

Mr. G.F. Hare, the Chinese scholar whose loss to the colony has been such a gain to the Federated Malay States, has paid considerable attention to this subject, and he has compiled a code, to be applied to all non-Christian Chinese, Malay and China-born alike, embodying Chinese law with modifications to suit the altered state of Chinese family life in Malaya. The scope of the enactment is to provide for the registration of betrothals, marriages, and adoptions; for the settling of disputes as to legitimacy and the custody and guardianship of children; for the granting of separation or divorce; and for defining the law of inheritance among persons of Chinese nationality. By the courtesy of Mr. Hare I have been favoured with the perusal of a portion of the draft, and I think I may with truth say that no contribution to a knowledge of Chinese laws and customs like it has yet been given to the world.

To sum up—I think, with Warren Hastings and Sir William Jones, that the true way to govern native races is to apply to them, in questions of their social relations, their own law, so long as there is in it nothing repugnant to our moral ideas. But, whether owing to carelessness in drafting the original charter, or to the too strict interpretation of the Judges, this was not done here. The result has been profitable to the lawyers, as most Chinamen with property make wills, and what with making wills and breaking wills, the lawyer finds plenty to do. Although we may regret that Chinese customs were not recognized when the law of the colony assumed its shape, it would be a very different thing to introduce them by Ordinance when the English rules have been recognized so long. The family life of the Chinese has changed, the position of women has improved, and one can scarcely imagine our President introducing a Bill to deprive females of their rights of succession to the property of their husbands and fathers. The recognition of adoption appears to me to stand upon a different basis. It had its counterpart in that wonderful system of Roman jurisprudence, and I cannot see that it could not safely be permitted under our law. The matter cannot in any way be considered a pressing one, and when the Code which is being prepared for the Federated Malay States has been completed and passed, it will be for the Protector of Chinese and the leaders of Chinese thought to consider how far its provisions can properly be extended to the colony.

Notes

1. See Constance M. Turnbull, "Communal Disturbances in the Straits Settlements in 1857", *Journal of the Malayan Branch of the Royal Asiatic Society* 31, no. 1 (May 1958): 94–144.
2. Ibid., p. 96. See also Rachael Leow, *Taming Babel* (Cambridge: Cambridge University Press, 2016).

14

THE ADMINISTRATION OF LAW AND ORDER IN THE COLONY IN ITS EARLY YEARS

President's Introductory Address

18 April 1903

by *W.R. Collyer*

Editors' Note

W.R. Collyer was a prominent lawyer and jurist who had earlier served in Sierra Leone, Gold Coast and Cyprus before arriving in the Straits Settlements in 1892.[1] In 1903 he was serving as the Attorney General when he provided the introductory address as the President of the Society. His address took up a question central to the history and development of the colony—the application of law to Europeans. In the early days, according to Collyer, it could be said that Europeans in the colony were "amenable to no authority in the place". This produced a contradiction between the equality before the law proclaimed by Raffles and the double-standards between Europeans and Asians which emerged in practice. The transfer of the colony to the Crown meant for Collyer that the present contradiction was no longer between Europeans and Asians, but was now between the interests of business and that of legal order. Giving the example of the then recent curtailment of the jury system in the interests of traders he argued that this policy was creating an opposition between civic duty and the pursuit of business. It also raised the question of whether the colony was simply a place to make money or a place in which the legal order had intrinsic value. In his opinion this in turn expressed the nature of colonial society in the Straits Settlements.

For my subject tonight I am indebted to Mr. Buckley's *Anecdotal History of Singapore*. Of course you have all seen the book, and I suppose many of you must have read it. It is a very wonderful storehouse of facts, and tells the history of Singapore in an original manner. It is kaleidoscopic in its variety, the events jostling one another as they do in an unselected and unedited diary. It depends on no attraction of style, and no artificial allurements of typography or "get-up", but simply on the enthusiasm and loving research which the author has bestowed on his work. It is full of surprises, and the interest never flags from the beginning of the book to the final chapters; one of which treats with, and is characteristically entitled, "Climate, Rainfall, and Amateur Theatricals", and the other deals in rather a mournful tone with the handing over of the East India Company's Settlements to the Crown.

Perhaps the points which come out most clearly in the book are the great difference of the physical surroundings of the early settlers from our own and the great similarity of the social and administrative questions with which they had to deal and with which we are still grappling. The administration of justice was the point which naturally attracted my attention most; and there I met with one of my surprises, which, as Mr. Buckley would say, will be mentioned hereafter.

At the date of the first treaty with the Temenggong the Residency of Singapore, as it was called, was placed, under the Government of Fort Marlborough at Bencoolen. The servants of the East India Company were brought under the regulations applying to that factory, but no formal or technical cession was made; and though practically Sir Stamford Raffles assumed the entire functions of government, including the preservation of law and order, technically speaking the law applicable to the place was the Malay law and that only; and Sir Stamford Raffles in his original instructions to Major Farquhar, whom he left in command on his return to Bencoolen, makes no mention of the administration of justice. This, however, was not neglected. A Court, in which the Resident presided, sat every Monday, with the Sultan and Temenggong, to hear both civil and criminal cases. Later, in 1823, Justices of the Peace were appointed. A Court was formed consisting of the Resident and two magistrates. Juries were established to try civil cases, consisting of either five Europeans or four Europeans and three respectable natives; and, to show how English ideas predominated at that early period, we find that gambling and cock-fighting were both strictly prohibited. These regulations were promulgated shortly before the actual cession of the Island of Singapore, and I cannot help thinking that the existence of such regulations tended to hasten that event. The arrangements for the cession were made in June 1823, and confirmed in the following year. Before leaving Singapore in June 1823, Sir Stamford Raffles issued his celebrated Proclamation, in which he speaks of provision having been made for the establishment of an efficient magistracy, and lays down the principles upon which justice is to be administered in the Settlement.

The minute of Sir Stamford Raffles on his regulations is well known, and deserves careful attention. He deprecates the introduction of English law in a crude state, insisting that justice should be so administered that the legal and moral obligations should never be at variance. He deprecates the habit of wearing weapons, but does not go so far as to suggest its suppression. He is more definite in his views as to gaming and cock-fighting; he considers it the duty of Government to suppress both these practices as far as possible without trespassing on the freedom of private conduct. Opium and spirits are apparently not considered by him as potential sources of public revenue, but he points out that the use of these dangerous luxuries may be suppressed by exacting a heavy tax in the way of license from the vendors. He enters on the question of the position of women in a manner which shows that he would have been an able Protector of Chinese; and, in anticipation of modern legislation, he suggests that it should be declared unlawful for any person whatever to share the hire or wages of prostitution, or to draw any profit, either directly or indirectly, by maintaining or procuring prostitutes, or for any parent or guardian of a female, or for any other person, to ask or receive, directly or indirectly, any reward for bestowing a female in prostitution, any law, custom, or usage of the country in which such female or her parents were born notwithstanding. He would leave it, he says, for a jury to say what by local usage constitutes a legal obligation on the man to support the woman,—or, in other words, a contract of marriage,—and what a connection of prostitution. I have quoted his suggestions on this subject at length, because it appears to me as if he had been considering the subject with a view to legislation, and his carefully-chosen phrases have something of the ring of an Act of Parliament about them. In later times we have followed Sir Stamford's counsel, though with somewhat faltering steps, in most of his recommendations.

One suggestion, by which he shows that he prefers the Oriental to the Occidental usage, has never been adopted; and I must confess I think it would be better if his advice had been followed. He thinks that, in order to uphold the sanctity of oaths better than it is upheld in England, the oath should never be administered in a Court of Justice except as a dernier resort. I believe that the British method of administering an oath in a perfunctory manner to every witness has no doubt brought the ceremony of taking the oath into contempt, and tends to diminish the horror which all mankind has at one time or other entertained for false swearing. On the whole, the minute is a capital guide to a working magistrate in the circumstances of the new Settlement, and with an efficient magistracy appointed, and sufficient power at their back to make regulations having the force of law, one would have supposed that nothing was wanting to ensure a sufficient practical administration of justice. Justice appears to have been dealt out with promptitude and without favour to the Malays and Chinese, whether original inhabitants or strangers within our gates.

But here follows the surprise. No sooner had Sir Stamford Raffles departed for Bencoolen, apparently leaving everything settled, than we find Mr. Crawfurd, the Resident, writing to Calcutta complaining that British subjects are at present amenable to no authority in the place, and that the ill-disposed among them have always the power to set the authority of Government at defiance. This representation appears to have been called forth by the conduct of a Mr. John Morgan, whom the Resident decides to send to Calcutta with a view of placing him at the disposal of the Governor-General in Council—a course forced upon him "by a consideration of the various outrages committed by Mr. Morgan on the persons and property of private individuals, British as well as native, and the insults and contempts offered by him to the local rules for the administration of justice and towards the persons whose duty it was to administer them." The outward and visible sign of Mr. Morgan's innate rebellious spirit appears to have been that he fired off a morning and evening gun from his schooner in the river, and imprisoned the master of a vessel consigned to his house. He, in fact, proclaimed his immunity as an independent trader from the East India Company and all its rules, and asserted a position analogous to that, of the interlopers of old days, who obtained such rough justice from the Company wherever the Company was strong enough to deal with them. And this is, no doubt, the light in which the Resident regarded him, for the ground he took up, and apparently the only ground he thought safe in dealing with Mr. Morgan, was that he was in the East Indies contrary to law—that is, without a license from the Court of Directors, and without the necessary certificate from the Chief Secretary to Government, and that therefore he could be expelled as an interloper.

It is difficult to see how it came to pass that at Singapore, which was a part of the establishment at Bencoolen and attached to the Bengal Presidency, an "efficient magistracy" should have been so inadequately furnished with powers as to be unable to take cognizance of outrages committed by a British subject on either natives or Europeans. Even if Sir Stamford's magistrates were only capable of exercising jurisdiction as delegated to them by the Malay Sultan, it is not easy to see how a British subject could stand absolutely outside the law. But this appears to have been the opinion, not only of Mr. Crawfurd, but also of the authorities at Calcutta.

I can hardly believe that Raffles, when he solemnly laid down, in his parting minute, the maxim "let all men be considered equal in the eye of the law", could have intended to sanction a situation in which the law was enforced to punish a Malay for cock-fighting and was powerless to redress an outrage committed on the person or property of a Malay by an Englishman, and one wishes to believe that Mr. Crawfurd was wrong in his view of the situation. But if he was technically wrong he was practically right, and the necessity of the establishment of some tribunal of a higher grade was recognized on all hands, and Mr. Morgan's case no doubt hastened the reconstruction of the judicial system in a manner more adequate to the requirements of the colony. As to Mr. Morgan himself, he was arrested and "placed in the mainguard" like a sort of prisoner of war, but released on apologizing for his "outrages". I do not think these can have been of a very serious nature, and I see that the name of "J. Morgan, merchant", appears in the list of magistrates for 1823, and I see no reason to suppose that it is not the same person.

It may be observed that the same difficulty had occurred sometime before in the Settlement of Penang. The origin of that Settlement was in some ways analogous to that of Singapore, though it lacked the guiding hand of Raffles. Captain Light, thinking the island a good commercial station and good for the production of spices, made a settlement there without much ceremony, taking over the island on behalf of the Crown in the name of the East India Company. The island never appears to have been formally ceded by any one; and it was always regarded by the settlers as having been an uninhabited island which had come into their possession by the mere fact of settlement. Any dominion of a native rajah was unrecognized; and if their view was correct, or even if the sovereignty of the island was in a barbarous power having no law, the settlers should have been considered as importing their own laws with them, so far as they were applicable to the surrounding circumstances. They preferred, however, to consider themselves as living without law in a lawless country, and the inconveniences followed which might have been expected. After a period of almost incredible disorder which might have been avoided, the mischief was remedied by the establishment of a Supreme Court in 1808.

Probably if the new Settlement had been regarded as directly under the Crown, instead of the East India Company, the difficulty would not have been so great. It must be remembered that the East India Company had not yet ceased to be a trading company, and the details of administration had not yet come to be the main object of the Company's existence. No power of administration appears to have been given to

Captain Light by any competent authority. He and his assistants ruled the natives, not by virtue of a cession from the Rajah of Kedah, nor as magistrates guided by English common law, but by a necessary assumption of power backed by superior force; but his position (and for some time that of his successors) in relation to the European settlers remained so undefined and so weak that even the most serious crimes committed by Englishmen remained unpunished. One John Sudds was charged with the murder of a man named Smithers. The charge was investigated by a military tribunal specially convened for the purpose, at Fort Cornwallis, and he was sent to Calcutta for trial, but was there discharged, as it appeared that no Court had any jurisdiction to deal with the case. The inquiry by a military tribunal looks like a lingering memory of the procedure under the early charters of the seventeenth century, when power was given to the East India Company to try serious offences by "martial law".

It is interesting to notice that our methods are not so far in advance of those of our predecessors, but that in the year 1902 there occurred a failure of justice analogous to that which I have just mentioned as occurring at Penang in the beginning of the last century. The Cocos Islands murder went unpunished, not from a want of power, but for want of a proper organization and distribution of the power. There was again something like the old difficulty of defining the exact position of the Settlement in relation to the law, and when the need came there was no particular court or department capable of carrying the law into effect. The characteristic difference between the two cases is that in the old case it was an Englishman who defied the law and saved his neck, while in the modern instance it was a Chinese coolie, who would unquestionably have had but a short shrift in Pulo Penang at the beginning of the century. Considering the advantages we have in the facility with which important matters can now be discussed and authority make itself felt across the intervening world, we certainly must not blame our pioneers in administration for their occasional administrative failures.

The gradual growth of British administration in the East is interesting. At first it was of a purely maritime character. The captains of the ships governed the crews, and the "General" as he was called, or commander of the fleet, governed the captains; and originally, when factories were established, he seems to have had control also of the servants of the Company on shore, just as if they had been parties casually landed from the ships, to be recalled by the sound of the gun. In their relations with the native inhabitants of each place they were in theory subject to the laws of the country. On the first establishment of the factory at Surat, in the beginning of the seventeenth century, a treaty was made with the ruler of the country by one Captain Best, providing that in the administration of justice "right should be done in all questions, wrongs, and injuries that shall be offered to us and our nation". At the same time justice in criminal cases among the servants of the Company themselves was administered by virtue of a Royal Commission under the Great Seal, which empowered the Commissioners to punish and execute offenders by martial law. What were the exact powers so described, or how the King came to have power to grant them, might, I think, at the present day be an interesting subject of controversy. But there is at least one record of a conviction under the King's Commission, which took place at Surat on 28 February 1616, when one Gregory Lellington suffered death for the murder of one Henry Barton "in or near the town of Surat in the dominions of the Mogul".

The first regular tribunals in the East Indies were established under the Charter of 1661. By it the East India Company was empowered to appoint governors and other officers in their several factories. These governors were to exercise civil and criminal jurisdiction in the factories according to the law of England, and when there was no governor and council competent to deal with the offence the offender might be sent to some other plantation or fort where there was a court competent to try him. Powers of a like nature were given to the Company in Bombay in 1661. The courts so established seem not to have worked well, and it is suggested by Mr. Kaye, the author of a book on the history of the East India Company, that one principal reason for their failure was the provision that the Company's servants in case of appeal should be sent home for punishment. The Charter does not say "for trial", but I suppose that is what was meant. It seems doubtful, too, whether the

Company's courts had any jurisdiction to try an European who was not one of the Company's servants.

As to the position of natives who, by treaty or otherwise, came under the jurisdiction of the Company, the power over them was derived, not from the King of England, but from the Mogul potentate. There was no question as to their receiving ample justice according to European ideas. We see from the records of the Court of Justice at Bombay in 1724 that native women accused of "diabolical practices",—that is presumably of witchcraft,—"it appearing to proceed from ignorance", were sentenced to receive eleven lashes at the church door. Such a proceeding would have been more in place in the days of James I, but no doubt even in 1724 this application of English ideas would have been approved by some contemporary English divines.

Further letters patent in 1726 instituted Mayors' Courts in Presidency towns. These, however, were not a success; the law they administered was not suited to the country, and appears to have been administered both ignorantly and oppressively. When the Government of India, instead of merely managing factories, had to govern provinces, a slovenly and corrupt administration of the law became unbearable, and in 1774, by letters patent issued under the Regulation Act of 1773, the Supreme Court was constituted, having jurisdiction in Calcutta, Fort William and the limits thereof, and the factories subordinate thereto. This reform brought Sir Elijah Impey and his colleagues to India, and then began a long contest between the administrative and judicial branches of the Government, of which the case of Nuncomar, commented on by Macaulay and others, is a leading example. The first English judges seem to have come with ideas extravagantly insular and very much unsuited to their new surroundings. It was one of these, I think, who, noticing the bare-legged Indian punkah-puller of his Court, thus expressed his aspirations to his brother judge: "I hope before we leave, this country, brother, we may see that poor fellow wearing as good a pair of stockings as you or I." He little thought of the discomfort such a change would cause to the object of his commiseration. With the best intentions no doubt, some grotesque injustice was done; but never from that time could there be a doubt whether a power existed in the Company to call the white man to account for his misdeeds. The time was past when the officials in the factories, doubtful of their jurisdiction, and with a hazy remembrance of the old "interloping" days, considered piracy to be the safest crime to convict a prisoner of, when it is said that one of them convicted and hanged his own groom for piracy in having taken his horse two days' journey into the interior of the country.

I have made this somewhat long digression to endeavour to account for the difficulty found by Crawfurd, and others in his position, in the management of his British population. The Company's authority being derived from two sources,—that over the natives, as a rule, from treaties with the native powers, and that over Europeans from Acts of Parliament and Orders-in-Council,—it is not strange that these two branches of authority did not always develop *pari passu*. We see at Singapore a much earlier development of the systematic government of the natives of the place than of the practical application of the law to the colonists themselves. The former, no doubt, was considered by Raffles of the greater importance. It was of the utmost moment that it should proceed on right lines from the earliest days of the Settlement, whereas the government of the English themselves was sure to come in time, and might be left for a time to take care of itself. He was a man who, being eminently qualified to govern others, found no difficulty in governing himself, and perhaps he was too apt to expect his fellow-countrymen to resemble himself in the matter.

In 1826 Prince of Wales Island, Singapore, and Malacca were incorporated into one Settlement, and a common Court of Judicature was established. It had difficulties to contend with at first in the scarcity of persons of legal education ready to take the judicial posts, but from that time there has been no lack of judicial and forensic vigour in the Settlement. That this vigour was sometimes ill-directed, and sometimes vented itself in acute dissensions between the Bar, the Bench, and the executive authorities, is a matter of history which I need not pursue. Is it not written in the chapters of the Historical Preface to Kyshe's reports, which is in fact another anecdotal history?

The Courts having been well established, we get from Mr. Buckley's work glimpses of their early working; and one of the most prominent features is the active part taken, not only in judicial, but in all sorts of administrative matters, by the Grand Jury. The original Charter of the

Supreme Court of Penang expressly gave to the Grand Jury the right to make presentments on all kinds of affairs, and the same privilege was enjoyed by the Grand Jury at Singapore. From their presentments we can judge what were the exigencies of the time and the trend of public opinion, and we see how identical the questions of early days were with those which now occupy the attention and provoke the strictures of the daily press.

Thus in 1844 we see that the Grand Jury recommend the keeping of the verandahs clear of obstructions, at the same time suggesting that legislation on the subject was necessary.

In April 1846 they present the ineffective state of the police and sundry nuisances.

In April 1849 we find them presenting certain wells in Commercial Square as nuisances and recommending the substitution of pumps. They also present the obstructed state of the mouth of the river, and the inefficient condition of the Tan Tock Seng Hospital. For the support of this institution they recommend the establishment of a pork-farm, which they say is favoured by some leading Chinese. There appears to be some unconscious naivete about this suggestion, which would certainly leave the pockets of the Grand Jury untouched, and might bring in a considerable revenue to some of the influential Chinese.

The same Grand Jury presents the nuisance of native processions and cracker-firing, and suggests their restriction to places where they will not constitute a public nuisance.

In 1852 we find them making a strong presentment about secret societies, and about the sale of poisons in the bazaar. They also appear to have visited Raffles Institution in a body, and to have examined the boys. They find no fault with the system of education pursued, but present the grounds of the Institution as requiring drainage, and recommend the removal of the school to some more central position. They generally regret the backward state of native education, and recommend that object to the authorities as the only effectual means of promoting civilization and checking crime.

It is interesting at the present time to note that in 1858 the Grand Jury asks for the establishment of a mint at Singapore for the coinage of dollars and subsidiary silver and copper coins. This was no doubt intended to show their opposition to the proposal of the Indian Government of the time to substitute the rupee for the dollar as the standard coin of the Straits. The recommendation of the Grand Jury was not carried out, but no doubt it had its effect in the coinage controversy.

It is clear that the jurymen conscientiously did their duty in making presentments on every conceivable subject connected with the administration of the Settlement. I cannot help surmising that they must sometimes have been a thorn in the side of the executive authorities. But it cannot, I think, be denied that these presentments had considerable value as an expression of public opinion. They were made after due deliberation, in open court—that is, in the most public manner possible—to a judge who was independent of the executive power, who was probably not prepared to listen patiently to nonsense, and whose assurance that the matter would be represented in the proper quarter was probably as valuable as some of the assurances of consideration given in legislative assemblies for the amendment of the law. Occasionally the judge appears to have gone further than this, and to have promised his assistance in the accomplishment of their wishes. The presentment as to the inefficiency of the police was followed by the separation of the duties of Superintendent of Police from those of Sitting Magistrate, and the appointment of the well-known Mr. Dunman as Superintendent. It ultimately resulted in a change which I think cannot have been intended by the Grand Jury, in the control of the police being withdrawn from the Court of Quarter Sessions, in which it had hitherto been vested, and taken over directly by the Government.

The Grand Jury in fact performed some of the functions now performed by the unofficial members of the Legislative Council; and so long as there was no such Council sitting in Singapore, the Grand Jury was as good a substitute as could be devised. They were a strictly constitutional body, and did their duty as well as a perfectly independent and entirely irresponsible body can be expected to perform it.

Here I may mention a subject which comes up again and again in connection with the administration of justice—the extremely thorny subject of gaming. Sir Stamford Raffles, like most thoughtful men of his time, had a great horror of the habit of gambling, and fully appreciated the resulting evils. He appears, however, too sanguine as to the possibility of keeping it in check by the enforcement of a rigorous prohibition. His successors were perhaps less penetrated by the idea of the intrinsic evil of the habit, but certainly less sanguine as to eradicating it by a vigorous exertion of power. A gambling-farm appears to have been sanctioned by Mr. Crawfurd shortly after Sir Stamford's departure, as a temporary measure. Sir Stamford protested against this, and the Indian Government wrote a despatch, in September 1820, agreeing entirely with Raffles, and saying that the farm should not be reinstated, but expressing a willingness, if Mr. Crawfurd thought on further experience that the relinquishing of the farm would not be advantageous, and the restoration of the farm would not be injurious to the morals of the people or respect to the British Government, the Government was prepared to reconsider the matter. On receiving a despatch which might have been written by Bunyan's "Mr. Facing Both-ways", Mr. Crawfurd knew how to read between the lines. The farm went on until 1829, and appears to have produced as much as $30,000 a year, which I suppose was then a considerable sum. In 1827 the Grand Jury presented the gambling-farm as an immoral nuisance, and the Recorder is supposed to have said (but I do not think it could have been in open court) that "he did not think there were thirteen such idiots in the place". He evidently did not see that there was any greater immorality in raising a revenue from gambling than in raising it from drinking or opium-smoking. The argument that drinking, and in some cases the use of opium, may be considered a necessity did not appear to him to make a difference, and I am inclined to think that the majority of robust minds take his view. Those who consider gaming of any kind as in itself immoral can, of course, never be persuaded that a gambling-farm can be otherwise than an immoral nuisance. But neither can those who look upon drinking whiskey as in itself an immoral act be persuaded to think it right to raise a revenue from spirits. The view of the Grand Jury, however, prevailed, and I suppose it shows the trend of the public opinion of that time. The results are still with us. We have not put down gaming-houses or public gaming. In the nature of things, we who play bridge and patronize the totalizator cannot do so. We have perhaps somewhat checked the gaming habit, but at a great expense of power, and by exertions which tend to demoralize the police, while we, perhaps unjustly, incur a suspicion of meting out the penalties of the law in one way to the Oriental and in another way to the European.

Since the transfer from the Indian Government to the Crown, the Courts have had but little anecdotal history. Their capacity and powers are well known, and there are few surprises, except perhaps an occasional verdict of a jury. The Grand Jury is a thing of the past, and the Petit Jury was reduced from 12 to 7 and given a majority verdict about 1873. No doubt these changes were necessary, but they were only indirectly made in the interests of justice; their primary object was to lighten the citizen's burden and facilitate the despatch of business.

The older institutions of England, especially those which we owe to the Saxon temper and tradition, all appear to be intended to make the preservation of law and order as far as possible the work of the people themselves, individual independence being closely bound up with individual responsibility. Our early advancement in these ideas is sometimes put down to our "representative government", but I believe that the parish constable and the juries of the hundreds and leets had more to do with it; and one cannot help regretting that changes should be necessary which take away from the ordinary citizen at once the responsibility and the personal interest he should feel in the administration of justice. In the old days 13 good and sufficient men sat as grand jurors, and prisoners were tried by a jury of 12, who had to give an unanimous verdict, yet we do not hear of the Grand Jury presenting the system as a nuisance or an unwarrantable interference with the grinding of the money-mill. Obviously much leisure must have been theirs to make this possible, and no doubt, under the changed conditions of life here, the change was necessary. Still, though the practice changes, it is to be hoped that the underlying principles will never be forgotten.

Note

1. "Death of Mr. W.R. Collyer", *The Singapore Free Press and Mercantile Advertiser*, 30 October 1928

15

THE REFORMATION OF BRITISH MALAYA

Essay

15 November 1907
by *James Aitken*

Editors' Note

A more critical tone towards colonial government was also evident in James Aitken's essay of 1907. Aitken, a Queen's Scholar from Singapore and a lawyer who practised alongside Song Ong Siang, came to criticize in the Society what he saw as the failings of British policy in Malaya.[1] The central issue of the ensuing debate with Arthur Knight was the standards to which British colonial policy was to be held. For Knight, British achievements had to be understood in relation to the condition in which they had found the Malay Peninsula and the improvement of this condition. Aitken, on the other hand, was concerned with the British failure to attain for the colony a fuller level of economic and social development and for the unevenness of their achievements. This debate came to focus particularly on the position of the Malays, and British responsibility to include them within the development of the colonial economy and colonial society. On his part Aitken would argue in a manner that was a precursor of later debates around affirmative action that whilst the Malays were "not likely for a long time to reach the standard of the European, Chinaman, or Tamil, he should be encouraged by Government, and the other races should even be slightly handicapped in order to advance him". Arthur Knight's critical response similarly emphasized objections to affirmative action which anticipate arguments raised in future debates. For him the current status of the Malays was an outcome of their nature. He argued that they had the formal right to study medicine and join the legislative council but lacked the inclination. He was of the opinion that their improvement could not therefore be forced. Moral reform and improvement for Knight appeared to be confronted with the reality of racial difference.

For the purposes of this paper British Malaya may be taken to be the Straits Settlements and the Federated Malay States, leaving out of account Labuan, British North Borneo, and Sarawak.

A great deal has been done in the past to improve, better, and transform this part of the world by the suppression of piracy and slavery, the establishment of law and order, the introduction of railways, roads, and telegraphs, the improvement of harbours and wharves, the founding of hospitals, the advancement of medical science by the creation of a school for medical research, the introduction of lawyers and competent judicial officials in the Federated Malay States, the improvement of sanitary conditions, and, last but not least, the steady growth of the press. A great deal, however, remains to be done to improve this part of the world, and it is the future reformation of British Malaya that will be dealt with in this paper.

I cannot do better than begin with the Malay. The great blot on all the progress of the past is that the Malay, the original native of the soil, has not received that consideration and attention which he deserves. It is not because it is impossible to improve him, but it is because he is neglected and overlooked, that he has not made any progress to speak of. A Malay cannot or will not put his hands to certain kinds of hard or dirty manual labour, but he nevertheless takes to and does satisfactorily other kinds of work which require skill, dexterity, and nerve. He will not, for instance, pull a rikisha or carry heavy loads, but he is successful at building his own house and boats, handling telephone wires, acting as seaman, captain, or engine-driver of small steamboats, and more recently as chauffeur of motorcars. He has unbounded energy for sports, as we have all noticed on the football field and in the Singapore New Year Regatta. It is because the Malay has been overlooked that, after all these years of British rule, there is not a single Malay medical man or surgeon with modern ideas amongst us. Think of the amount of good such a man would do, the lives he could save, the superstitious practices and mistaken ideas about Western medicine he would gradually wipe out. Suppose, for example, a Malay was suffering from *beri-beri* and was told by a European to go to hospital. His Malay friends might get round him and tell him that he would have both his paralyzed *beri-beri* legs cut off if he did so, and to save him from that fate they would bring in their *"pawang"* or medicine-man, who would perhaps practise witch-craft, and, in their opinion, if that could not cure him nothing would. We certainly should have a Malay or Malays in our midst, if not skilled in medicine, at least proficient in one of its branches. Ambulance lectures were a short time ago given to Malay policemen in Malacca, and they seemed to take an interest in the subject and passed the usual examination that followed the lectures. What are such lectures but elementary lessons in medicine and surgery? If an ordinary Malay *"mata-mata"* can be successful at amateur surgery, surely a Malay who has devoted years to the subject would do some good at it. The Malays I believe have not made any progress to speak of because they have not learnt that it is quite possible for them to attain knowledge as the Japanese and other nations have done, that other civilized peoples have at one time been in the same state of development as themselves, and that it is only application and self-confidence that will bring them up to the same level as other races who have made great strides in civilization.

Think of the difference it has made to the Chinese population here to have first one and later more than one Chinese practitioner skilled in Western medical science in their midst. Hundreds through mere ignorance would have died rather than submit to the simplest operation by a foreigner, whereas they have confidence in and trust themselves in the hands of one of their own countrymen, who can make himself understood to them in their own language and knows thoroughly the habits and the peculiarities of the diet of his patients. It is not because they are incapable of study that there are no Malay doctors. It is because they have not been given the chance. At first they should be encouraged by being allowed to pass in medicine with about one-half of the marks required of other nationalities.

In the State of Johore there are Malay lawyers, and in the Philippines there are Filipino doctors who qualified in Spain, and some of them have no doubt since qualified in America; and what, after all, is a Filipino but a Malay? One of the members of the Commission appointed to enquire into the opium question in the Philippines was a Filipino doctor and member of the Council. Why should the Malays not boast of a Malay doctor? Why should they not be as advanced as their brother the Filipino in classical music? In the Federated Malay States the Malay is being assisted by Government to improve his position by the promotion of Malay art and industries, but I regret to say that this is not being done in the Straits Settlements. As the Malay is not likely for a long time to reach the standard of the European, Chinaman, or Tamil, he should be encouraged by Government, and the other races should even be slightly handicapped in order to advance him. Now, how is this to be brought about? It will never take place so long as the Malay, unlike the Chinaman, is excluded from representation on the Legislative Council. If as yet there is no Malay of sufficient standing and talent, with a good knowledge of English, to take his position in Council, let a Government official or some other person be selected to study the interests of the Malays and all questions which affect them, and his duty should be to continually watch and promote their interests. When we turn to the Municipal Commission the state of affairs is the same. No Malay has, to the best of my recollection, ever sat or been invited to sit on that body, and no one has been chosen expressly to represent that section of the public, with the result that their quarters, in Gaylang for instance, are in a most insanitary state. It is certainly otherwise with Chinese affairs. They have, in addition to re-presentation on the Legislative and Municipal Councils, a Chinese Advisory Board and a Chinese Protector, in addition to the protection afforded them by their Consul.

With regard to the Tamils in the Straits and Federated Malay States, who number about one-third of the population, it is also, I think, a pity that we do not have an expression of their views in both the Municipal and Legislative Councils and in the public press. When a Bill is introduced in the Legislative Council with reference to Indian labour, for instance, we have the views of the employers of labour on the matter discussed at great length in the newspapers, but not a word is generally urged on behalf of the labourers; their grievances or views are not put forward. Now, I dare say, if they were represented and their views expressed, the legislation would be more satisfactory, and it might lead to an increase in the immigration of such labourers to this part of the world. Government officials may try to protect the interests of these people, but that is not sufficient. We do not want them to be regarded as dumb animals. For instance, if they consider the conditions of indentured labour no better than slavery they should come forward and say so, with suggestions to improve such conditions, and let the matter be discussed in public and in the public press. If, again, the Tamils, including Chitties, who are living here, think that Government is not encouraging Tamil emigration to Malaya by not providing Tamil schools for Tamil children, or by not seeing to the immediate construction of a railway to India which would enable Chitty women and Indians of a better class to find their way to this part of the world without losing caste by crossing the sea, let their representative fight such questions for all they are worth.

The next matter I would refer to is bribery and corruption in British Malaya. While it must be admitted that the heads of departments and officers in the higher positions are above the mere suspicion of bribery, and that some of the subordinates are not in positions to command bribes, while a few others are men of such integrity of character that they would live on rice and salt fish, or bread and water if you like, rather than taint themselves with bribery and corruption, yet those whose work brings them in contact with some of the subordinate staff in certain departments, from the office peon upwards, say that the amount of bribery and corruption that goes on is something appalling, and that no honest man can hope to do business successfully with such departments. A Chinaman quite recently asked me if I thought a certain contractor was making money, and whether in that contractor's business there were opportunities of charging for twice as much material as that actually supplied. What are the causes of this unsatisfactory state of affairs? The first is that Chinese encourage bribery, as the offering of bribes is as natural to them as gambling. An honest subordinate might refuse to accept these bribes, but when there is rank corruption around him his work might be made intolerable, and life a misery to him, if he does not stoop to bribery. We have the case of a man here who was blinded with oil of vitriol, and what was the motive? Revenge, because this honest man was a spoke in the wheel of those who wished to profit to the full extent by bribery. Another young man who tried to put down dishonesty here went into the Lunatic Asylum for two weeks. Life, he said, was made so unbearable to him by those who were tarred with the brush of corruption that it drove him crazy. The second is extravagance in living and the low tone of morality among a large number of those educated in the Straits, and elsewhere too I am afraid. The third and most important cause is that the officials in higher positions, who are above suspicion, allow their subordinates too much power. They do not come sufficiently into direct contact with the people with whom their departments have to deal. To illustrate what I mean, let me refer to an instance where the higher official formerly did not, but now does come into direct contact with the public. In former years, when a man wished to obtain a summons or a warrant in the Police Court he would go to an interpreter and a clerk, who would take down the information, which would afterwards be submitted to a Magistrate for a summons or a warrant. If no bribe was forthcoming the complainant might be put off. If a sufficient inducement was offered, all the necessary tips would be given the complainant to bolster up a false or a bad case, for the purpose of obtaining a warrant which might have been refused if, as at present, the Magistrate sees the complainant and takes down his statement and examines him himself. As long as a high official leaves his subordinates with too much power, so that they virtually sanction licenses and approve of contracts, work done and materials supplied, and practically control other matters, so long will there be glorious opportunities to the subordinates for graft. A great deal of bribery and corruption could be put a stop to if officials who are heads or sub-heads of departments would, wherever possible, deal direct with contractors or persons having business with their departments. In fact I think a rule should be made in Government and Municipal service that any member of the public shall on alleging that there is bribery and corruption among the subordinates of a department, and without being called upon to prove it or being liable to answer in damages for such allegations, be entitled to receive his orders direct from the head of such department, and demand that the head of the department himself shall in every particular approve of his work, materials supplied, or whatever else it is, independently of the subordinates and of their suggestions, recommendations, or arguments. At present the state of affairs in many departments is unsatisfactory. If a man attempts to write to or approach the head of the department when he considers the subordinates are trying to squeeze him, he is probably referred back to the subordinates, who then have an opportunity of showing the individual that it is they who virtually control the department, and not the head. If the man, however, chooses to prosecute one of the subordinates for bribery, and this is seldom done,—it may result in the prosecutor and his witnesses being fined for malicious prosecution, so cunning and clever are the people who take bribes in screening themselves and getting innocent folk into trouble, if necessary.

From bribery and corruption I shall pass on to the subject of brothels, because they give rise to an endless amount of disease, misery, and vice in our midst. The great majority of Chinese in Malaya are a strictly moral people. It is only the Cantonese river-boat girls who are given to prostitution. Although we have 150,000 Hokkien, Teochew, and Hylam Chinese in Singapore, and there is no law suppressing it, there is not a single Hokkien, Teochew, or Hylam public brothel. With the Hylam it is impossible, because they believe that a high state of morality cannot be maintained if they allow their woman-folk to go abroad. So strong is this custom that no Hylam would dare bring, or even smuggle his own wife, mother, or sister away from his native land in defiance of his countrymen at home or abroad. The Japanese, on the other hand, come here only in small numbers to carry on respectable trades, but their women come in large numbers, and they have no other calling than prostitution, with Singapore as a distributing centre for the disposal of some of them as personal chattels. Why and how are they here and all over the East in such numbers, though the law in Japan prohibits the emigration of Japanese for such purposes? It is because the Japanese are on the whole an immoral people so far as prostitution is concerned; and further, because, however high their repute for being above bribery and corruption in other matters, in this matter at least the Japanese officials concerned must surely be a deplorable failure, or we should not have thousands of Japanese prostitutes all over the East. If certain Japanese officials are blind to the breach of their own law for monetary considerations, the British Government are also to be blamed for receiving into their midst hundreds of women who could only have got away from their country by being kidnapped, or, if they were parties to the transaction, by fraud and deception practised by themselves and bribery on the part of officials, in order to enable them to be smuggled out of their country.

The next matter I will briefly refer to is education. One great defect in the education here is that the men in high Government positions and controlling education have nearly all been educated in England and received a classical training, and they naturally consider that what was good education for themselves must be good for children here. What is the result? Instead of finding Chinese, Tamil, or Malay among the languages prescribed for examinations in connection with English education here, we have French and German. Now, French and German may be of importance in Europe, but to a lad here they are almost worthless. All the French and German he will need in connection with his English can be obtained in a list of foreign words and phrases at the end of a small dictionary. After he has left school he may probably never utter two sentences of French or German for the rest of his life, and if he does use any French words it will probably be those which people who have never learnt French are quite familiar with, as such words have become part of the English language. The languages they should teach, if foreign languages are to be taught here, are, first, the Hokkien dialect of the Chinese, because by far the great majority of Chinese here are Hokkien, and the Teochew, who come next in numbers, understand it. All that would be required would be instruction in conversation only, as the study of the written character would mean a stupendous task, and it would be overburdening and hampering a boy who had English studies to keep up at the same time. The next language that should be taught is Tamil, a language that belongs to the same big family as the European languages, and is, in many respects more highly developed than them, if a highly inflected language and a more perfect alphabet and phonetic system of spelling is an indication of superiority. Another advantage of teaching Chinese or Tamil as a foreign language is that you would be able to get your teacher at about one-fifth of the cost of a competent teacher of French or German, and one would have heaps of opportunities in life after of practising them here. Thousands of Chinese boys here are educated in English, and they have opportunities of speaking Chinese at home, and it seems only fair that other boys who will find Chinese useful to them in life after should be given an opportunity of learning that language if they desire it, so that when necessary they might deal with Chinese from China direct without the intervention of an interpreter. The Tamil and Chinese classes should be open, to both Chinese and Tamil Straits-born children, in order that they may be made familiar with the mother-tongues of their forefathers.

At the present time about 50,000 Indian labourers arrive annually in the Straits Settlements and the Federated Malay States. A large number of Straits youths must come in contact with these people, and it is deplorable that they are not able to converse with them in Tamil. Next to Malay and the Hokkien dialect of Chinese, I should think Tamil is spoken by more of the inhabitants of British Malaya than any other language. You have a Straits youth educated at the Medical College here, and then placed in some hospital where he may come across scores of Chinese and Tamils and not be able to ask them in their own language the most ordinary questions as to their symptoms, the state of their health, and other facts which would enable him to deal successfully with his patients. Take another lad who is on an estate or mine where Tamils are employed. How can he work those coolies satisfactorily if he cannot convey orders and give instructions to them in Tamil? A second great defect about the education here is that too much importance is attached to the classical side, and commercial education appears to have a secondary place and does not receive much encouragement in the shape of big prizes or scholarships. If the attention commercial education deserves were given to it there would be no need for busy gentlemen in the town to waste their time over Chamber of Commerce examinations. A third great draw-back to the education here is that very little attention is paid to physical drill. Some schools have their playgrounds, but there is absolutely no systematic physical training during or after school hours, as in most schools in Europe. The result is that hundreds and thousands of Chinese and native children who live in crowded parts of the town grow up weaklings, and create progeny who are worse weaklings, and contribute largely, I venture to think, to the high infantile mortality in this colony. There are so many conveyances here nowadays that children do very little walking. A little over twenty-five years ago they had no rikishas or trams, and two, three, and four miles a day to school and back was quite a common thing for them. Now a boy has his rik even for a trifling half or quarter of a mile to school or elsewhere. In the old days children had to walk, and a trudge of four to six miles out in the country and back the same day was a common thing for them. At present it would not be dreamt of. At the age of twelve I remember my schoolmaster asking the boys if they had been to the top of Bukit Timah, the highest hill in Singapore. The next Saturday another boy and I, who had not seen Bukit Timah, set out on foot for that hill. We passed Bukit Timah entrance, and as there was then no sign-board we did not think it could be the highest hill. We walked about two miles further-on, until we came in sight of what now looks like Bukit Panjang. We went some distance through a lalang path, and as we had our doubts about it being the highest hill we turned back. On reaching the police station at the seventh mile we asked to be directed to Bukit Timah, which we were told we had just passed. We walked back again to the entrance and up the road, which was little better than a jungle path in those days, and were soon viewing Singapore from the top of a wooden stage, there being no bungalow then. Ninety-nine per cent of the town children in Singapore could not undertake such a task today without collapsing. If the children were systematically drilled and properly fed, it is my firm belief that they would be as healthy and strong as most children in other parts of the world. There would be no necessity then for

Europeans with limited means to stint themselves to send their children home for their health and education. The children would grow up to be healthier fathers and mothers than we have at present in our midst, and there would be an appreciable improvement in the death-rate of infants. I have noticed a marked improvement in the physique of the Straits-born Chinese who have gone in for volunteering, and I am sure that the death-rate of their children must be considerably lower than the weak, sickly-looking, undrilled fathers who are not volunteers. If statistics could be furnished on the subject, I feel almost certain that the mortality of infants of Straits-born Chinese excluding volunteers would be much greater than that of the more robust Chinese men and women from China.

While we are on the subject of the death-rate, I might say that if we were to leave out the unhealthy occupation of the rikisha-puller in a tropical country we should probably find that the death-rate of Singapore is not quite as bad as it is supposed to be. In Japan, which has more favourable climatic conditions, the rikisha-puller is protected by having only one person to pull at a time. While I do not say that this should be the case in Singapore, I certainly think that he should be at liberty when pulling two passengers up a slope, or over loose ravel, to require as a matter of right, when it is not raining, that they should walk up the slope or over the loose gravel, and that he should also be able as a matter of right to call a halt of a few minutes after any distance over three miles, for the purpose of having a drink, feed, or rest. Another means of reducing the death-rate amongst this class is to appoint a medical examiner, whose duty would be to license those only who are physically fit and to weed out those who have become gradually unfit for their occupation, so that they might take up other callings which may be less profitable to themselves, but would prolong their lives.

I should next like to touch upon the desirability of reform in medicine here. If I were a medical man I dare say I could say a very great deal on this subject. The establishment of a medical school in Singapore and of a school for medical research at Kuala Lumpur are important steps taken in the advancement of medical science and knowledge here, but I believe the general opinion is that in medical matters we are not up to date. A lady who had served as a nurse in one of the missions in China said that when she was shown through the General Hospital here some years ago she was surprised to find that it was not as well equipped for surgical purposes as some of the large mission hospitals in China. In European towns of the same size as Singapore there are throat, ear, and eye hospitals, asylums for the deaf and dumb and the blind, and homes for inebriates, but in the whole of Malaya there is not a single institution of the kind.

The next subject I will touch on is law. A deplorable defect about our system of laws is the lack of uniformity between the Straits Settlements and Federated Malay States. If the Straits Settlements follows the English Civil Procedure, the Federated Malay States adopts the Indian Civil Procedure. When the Straits Settlements devotes a great deal of labour in preparing a new Civil Procedure Code to suit local requirements, the Federated Malay States are not asked to co-operate, and the difference is maintained, to the great inconvenience of Straits' lawyers, who are sometimes retained for Federated Malay States' matters, and also of Straits' judges and judicial officers who may be transferred to the States, or vice versa. In education I notice they are having one common head, and they propose to have a common code for the Straits and Federated Malay States, and it is high time they did the same in law. The lack of uniformity in law means a lot of time and energy wasted unnecessarily. In a criminal matter, for instance, a Straits' lawyer finds he cannot advise a client from the Federated Malay States off-hand, because the Criminal Procedure there is not identically the same as in the Straits, and the lawyer here has to study their Criminal Procedure Code closely before he can advise in such a case. If they wish to introduce English laws into the Federated Malay States, why not simplify matters by adopting legislation which Singapore has found good enough for its purpose? And Singapore, in its turn, should have its laws made as nearly as possible identical with the laws of England. If divorce jurisdiction, for instance, is exercised in Courts in England, the Courts here should have like powers; and I am glad to say steps are being taken to rectify that defect. In due course, no doubt, a divorce and a Deceased Wife's Sister's Bill will be introduced.

A great many other reforms might be effected for the advancement of British Malaya, amongst which might be mentioned the establishment of a Government or Municipal department for the control of foodstuffs and drinks, which would see that none but genuine articles were sold, and that no articles of food, spirits or other liquids, manufactured in Singapore were labelled as coming from places which are noted for such products, and thereby damaging the reputation of articles coming from such places. For instance, when I was a boy I remember going to a house in Kampong Sultan, where I saw a Chinaman making and bottling syrups and labelling them as coming from Bordeaux; and the same kind of thing is going on in Singapore today. In conclusion, I would say that one of the greatest reforms would be dispensing with the Crown Agents' system of interfering with local affairs and contracts, as the colony is well able to look after its own affairs, and, judging from past experience, would do its own work more cheaply and satisfactorily than the Crown Agents.

CRITICISM
by Arthur Knight

The subject on the Syllabus for this meeting is "Tropical Administration". Mr. Aitken has altered this to "The Reformation of British Malaya". This is really the same subject, only limited to the local aspect of it. But then, in the essay which you have heard read, comprehensive as it is within the limits stated, the writer confines himself almost wholly to his estimate of the *defects* of the present system and to the particulars in which he thinks reformation is necessary or desirable.

The Essayist, it is true, begins by a brief—very brief—acknowledgement of what has so far been done in the way of improvement. In this he includes the introduction of lawyers in the Federated Malay States and the steady growth of the press. These are comparatively recent in the Native States. The first of the two, considering his profession, the Essayist would naturally not omit, though possibly there may be people who would think there might be something to say on the other side. But both these improvements are the result of personal enterprise, while it is to what he considers defects in Government policy that the Essayist proceeds chiefly to advert.

"Many of the improvements", we are told, "are of a second-class order." Here I cannot but think that more justice should have been done to our achievements in the Malay States of the Peninsula, which have roused the admiration of all who have had the opportunity of studying them. Here, some thirty years ago, was a country absolutely neglected by Europeans, with no proper Government, with a population of peasants suppressed, robbed, and enslaved by their chiefs; without an inch of proper road, and with the waterways obstructed by stockades, at which heavy tolls were exacted from every passing boat. Why, people who do not know the facts could hardly believe that such a country as they now see was in such a condition a generation ago as I have briefly indicated.

Here is a country which, as I have said, was neglected by Europeans. It was, in fact, taken in hand at last because it had got into a state of partial anarchy which threatened the peace of our own colony. And then, instead of seizing and incorporating the territory, we recognize the status of the rulers, guarantee them handsome allowances, and assist them to organize a firm and impartial government, under which the people have liberty and protection, and are comfortable and contented; while the produce of the country, without burdensome taxation, has enabled the construction of hundreds of miles of railways and fine roads, and other blessings, some of which the Essayist has briefly specified.

Well, what are these "second-class improvements"? "Instead of being able to travel at the rate of 50 or 60 miles an hour, a train in the Federated Malay States attains a top speed of about 30 miles an hour." Can the Essayist be serious in looking for an English express in Malaya? To what end? Such a thing is not thought of even in India. And does he not know that such a speed would require much stronger railway construction and rolling stock? Result, that it could not be run at present rates. And then we come to the steamships. The railways are constructed and run by Government; the steamships belong to companies and firms. The position is, therefore, entirely different: it is for the owners to judge what pattern of ship is best adapted to the circumstances. Two things are fairly well known: first, an increase of even a knot in speed entails a disproportionate increase in cost; second, more power, and therefore, greater expenditure, is necessary to keep up a given speed in the tropics than in cooler climates.

Again, the Essayist is surely hardly reasonable in his complaint that we cannot yet run from Singapore to Rangoon or Bangkok by motorcar. Why should Prince Borghese have the influence to get such a passage made? There was no such preparation made for him in Siberia. He certainly did not, as the Essayist implies, "travel 6,000 miles in a motorcar without a break" in Russian territory, though he managed with great difficulty to effect the journey. And it is certainly not "absolutely out of the question to traverse short distances of from 100 to 200 or 300 miles by the same means" in the Federated Malay States, as it has been repeatedly done without difficulty.

Then in another part of his paper the Essayist imputes blame to the Government for "not seeing to the immediate construction of a railway to India which would enable Chitty women and Indians of a better class to find their way to this part of the world without losing caste by crossing the sea". A railway from Calcutta round the northern coasts of the Bay of Bengal to Burmah has often been discussed, and it might thence be extended farther south; but how could our Government undertake such a tremendous work? And if such a railway were constructed, what does the Essayist think would be the cost of the journey, which is now made by sea for a few dollars? Then I do not know that there is any particular demand here for "Indians of a better class"; and if Chitty men do not lose their caste by crossing the kala pani; neither would their women.

I should doubt whether the time has come for going to the expense of laying a telegraph line to Pekan, which is not now, as the Essayist styles it, "the capital of Pahang", in the usual sense of being the seat of Government. I do not think the Government would be justified in incurring such an expenditure; and if there were really a demand for it, it could be done by private enterprise.

Turning now to more serious matters, the Essayist says—"The great blot on all the progress of the past is that the Malay, the original native of the soil, has not received that consideration and attention which he deserves." This can only refer to the Peninsula—where, if not the original native, the Malay has been owner of the soil for centuries—because as regards Singapore and Penang, the Malays can hardly claim to be more the original natives than other races.

Now, taking first Malacca, comprising a larger area than all the rest of the colony put together, and almost wholly agricultural, the main object of our Government has been to promote the good of the Malay peasant, with the result that, before our protection of adjoining States, the population tended to increase by migration. In the Federated Malay States it has been often observed that the Malay, the native of the soil, is very much thrown in the background. I should be sorry to impute this to Government neglect. It is really the inevitable result of circumstances: the Malay has done nothing to develop his country; this has been done, and is being done, by other races, and the Malays are now in these States actually in the minority. But it would be impossible to be more truly interested in the Malays and their well-being than many members of the Civil Service who have learnt their language and served among them—most of all Sir Frank Swettenham. Much assistance is given to the Malay peasantry by the Native States Service. Then there is a very extensive system of schools, both in the colony and in the Malay States, for the Malays as well as for other races. Sir Frank Swettenham, in his book *British Malaya*, says—"The most promising boys in the vernacular schools are helped, if they desire it, to pass on to a school where English is taught." And again: "Special efforts have been made to provide a suitable education for the children of Malay Rajas and chiefs; but the Government has not aimed at educating the children of any class or nationality to unfit them for the lives they will probably have to lead." The Government has also tried to introduce agricultural and technical schools and classes, but an intelligent boy can so soon secure remunerative employment that the tendency is to leave school too soon: the very thing that is observed in Singapore. There has always been kept in view the education of the Malays for employment in the administration, even in responsible positions, and this has met with considerable success. The State Councils are largely composed of Malays holding high administrative posts. Large numbers of Malays are employed in the police, in the forest and survey departments, in clearing and building huts, etc.; but long hours of indoor work do not suit the Malay. The official lists of the Malay States contain in subordinate posts—clerkships etc.—numerous Tamils and Sinhalese; of course Malays would be gladly accepted if they were willing and able. As the Essayist says, they also get employment on steam-vessels, and as chauffeurs of motorcars. I quite agree that it would be an advantage for Malays to study medicine, but they cannot be forced to do so, and they are not debarred from doing so if they choose. There is, as the Essayist has mentioned, now a medical school in Singapore; I do not know whether any Malays have taken advantage of it.

But then, we are told, the general advance of the Malay will never be brought about until he is represented in the Legislative Council. I fear the Essayist over-estimates the influence and power of an unofficial member of the Legislative Council. Moreover, the Malay is not, as he says, unlike the Chinaman, excluded from such membership. No one, whatever his race, can expect to be appointed to such a position unless, besides a knowledge of English, he has standing and position in the community. The same remarks apply to the Tamils. The Essayist further points out that neither of these races has ever been represented on the Municipal Councils; to which it may be replied that is because they have not been elected by the ratepayers. Moreover none of these Councils legislate for the Malay States, and the State Councils, which are, as already stated, largely composed of Malays.

The next subject of the essay is the prevalence of bribery and corruption in British Malaya. I am unable to judge whether this is more considerable than elsewhere. The Essayist, in his profession, has apparently been brought into contact with certain forms of the evil. In some of these he says improvement has been effected by a head leaving less to his subordinates. It is obvious, however, that everything cannot pass through the hands of the head of a big department, otherwise he might as well have no subordinates.

As regards brothels, I am one of those who have always regretted the repeal, by orders from home, of our laws for their control. If things are as the Essayist states in regard to the Japanese women, I think our Government should communicate with the Japanese Consul.

The Essayist gives at some length his views of the points in which the system of education here might be improved, and on the whole I think them worthy of consideration. But he considers that instead of including French and German among the languages prescribed for examination, we should have Chinese, Tamil, or Malay. Now, it is in the examination for Government Scholarships that French and German are included. These are competed for by boys who are aiming at higher education, and Chinese, Tamil, or Malay could hardly be substituted here. It would be useful for boys to have at least a colloquial knowledge of these languages, but it could hardly be made a part of ordinary schooling. Encouragement of commercial education and of physical drill I quite agree with; the Essayist's note of the change from his early days in the matter of riding and walking is very just.

The occupation of jinrikisha-pulling, which is incidentally mentioned, is certainly a very trying one, and I fear many of the coolies are short-lived. The proposal for licensing them was fully considered years ago, and reluctantly abandoned as impracticable. There are about 25,000 gullets in Singapore, and it would be impossible to identify them unless each man was marked with a badge on his skin. A badge buckled round the arm could easily be transferred by one man to another.

I agree that our hospitals are capable of much improvement. I have heard our General Hospital here spoken of repeatedly in the very strongest terms of disparagement.

Doubtless the Essayist is right, from his professional experience, in advocating as much uniformity as is in the circumstances practicable between the law in the colony and the Federated Malay States, and I am under the impression that measures in that direction are in progress.

The essay closes with a paragraph with which I am in entire sympathy. I do think that something might be done by legislation to exercise greater control over the sale of articles of food and drinks, especially the latter, for the poisonous liquors which are largely sold here are doing untold harm. And finally, I am quite with the Essayist in his advocacy of getting rid of the Crown Agents' monopoly. I would as a rule purchase here what can be obtained here, and in the case of contracts for works I would give local firms the liberty of competing. But, you see, in this matter we are under the rule of the Colonial Office.

The essay which you have heard read can hardly claim to be philosophical; nor can my criticism. We have simply been discussing local matters from a practical point of view. You have found my paper rather scrappy, but that could not be helped as I was desirous of dealing with the subjects seriatim.

Note

1. "Obituary: Mr. James Aitken—Doyen of the Singapore Bar", *The Straits Times*, 28 May 1928, p. 7.

III

The Colonial Order and the Chinese

16

CHINESE LOCAL TRADE

Essay
10 August 1901
by *Tan Teck Soon*

Editors' Note

Alongside Lim Boon Keng, Tan Teck Soon was the other prominent, and longest serving, Straits Chinese voice in the Society. In their contributions, both challenged the less than liberal and often stereotyped views of the Chinese held amongst some prominent members of the Society (see Section 2). Although Tan's main intellectual interests were focused on cultural and educational concerns related to Chinese and Western societies, this atypical presentation sought to share with his European audience insights into the Chinese conduct of enterprise and business—both the positive and negative aspects. The essay is noteworthy in outlining the case made by the acculturated English-speaking Straits Chinese elite which not only saw themselves a match in educational and social achievement with the British but also felt it necessary to emphasize the economic contribution the Chinese had made to Malaya. The Chinese, Tan argued, had developed the land of the Malay States at a time when the British had avoided intervention and had worked to facilitate trade into the interior, often in precarious circumstances and without government protection. Coinciding with the growth of Chinese nationalism amongst the overseas Chinese in Malaya, Tan, who had been educated in China and whose writings reflected upon the rise of a modern China, highlighted the importance of the China trade to the Peninsula and the difficulties faced by the trading community. Responding to the paper, J.M. Allison, a member of the Legislative Council and a manager of Barlow & Co, prominently involved in the rubber trade, had little sympathy for what he saw as Tan's "exaggerated account" of the plight of Chinese traders. Disputing various points in the presentation relating to the contribution of Chinese traders and the Chinese population as a whole in Singapore, his main counter argument was to emphasize that Tan overlooked the benefits of trade under the British flag which provided the basis of prosperity for the trader and the colony.

In endeavouring to write an essay dealing with Chinese local trade for discussion at a meeting of this Society, I must first apologize for introducing into our syllabus a subject to which some objection could justly be made as hardly coming within the scope of the Society's aims and objects as evidenced by its rules. And yet, as residents of a colony whose prosperity depends so largely upon trade, it is a subject which constantly intrudes itself upon our notice, and is therefore deserving of some slight attention even at the hands of professed philosophers. The recent establishment of the Commercial Intelligence Branch of the British Board of Trade is significant, and reveals the necessity for accurate information in regard to trade matters; and so important is Chinese commerce that we have had lately Commercial Missions from Blackburn and Lyons appointed to study its conditions, so that it would perhaps not be entirely out of place for us here to inquire how far local circumstances modify the statements made by the selected experts in their published reports. While all of us are perhaps more or less familiar with the statement that Chinese trade is the backbone of our commercial prosperity, it is possible that very few among us have ever ventured to inquire into what is comprised under the term "Chinese trade", how is it usually conducted, and what is its exact economical value in the development of the general trade of the colony? I shall therefore merely attempt to discuss the subject from a purely academical standpoint, leaving out all references to statistics, and craving my critic's and the society's indulgence for any misstatement or inaccuracy that may appear therein.

Although the Chinese are not *bona fide* natives, yet, owing to their numerical superiority, nearly the whole internal trade of the colony is in their hands, and a considerable proportion of this is exclusively dealings among their own nationality. They are, therefore, producers as well as importers, distributors, and exporters. As the principal purveyors, supplying the natives with the chief necessaries of life, they form an intermediate link between the distant Malay kampongs and the chief centres of trade. It is often an instructive as well as interesting spectacle to observe them far away amidst the jungles of the Malay States, sometimes for months without any intercourse with their own countrymen, patiently and perseveringly maintaining their position, and selling and purchasing among the natives who surround them on all sides. These traders are mostly Hokkiens from the Ying-chun sub-prefecture. While the Straits-born Babas are by affinity of language, custom, and temperament perhaps more fitted for such enterprises, yet they have never seriously attempted to avail themselves of the opportunities offered them. They positively dislike the solitary, monotonous existence, without any of the usual amenities of civilized life, and with only the barest prospect of making a fortune. The Ying-chun Chinese, on the other hand, patiently adapt themselves to their environment, make friends with the natives, learn their spoken language, make themselves indispensable to all around, and quietly pocket all the compensating advantages of their position. Their *modus operandi* appears to be somewhat as follows: a newcomer from China, or a return immigrant, would scrape together from friends and other accommodating creditors sufficient means to buy a cartload of such necessaries as rice, salt, salt-fish, tobacco, kerosene, matches, sugar, biscuits, manufactured cotton goods, umbrellas, etc., and proceed to a distant village some miles from the nearest trading centre, and at once commence operations by building a hut, planting a small vegetable garden for his own requirements, and opening a *kedai*. From his experience of officialism in his own country, he is always deferential to the Penghulu and other persons of standing, and is ready to give credit to the respectable among the villagers. His shop is soon the rendezvous of the natives, who resort thither on all occasions or when they have leisure. For such among them who possess jungle produce, such as gutta, garroo-wood, rattan, gum damar, areca-nut, etc., the shopkeeper is ready to barter in exchange for the goods of his shop. He cheats them outrageously both in weighing and in calculation, but he does all this with such apparent good-nature and friendliness that complaints are seldom made. The goods thus obtained are carefully stored until, after a few years' collection, the man finds he has sufficient to load two or three carts, when, after first disposing of his shop, good-will, and stock-in-trade to a successor, he would start with his goods to the port of embarkation. Here he would dispose of them to the best advantage, pay off his creditors, and he is then ready to take a trip to China to enjoy a holiday with his family. From personal inquiries made, I find that after paying off their creditors, these men would only realize an average of $200 to $300, which would thus represent the net savings of perhaps three years' trading. This would appear to equal the average earnings of a day-coolie in town, or that of a household servant, but of course the business experience which the man acquired in his trading ventures would be invaluable to him in his future career. The special feature of interest attached to even a cursory contemplation of this branch of Chinese commercial enterprise is, however, the conspicuous exhibition among those who engage in it of the great moral qualities of thriftiness and frugality, as well as patience and perseverance, as a national characteristic.

Dealing next with the product of Chinese labour, we find that as regards these Settlements the greater bulk of the new immigrants from China are engaged in planting enterprises, while in the Native States mining is the chief industry. So important is the demand for labour on these objects that the Legislature in these places have framed laws both to regulate the traffic and supply, as well as to protect the immigrants. As is well known, the chief planting industry for Singapore and Johore comprises the cultivation of gambier, pepper, and pineapples, while in Malacca tapioca is almost exclusively planted, and in Penang sugar-canes. Some ventures have also recently been attempted in Malacca to cultivate gutta-trees. The Penang estates, however, mostly engage Tamil labour, and their system is already familiar to all. The Malacca plantations are almost entirely in the hands of great capitalists, who engage their labourers, usually Hainanese, monthly or annually. The chief interest for this branch of Chinese labour centres, therefore, in the gambier and pepper-planting industry, especially that of Johore. This Native State, although so close to Singapore, has never been much interfered with by the British suzerain, consequently, under the enlightened encouragement of the native rulers, and especially that of the late Sultan, the Chinese have been enabled to organize an entirely unique and perhaps efficacious system of land-tenure and cooperative cultivation in this connection. When the gambier and pepper trade first became important, large tracts of jungle-land were cleared and placed under cultivation. These planters are mostly Teochews from the districts surrounding Swatow in China. The system in vogue is usually somewhat as follows: a Chinese who had previously succeeded in securing the confidence of a number of gambier and pepper traders in town, generally five or six, would first proceed to an unoccupied district in Johore or Muar, and select a tract of jungle-land for his purposes. This land is usually situated close to the bank of some river or stream navigable for boats. For purposes of transport and communication with the town the river is a *sine qua non*, and consequently both the man who opens up the district as well as his principal habitation are in Chinese designation intimately connected therewith. He is thus styled the *kangchu*, meaning the river lord or chief, and his shop or village is the *kangkha*, or river depot. The *kangchu* would first petition the native authorities for permission to occupy the land, and on this being granted, special privileges are attached to his title. As far as the officials are concerned, he is the *penghulu* over the actual Chinese planters, and on appointment is invested by the ruler with a *"lembing"* or spear in token of liability to the military service of the State, with a rattan as symbol of police supervision, and with authority to handcuff and confine in the stocks transgressors generally. Over the planters and other settlers he is monopolist for opium, spirit, gambling, pawnbroking, and pork. His position is therefore one of considerable affluence, some of the richer commanding an annual income of several thousand dollars; but he had to pay the State for his appointment a single fee of $100, and levies a land-tax on the produce for its benefit also.

Besides these, he has, of course, to arrange with the different revenue farms as regards contributions for opium, spirit, etc. He has, moreover, to construct and maintain in repairs the paths leading to the several plantations under his control, as well as provide for the upkeep for the river communication. Latterly his district has been properly surveyed and demarcated, but formerly he usually exercised control only from the riverbank to the nearest watershed. For opening up the jungle and planting he arranges with a number of semi-dependent planters, to each of whom is allotted sufficient acreage for present cultivation as well as for future expansion. These planters are induced to undertake the enterprise by an arrangement under which for the first eighteen months or so the *kangchu* has to supply them with all the necessaries of life, implements of husbandry, and seeds and cuttings. The cost of these would be debited to the planter's account in the *kangchu's* books. When the first crop is ready for the market, a settlement would be made all around. The *kangchu* then distributes the planter's debts to each of his own creditors, the town traders, apportions the plantations among them, and transfers the produce only by a legal deed called a *"pajak"*. Henceforth each planter would be financed by his own town trader, but must dispose of his produce only to his shop until his debt is all paid. The trader supplies him with rice, grocery, and money for further planting, all at stipulated prices, and receives his produce in exchange, with deductions for weight according to a defined scale, and at prices regulated by his guild (the Gambier and Pepper Society), about 30 per cent, below the actual market value. The planter, however, retains his right to become his own trader, or to exchange for another more liberal financier, by paying off his debt at any time at a pre-arranged percentage of reduction. He has also his own guild for the protection of his interests, so that in these bargains and negotiations he is not so completely under the thumb of the capitalists as would naturally be supposed. For the transportation of the produce from the plantations to town another socialistic combination is effected. The several traders interested in a river or its vicinity and the *kangchu* would furnish the necessary capital between them to build a gambier *tongkang* of sufficient capacity to carry off the produce in fortnightly or monthly trips. This boat would then be manned by some half-a-dozen boatmen, one as steersman and the others as assistants generally. The freight of produce is placed at as low a rate as possible, chargeable to the planters. At the end of the month this is divided among the boat-people at a fixed proportion, the *kangchu* also receiving one share as nominal owner. A deduction is also made monthly until the capital account is paid off. The boat people, however, have to be personally responsible for the safety of the cargo, and have to pay from their earnings for all damages, even when these are clearly due to natural causes or to pure accidents. With the exception of freight on produce, all other cargoes for the plantations or the *kangkha*, and all passengers to and fro, are carried free of charge. Owing to its importance and the vested interests which have in time grown around this traffic, no competition is ever permitted. Even when a boat is undergoing repairs, the planters are not allowed to ship their produce by a neighbouring boat. Should the market price of their goods induce them to do this, they quietly submit to doable payment, once to their own boat-people and again to the actual carrier. This arrangement effectually prevents their adoption or encouragement of rapid steam service, though where the latter has already existed they are not behindhand in availing themselves of its existence. In a way this illustrates the immense difficulty experienced at the present time in China in inaugurating steamers on the inland waters. But for us the chief interest is without question the cooperative and socialistic tendencies so manifest in all Chinese commercial undertakings. As regards the Singapore pineapple planting industry, which has so largely developed in the last few years, the principle of financial advances for capital account, and of exacting payment at a reduction of the actual market price, is similar to the above. The main difference is, however, that here the *kangchu* is not a recognized institution, and the planters enjoy, therefore, greater liberty in regard to procuring the necessaries and luxuries of life.

As is only natural, the mining industry of the Native States has already had considerable attention paid it by their several Residents and Mining Superintendents, and full details could readily be procured from their reports on the different systems in vogue among Chinese miners. From the Chinese point of view, great importance is attached to the effectual working of the system for deriving a profit from the necessities of the miners. Like all importers of Chinese labour, the mining towkays retain in their hands the claim to supply their workers with all opium, rice, and other necessaries, either directly or through a shop established and controlled by the Kongsi manager. Under this system, not only could they rely upon realizing a substantial profit each year from their coolies, but so long as these latter are in a position to earn anything from their labour in the mines, the towkays could expect to be handsomely reimbursed for all their outlays. This explains how it is that even under the most adverse conditions, as regards a falling market for tin, so many Chinese mines could still manage to continue in operation. In fact, wherever Chinese labourers congregate in any number, their mere existence creates material values, and a large profit is realizable by their purveyors, not only through the sale of the necessaries of life, but also in pandering to their vicious and other immoral habits. This is so apparent in the Native States, and in the tobacco plantations at Deli, as to be readily remarkable by anyone who would take the trouble to appraise the different economic values of any Chinese *kangkha* or mining village as compared to an ordinary Malay kampong, even when the latter contains the larger settled population. From the mere revenue point of view this would doubtless be deemed an improvement, but I am afraid the same cannot be said from the purely moral standpoint.

Turning next to the export and import business of the colony, the first thing to be noted is the entire absence of any Chinese share in the direct wholesale European trade, while they almost monopolize the local and China business. As regards European imports, all orders are now effected by indents through local European firms upon payment of a small commission, and ever since the instability of local exchanges these firms have found it convenient and safer to confine their dealings with the Chinese upon this system, except, of course, in such staples as manufactured piece-goods, wines and spirits, hardware and rough goods generally. The Chinese traders, mostly natives of Swatow and Hainan, accordingly restrict their ventures to merely such goods as are already favourably known and easily saleable in the local markets, and there is perhaps a lack of enterprise shown either in developing any new line of goods or in pushing forward new brands. Keenness of competition has likewise tended to somewhat demoralize the import business, especially in manufactured goods. For instance, a Chinese trader would discover that a certain sample of handkerchiefs eighteen and a half inches square had easily found favour among local purchasers. Exercising his ingenuity rather than his business enterprise, he would then proceed to the same or a rival European firm and order the manufacturer to send him the same quality of goods but of smaller dimensions, say only eighteen inches square, of course with a corresponding decrease in the cost, and until the trick is found out by competitors he would derive some considerable profit by selling the new goods to customers at the same old price. In the report of the Blackburn Commercial Mission (1896–97) Mr. Consul Bourne pertinently remarks that "in trade, as in language, literature, and etiquette, there is the same tendency among the Chinese to find scope for great subtlety and ingenuity, to which the great world of progress is closed by intension, so to speak, over a very narrow and much-trodden field." The export trade in tin and produce is also entirely in European hands. Manufacturers of preserved pineapples likewise, when the local demand is limited, ship off their goods to Europe through some European agency. In this connection, however, they complain bitterly that they are thereby deprived of all means for controlling or checking the vagaries of their London dealers, who sometimes deduct large percentages from their account-sales for leakages and other damages. Another complaint is that they are not permitted to use their own labels or marks in any shape whatever on their tins, consequently they are deprived of all advantages resulting from the possession of well-known or favoured brands. This they attribute to combination among intermediate buyers and agents, and there is therefore a movement on foot to effect a rival combination among local manufacturers, and to establish a trustworthy agency of their own in Europe for the protection of their interests as well as to push forward their trade and brand, but whether the scheme will assume any practical shape is still undetermined. The necessity is, however, clearly felt, and no doubt action will in the course of time duly follow.

The importation of local food-stuffs from surrounding countries and the traffic in purely Chinese requirements are, as already remarked, entirely in Chinese hands. Of rice the qualities imported for local consumption are mostly from Siam, while the products of Burma and

Annam are usually sent to the mines and plantations. Large re-exports are accordingly made to meet the requirements of Malacca and the Native States, and when prices are favourable it is even shipped off to Java, Borneo, and Manila. Owing to the employment of modern milling machinery at the producing-centres, mostly white rice is now imported, and the old stone rice-hullers, so commonly seen some thirty years ago in local rice shops, are now seldom met with. Three separate guilds control the trade, one for Siam rice, one for Rangoon, and one of local dealers. Their interferences, are, however, chiefly confined to questions of payment, such as the proper percentage of copper coins (the enactment of "legal tender" notwithstanding), period for settlement, and discount for cash bargains; but sometimes they are readily employed even for such purposes as the coercion of European traders, as the forcing a certain large shipping company to pay claims for damages and losses on uninsured cargoes.

Importations from China comprise what are usually known as Canton goods, mostly confined to Canton dealers. This trade is in point of fact merely a portion or adjunct of the Chinese home trade, although the Chinese Customs Statistics regard it as foreign. The local trade in Japanese matches should also be included in this classification, as, apart from manufacture, all the dealings, financings, and handlings are done by Chinese. The immense proportion of this branch of our local trade and its continual expansions forcibly illustrate how independent the Chinese are of the trade of other lands. Except in regard to wearing apparel and such necessaries as kerosene, tinned provisions, and cutlery, even the Straits-born Babas are largely dependent upon China for their requirements. In one of the recent articles in the *Fortnightly Review*, Sir Robert Hart has forcibly pointed out that:

> Chinese have the best food in the world, rice; the best drink, tea; and the best clothing, cotton and silk. Possessing these staples, and their innumerable native adjuncts, they do not need to buy a penny's worth elsewhere; while their empire is in itself so great, and they themselves so numerous, that sales to each other make up an enormous and sufficient trade, and export to foreign countries is unnecessary.

For the goods they receive from China they ship back tin, sugar, rattan, beche-de-mer, planks, etc.

It is, however, as distributors in our large and growing trade that the largest number of individual Chinese are personally engaged. Whether as shopkeepers, peddlers, or hucksters, it is to their enterprise and perseverance that the colony is indebted for the large expansion of its trade, not merely inter-Settlement, but also with Netherlands India, the Philippines, Indo-China, Siam, Malaya, Burma, and other countries. As commercial travellers they penetrate into many islands where a white man is never seen. In the past they have watered with their blood many a savage territory, and paved the way for the introduction of civilization and better government into many lands. The millions sterling worth of goods imported into this colony annually could not have been so easily disposed of if it had not been for their industry and venturesome spirit to discover and open new markets in all directions. Where steamship communication is duly established in the Archipelago, they travel about as passengers, taking with them their goods on board, which they dispose of from port to port en route, wherever they could find an opening. But the risks they run and the dangers they encounter are even now considerable. Oftentimes they have to wait until some subsequent trip of the steamer for the payment of their bills. And not only this, but, being under no governmental protection, they are often considered fair and easy game everywhere, and have to put up with innumerable inconveniences from every obstructive petty official, or are mulcted all sorts of deductions by every arbitrary State and grasping native chief. The obstacles placed in the way of the expansion and development of this branch of our local trade are therefore sometimes almost insurmountable, yet redress could nowhere be successfully attempted, so little notice is taken of these traders and their grievances. Yet they continue to struggle along, always buoyed up by the hope that the industry must have its ultimate reward, if not in their own favour, yet for the benefit of their successors. The grievances of the "*lekin*" collection and the hindrances to British trade in China loom largely before the eyes of the British Government and the British public, but the difficulties of the same and kindred character experienced by these traders also result in permanent injury to the same British trade in the Eastern Archipelago. If the one deserves the strongest support and protection, surely the other also should not be neglected and ignored.

CRITICISM
by J.M. Allinson

With a skill quite his own, the Essayist has endeavoured to make an uninteresting subject both instructive and interesting. I think, however, that both Mr. Tan Teck Soon's and the Society's time could have been more profitably employed in discussing some other subject, more in sympathy with the aims of this Society.

We are treated to a preface, in which the Essayist apologizes for introducing the subject, and attempts to raise the level of the same by reference to such high-sounding institutions as:

> The Intelligence Department of the British Board of Trade.
> Commercial Missions to China from Blackburn and Lyons.
> Economic value of Chinese trade to the Colony.

The Essayist then plunges into his subject, and introduces us to some of the "ways and means" by which our Chinese friends make both ends meet. It does not matter if these ways are not our ways, we have a standing proof (in the wealth of the Chinese community) which controverts the proverb that "honesty is the best policy". The Essayist grows eloquent in picturing the Chinese colonist who, in the most philanthropic manner, isolates himself in the far distant Malay States, and, with a smile that is "childlike and bland", cheats the natives outrageously both in weighing and in calculation. To me the picture is a sordid one, and one unnecessary to the text.

The Essayist remarks that we are all probably more or less familiar with the statement that "Chinese trade is the backbone of our commercial prosperity." I cannot say I have heard it put exactly in this way. I think it would be more correct to say that the Chinaman is the backbone of the colony. It is from the individual coolie, who works in this colony as no white man can (or other native will), to which we must trace the first steps in the colony's prosperity. Without labour, capable of endurance, without the national characteristics of perseverance, diligence, and thrift, this colony would never have flourished as it has done. It is, therefore, the merits of the colonist individually, be he labourer, artisan, or trader, that form the backbone of this colony.

From this onward the Essayist tells his tale well. He describes the planting industry as carried on in Johore, and incidentally introduces us to something like a "shipping conference", in which the shipper of gambier and pepper can only ship by certain *kangkha* boats, or pay double freight. A point is also made of the cooperative and socialistic tendencies manifested by the Chinese in their commercial transactions. Mining is touched on, and a sad but true account is given of the effects of Chinese mining arrangements. I have seen with my own eyes the derelicts cast adrift from the mines, to be supported, until death ends their miserable existence, by a humane but inconsistent Government. The import and export trade of the colony is referred to, and again the immoral tendencies of the Chinese are brought into prominence. Take my word for it, to cheat is no monopoly of the Chinese; it is rampant in all commercial communities, and in all countries. I personally have dealt with the Chinese for over twenty years, and I can look back with great pleasure to my connection with the Chinese merchants of Singapore.

In the closing paragraphs the Essayist treats us to a somewhat extravagantly drawn picture of the importance to trade of the Chinese commercial traveller, and gives us an exaggerated account of his perils by land and by sea. And further, we are treated to some quite irrelevant comparisons between the obstacles to trade in China proper and the hindrances met with by our friend the Chinese commercial traveller, whose case the callous British public is charged with having neglected. These nicely-turned phrases really mean nothing, and have been artistically introduced to give importance to a subject really devoid of much interest except to those actually connected therewith.

I have to note a strange omission, and it is—that not a single word is said as to the singularly favourable conditions under which the Chinese trade has been and is now carried on. In this colony, under the protection of the British flag, equal rights, civil and religious, are enjoyed by all races, and in this colony only is trade absolutely unhampered. Just beyond the shadow of our flag, we are surrounded with countries where trade is strangled by protective tariffs, where class legislation refuses to the Chinese equal laws, and where he is taxed as we tax dogs in Singapore.

17

LOCAL EDUCATIONAL PROBLEMS

Essay

16 August 1902
by *Tan Teck Soon*

Editors' Note

In one of several presentations that he made to the Society on education, Tan took up the issue of the modernization of Chinese education which he saw as central to the question of social reform amongst the Chinese. His essay is also notable for the attention it gives to the educational challenges faced by other communities and his criticism of British neglect. A notable intellectual and social activist, Tan, anticipating Furnivall's much cited work on the emergence of the plural society almost fifty years later,[1] was critical of the development of the colonial plural society in which "except as regards the strenuous pursuit of dollars, each leads a life of his own entirely indifferent to the existence or proximity of the other". This was particularly true of the Europeans who, he argued, lived a separate social existence in the colony, governing only with regard to their own ideals and making only "feeble and spasmodic attempts" to understand and influence non-European populations.

Tan's essay can be seen as an early pioneering call to the British for a greater focus on modernizing and reforming Malaya's different communities. At the same time it is not surprising to find in his discussion on the Malays important discursive overlaps between Straits Chinese and European thought. The Malays were defined by Tan as characterized by a laziness induced by the tropical climate. Thus their "want of stamina and character is inherent, and if entirely left to itself the race will in all likelihood degenerate and die away in a not very distant future". And whilst he would argue, alongside other members of the Society, that racial mixing was slowly improving the Malays, he also reasoned that as the "child of the soil" the Malays required special protection from the British, as well as the education of Malay women and the formation of model farms to teach them agriculture. These were themes which European members of the Society were also inclined to support (see Section 3).

In attempting to lay before the Society tonight a short summary of the conditions of local education and the problems appertaining thereto, I am conscious of the utter impossibility of treating the subject exhaustively, notwithstanding its absorbing importance, as well as the immense difficulty of elucidating and understanding its real and full significance. In a community such as ours, whose constituent elements are so diversified, and whose characteristic civilizations are so mutually antagonistic, it must be admitted that mere generalizations on the subject indicated must inevitably be one-sided and incomplete; while any attempt to arrive at clear and definite conclusions must also be partial, if not altogether impracticable.

In the first place, let us glance at the different racial elements and nationalities composing our community. At the head thereof is the governing European, with his dominant civilization and institutions. He comprises but a small minority of the settled inhabitants, but his importance is supreme, for he possesses power, intelligence, and adequate means to enforce his will and authority on the rest of the community. His previous training and education may appear to be the most perfect of its kind, yet it would nevertheless be permissible to us to ascertain whether for his present sphere of duties he thoroughly appreciates his position, and is in every respect as perfectly equipped to maintain it. As an alien of a different civilization, with ideals and aspirations of perhaps a different character, it would be presumptuous on my part to endeavour to pass any conclusive judgement on such points. But the fact could not be concealed that the European here lives entirely in an atmosphere of his own, separated socially and morally from the other sections of the community. As a governor he legislates only from his own ideals, and from his own standpoints of political economy. He enforces respect for and obedience to his laws merely by the power and surveillance of the police. He punishes in a manner that suits his own prejudices, and, it must be admitted, in accordance to his own sense of justice. He associates but rarely with the others. His relaxations, amusements, and sports are thoroughly national, and congenial only to his own tastes and habits. His public press and popular literature reflect his own ideals and indicate his own national bias. In a word, he lives and moves in a little world of his own, connected, it is true, with the rest of mankind, but by means of his external institutions and relations merely. Internally but feeble and spasmodic attempts have been made to understand and comprehend the natives who surround him on every side, to influence them by moral or social means, or even to inspire and elevate them by intellectual and educational methods.

Economically, however, the European maintains a more extended intercourse with the other members of the community. Through commercial transactions, financial arrangements, and industrial pursuits, there exist certain points of contact for them to meet and co-mingle with each other. But even in these points the contact is superficial, and unproductive of important and lasting results. Community of temporal interests may indeed produce and foster a certain measure of mutual respect, forebearance, and sympathy, but it is incapable of any assimilative effect in face of the barriers erected by national character, by egotism and prejudice, and by competition. The one is in the majority of cases the employer, creditor, or teacher; the others are subordinates or dependents on favour. The European seldom enters spontaneously into the difficulties, feelings, likes and dislikes of the native; while the latter, taking advantage of his position and opportunities, not unfrequently repays any kindness done him by the former with positive injury and ingratitude. On the whole, therefore, I think it must be admitted that even economically, in spite of commerce and industrial pursuits, the European is as much isolated from the rest of the community as in other respects.

But although separated from each other in civilization and habits, the European could not entirely ignore the natives living under the same political rule as himself. The necessary education of a local character to meet his case is, therefore, mainly of a political nature also. The definition that education is a mere system of instruction, intended to fit men to fill up useful situations in life, is therefore in his case further extended to include discipline and experience. Mere cultivation of the intellect in the various branches of knowledge should thus be supplemented by other agencies, moral as well as intellectual, capable of developing and improving the powers of the understanding. Hence the education to efficiently fit him for his present exalted sphere is akin to that comprehensively embraced under the term statesmanship. And statesmanship not merely of that local parochial order which concerns itself with the affairs of one's particular nationality, but universal and transcendental, capable not only of evolving order out of chaos, but also of conciliating, harmonizing, and elevating conflicting civilizations and interests into unity. It is what in Chinese classical language is styled the "Great Study", the system in which schools and regular courses of instruction form no part whatever. This is the problem which our European friend has set before him, the burden which his status of a "white man" imposes upon him, and which each has to conscientiously solve in his particular career, And to his wise and skilful solution thereof will depend not only on the welfare but also the future destiny of the whole community, as well as the destiny of his own Imperial race. So far as it would be possible for an alien to judge, I think it must be fairly and positively acknowledged that our European fellow-residents, with but rare exceptions, have hitherto consistently maintained the high and characteristic qualities of the race for sober, clean-handed justice, for impartiality, and for efficient discharge of official administration.

Coming now to the native sections of our community, the first thing that calls for special remark is a similar isolation and separation of interests, not only as towards the governing powers, but also even among the various elements of the native races themselves. Except at the request and instigation of the authorities, spontaneous endeavour has seldom been made on the part of the natives themselves to combine together for the celebration of any event of national importance. The much-lauded loyalty, cooperation, and liberality of all races in the recent celebrations were, let us hope, not exceptional and unique, but it requires a deeper insight into racial traits and a more elaborate analysis into motives to assure one as to their hearty genuineness. The characteristic indifference and apathy of the Asiatic towards governmental measures and administration for the public good are especially manifested in matters of local legislation. Few, if any, voluntary attempts have ever been made to investigate or comprehend provisions of a new Ordinance affecting even their highest interests; in fact, these have never been published or promulgated in the vernacular for their especial behoof. Criticisms, protests, or oppositions of any kind have hitherto been usually undertaken only on the advice or under the initiation and guidance of interested leaders. Whenever a law threatens to invade the sanctuary of their social life, however, their habitual means of defence and resistance have been secrecy, evasion, bribery, or passive inertia. These it was which have rendered so many of our best-intentioned sanitary and other ameliorating laws ineffectual, and their execution difficult. Penalties for detected breaches would be cheerfully paid, but the same offences would be unhesitatingly repeated at the very next opportunity. In fact, as Kipling has pertinently observed, "East is east and West is west, and never the twain shall meet." The only remedy for such an anomaly, if remedy there be, is perhaps better and increasing mutual knowledge, and more extended intercourse and exchange of ideas between governors and governed.

But even among themselves the native races seldom display any mutual sympathy or even antipathy towards each other. A Hindu coolie or cart-driver would voluntarily and even faithfully serve a Chinese labour contractor; he may even offer up vows and prayers to his own Samy for the welfare and prosperity of his employer; but he would as unhesitatingly desert him and take service with a rival establishment whenever his interests urge him so to do. A Mohammedan householder may vehemently object to the establishment of a Chinese pork-butchery in his immediate neighbourhood, but he would at the same time be as callous towards a stall-hawker vending the cooked meat in front of his house. In fact, except as regards the strenuous pursuit of dollars, each leads a life of his own entirely indifferent to the existence or proximity of the other. While such a contingency would undoubtedly prevent any effective combination among them for purposes of resistance to governmental measures, it is nevertheless a positive disadvantage in cases of practical administration especially of a remedial or ameliorating nature. Individual national conditions and necessities would have to be analytically studied and considered by themselves, while in some cases perhaps no synthetical application would ever be practicable. In matters of local education, therefore, the problems will have likewise to be studied from each individual national standpoint.

The Malays are natives of the soil, and as such could claim the special attention of the Government to their circumstances and environment. In this colony they are mostly agriculturists, fishermen, sailors, policemen, petty hawkers, and domestic servants, such as syces and gardeners. Their children are accordingly trained to follow more or less in the footsteps of their fathers. Educational establishments among them are for the present restricted to vernacular schools, where instruction is given in Arabic and Romanized Malay. The aims of such schools are, in the words of a former Acting Inspector of Schools (Mr. R.J. Wilkinson), "the bestowal of an elementary education, such as will enable a villager to keep simple records, and to so protect himself against the petty swindlers who in our mixed population are ever ready to prey on ignorance." But the Inspector continued in the same report to remark—"the spread of instruction does not necessarily create a recognition of its importance nor does it lead the people to really believe in Western sanitary ideas. The limitation of the curriculum to the three elementary subjects prevents the growth of a class of educated men, and allows no scope for the exercise of real influence upon the habits and modes of thought of the race."

From the subjective standpoint of the Government such results are in themselves deplorable enough, but the judgement, I am afraid, does not indicate sufficient insight into the real stakes at issue. The educational problem which a Malay has to set before him is not the acquisition of mere means to some ends, but it constitutes the very ends in themselves. It is not the mere recognition or appreciation of some higher ideals of life, but it involves the necessity for living itself. The Malay is no longer an important factor in economical or commercial considerations, his want of stamina and character is inherent, and if entirely left to itself the race will in all likelihood degenerate and die away in a not very distant future. The system of agriculture to which he is best accustomed is not such as would tend to stimulate him to continual efforts. Nature has been most bountiful in his behalf, freeing him from such onerous labours as irrigation and fertilization, which vex and burden Chinese husbandry. He is too lazy even to gather in the produce of his plantations, preferring rather improvidently to farm out both the labour and proceeds to others. It would thus be a hopeless task perhaps to rouse him to enthusiastic and persevering exertions for his own salvation. But his preservation should be the aim of all his sincere well-wishers, and the exertions for his own salvation. But resources of robust statesmanship should not be so readily abandoned or exhausted for his amelioration. To ignore him altogether would be most prejudicial and fatal to British supremacy in this colony, for he is a child of the soil, and although, according to the last census, the total Malay population forms but 37.5 per cent of the whole population of the colony, the proportion in respect of those under 15 years of age shows that the Malay element preponderates to the extent of 59.7 per cent of its separate total. To be productive of good results, education undoubtedly requires more promising material to work upon. But even should the male element itself prove to be a failure, it would nevertheless be good policy to try to influence it through the education of its womankind. Even now there linger in many districts of Malaya traces of matriarchal institutions. Throughout the Peninsula, female agricultural labour continues to be the more constant and reliable factor of the two. In the history of other progressive civilizations, it was precisely at the stage where husbandry had become prominent that matriarchal institutions had given place to patriarchal, and polyandry to monogamy. But here, apparently owing to the influence and sanction of Mohammedanism, evolution seems to stand still in respect of land tenure and labour, while it skips over to polygamy in regard to marriage observances. Thus, female labour becomes doubly attached to the soil, by tenure and by actual labour, and any endeavour to elevate the race in regard to agricultural improvements should therefore be conducted through the actual tillers of the land. Novel and revolutionary though the experiment may be in idea, it is nevertheless the channel through which Nature herself has worked, and is now utilizing for the future advancement of the race. Intermixture of blood through foreign marriages has undoubtedly been most beneficial in many cases. And although the Eurasian product as witnessed in Malacca may be pronounced an experimental failure, still it cannot be entirely viewed as a decided deterioration or retrogression. On the other hand, perhaps owing to natural affinity, the Straits Babas and the Jawi Pekans must be considered as decided improvements, and the same may be said of the coming future races of the whole Indo-China. Throughout Burma, Siam, Annam and Cochin-China, Nature proceeds in a similar manner to develop and improve future generations, and the efficient equipment of local female education by State or other measures would be but assisting Nature in her own Processes. To the personal charms with which the sex is endowed by maternal Nature, it would be but to add the accomplishments of Art. And even should the experiment fail in its main object of attracting more virile races, owing to the prejudices of religious fanaticism and other causes, the influences of such an educational policy upon the male element of the race itself would be incalculable. As regards ways and means, the improvement of household duties by practical lessons on domestic cookery, on needlework, embroidery, and weaving, would undoubtedly produce beneficial results in the family circles, and thence react over the whole race. In agricultural pursuits also variations could be introduced by means of model farms to initiate the *rayats* into new improvements in fertilizers, in systems of irrigation, modern implements and tools. And by object lessons in farm-stock raising, vegetable gardening, and fruit-canning a whole series of cognats and new productive industries would be open to their selection and for their future amelioration.

Dealing last with the Chinese aspect of local educational problems, I must premise that this portion of the subject bristles with difficulties throughout. In the first place, it is remarkable that, in spite of their numerical and commercial importance, the local Government does not concern itself in any way with purely Chinese education. The reason for this, as given me by a former Protector of Chinese, is that Chinese education is mostly religious. This would perhaps sound frivolous to those who are unacquainted with the nature of purely Chinese education. If Confucianism should, however, be viewed as a religious tenet, and not as a mere system of ethics, then Chinese education would certainly be considered religious. And there would be nothing of importance left to teach in Chinese after Confucius and his teachings have been eliminated from the curriculum. Therefore the neglect of Chinese education by the local authorities is so far intelligible. And yet I am afraid the dangers and risks of complete nonchalance and indifference have not altogether received proper and adequate attention. According to the last census the total number of Chinese children under 15 is given as 42,257. Of these the Report of the Educational Commission of April last gives only 7,708 boys, or a little over 18 per cent, as the total enrolment at English schools last year. The remainder must therefore be receiving private education of some kind or other, or none whatever. The dangers of illiteracy need not be specially referred to in this connection, we are already reaping some of its fruits in the establishment of Reformatories in our midst. But I believe it must be evident to those in authority, and to their special advisers, that even quietly permitting a purely Chinese education by private means to the bulk of the future population of this colony would not be conducive to the supremacy of British ideals, or to the security of British political ascendancy in these Settlements. The teachings of Confucius undoubtedly encourage loyalty, but it must be remembered it is loyalty to the "Son of Heaven", the Sovereign of the *Chinese* and not of the *British* Empire. The tendency is not merely sentimental, nor is it only skin-deep, as even the most loyal Straits-born have been from time to time affected and influenced by its existence. It springs from environment and from racial consciousness, and the problem would therefore be how best to circumvent and overcome its force. Mere multiplication of English schools would not meet the difficulty, as the curriculum there, where not purely sectarian, is colourless, and lacks distinctive aims and specializations. The true solution of the problem would perhaps lie in the initiation of a bold policy, firmly grappling with the dilemma and meeting the difficulty face to face. To obliterate or prohibit Chinese education altogether would be a hopeless endeavour. But the curriculum could be reformed, new textbooks could be introduced, and modern ideals adopted and practised. As regards local English education, the problems must be considered from the native as well as the European standpoints. The European desires to procure clerical and other assistance in his several enterprises; he aims at spreading the benefits of his civilization to the "gentlemen who sit in darkness", or to improve them "off the face of the earth". He therefore considers the progress already achieved exceedingly unsatisfactory and slow. But the native only aims at the best and easiest means of procuring the wherewithal to feed and clothe his body; his aspiration at school does not extend beyond the acquisition of an enlarged vocabulary and the most elementary knowledge, and he therefore looks upon all attempts at intellectual improvement as mere piling on of the Brown Man's burdens. With such complicated and contradictory views, it would be impossible to arrive at any definite solution without calm and exhaustive studies of the issues involved, and I would therefore plead the indulgence of the Society for my failure to do so, as I possess neither the time nor the space for such purpose.

CRITICISM
by A. Knight

I must confess to feeling some disappointment with the able and interesting paper we have just heard read: the Essayist lays great stress upon the difficulties inseparable from the highly diversified elements of our population, which he looks upon as the main source of the problems which present themselves to the authorities, but he offers us very little guidance to their solution. In fact, he concludes by saying that he possesses "neither the time nor the space for such purpose".

Moreover he dwells upon the variety of races chiefly as presenting difficulties in the way of administration—which, of course, is undeniable—and only secondarily as offering educational problems. There is, therefore, but little for me to criticize.

The Essayist refers only in the most cursory manner to one of the principal divisions of our population—the natives of India—and it may be regarded as somewhat curious that the only race in whose behalf he makes any definite recommendation is the Malay.

It is gratifying to find that the Essayist feels justified in speaking in commendation, on the whole, of the attitude of the European towards the native races, though he says that the white man has made "but feeble and spasmodic attempts to understand and comprehend the natives who surround him, to influence them *by* moral or social means, or even to inspire and elevate then by intellectual and educational methods". He regards the natives as quite as much accountable as the white man for the want of sympathy, or the imperfect sympathy, between East and West, and points out that the same want exists between different sections of the Asiatic population.

Now, as to the Malays, the Essayist rightly remarks that "Educational establishments among them are for the present restricted to Vernacular Schools", though, of course, there is nothing to exclude them from English schools, which a few in the towns do attend. Now, these vernacular schools cost in the whole colony something like $80,000 per annum and I think it open to question whether they are worth the outlay. I remember an intelligent Government servant, who has long retired on pension, and who had much to do with Malays, once expressing a strong opinion to me that the support of these schools was a waste of money. What, he asked, was the use of teaching the Malays to read in their own language, when they had practically no literature, and we were not providing them with any. The money, he thought, would be better spent in teaching them English. I have some sympathy with those views. Certainly the aims of the present schools, as expressed by a former Acting Inspector of Schools in words quoted by the Essayist, are far from being elevated in their character.

The proposal of the Essayist for the preservation and elevation of the Malay race is a remarkable one, but bears rather upon social improvement than upon education in the ordinary sense. In the first place he suggests that the women should be given "practical lessons on domestic cookery, on needlework, embroidery, and weaving". I doubt whether we have anything to teach them in these branches, in which Malay women have the reputation of being fairly proficient. As regards general education of females, I suppose the Malays favour it as little as other Eastern races; but a good number of vernacular girls' schools have been founded and have met with some success.

Then the Essayist suggests the establishment of model farms to initiate agricultural improvements, and to institute "object-lessons in farm-stock raising, vegetable gardening, and fruit-canning". I think these suggestions are worthy of careful consideration. The agricultural shows held occasionally in Province Wellesley and Malacca will not be without their good effects, but I think more might be done. For "fruit-canning", however, I would substitute fruit-cultivation. Some of the native fruits in this part of the world are delicious, but I feel certain that they could be immensely improved by some such careful cultivation as the fruits we get in our own country, instead of growing practically almost wild.

Dealing last with the Chinese aspect of the subject, the Essayist says "it is remarkable that the local Government does not concern itself in any way with purely Chinese education." How can it? If the Chinese want education on their own lines, they surely know how to get it and it seems scarcely practicable or desirable that the Government should furnish it. Indeed, a few sentences further the Essayist speaks of Chinese education as a positive danger, unless "the curriculum could be reformed"—a task which the Government could scarcely undertake.

Finally as regards English education, which it is generally admitted the Government should foster, the Essayist has very little to say beyond the statement that the European wants "clerical and other assistance", while the native simply wants to earn a living. Speaking generally, this is probably true; but so it is, to a great extent, *mutatis mutandis*, in other countries. People have to be shown the advantage of better education. If employers were to insist on a higher standard, those who looked forward to employment would aim higher. Already there are not a few who do aim at improving themselves even after leaving school.

The Essayist states that "according to the last Census the total number of Chinese children under 15" (i.e. boys and girls from birth to 15) "is given as 42,257", and that "the Report of the Educational Commission of April last gives only 7,708 boys, or a little over 18 per cent, as the total enrolment in English schools last year." I make the grand total of enrolment 7,888 (Appendix II), and this is made up of 6,219 boys and 1,469 girls. From data furnished by the Education Commission Report, the number of Chinese boys at these schools may fairly be estimated at about 4,000, with Chinese girls not more than 200. In the same report it is correctly stated that the census of 1901 gives the number of Chinese boys between the ages of 5 and 15 as 16,144 so that taking these as the school ages (though a boy is hardly likely to be sent to school as early as 5) the enrolment is about 25 per cent. On the face of it this appears not quite satisfactory, but then the circumstances must be considered. There is, and I apprehend can be, no compulsion. I do not know that Chinese immigrants who have children can be expected to send them to English schools to any extent: moreover, many of them are agriculturalists living far in the country. There is nothing that I am aware of, to prevent Chinese, or any other people, living in or near the towns from obtaining for their sons such English education as is to be had in existing schools. It is cheap enough in all conscience: no class is better able to afford it than the Baba Chinese; and if there were an evident demand for additional school accommodation, I am sure it would be supplied.

Now, the number of Straits-born Chinese children between the ages already stated is 6,784, and of this number, 3,679 are from 5 to 10 and 3,105 from 10 to 15. Of the total number, 859 are returned from Province Wellesley and the Dindings, where they are not within reach of an English school. I have no doubt that the great majority of the Chinese at English schools (whom I have estimated at 4,000 in all) are of Straits-born parentage, and if so, it would appear that most of the boys of that class of school age are under English education.

The Essayist does not deal with the defects in our schools—some, at least, remediable—to which such prominence is given in the Education

Commission's report. Even as they stand, I am of opinion that boys of fair intelligence, with the encouragement of their parents, can, and as a matter of fact do, obtain a very fair education.

Regarding the general complaint of the very imperfect education with which most of the boys leave the schools,—one of the merchants to whom questions were addressed by the recent Education Commission suggested that firms should be asked to employ only those boys who have passed a certain standard. This seems sensible. No one who has been for many years in the Government service here can fail to notice the general improvements in the clerical staff of Government. I remember the time when a boy was taken on without examination—often because he was the son of his father who was an old public servant. Now a Government clerk must not only have passed the higher school standards, and have attained the age of 17, but he must undergo a special examination before admission and a further examination before he can be passed to a higher grade. In the old days a clerk would write a beautiful hand, but often had so little knowledge of English that in making a copy of a written minute, if he was puzzled with a word in the manuscript, he would put in anything that he thought it resembled in appearance without a least regard in the sense. Now the handwriting is seldom so good but there is much better knowledge of English. Can't other employers use similar methods to secure a similar result? Is it that the demand is so in excess of the supply that employers have to take what they can get?

The Essayist has nothing to say in criticism of the existing system of education, or of the Scholarship system. Does he, for instance, approve of the so-called Queen's Scholarships? I confess that I have long doubted whether these scholarships benefitted the colony in proportion to their cost, or anything like it. I agree with Dr. Brown of Penang that the money might be spent to much better advantage.

There are other points in which I am disposed to agree with the views put forth by Dr. Brown in his memorandum on the Report of the Education Commission. There is the question of the taking over by Government of the Penang Free School. Dr. Brown points out that this school has hitherto been largely supported by the Chinese and other communities in that Settlement, and he considers it a distinct disadvantage that anything should be done to, as he expresses it, "perpetually disenfranchise the educational interest of the public". He avowedly writes from a Penang point of view but does not the same principle apply to Singapore? The Chinese are the wealthiest community in the place, and they are increasing in wealth and numbers. The Straits-born Chinese are permanent residents, and need education for their children; with a few honourable exceptions they have done little for the promotion of education; but they are not deficient in liberality, and would, I feel sure, if the matter were made clear to them, be ready to assist largely in providing the means of putting the existing schools on a better footing.

I also agree with Dr. Brown in his view as to the separation of Secondary from Elementary Education. But it is unnecessary, and would be out of place for me to go further into questions which have been so fully considered and discussed by men who have qualifications which I do not possess for forming judgements on them; I will therefore now leave the subject in the hands of members.

Note

1. J.S. Furnivall, *Colonial Policy and Practice: A Comparative Study of Burma and Netherlands India* (Cambridge: Cambridge University Press, 1948).

18

OPIUM VERSUS ALCOHOL

Essay
10 July 1908
by *Lim Boon Keng*

Editors' Note

One important element of the social reform movement amongst the Straits Chinese was the anti-opium movement which called for the prohibition on the opium trade in the colony and treatment for opium smokers.[1] As early as 1894, Straits Chinese members took the lead in representing the anti-opium cause at public meetings in Singapore. In doing so they challenged the view common in European circles, and expressed in the papers to the Society, that the Chinese community was averse to the banning of opium,[2] Lim would continue to write on the issue in the *Straits Chinese Magazine*, seeing the issue as an opportunity to mobilize the Chinese community in Singapore.[3] As highlighted in his paper to the Society, Lim was foremost in the use of medical arguments which highlighted the deleterious effects of opium, as well as in rebutting the belief that without opium, worse abuses would follow. Although he perceived that alcohol was no less an evil, Lim suggested that this abuse was less common amongst the Chinese, easier to detect, and more easily treated. Together with his brother-in-law, Yin Suat Chuan, he founded in 1906 the Singapore Anti-Opium Society, and ran an experimental rehabilitation centre funded by Baba merchants. This influenced Wu Lien-teh to establish a similar clinic in Penang, where an anti-opium movement also emerged. The movement was also supported by prominent missionaries active in the Straits Philosophical Society: W. Murray and William Shellabear, whilst D.J. Galloway would sit on the Opium Commission in 1908. The Commission studied the opium problem and put forward recommendations to restrict, but not to prohibit, opium, thereby protecting the colony's revenues.[4]

Lim's essay and J.G. Campbell's response highlight that, beyond moral reform and economic concerns, ideas of race and racial susceptibility to substances such as opium and alcohol were important to debates on social policy and reform.

Gentlemen, in my humble opinion, there is not much to choose between opium and alcohol, at least from the ethical and scientific point of view. It seems a great pity, indeed, that public discussion of the evil of the opium habit has led to the studious elaboration of facts and fancies into a very taking kind of hypothesis that as compared with alcohol-drinking the opium habit is, after all, a very desirable kind of virtue. Moreover, it is also commonly taught by certain wiseacres that mankind must need to have some sort of narcotic to stupefy the over-active processes of the higher nerve-cells, and that if denied opium the Chinese, for example, would be driven by inexorable fate to consume alcohol instead. It need scarcely be said that these generalizations are of such a character that they are nothing else than baseless assumptions. The antinomies of human life and character are part and parcel of the very cosmos whereof man constitutes only an infinitesimal unit. No one cognisant of the most rudimentary principles of physiology can be ignorant of the diverse organic needs which are deeply implanted on the human organism. That, subjected to the toxic influence of tea, tobacco, alcohol, opium, and such-like substances, the nervous to the changes set up [sic], is a foregone conclusion. But this does not justify us in the least in concluding that normal people will be impelled to drink alcohol if the law makes opium difficult to obtain. It is quite necessary at the outset to emphasize these few misconceptions, which, thanks to the blatant advocacy of many newspapers, bid fair to become the shibboleths of the man in the street.

Now, in the first place, both opium and alcohol are poisons, that act powerfully in paralysing the function of the nervous system. They are therefore classed together as narcotics. In many details their action differs, but in the main their ultimate toxic influence on the cells of the brain is identical. The resistance of the nervous system to alcohol being greater, the symptoms of intoxication unfold themselves seriatim at a slower rate. In the case of opium, the preliminary stages of excitement, hilarity, and so forth, so typical of alcoholic poisoning, are suppressed, and the full effects of paralysis set in immediately, so that medicinally opium is still the most powerful anodyne at our disposal. The fact that opium and alcohol are both narcotics, and that, of the two, opium is a more powerful poison, must always be borne in mind. We shall soon see that alcohol as a beverage, and even as a medicine, is a very dangerous thing to play with. Hence we must infer that opium is still more dangerous. The value of opium as a medicine must in no wise be confounded with the seductive influence which opium exerts upon the mind of its victims. Everyone knows that opium is a very useful drug. But its great value as a medicine does not justify the special pleading which strives to mislead the uninformed into thinking that indulgence in opium is not more harmful than the smoking of cigarettes.

Alcohol has little or nothing in its favour. It should be totally condemned as a food, because it is such a treacherous enemy, once it gets installed as a necessary article of consumption. Being itself the by-product of metabolism, it is a very energetic protoplasmic poison, inhibiting the activity of the very organisms whose cellular energy has resulted in its production. It delays the oxidation of the tissues, and leads to fatty degeneration. It hinders the processes of growth, and, by its inhibitory action on the phagocytes and other cellular elements concerned in the establishment of immunity against microbic infection, alcohol therefore predisposes the system to the invasion of the germs of infectious diseases. Moreover it is the direct cause of many chronic ailments, and of some very serious organic disturbance of the liver, kidneys, and the nervous system.

But from the social standpoint, the greatest objection to alcohol lies in the fact that it induces drunkenness in a fairly large proportion of those who drink alcoholic beverages. It is unnecessary for the purposes of this paper to dwell at length on the phenomena of acute alcoholic intoxication. From the cheerful loquacity of the man who is "drowning" the cares of business with his fourth "*stengah*", to the acute mania and subsequent paralysis of the soldier or sailor who gets "dead drunk" on a spree, there is an infinite series of graduations, varying in intensity and character with many circumstances. In many cases the paralysis of the power of control, together with the presence of hallucinations or auto-suggestion, may lead to serious consequences to the drunkard, as well as to those brought in contact with him. In Scotland the wives of many poor working-men in the large towns look forward with horror to the return of their drunken husbands on a Saturday night, unless they have taken the precaution to fortify themselves with a good strong dose before returning home. The amount of mischief committed by drunkards is appalling, and altogether, both from the social and the economic side, one must come to the conclusion that alcohol is nothing else but a curse in Europe.

From personal knowledge and experience, I fully concur with this brief resume of the effects of alcohol. It is not the intention of this paper to minimize in the slightest degree the fearful consequences of the alcoholic habits among all races the world over.

It is rather distressing, however, to those who know the evil results of the opium habit to find that, for some time, a certain number of popular newspapers, as well as not a few men of influence and ability, have been trying to disseminate the view that indulgence in opium is such a trifling affair that it may be compared with the use of cigarettes. Moreover, many persons, who ought to have known better—both from the positions they held and their long residence among Chinese—have freely expressed the opinion that opium has been of benefit to the individual as well as to the State. A number of would-be experts have come forward to assure us that the opium habit has contributed to the reduction of crime. This opinion has been arrived at in a very curious way. It is pointed out that opium is not known as a primary cause in producing sets of violence, whereas we all know how often alcohol is responsible for the drunken brawls, fights, and also for crimes of a serious nature. It is thus confidently held that victims of the opium habit pass their nights in peaceful slumber, and are all estimable members of society. At least this is the opinion openly espoused, although it is very likely those who are responsible for it will not care to associate intimately with the victims of opium.

Both alcohol and opium are very injurious to the growing nervous tissues of the young. The degenerative changes and chronic diseases which alcoholic drink can give rise to are paralleled in a far worse degree by the altered metabolism induced by the presence of morphine in the system. Whilst we at present do not possess an adequate knowledge of the microscopic and macroscopic changes in the nervous tissues caused by chronic opiumism, we know enough to infer that the prolonged intoxication must cause profound alteration in the modulus of protoplasmic activity in each neuron. By interfering with the secretion of the digestive juices, opium commences a frontal attack upon the vitality of the human organism. The consequent indigestion undermines the system and prepares the way for diverse flank attacks by diseases which develop in the train of indigestion. Growth is hampered, the normal development of the intellect and character is interfered with, and premature senile changes are ushered in. The youth becomes sallow and aged. The bright countenance is replaced by the wrinkled and careworn features of the opium habitue. The lustre of the eyes is lost, and the eyes seem heavy and dreamy. The gait is deliberate and slow. In every respect, life seems to have lost its freshness. This is not an exaggerated picture. The paralyzing effect of opium upon the nervous centres is very well known. Through its action on the nervous system, opium leads to defective nutrition of the whole body.

On full-grown and healthy adults it takes a longer time to cause these profound changes. But sooner or later these traits are developed. While opium-smoking, when the habit is acquired in adult life, does not necessarily shorten life perceptibly, there is no shadow of a doubt that it greatly increases all the inconveniences incidental to old age. On the wrong side of fifty, opium makes itself felt mainly in the altered mental habit and in the change of character. It also seriously increases the risks to which the aged are predisposed. Thus we see that as regards age we can discover no reason for the opium habit.

There is also a very common belief that great numbers of habitues use a moderate amount of opium only, and that we must distinguish the beneficial use from the abuse of the drug. Here our experience of the so-called use of alcohol by a considerable number of people is cited as an analogy; but the comparison is quite misleading, because, although the narcotic effects of the two drugs are like, the power of morphine in impressing upon the nervous system is much greater. Besides, opium enslaves the mind in its own specific way.

Both substances produce sooner or later a marked tolerance. In the case of opium, the quantity that at first produces marked nervous effects in a short time ceases to have the same efficacy. It has, in fact, lost all its charms. This is true also of alcohol in some individuals, although in the case of opium the tendency is for the habitue to continually increase the dose in order to get the craving fully satisfied. Of course, the desire to increase the quantity of drug is limited by various circumstances. Even the pangs of the opium pains cannot obtain for the unfortunate victims the opium they desire without sufficient means. The life of the majority of smokers is thus an eternal round of blasted hopes, and an ever-anxious expectation of an opportunity for a larger indulgence. The maximum quantity procurable for the time being has become the minimum dose to allay the discomforts of the craving.

Before discussing the phenomena of the craving, let us remember the two sets of conditions to be fulfilled daily by the habitue before he can even think of adjusting himself to his environment, and of doing his day's work. In the first place, a habit has been created—a world by itself wherein the habitue finds himself enshrouded in his own egotism, indulging to the full, amidst the fuliginous haze of reminiscent concepts and narcotic dreams, in a sense of well-being, which reconciles him in a wonderful way to discomforts and pains. The whole of his mental life is in time altered, but the change is insidious, and the victim will protest vigorously if any interested friend, unaware of his weakness, happens to call his attention to it. Generally, the desire to gratify the pleasures of the drug resembles that mental habitude which indulgence in various habits invariably produces. The gambler feels miserable if denied his opportunities. The pain and disappointment may be nearly as acute as those of the drunkard or of the opium sot. The mental anguish of the habit is something quite apart from the real physical changes in the body which characterize the conditions known as the craving.

When the mental longing and anguish have reached their acme, a train of painful symptoms begins to appear. These indicate a general nervous breakdown, and are, in fact, sequelae of the bursting of a great nerve storm. They are not always identical in all persons. Protean in form and in the mode of onset, the craving is always intensely painful, and is often of sufficient severity to drive the victim to suicide. Sneezing, yawning, fits of coughing, diarrhoea, gastric pain, profuse sweating, sleeplessness, muscular pains, are a few of the usual concomitants of the attack. Very few individuals, indeed, have the moral courage to go through these without crying for the drug, and without using every effort to obtain it. Once a person has become a slave to opium, it requires more than a pious resolution to throw off the yoke. And remember—every user of opium within six months at the latest both acquires the habit and suffers from the craving. Now, in this respect alcohol is a much safer substance. The experiment with alcohol has been carried out for us on a vast scale in the armies of Europe. Out of the thousands of soldiers who indulge in alcoholic beverages, there are scarcely 10 per cent of them drunkards, who require to be intoxicated three or four times a day before they can feel fit. Now, in the case of opium nearly all must have their daily dose, or all would be placed *hors de combat* and be useless. Personally I think indulgence in alcohol is bad for any one at any time, but I think the use of opium is even more dangerous, not because it leads to sickness, crime, or insanity—although, in its peculiar way, it predisposes to all—but because it makes life merely a shadow of what it should be.

European enquirers, who have been impressed with the awful results of drunkenness in Europe, find that opium does not directly lead to crimes of violence. They fail to find men fighting in the streets. The wives and children are not attacked at home. The opium wretches seemingly attend to their duties, unlike the drunkard, who is a nuisance to everyone and keeps away from his work. No wonder, then, that the average European, who knows so little of the real life of the people around him, is impatient with those who are striving to bring home to all civilized governments their responsibility in deriving a revenue from a means of moral and physical degradation of the people. The Chinese Government repeatedly refused to legalize the traffic, and the world knows that Commissioner Lin of Canton consigned to the flames £2,000,000 worth of opium. The Japanese Government strenuously forbade the importation of the drug into Japan, and, when Formosa was ceded them, took immediate steps to control the opium trade and to register all smokers, with the object of ultimately stopping the habit altogether. The Chinese Government is often accused of insincerity, and an attempt is made to prove that China has raised this anti-opium crusade merely to stop the importation of Indian opium. This hypothesis is quite absurd. The wishes of the Chinese Government are often, like those of other governments, not fully realized. The difficulties to be encountered are unparalleled. Besides real obstacles inherent in the work of real prohibition, China has to consult interested foreign governments. If China is given a free hand, in ten years the habit will be rooted out to a very large extent. But of course, as long as Indian opium can be imported, no efforts of the Government can be of the slightest use. Moreover many people nowadays forget that the enormous acreage under poppy in China has been the result of the desire of the Government to encourage their own production to oust Indian opium, and then to stop the growth as a question merely of internal policy, But, thanks to the co-operation of the British Government, the dreams of the Chinese are to be realized—a real effort is to be to deal an effective blow to the opium habit. But, strange to say, while Europeans now think it wrong to force China to buy opium, they are trying to prove that there are only 2 per cent of smokers in China, and that British colonies like Hongkong and the Straits Settlements will be financially ruined if the Chinese cease to use opium. Besides, they are for the first time solicitous for the welfare of "the Heathen Chinese", fearing that they may help to swell the profits of British and German manufacturers of alcoholic drinks! The ordinary European takes little or no interest in the Chinese. He is not qualified to judge at all in a matter of Chinese tastes and habits. Alcohol has been in use in China for many centuries—in fact, ages before Europe was even a civilized country. Dr. Giles has, indeed, pointed out that a great number of great writers in Chinese literature have written enthusiastically in praise of wine. Yet history and modern experience tell us that the Chinese are not a drunken race. There are millions of Chinese in every city who neither drink alcohol nor smoke opium.

But, of course, certain new races, like the Maoris, the Malays, the Negroes, and the natives of Polynesia, are very susceptible to the attractions of the cheap poisons imported from Europe under the names of champagne, wines, and brandy. The demoralization of these races has been a sad result of the spread of European civilization; and, alas the Chinese blame the British Government for the wars that cripple the resources of their Government to effectively deal with opium, and that ultimately compel the Chinese to acquiesce in the legalization of the opium trade. In British settlements there is a tendency among Chinese to use the cheaper kind of spirits, and yet we do not see the same amount of drunkenness as might be expected. We must conclude, therefore, that alcohol is especially dangerous to certain races. The white peoples of Europe were formerly more addicted to alcohol than they are now. In the last thirty years there has been a great diminution in the use of alcoholic beverages of all kinds. It is a matter of common knowledge that a couple of centuries back an English or Scotch gentleman scarcely ever returned sober from a feast.

The fascination of opium is particularly tempting to those hard pressed by labourious toil. The strenuous life so vigorously advocated by some is responsible, to no small degree, for the desire for some sort of narcotic to give a short respite to the overstrained nerves. Among the Chinese, the ceaseless toil of the poor, the peculiar habits of the people, the absence of physical exercise, and the strenuous endeavours of the men in all pursuits render the race peculiarly susceptible to the influence of opium. But the victims of opium are no longer confined to the Chinese. All over the world there are now miserable habitues. In England, since the time of De Quincey, the prevalence of the opium habit has been steadily increasing. It is probably as common in France and the United States. The French garrisons in Indo-China succumb to the habit in large proportions. Australian whites are also not immune; and we know how eagerly Malays take to it. If anything, the opium habit is universal, and is probably more extensive than the alcohol habit. When we total up all the habitues in Turkey, Persia, India, Burmah, Siam, Indo-China, Netherlands-India, China, Europe, and America, we shall find that the number of victims is really appalling. No race is immune to it. The most cultured white is as susceptible to it as the happy-go-lucky unsophisticated Malay. And amongst all these, once the habit is established, the victims must sacrifice daily at the shrine of the demon, and, if possible, they will go on increasing the quantity consumed. The poor is limited by his means, the rich man spends every available opportunity in his indulgence.

From the social point of view, the opium habit is extremely dangerous. Like all bad habits, it is contagious. The opium habitue is naturally secretive and selfish, and in this respect is the reverse of the drunkard. The victim of the opium habit neglects most of his social duties, and should he attempt to fulfil them, he would probably not succeed. Always slow and perpetually behind the time, without being conscious of it, he is gradually left behind, and very soon lives entirely in a world of his own.

Economically, the loss to the family and the State is incalculable. Besides the cost of the drug, we must take into consideration the fact that the habitues cannot perform their work effectively, so that they really earn less money than non-smokers. No employer of labour prefers opium-smokers, they only tolerate them *faute de mieux*. The fiction that without opium the Chinese miners cannot carry on their work is the invention of those wealthy monopolists who sweat their coolies and work their miners by the profits on the opium sold out in lieu of cash. The Government loses in the long run. It taxes 10 per cent of the population, and in a few years these habitues—10 per cent of the population—cease to be effective labourers. A great deal of crime is really due to opium, although there are no available statistics to support this view. But a little reflection will enable us to see the connection between crime and opium. When pressed by the sufferings due to the craving, opium habitues must steal or swindle—they sacrifice everything to get the drug. When caught, the fact that they were driven to crime by the desire for opium, or by the poverty which was the result of their indulgence, does not receive any notice. On the other hand, when a drunkard commits anything, the fact of his drunkenness is always noted. Hence police records tell us scarcely anything of the connection between opium and crime. But anyone who knows the real life of the poorer classes knows that the opium-smoker is frequently a criminal, and, in many obscure and indirect ways, it is the opium which is at the bottom of the crime. An unexpected confirmation of this view may be found in the notorious increase of petty thefts, burglaries, and similar crime on the approach of the Chinese New Year. In this case, the poor are tempted to steal and rob because custom—that hard taskmaster—demands extravagant habits, fine dresses etc., at the New Year feasts. In exactly the same way, the opium habitue, driven to the last extremity, resorts to crime to appease his terrible needs.

Look at it in whatever way you like, the opium habit is a frightful curse. It blights the manhood of a nation. It dries up all noble aspirations. It enslaves the mind and impoverishes the body. A nation infected with chronic opium intoxication is fore-doomed to annihilation, if not by conquest, certainly by degeneration of individual units. A nation of drunkards would at least have the manliness to toast the health and prosperity of the nation, and would at least have a last bacchanalian orgie in order to meet the enemy; but your opium habitues would first take care to secrete enough opium for the day of trouble, and when they would be wanted at the cannon's mouth to die for their country, they would most likely be found in some dark corner, quietly fortifying themselves with opium before the enemy should come and disturb them. This is no fanciful caricature, but is drawn from actual facts in the history of modern times.

In conclusion, we must maintain that every civilized state should endeavour to restrict the use of alcohol as much as possible, and should absolutely forbid the use of opium, except as a drug to be employed only by duly qualified physicians. Aside from cane and prejudice, and especially dissociated from questions of gubernatorial finance, this is the only possible view in accordance with the dictates of philanthropy and morality, as well as with the unbiased findings of science.

CRITICISM
by J.G. Campbell

Mr President, Dr Lim Boon Keng, and Gentlemen,

In endeavouring to criticize a paper written by a medical man on what is as much a medical subject as it is anything, I am at no little disadvantage. Nevertheless I am going to endeavour to do my duty as a critic, and I shall commence by differing with Dr. Lim Boon Keng in his statement (or humble opinion, as he himself calls it) that there is not much to choose between opium and alcohol; why shall appear later. Further, I do not think that public discussion of the subject has yet led to that elaboration of facts and fancies which produces the hypotheses that, compared with alcohol drinking, the opium habit is a desirable kind of virtue. It is true that in these, shall we say? degenerate ways, it is the custom to make heroes of some of our ancient villains. We are taught by some (higher Critics, I presume) that Nero did not fiddle while Rome burned. Why, bless you, we have no evidence that there were fiddles in Rome at that early date.

A modern novelist assures us that Satan suffers unutterable agonies when he succeeds in leading a poor mortal astray, and, several modern novelists preach immorality as morality; but we have not yet been by merit raised to that bad eminence of preaching the desirable virtue of opium-smoking.

Dr. Lim Boon Keng scoffs at the idea that only 2 per cent of the inhabitants of the Chinese Empire smoke opium, but it will take more than mere scoffing to get behind the facts and figures contained in the paper by Mr. Clementi, assistant Colonial Secretary in Hongkong. I do not enter into these, as I have no doubt you all have read the report as published in the *Singapore Free Press* on Saturday 27th June last.

May I venture, before dealing with the statement that there is not much to choose between opium and alcohol, to suggest that the paper read to you this evening makes little or no attempt to show whether there is anything to choose or not? Dr. Lim Boon Keng, having delivered himself of this "humble opinion", straightaway indulges in wholesale fulminations against both evils so far as the individual is concerned, and draws for us, as a climax, a lurid word-picture of the glorious position of the people who are exterminated in a bacchanalian orgie, deliberately organized with a view to celebrating the event; and compare it with the miserable cowardice of the people who are exterminated only after being found in various hiding-places (if they are sufficiently vertebrate to worry to seek these), whither they have retired to indulge their particular vice in a manner so irresponsible that it could hardly drag from a stoic a single word of praise.

We are told that the Chinese are not a drunken race; that alcohol has been in use in China for many centuries—in fact, ages before Europe was even a civilized country—and that Dr. Giles has indeed pointed out that a great number of great writers in Chinese literature have written enthusiastically in praise of wine. In this, I agree with Dr. Lim Boon Keng, and I suggest that had the learned Essayist continued to view his subject from a national, or rather a racial, instead of an individual standpoint, he would have found that alcohol is immeasurably the greater evil.

Alcohol is a very stringent selective agent, and as any particular disease will weed out the particular individuals of a race who are most susceptible to it, leaving the race in the course of time immune, so will alcohol weed out the particular individuals of a race who are most susceptible to its charm, and the race should grow more and more resistant, less and less prone to excessive indulgence.

Such is the case with the Chinese, the Southern Europeans, and to a lesser extent the Northern Europeans. Dr. Lim Boon Keng admits that in Northern Europe, or at any rate in Great Britain, excessive drinking is not so common as it was two centuries ago, and we know that a few years ago a Chancellor of the Exchequer in a British Parliament pointed out the decrease in revenue from excise duties, which was due directly to the reduction in the quantity of alcohol consumed by the nation. I do not know how long it is since the Chinese became a temperate if not teetotal race, and I doubt if Dr. Lim Boon Keng will venture to say that they have always been so.

Alcohol, however, does not cause a race to degenerate, and we find the most degenerate races among those who have not known it, such as the Esquimaux, the Tierra del Fuegians, and the Australian Blacks. The longer alcohol has been known to a race, the more temperate it is, irrespective of education and environment. It will, I think, be admitted that the Northern Europeans as a race have a better and more civilized environment than the Southern Europeans, and also that they are better educated; but if not, it must be conceded that they are more civilized and consequently better educated, and that they have a superior environment to West Africans, and among the Southern Europeans and the West Africans alcohol has been known for a longer time and excessive drinking is much less common.

Nevertheless, so great is the evil of alcoholism that when introduced to a race that have not previously known it, that race, unless sufficiently strong numerically, will be wiped out.

Alcohol was known to the Northern Europeans certainly before the fall of Rome, and yet, after all these centuries, the Northern Europeans have not yet acquired immunity from excessive drinking.

Opium has been used in India extensively for several centuries. The use of it prevails widely in that country. Very generally the crude drug is used. Sometimes, however, as is the case in Rajputana, a watery decoction known as "Kusoomba" is used. Opium-smoking is also widely practised, and for that purpose is used the watery extract "Chandul", from which word I take it the local word *chandu* is derived. In *Criminal Investigation*—a translation and adaptation to Indian requirements of *System der Kriminalistik* of Dr. Hans Gross, by John Adam and J. Collyer Adam, both barristers-at-law practising in Madras—it is stated that opium, both in its solid form and as a decocation, is so familiarly known throughout India that no Investigating Officer needs any description of it. Archdall Reid, in his *Principles of Heredity*—to which I am much indebted for my information on the effect of alcohol, and whose theory I have followed in this criticism—says with reference to opium,

> There is no evidence that the use of opium has caused any race to deteriorate. Indeed it happens that the finest races in India are the most addicted to its use. According to the evidence given before the late Royal Commission on Opium, the natives of India never, or very rarely, take

it to excess. When first introduced into China it was the cause of a large mortality; but today most Chinamen, especially in the litteral provinces, take it in great moderation.

This last statement is corroborated by the figures in Mr. Clementi's report, to which I have already referred. Dr. Lim Boon Keng has ignored this report, and addressed himself solely to the evils of the excessive consumption of alcohol and opium by the individual. Although he has not given so much attention to the cravings of the dipsomaniac as has to those of the opium habitue, yet he has, quite correctly so far as the individual is concerned, stated that there is little to choose between them; but submit that as a national evil alcoholism is a greater and longer enduring evil.

Let me again quote Mr. Archdall Reid:

> An interesting parallel obtains between diseases and narcotics. Against some diseases, for example tuberculosis, immunity cannot be acquired by the individual. Against others, it can be acquired with great ease. Between the two extremes lie all other diseases. The power of acquiring immunity is a short cut by means of which the tedious process of evolving inborn immunity is avoided. By a single process of evolution provision has been made against many maladies. The most death-dealing diseases are those against which immunity cannot be acquired, or can be acquired only slowly and with difficulty (e.g. Malaria). Alcohol resembles tuberculosis in that little immunity can be acquired against it by the individual. Without very greatly increasing the dose, the drinker is able to reproduce the immediately poisonous effects (intoxication) which he felt on the first occasion of using poison. It is just these poisonous effects that he seeks to renew. The mortality caused by alcohol in a race new to it is very great, and tends to produce inborn immunity—that is, to evolve a race which does not desire the immediately poisonous effects, and which, therefore, drinks in moderation. Against tobacco complete immunity may be acquired. Nicotine is very poisonous to the beginner, but not only does the habitual smoker acquire the power of tolerating immensely increased doses, but he never craves to renew the immediately poisonous effects which he felt when he first used the poison. In other words, all smokers smoke in "moderation"; that is, they do not seek to intoxicate— to immediately poison themselves with nicotine. The mortality caused by tobacco is so small as to be negligible. As a consequence—and in this it resembles chicken-pox—evolution results from racial experience

of it. Races who have long used it desire it in quantities as large as races that have had no previous experience of it. Opium lies midway between alcohol and tobacco. Immensely increased doses can be tolerated by the habitual user, but if he belongs to a race which has had no previous experience of opium, he generally desires to reproduce the intoxication he felt on the first occasion of using it. Opium, like measles, is therefore the cause of a large mortality. The resulting evolution tends to render the race "immune", so that it no longer desires opium in such quantities as to produce intoxication. It would appear, therefore, that the power of tolerating increased quantities is a great advantage. The race does not start from the scratch. It evolves immunity much more quickly and easily than in the case of alcohol. After an experience of a few hundred years the natives in India appear quite "immune". After two centuries the Chinese have evolved far towards immunity. But a disastrous experience of thousands of years has not rendered North Europeans fully "immune" to alcohol.

Notes

1. Toda Kenji, "Anti-Opium Movement, Chinese Nationalism and the Straits Chinese in the Early Twentieth Century", *Malaysian Journal of Chinese Studies* 1 (2012): 85–100; Cheng U. Wen, "Opium in the Straits Settlements, 1867–1910", *Journal of Southeast Asian History* 2, no. 1 (1961): 52–75.
2. "The Anti-Opium Meeting in the Town Hall", *Daily Advertiser*, 7 March 1894.
3. Lim Boon Keng, "The Attitude of the State towards the Opium Habit", *Straits Chinese Magazine* 2 (1897): 47–54; "The Opium Question", *Straits Chinese Magazine* 10 (1906): 149–51.
4. Wen, "Opium in the Straits Settlements 1867–1910", pp. 71–72.

19

THE CHINESE IN BRITISH MALAYA

Essay
10 February 1910
by *Lim Boon Keng*

Editors' Note

"The Chinese in British Malaya" is one of Lim Boon Keng's clearest and most detailed writings on the history and position of the Chinese in British Malaya. The first half is devoted to documenting the migration of the Chinese to Malaya and describing the different dialect groups and their economic activity in the colony. Yet, more than a straightforward historical essay, the presentation sought to analyse and reflect upon the effects of life in Malaya upon the Chinese in a way which highlights Lim's concerns around race, social Darwinism and nationalism. One significant factor that he identified was the effect of mixing Malay with Chinese blood; and his belief that life in the tropics was tending towards the degeneration of the resident Chinese race and was producing inferior offspring who "despise labour". This, Lim argued, was mitigated by "Chinese blood from China" which continued to arrive in Malaya to check "the degenerative process". The education of girls was also seen to delay "degeneration", yet "unless young people are removed from the tropics, there seems very little hope of maintaining the stamina and the virile qualities of the race—attributes due principally to the Chinese environment".

For Lim what was partly to blame was the system of education in the Straits which, unlike the system employed by the Dutch, he saw as deleterious to the handing down of trading instincts and other aspects of Chinese culture. He also rejected the idea of "Europeanization" which he argued was "unattainable and undesirable". To halt this degenerative process, he advocated a return to the teaching of Chinese morality and an education system mixing manual labour with an academic curriculum. Such an approach in his view could lead to a positive re-sinicization emerging out of the climatic and social conditions of the Malay Peninsula.

At the same time, Lim's concerns around race and social Darwinism led him to also address the position of the Malays in the colony in a manner which reflected the European thought of the Society's members. This led him to argue that whilst the Chinese could be left to reform their own community, the Malays would require "special care and protection". Referencing the Mukim regulations in Malacca, Lim argued that without such policies the Malays would soon disappear.

Gentlemen,

Some time ago I spent a long time, one afternoon, watching a huge army of ants, passing in a seemingly ceaseless procession from one part of my garden, towards another. The myriads of this throng seemed actuated by a common purpose, and no disturbance by water, fire, or other calamity along the route could check the steady advance. It seems that the continual immigration of Chinese into the Malayan world is parallel to this common garden episode, and is due probably to analogous causes.

To study the effect of Chinese immigration, I propose (1) to consider the character of the immigrants; (2) to discover the changes in them due to their new environment; (3) to account for any progress of the localities due principally to their exertions; (4) and, lastly, to compare the British, Dutch, and other government systems in vogue in Malaya with reference to the settlement and development of Chinese communities.

(I) The character of the Chinese immigrants. It is a well-known fact that the people of China do not have the same anthropological features nor have the same ethnological traits all over the immense Empire. The inhabitants of the Southern provinces differ in language, physique, and other characteristics from those in the Central and Northern provinces. The difference in many cases is as great as that existing between the Celtic races of North Europe and the Graeco-Turkish inhabitants of modern Greece.

The Malay Archipelago was first visited by the Chinese many centuries ago. During the Tang dynasty, the well-known Buddhistic pilgrim made an extensive tour of India, and included in his route the then Buddhistic kingdom of Central Java. Chinese junks seem to have traded with the Malay islands, and to have visited the Zanzibar costs of Africa. Malacca had a Chinese colony before the advent of the Dutch, and Kelapa, or Batavia, and Bencoolen were flourishing centres of Chinese trade in the eighteenth century.

Chinese adventurers had penetrated into every remote corner of the Archipelago, extending from Luzon in the North to Timor in the South, and throughout the whole extent of the Malayan region from East to West. An extensive trade in the spices and peculiar products of these rich islands had been carried on between China and the Archipelago, and immense wealth had accrued to the pioneers, so that the peoples of Fukien and Kwangtung had for five centuries looked upon Malaya as a veritable El Dorado. Tradition also has ascribed many wonderful miracles to the Chinese eunuch Sampo, who, like another saint of a different creed, visited these shores partly for religious and partly for political reasons. The most curious example of how a legend could grow up to account for an established fact is in connection with the well-known fish known as *ikan talang* and the fruit of the cashew tree. The fish, as is well-known, has two or three transverse blackish markings on the body. The Malays have long believed that the fish is poisonous, and, if eaten, may cause the skin disease known as the Sopak-pinta. Out of this has grown the legend that Sampo found the fish in a fisherman's basket, and, recognizing its poisonous character, lifted it up and threw it into the sea, thus leaving on it the impressions of his fingers as an everlasting warning to the people. In like manner, Sampo is said to have squeezed out the seed with its acrid covering out of the juicy fruit, so that posterity may now enjoy the acid fruit. Of course we know what looks like a seed with its testa is the fruit itself, while what is eaten, and is considered by the uninformed as the fruit, is only the succulent peduncle. But here we have a legend extensively believed in by the Chinese in the whole of Malaya.

Passing now to more practical matters, we can notice that the Chinese have imported into these parts all their customs, usages, and habits. The passion for gambling, being universal, has been taken advantage of by the Dutch as a means of extorting further revenue from a people whom they have never understood. While the Chinese are generally very tolerant towards all forms of religion, they have, on the whole, resolutely maintained their religious observances wherever they go.

They have built temples to honour their national heroes and saints everywhere, and have also established Buddhist temples and monasteries in many places. Christianity has made hardly any impression upon the Chinese abroad, but it must be said that the missionaries, save the Catholic padres, have done little any way. The splendid charter, which the genius of Sir Stamford had given to Singapore, had allowed the Chinese to cultivate their religions in a manner that they could not do even in China. In Spanish territory the Chinese had been cruelly persecuted by the priest-ridden Government, while in Java the political unrest of the native tribes gave the Dutch many opportunities to oppress the Chinese, since the latter were then the intermediaries in all affairs, as they have since remained the principal middle-men in the trade of Netherlands India. In the sphere of British influence alone have the Chinese found a nation which could appreciate their sterling qualities, and the Chinese wanted only common justice and fair-play, which, fortunately for all concerned, have been the main attributes of British policy in the Malayan region, as well as elsewhere.

Under these advantageous conditions, the Chinese have flourished exceedingly, and have flocked in great numbers into every region of British Malaya. It is curious, however, to note that the people from certain districts of China have specialized in their trades and occupations.

The Hakkas, from Canton, are mostly miners, agriculturists, tin smiths, and pawnbrokers. The Cantonese proper are fitters, dock labourers, stevedores, bakers, carpenters, painters, miners, and merchants. The population of the villages near Canton come here to do the agricultural and mining work. The Teochews, from Swatow, are our planters and retail shopkeepers, as well as merchants. The Hylams, or natives of Hainan, have for generations been satisfied to work as house servants, and are the only class of Chinese, who, like the high-class Brahmins, have absolutely refused to permit the emigration of their women. The Hainanese consider the good name of their women so highly that the population, as a whole, exert such a moral influence that no one has apparently dared to induce a woman to come here.

The Fukienese were the earliest of the people to come South. They were the principal inhabitants of Malacca and Penang. They are principally merchants, traders, hawkers, and vegetable gardeners. For many years the principal immigrants of Fukien came from the neighbourhood of Amoy; but since 1880 a numerous horde of people have migrated from Foochow and its dependencies. These people are now the rickshaw-pullers of the Straits, and recently great numbers have gone into the country to work on rubber plantations. Amongst all these, we have the small but important community of local-born Chinese and the evil or beneficent influence of the Government of a Malayan state can be read off, as from an indicator, from the social and intellectual condition of the local Chinese, born and brought up in their Malayan surroundings. In my humble opinion, the present position of the Straits-born, Chinese is the best possible criterion of the wisdom of that British policy which primarily we owe to the sagacity of Sir Stamford Raffles.

The languages of the Kwangtung and Fukien provinces are very different. Each has several very important dialects. Each variety requires special study. So long as these differences prevail, the Chinese could never move in a body over any important question. Owing to this very cause also, the Chinese have remained till very lately so clannish and conservative. The Fukien dialects, however, are generally understood by most Chinese who have lived in Malaya, except in mining districts populated mainly by the Hakkas and Cantonese. Malay, therefore, has been the *lingua franca* of this immense Chinese population, and is the medium of communication between the Chinese and the Malays and Europeans.

The existence of innumerable guilds, societies, and temples has made it possible for the Chinese to make a concerted movement wherever their interests appear to be threatened. The Secret Societies, however, belong to a different category altogether, and exert a dangerous influence upon the ignorant masses. Within the last four years, Chambers of Commerce have sprung up like mushrooms everywhere, and in 1907 was held in Shanghai a memorable meeting of all the Chinese Chambers of the world. The present writer was the delegate of the Singapore Chamber, and had the privilege of meeting delegates from every important town in Malaya, Rangoon, Vladivostock, Japan, America, and Australia. Last year the heads of these mercantile bodies organized a gigantic exhibition at Nanking, and brought together, in that ancient and historic city, innumerable objects of art and industry from every conceivable corner of the Malay Archipelago. The manufactures of the Chinese abroad were for the first time in history, compared with home products, and it must be confessed that though the work done abroad bears traces of European influence, upon the whole, it cannot be said to be superior to Chinese workmanship in point of detail and finish. These differences must be due to the economic conditions of labour existing in China and in the Chinese settlements abroad.

The moral character of the Chinese as a whole has not been adequately understood. Most European writers have dealt with extraneous features that are unfavourable and unjust to the people. Naturally the grotesque side and the inevitable defects of the race have been grossly exaggerated. What are the universal failings of mankind have been elaborated into the characteristics of the Chinese race. Mr. Arthur Smith's well-known work must be well-known to all. The best reputation of his satires and slanders is to be found in his recent apotheosis of the Chinese. But the latter know well enough they are human. They do not claim to be God's elect on earth, nor do they admit they are morally inferior to the most civilized peoples of other lands. It would be foolish, however, to ignore the fact that the Chinese do not look at things from the same standpoint as Europeans. This is not surprising, for the peoples of Europe have changed their religions and other opinions very materially within the last century. Most of the trouble between the Chinese and Europeans has arisen from misunderstanding, and from racial prejudice. In many cases the susceptibilities of the Chinese have been ignored, while the Chinese, on their part, imagine that the Europeans design something harmful to themselves. Doubtless, to a modern mind, the figment of the educated Chinese mind is something ludicrous or absurd, but the intellectual ken of an oriental proletariat must be viewed from a special standpoint, with due reference to the actual state of education. Let us illustrate these general statements by a few concrete examples. Take the first attempt to establish a postal service for the Chinese in Singapore many years ago. It resulted in a riot. The people, somehow, thought the Government had intended to tax all their home letters, as well as their scanty savings, which their filial instinct had reserved for the parents in China. But when Government re-introduced the postal arrangements the Chinese welcomed the convenience. A few years ago, an energetic medical officer desired to get complete statistics of the causes of death in the Straits Settlements, and he issued an order that all uncertified deaths should be sent to the public mortuary for post-mortem dissection. Now, of course this would not be tolerated even in England. The Chinese and Mohammedans nearly broke out into a serious riot, but fortunately the Governor had the wisdom to countermand the order immediately. The Chinese do not like post-mortem dissection, but in cases where justice demands that such an examination be made, they have always philosophically submitted to it, only premising that they be allowed to bury the corpse in their own way. The Englishman's house is proverbially a castle. The Chinese have always held the same notion, for China has been for ages the most democratic country in the world, despite her tyrannic and despotic Emperors. In China, it may be said that the rulers have been able to exercise their absolute powers mainly on paper and in the name of justice only on breakers of the law. If a person does not infringe the law, then in China he has quite a surfeit of liberty, there being no rules nor regulations to bind him, save only the goodwill of his neighbours. Hence it is that the Chinese dislike domiciliary visits of municipal agents, and prefer to purchase immunity by bribes. The municipal authorities ought to recognize this fact, and should adopt such regulations that the people themselves might thoroughly understand the reason for these visits; and moreover, only men of high character should be employed in the Service. The town should be divided into wards. Each ward should have a ward committee, who should assist the sanitary inspectors in their work. Instead of mulcting fines, the sanitary authorities ought to assist in the people carrying out sanitary work. At present much time is wasted in the police court, where, at one time, the hearing of municipal cases was the merest travesty of justice. On one occasion there was a long string of cases. As each delinquent one came up, the question was put "Guilty or not guilty!" and the result of each case was a fine of $5 for those who pleaded guilty and $10 for those who had the temerity to say "not guilty". The last man on the list was a Chinese philosopher. He refused to say yes or no, but handed the magistrate a five-dollar note! He was told that he must plead one way or the other. Then said he, "I cannot speak the truth, for you will fine me ten dollars if I do so; I prefer to pay five dollars without saying any truth! The Court and the audience smiled, and the man was let off without a fine. This case reminds me of a puisne judge who is now no more in our midst. He was an unusually acute observer of men, but even he frequently misjudged the character of the Chinese who appeared before him. He once casually remarked to the Court, "Here comes a pack of lies" as a particular witness was entering the witness box. The witness looked fiercely at the Judge, and then walked out of the box again, to the consternation of the Court "Where are you going!" said the Judge. "My lord", replied the witness in good English. "As you already know what I have to say, it is needless for me to speak." The Judge collapsed and had to speak kindly to the indignant man. These are only a few instances of the hardships caused to the Chinese by the prevailing anti-Chinese prejudice. Fortunately we have a special department, under the guidance of the Chinese Advisory Board, to advise the Government, and an experience of many years has proved the wisdom of the policy initiated by Mr. Pickering, who had lived in China for years.

Physically and intellectually, the Chinese can hold their own with any people. Most of them have acquired all sorts of immunity against infectious disorders before leaving home. They fear nothing but failure. So, like the ants, they swarm into a primeval jungle, conquer it, and settle on it. In this way, they have slowly but steadily converted jungle into plantation, and turned miasmatic mud flats into flourishing cities. In less than a century, through ceaseless activity—mostly unaided, save only in the maintenance of order and security by the Government—this endless stream of human flesh and blood has flowed into these islands and made civilization possible. In this race movement there is a tenacity of purpose that brooks no interference, and, despite all horrors and obstacles, like the instinct of the hive, impels the masses onward to their destiny.

(II) The effects of their Malayan environment on the Chinese may be well studied in the numerous colonies of local-born Chinese in all parts of the Malay Archipelago. The admixture of Malay blood is undoubtedly a disturbing factor of great importance. The close affinity in many qualities between the Dyak, the Japanese, and the Sinico-Malays deserves a careful etymological and anthropological enquiry. The descendants of the Chinese are still a hardy race—better in many ways than the descendants of some European races quite similarly situated. In spite of many good qualities, these people show distinct stigmata of degeneration, with obvious traces of Malay characteristics. Generally speaking we find that the old families have come to the parting of the ways, and are at present thrown upon the horns of a dilemma—complete Europeanization or assimilation of more Chinese culture. Defective education, abuse of wealth, intermarriage of relations contribute materially to bring about impending social disasters. Whole families are not in process of being polished off the surface of the earth by those scavengers of effete individuals with spent-up energies—namely; the scourges of civilization—alcoholism, vice, and insanity. Fortunately the infusion of Chinese blood from China has frequently checked the degenerative process. In any case the dissolution of many of the older families seemed only a question of time. The education of the girls may help to delay matters, but unless young people are removed from the tropics, there seems very little hope of maintaining the stamina and the virile qualities of the race—attributes due principally to the Chinese environment, which itself is the outcome of six millenniums of ceaseless social struggles.

Physique—The offsprings in these parts tend to become smaller and shorter, and in every way more delicate. Perhaps a great deal is due to the pampered lives most of these people lead. In innumerable cases, while the father is a strong man, the children are in all cases much shorter in stature, and are certainly much more slender in build. There are exceptions, of course, but the general statement applies to most places in my knowledge. The children are certainly better acclimatized, but tend to become more and more like the Malays. If entirely cut off from association with Chinese, they would revert to Malay ways in every particular, just as the descendants of the Portuguese in Malacca. The Chinese family system has helped to keep together the ties, without which the social changes would have been greater.

Although an elementary knowledge of English is now prevalent amongst them, there are few who are successful merchants. Those who have inherited great business either relegate the control to Chinese from China or soon ruin the whole concern. It is a great pity that the education given them has, in my humble opinion, done harm rather than good. Unlike their fathers, they despise labour, and prefer the easy going dependence of a clerkship to any kind of work involving toil. Hence, we are continually recruiting artisans from China, and the local-born population had grown up to sell the gang of our "idle-rich", our horde of clerks, and our increasing band of masters. This is a problem that the Government and the Chinese should face at once. This state of affairs is due to the system of education, which, in the most majority of cases, leads you nowhere! This is the result of an unsuitable form of education. In the Dutch Indies the Government used to do nothing for the Chinese: the few who obtained a European education left the Chinese kampong and, like fish out of water, endeavoured to live as Dutchmen. The bulk of the population, thus isolated by law and social circumstances, has inherited unimpaired the trading and other useful instincts. The native-born Chinese, therefore, continue to work and trade after the manner of their forefathers. On the other hand, in Manila, where the padres used to control government policy, the children of the Chinese, unless taken back to China, became indistinguishable from the Tagalog or Filipino in all respects. The present writer considers that complete Europeanization is unattainable and undesirable. The other alternative, then, is to teach the old Chinese morality, and to have elementary schools which combine manual labour with the usual lessons.

(III) On the whole, the Chinese have helped to build up the property of most places in Malaya—by supplying an efficient labour force, by contributing to the financial support of the local government though the taxes paid by them, and by carrying on an extensive trade in the hinterland beyond the reach of the civilization. Time forbids my dealing in detail on this part of the subject. The only thing needful to obtain a sufficient supply of Chinese labour is to treat the men justly, and, to reward then properly for extra exertions. Then there is no other labour in the world that can bring to bear upon any piece of work within a given time more muscular energy and intelligence combined. This is the secret of Chinese undertakings on a huge scale brought to a successful issue.

The opium revenue is, of course, really a tax, mainly borne by the Chinese. It has been held by some that any new taxation introduced in lieu of the loss of the former should also be saddled upon the Chinese. So long as the place is a profitable field for work, no tax will deter the Chinese—as witness the enormous taxes imposed by Canada. The question with Malaya is, whether it is wise to kill the goose that lays the golden eggs. Once we disperse the brain-workers in the Chinese communities—and any harsh law will tend to drive them away—the stream of the immigration will be changed. Annam was formerly largely resorted to by the Chinese, but, owing to the vexatious taxes, few Chinese, unless those already with vested interests, would care to go there. Lately, the French Government has discovered that they must introduce Chinese labour to exploit the enormous agricultural resources of that rich colony. The Dutch have been obliged to give Chinese labourers more humane and more reasonable treatment, since the Chinese Government has begun to look after the interests of their subjects. On more than one occasion, the question has arisen in China of stopping migration to a Dutch colony. The Philippine islands sorely need the persevering industry of the Chinese in order to reap the full benefits of the introduction of modern scientific equipment and ample capital. But the best of resources and the most capable experts with unlimited funds, are of no avail without an efficient labour force. For this reason, those who understand the real situation are agitating for freeing the Philippines from the incubus of Chinese exclusion laws. It seems to me that such immigration can be checked by taxes just as well as by exclusion laws. How can the Native States be developed without the enterprise of Chinese pioneers in mining and agriculture? How much of the trade, which maintains our largest European firms in such prosperity, depends upon those numberless and fearless itinerant traders, who penetrate into the remotest village as well as the haunts of savage tribes? As soon as you make it unprofitable for these men to carry on their risky business, you will find that the greater part of the trade of British Malaya will disappear. It is also remarkable that the greater portion of this distributing trade is carried on entirely on credit. The country petty tradesman takes away a few hundred dollars' worth of goods, and returns in from three to six months, either with cash or produce to settle his account. The middleman relies on the good faith of these distributors, and is seldom cheated. When the sudden change of the Straits currency took place, and importation of coins was prohibited, a great blow was dealt at the commerce of the colony, from which the community has scarcely recovered. Primarily the Chinese were the sufferers, but, as you are doubtless well aware, the whole mercantile body has since suffered from the slackness of trade. Riow was formerly a more important place than Singapore but, very shortly after the foundation of the latter city, the advantages of freedom soon told, and today Riow is only an insignificant appanage of our port.

(IV) In conclusion, let us compare briefly the conditions of the Chinese communities as they exist in the colonies of Holland, Spain, France, and England. The Dutch have waxed hot and cold in their treatment of the Chinese. Although the latter have amassed wealth in spite of hardships and difficulties, the majority of them do not like the system, and could they transfer their business elsewhere would eagerly do so. There is very little sympathy between the Chinese and the Dutch, and on either side, it is to be feared, there exists a feeling that the situation is to be tolerated as a necessary evil. The Chinese seldom learn Dutch. Recently the Chinese in Netherlands India began to spend large sums in establishing modern schools, in many of which the English language is taught. This caused quite unnecessary uneasiness on the part of Dutch officials, who have succeeded in opening Dutch schools for Chinese after the Government schools of the Straits. In Java the Chinese are almost entirely traders and shopkeepers and hawkers. They are heavily taxed. In Banka there are indentured coolies at the mines. In Sumatra and numerous other places there are large numbers of indentured coolies on tobacco, rubber, and other estates, many complaints have been made about the cruel hardships suffered by the men, and the Dutch Government has endeavoured to enforce such regulations as are dictated by the regimen of modern civilization. The frightful abuses that were reported in Singkep, Deli, and other parts of Sumatra have at last compelled the Chinese government to keep a sharp look-out in the interests of these unfortunate immigrants. But nowadays the Dutch are too wise to permit anything to happen that may jeopardize the steady immigration of Chinese into their colony. There is every prospect of an early reform in the vexatious regulations imposed upon the Chinese as a result of a century's misunderstanding and friction.

The Spanish regime is now happily over. But its mis-government is not only of historical interest, but may serve as a warning. The Chinese flourished because the country was exceedingly rich, and money could open the gates of paradise as well as of the inferno, both of this world and of the next. The bigotry of the Catholics drove the Chinese to join the Church, but only an infinitesimal fraction remain Christian. The children practically became Filipinos, and ultimately became the leaders of the insurrection that gave the Spaniards so much trouble. The Spanish colony made little progress, and the Chinese could only exploit the country by means of heavily bribing the officials.

The French in Saigon adopted a system alien to the Dutch and Spanish systems. The Chinese were discouraged, and, in spite of the splendid efforts of the French and the immense natural wealth of the land, the commerce of the country has not kept pace with that of British

Malaya. Were the Chinese given friendly treatment such as that accorded to them in the Straits, there could scarcely be a doubt that the trade of Saigon could easily be doubled. Even as it is, the Chinese are the most important members of the commercial community.

The immense success of Hongkong and the Straits and Federated Malay States is due, of course, to the combination of British statecraft and the enterprise of an ever-increasing Chinese population. The union has proved of mutual benefit, and besides there have grown up local communities of Chinese descent, thoroughly loyal to the Government, with good prospects of becoming a useful permanent population. But the secret of success depends upon the impartial administration of justice, and upon offering the Chinese ample scope for the exercise of their energy. In justice to the Dutch system, however, it must be said that the interests of the aborigines have not been overlooked. The British administration gives equal opportunity to all, but the Malays require special care and protection, and unless protected by the special laws, such as the mukim regulations in Malacca, the Malays will soon have to disappear altogether from places into which the well-equipped foreigners—Europeans, Indian, or Chinese—have migrated. Justice requires that the Malays should receive more attention from the Government, and the Chinese ask only for equal opportunity with the Europeans to share in the further development of the country in which they have so much interest, and to the successful opening up of which their predecessors for a century had contributed the best manhood of the race.

20

THE CHINESE REVOLUTIONARY MOVEMENT IN MALAYA

Essay
11 July 1913
by *Lim Boon Keng*

Editors' Note

Although a strong supporter of the British colonial administration (he was appointed a member of the Straits Settlements Legislative Council in 1895 at the early age of twenty-six), Lim Boon Keng played a prominent role in the Chinese nationalist movement in Malaya. He had close ties with Sun Yat-sen and Kang You-wei, hosting the latter in Singapore in 1898. In 1901 he authored *The Chinese Crisis from Within* (edited by Society member Rev. G.M. Reith), chronicling the reform movement in China. In 1906 Lim became a founding member of the Tongmenghui, an anti-Qing dynasty movement, established by Sun Yat-sen, and served as president after it became the Singapore branch of the Kuomintang in 1912. After the Qing dynasty was overthrown in 1911 he was appointed to various medical positions in China and became the personal physician of Sun Yat-sen. Significant to Lim's thought in this period was his belief that the Babas of Singapore, with their mixed culture, could play an important role in the reform of Chinese society.[1]

Lim's 1913 essay to the Society highlighted the importance of the Chinese of Malaya to the nationalist movement in China and also took stock of the nationalist movement itself. Listing down the effects of the movement including the removal of the queue, the adoption of European dress, the introduction of representative government and the emancipation and education of women, he also noted its tendency towards extremes. "Fanatics", he argued, influenced by the "crude socialism of the workmen of Australia" sought for "equality in all things, abolition of social, legal, and family distinctions and suppression of religion", believing that the "masses only require work". This materialist and radically egalitarian philosophy was antithetical to the Confucianism to which Lim had long subscribed.

In his view these questions had largely been resolved in favour of Confucianism, with popular opinion in Malaya and China defending Confucian values against attempts to abolish such teachings. Echoing his belief in the progressive role that the Baba Chinese could play in China's development, Lim perceived the support for Confucianism amongst the Straits Chinese as an expression of their openness to what was best in Western culture "while intending to maintain their old institutions that do not conflict with republican principles". The question of the importance of Confucianism to modern Chinese society became a source of debate between Lim Boon Keng and Lu Xun. Lu Xun, a critic of Confucianism, was seen by many as modern China's most important writer, essayist and poet.[2]

In his response, J.H. Roberts highlighted progressive European perspectives on the nationalist movement, emphasizing the role played by the migration of the Chinese to British Malaya, whilst also championing the Straits Chinese members of the Society as leaders which a new China could look towards.

This imperfect sketch is intended to be mainly historical. Read after dinner, it is not likely to promote digestion, but it is hoped it is not altogether a hypnotic.

The primary cause of the Chinese revolution is, no doubt, the antipathy between the Chinese and Manchus. It originated from the time of the conquest. The Manchus were ever afraid of a revolt, while the Chinese have plotted to overthrow the Tartar from the start. The astute diplomacy of their war victims was too much for the barbarians, who lost more than they gained in the terms of peace. The conquerors agreed not to trade, not to be farmers, but simply to remain as soldiers and pensioned grandees. Of empty titles they had more than enough, but they succumbed to the effects of parasitism as the Chinese expected. During 250 years the contest had continued. The first revolt was Wu Sankuei, the general who had invited the Manchus, while the penultimate rebellion was the Taiping or Universal Peace movement, carried on by pseudo-Christian fanatics, whose chief claimed to be the brother of Jesus, and, like the prophet of Arabia, issued direct the mandates of Heaven. The frightful excesses committed by them plainly showed that the leader's justified their treatment of idolaters by the examples of Hebrew leaders who claimed to be inspired. General Gordon aided the Government in the suppression of this dangerous theocracy, which had laid waste the fairest provinces and had deluged the country with blood. Of vast cities and busy marts only ashes and ruins remained. When the Manchus had regained the upper land, the rebels were punished with ruthless severity. The movement changed in character. It had already dripped its theocratic pretensions, and was now obliged to adopt secretive methods. It became a body of freemasons, who took the oath of vengeance against the Manchu dynasty. The secret society now known as the Triad Brotherhood spread into Malaya, and its activities fill many pages of Malayan history. In China the society was sternly repressed, but it was carried on all the same, especially in Kuangsi and Canton, where Dr. Sun Yat-sen joined the local society and made up his mind to convert the secret society into a political party. This work was very risky, because the Manchus would not tolerate any attempt to unite the Chinese masses on any political pretexts whatever. Soon after completing his medical studies in the Hongkong Medical School Dr. Sun was in the thick of a plot to capture the city of Canton. The authorities were wide awake. He escaped to America and London. In the latter city he was kidnapped, and the world first heard of him. On his release he came east and visited Singapore, where he found an old acquaintance Dr. Goh Kitmoh, who had a surgery in South Bridge Road. I met him first at this time, and have always found him the same sanguine idealist, ever planning for the uplifting of China.

After the war with Japan a great wave of intellectual unrest passed over China, and under the inspiration of the *savant* Kang You-wei a great band of essayists, whom many years ago I compared with the French encyclopaedists, came into prominence. The excitement infected even the morose Emperor Kuangsu, and it became his ambition to play the role of a Peter the Great of Russia, to avert for China the fate of Poland and Turkey. The result was a *coup d'etat*, which led to the flight of Kang and the massacre of his chief assistants. After visiting Japan the exiled scholar came to Singapore, and lived at Boat Quay under a police guard sanctioned by the Governor, Sir A. Swettenham. Mr. Liang Chichao was meantime forming Loyalist Associations in America and Australia. At that time Dr. Sun thought that he could convince Mr. Kang of the futility of trying to prop up the tottering throne. He was on a mission to raise a revolt near Canton, and came here as a ruse in order to put the authorities off the scent. Unfortunately Mr. Kang's friends wired from Japan that there was a plot to kill Kang. The latter put the telegram in the hands of the police who were guarding him, with the result that Dr. Sun's party had to return to Japan, in this the two leaders never met to discuss the plan of union. It says a great deal for the pair that he never said an unkind word of Mr. Kang, through whom his plan, elaborated for months, had been ruined.

The Kang-Liang party made a great deal of noise, but it was to be expected that loyalty, that means exile or death at the hands of the officials, could not last. The Peking government treated the Kang party with the same impartiality as regards methods of repression as the avowed enemies of the dynasty, but to the end the loyalists argued, but did not fight for their cause. Mr. Khoo Siokwan, a Boat Quay merchant, ran a paper in the Kang interests, while an opposition paper, called the *Tunanjihpao*, was started by Mr. Teo Enghock and Tan Chulam in Hokien Street. Through his latter paper Dr. Sun came to correspond with the promoters, and on his visit to France he met a party of sympathizers on board the M.M. mail.

In 1904 there was a rising in Waichow, and after the failure of the attempt, numbers of refugees came to Singapore. In 1905 Dr. Sun again visited the Straits, and lived in Balestier Road. Dr. Huang Hing who became Commander-in-chief and Minister of War in Nanking, was then travelling with Dr. Sun. Mr. Wang Chingwai was visiting every port, and Lim Neesoon was an active member. In Penang Wang Chingwai made a lady convert, who went with him to Peking in a desperate attempt to blow up the Regent's palace. Wang and his friends were arrested, but the lady escaped.

In 1906 Kang's party set up a new paper in Cross Street. The party of revolution had a rival organ on the opposite side of the road. About this time great numbers of non-Christians apparently became interested in mission work, but in reality they were making use of the church as a cover for their propaganda. The Japanese have found that the same plan had been adopted in Japan and Korea. It was found that the scheme worked very well, as the missionary took credit for the evident excess of social work, and the Chinese could work without the interference of the Registrar of Secret Societies. Thus the revolutionary Society prospered exceedingly, and in spite of the vigilance of Consul Tso Ping-lug the members were able to propagate their views in Netherlands India, in Siam, as well as in Burma.

From the Straits the plan of campaign for the South was to a large extent arranged and financed. During ten years the struggle went on in spite of repeated failures. The outbreaks in Huang-Kang, Canton, Kuang-si, and Yunnan alarmed the Manchus, who, in a fatal decision made in the spring of 1911, resolved to govern China as the British rule India, and the reply of the army was the universal mutiny of the troops in the South. The young officers of the army were seriously disaffected. Numbers had been educated in Japan and had the new socialism, as well as the liberty idea, in the mind. In 1907 Dr. Sun had formed the "Sworn Brotherhood" in Tokio, and soon after a branch was inaugurated in the Malay Archipelago. Henceforth the feeling was gaining ground that the grant of a constitution would soon solve the revolutionary agitation, but Sun Yat-sen was never tired in pointing out that the promises were worthless. When the Peking Government sent out commissioners to study foreign constitutions, Wu Yueh hurled a bomb at them to show that the mission could end in nothing. The authorities did not know what to do. The attempt to evade the popular demand caused general dissatisfaction. When the people of Szechuan opposed the nationalization of railways the Hankow garrison mutinied and forced General Lei Juanhung to lead the revolt. Thus in a few weeks eighteen provinces were in a ferment and thirteen had already declared their independence. The bulk of the merchants had not taken a serious view of the situation, and did not wish to endanger their interests. They tried to remain neutral, and thus provoked the members of the revolutionary party. Owing to many causes the Chinese were split up into two factions. In many places new Chambers of Commerce were formed, and it has been clear that the bulk of the people in Malaya did not want a Socialistic Utopia all at once. The merchants are satisfied with the republic, but do not like the endless disputes of so many parties. Professional agitators, however, make things appear worse than they are.

Political parties have opened their societies in all ports in Malaya. The nationalists are the most active, but the republicans are the bulk of the old Conservatives. In towns the merchants are not taking an interest in the vexed questions of home politics. In inland places workmen belong to the Nationalist party.

At first many of the hot-heads created disturbances. Fortunately no serious trouble has broken out in the Straits. In Java the Dutch police was at its wits' end, and the military had to be called out to overawe the Chinese in Surabaya.

As Chinese abroad have a right to representation in the Parliament, every election will be contested in all ports. The Chinese are thus better off than the citizens of most countries, in retaining their political rights even in their sojourn abroad. Dr. Sun Yat-sen made Singapore his headquarters, and lived for some time in Orchard Road, opposite the police station. Fortunately the worst said of him has been that he is a dreamer of dreams.

A large number of noted Chinese lived here in exile. Most of them are holding important positions today.

The changes caused by the revolution are numerous, but we need only consider such as are important here. The queue has disappeared, and the people have taken to European dress. The modern solar calendar has been made official, and representative government has been introduced. Incidentally many local customs will be changed. Women have been emancipated. Girls are being educated. Some fanatics seek to destroy every religion, and think the masses only require work.

The new socialism is a good theme for discussion, but it will not be possible to carry it out. Our Straits Chinese are conservative, and in our midst less is heard of the crude socialism of the workmen of Australia e.g., which has found favour with a few of the radical extremes of the Nationalists. Such clamour for equality in all things, abolition of social, legal, and family distinctions, and suppression of religion! But the common-sense of the overwhelming majority does not favour such risky experiments, especially as all such questions had been settled in ancient China. When the Minister of Education, Mr. Tsai, tried to abolish Confucianism the whole country sent in protests, and, as a protest, Societies for promoting the Sage's teaching have sprung up all over China and Malaya.

The popularization of Mandarin as the *lingua franca* and of the Confucian ethics as the national were advocated by me twenty years ago, and these two questions have been settled in a satisfactory manner. In Malaya, Mandarin is now taught to children and Confucianism is being explained in the light of modern knowledge. In China, Confucian festivals have been recognized as public holidays by the Republic.

All over Malaya the Chinese contributed largely to the funds of the revolution. This is to be expected, when it is remembered that Malaya has been the place of refuge and exile of all the leaders of revolutions in China during a whole century. Their descendants are rich and prosperous, and, though they have never been to China, they believe it their duty to help in the overthrow of the Manchu dynasty. The idea that the revolutionists had an inexhaustible war chest in Malaya had a paralyzing effect in Peking, and telegrams mentioned of myriads of angry Huachiao (i.e. Chinese emigrants and their children) returning to seek vengeance.

The local Chinese have now an open mind for what is best in the culture of the West, while intending to maintain their old institutions that do not conflict with republican principles.

President Yuan Shihkai has the confidence of the majority of the Chinese nation, though a section of the nationalists distrusts him. He has keen admirers as well as violent traducers in Malaya, but on the whole his policy has found favour among the merchants.

The Dutch policy of setting the Javanese against the Chinese has resulted in the formation of a fanatical Moslem league on the lines of the Indian Swadeshi and the Chinese revolutionary societies. This awakening of the Javanese is a remote consequence of the Chinese revolution.

CRITICISM
by J.H. Roberts

Dr Lim Boon Keng's paper is of such a nature as to make criticism difficult. It is historical, and sets forth certain historical facts in a way that convinces one of their truth, and so makes criticism absolutely futile. I may be pardoned if I depart from the established rule and will endeavour to amplify the doctor's paper by examining the subject from a more general point of view.

Most Europeans are under the impression that China is similar to Great Britain or France, and that it has dialects similar to those of Scotland or Yorkshire. This is not, however, the case. China is more akin to Europe as a whole than to any one country in particular, and although the written language is used throughout the country, yet the spoken language differs so much that a man from the extreme south is incomprehensible to a native of the north. When two such men meet, the medium that is employed to express their thoughts, strange to say, is "Pidgin English". There are further great natural antipathies existing between the various provinces. These are quite noticeable even on the ships that frequent the Singapore harbour, for the deck-hands have generally one cook and the engine room staff another, if they come, as they generally do, from different parts of China. They will not eat, sleep or associate together, although they occasionally fight with each other.

Now, considering that the country is a continent, and that the inhabitants are embittered by racial hate and estranged by lingual difficulties, it is astonishing that sufficient unity and inertia has infused into the mass to make even an attempt at a revolution possible. It also shows the high standard of the courage and ability of the men who engineered the movement. It was a herculean task, and probably many of the leaders did not understand the magnitude of their undertaking. It is more astonishing still to realize how few were the real leaders, and how many medical doctors were associated in it with Dr. Sun and Mr. Kang. In the abortive attempt at a revolution in Canton, mentioned in Dr. Lim Boon Keng's paper, one of the most eager and active participants in the movement was Dr. Lim Boon Keng's assistant, and Boon Keng's father-in-law was the treasurer, who had at his disposal the money subscribed for the attempt, and which was deposited in the Chartered Bank at Singapore. A large sum of this amount was to be used to purchase arms and ammunition from England. Dr. Lim Boon Keng's assistant, Dr. T.B. Sia, gave me the assurance that these arms were not for the purpose of attacking the soldiers of the Emperor, but to quell any local troubles that might endanger the lives of the foreign inhabitants. After the Republic was declared, no opposition was anticipated. Another medical doctor, Dr. Tso, was also an active participant. He had come from Shanghai, accompanying a party of Mandarins who had been sent by the Emperor to study the political systems of other countries. I think Dr. Tso must have accomplished all the observations these officials desired, for they never left their rooms for three weeks. Captain Kinghorn, who was then master of the S.S.Arratoon Apcar, was approached with regard to landing the rifles in Canton, and he undertook to get the articles passed the Customs officers. How far Dr. Lim Boon Keng was connected with this attempt he never would say, but I often thought, by the way he avoided all conversation or reference to the matter, that he had had a considerable hand in financing the business. There is no doubt of the fact; however, that the conspirators gathered in his consulting-room, and generally discussed there their plans in the dark passage that leads to his room above the dispensary.

As the continental powers of Europe complain that London is the centre of all European conspiracies, so the Manchu Dynasty could with equal reason have complained that Malaya, and Singapore in particular, was the breeding place of all reforming efforts—revolutionary or otherwise. Every circumstance, natural and political, in the country was pregnant with revolution. The Chinese in Malaya had legal equality and equal rights with all peoples. Some of our Governors of the Straits Settlements and Residents in the Federated Malay States favoured them more than other alien peoples. They had also absolute freedom to acquire wealth, and instruments of education for their children at their disposal. The contrast, therefore, between their conditions and opportunities in the new, as compared with those existing in their own country, was certain sooner or later to be the cause of a political catastrophe. This is further realized when one considers the vast number of Chinese who return annually to China, and if this is multiplied by thirty to represent the returned emigrants of the last thirty years, the surprising amount of discontent in China that fostered the rebellion is understood. Not only so, but the different provinces of China gave their sons to different parts of Malaya. Ten or twelve years ago Kuala Lumpur and Ipoh had more people from Canton than Chinese from other provinces; Taipeng had more Hokkiens; and in this way the various states of China became permeated with discontent and revolutionary principles.

What Malaya contributed to make the revolution possible was—that it

1. Increased the intelligence and business ability of the Chinese, who came here as coolies and generally returned as towkays.
2. Gave the Chinese immigrants a basis of comparison between their old and their new life.
3. Developed their sense of justice, freedom, and equality; and made every immigrant on his return to his own land a political agitator for reform.
4. Made leaders in Malayan schools by the now abandoned Queen's Scholarship system.
5. Gave opportunities for acquiring wealth, without which the movement could not have been financed.
6. Gave opportunities to conspire.

This view of the revolution is different from that of Dr. Lim Boon Keng's in his paper, who describes the movements of the principal, leaders only; but a revolution requires more than leaders, for leaders are the organizers and directors of forces already in existence.

Malaya has from the earliest times been the favourite field of exploitation by the Chinese. The struggle for existence in China has probably reached a far more acute stage than in any other country in the world. This makes emigration imperative. The first influence that affects a newcomer when he reaches the port of Singapore is a sense of fuller individual freedom, which occasionally develops into rudeness to the red-haired strangers, as the Europeans are called.

Another influence that affects those who go inland to the Federated Malay States is the sense of immensity which the jungle produces. Instead of the small square patches of carefully tended and cultivated fields which they are accustomed to see in their own country, they come in contact with nature, in its wildest condition and most luxuriant aspect. No one can be in the jungle—not even a raw coolie—without thinking, and when one has begun to think for himself, he has advanced in self-knowledge, self-reliance, and self-control. These three alone lead to sovereign power. The struggle in China was a labour to coax nature to produce. His work here is to keep nature under control, or to wrest from it its treasures of mineral wealth. So the Chinese immigrant learns that there are conditions differing from those of his home-land, and that all things do not have their origin in China, as many fondly suppose.

Those who became traders gradually realized that there was a world beyond China, and, coming into business relation with these outsiders, sharpened their intelligence as well as enlarged their geography.

The immigrants further quickly realized that all men were equal before justice. Justice is the theoretical basis of Chinese jurisprudence, but the practical application of abstract equity was not so universal as it ought to have been during the *regime* of the Manchus. He finds in Malaya more practical justice and less theoretical ideas about it, and the comparison is to the disadvantage of his own country.

Now, one's own country is always the best in the world, and a native of China naturally drifts back to his own land at some period of his life. He is, however, a totally different man from the one who left. His knowledge of men and things has been enlarged. His national prejudices have been modified. Things which would have been accepted without comment, and as part of his natural life, cannot and will not be accepted now. Conditions which formerly would never have been disputed are more irksome and intolerable. In fact, a sojourn in Malaya made every Chinese emigrant on his return a political agitator for reform and a deadly enemy of the Manchu Dynasty.

Those who made homes in Malaya and had families naturally sent their children to the English School, because a knowledge of English was financially valuable. Education at first was an investment. The students were brought up to consider that the freedom which England gives to all her dependencies was their indisputable birth right. Any other condition but those of the Anglo-Saxon was pernicious, and ought to be changed. So there arose in time a body of educated men, accustomed to democratic institutions and the natural leaders of change and reform. The Queen's Scholarships of the Straits Settlements also allowed the cleverest students to study in England, and these, who were generally Chinese, on their return naturally became the advisers and guides of the educated portion of the Chinese community. Malaya therefore produced leaders.

Dr. Lim Boon Keng, realizing years ago that one of the greatest drawbacks to the unity of China was the language question, opened schools for and encouraged in every way the study of Mandarin. He realized further the limitations of local education, and for years lectured weekly on every conceivable subject—art, religion, science, etc. He also emphasized the fact on every occasion that religion is the spiritual development of a people—a growth from within, and not something adventitiously acquired from without. He therefore insisted on the Chinese studying their own history, classics, and traditions, and did much to revive a weakening love of their native land.

Along with Mr. Ong Siang, he published for many years the *Straits Chinese Magazine*. Even the quiet Tan Teck Soon gave an occasional address, and this was done to raise the standard of intelligence among their countrymen, and fit a few at least for the work that inevitably had to be done in the evolution of the Chinese race. The moral and personal example of these and the other leaders went far to enlarge and purify the aims, purposes, and ambitions of their countrymen, and by doing so they were effectually laying the foundation of a revolution, dethroning a dynasty and, who can tell? Probably altering the history of the world.

Had it not been for these long years of preparation, the Chinese would not have been so eager to part with their wealth at the call of revolution. But the crucial time came, the sinews of war were available, the leaders prepared and ready, and the mass of the people in the large seaport cities in a state of revolutionary agitation and prepared for all changes. Then the revolution burst. It is to be hoped that suitable men may be found to carry on the first successes to still greater achievements, but if the men cannot be found, then let China look again to Malaya, and two capable leaders at least, worthy of the traditions of their ancient kingdom, will be found in the Straits Philosophical Society.

Notes

1. Lim Boon Keng, "The Role of the Babas in the Development of China", *Straits Chinese Magazine* 7, no. 3 (1903).
2. Wang Gungwu, "Lu Xun, Lim Boon Keng and Confucianism", in *China and the Chinese Overseas* (Singapore: Times Academic Press, 2003).

21

SOCIALISM AMONGST THE CHINESE

Essay
12 December 1913
by *Lim Boon Keng*

Editors' Note

Whilst in his earlier essay on the Chinese revolutionary movement in Malaya, Lim Boon Keng suggested that he did not have the space to discuss the rise of socialism in China, his subsequent presentation to the Society a few months later in 1913 dealt with this topic. Initially tracing the Confucian origins of what he identified as socialist thought in China, he sought to distinguish this socialism from the modern socialism of Europe. Whilst Sun Yat-sen's socialism mirrored, for Lim, the socialism of Marx and Engels, Sun remained for him also a Confucianist. Lim also sought to contrast Chinese socialism with the "Jacobins" of the European nationalist movement and the Westernized radical ideas of socialism being produced in China by "rabid communists, syndicalists, and socialists, and few even graduating as nihilists and anarchists". This had culminated in the bomb-throwing in Peking in 1905, and attempts to uproot traditional Confucian culture. For Lim, Confucianists who "have striven to resuscitate the old Socialism based on ethics and the natural humanistic order" offered an alternative and more ethical model of modernity than the European socialism practised in Europe.

In any study of Socialism among the Chinese, the vast importance of the past economic history of the nation could not be overlooked. For thousands of years the Government of China has relied upon the economic principles of Confucianism and Chinese society has retained up to this day the peculiarities which patriarchic communism had imparted to it in the prehistoric era. The immense gulf separating the social conditions of the East and of the West explains the wide divergence of the methods of Socialism. The prevalence of serfs and slaves in Europe down to the modern ages, and the oppressed state of the labourers, who had in most Western States, become detached from the soil, explain why in the West the Socialistic movement has been carried on from the lower social orders. In China some form of Socialism has, until our own day, been always attempted by the Government, while the free people of China has been contented with their domestic and village liberties and immunities. Whereas in Europe the labourers had to fight against class prejudices and legal enactments to obtain the right to unite in self-defence, the Chinese have had for ages their artisan guilds and mercantile associations whereby employers and employees could meet on equal terms.

A cursory examination of the progress of Socialism from the earliest times in China will show how inapplicable and unnecessary are the European remedies for social inequality, with all their accompanying dangers and inconveniences of sabotage and general strikes.

The economic theory of the Sage founders of Chinese civilization was essentially democratic and cosmopolitan in principle, and further, was based upon the noblest altruism. The Sage rulers regarded themselves as the servants of Heaven, to accomplish for the people every conceivable happiness. The divine right of kings, in the sense of the Sacred Canons, is to nurture the people, to educate them, and to raise them to the highest excellence. Confucius, some two thousand years later, fully endorsed this teaching and strenuously preserved it, thus imparting upon the politics and administration of China the democratic characteristics which distinguish Chinese institutions from those of the West.

During the Chou period, the Duke of Chou, 1122 BC, consolidated the system of patriarchic communism by definite regulations. His system has been preserved by Confucius, and is known under the style of the Ching-tien. Ching is an ideogram for a well; Ti'en is a field. It is the system in which the unit is a Ching or plot of nine squares, each of 100 acres. The central plot was the public land, and was cultivated by the joint labourers of the families living in the eight other plots. The produce of the common field belonged to the State, and out of it the public funds paid for the education, the upkeep of granaries, asylums for the aged and feeble and maintenance of a standing army. There were rarely other taxes except those levied at the market, where the people sold or bartered their goods. Within their own lands the people owned all they produced. After sixty, a man could claim relief from the asylum, and the land occupied by him reverted to the State. The whole system is minutely described in the "Chou-li" or "Institutes of the Government of the Chou Dynasty". It was a species of communism without the inconvenience of a common purse, and without the obliteration of individualism. Each area of nine plots formed a Ching, the unit of land administration. The people living in it constituted a miniature republic, combining for police and other civic purposes, and also served as recruits for the militia in times of war.

With the decay of the feudal system, and the encroachment of the nobles upon the authority of the central government, this form of Communism passed away. By the time of Mencius it had almost ceased to exist. Confucius approved of the Ching-tien system because it prevented the rulers from oppressing the people.

In the Cannon of Rites, or Li-Ki, there is a striking reference to the condition of the ideal republic, in which are to be found the kind of social state for which the Socialists of Europe have been clamouring. It is nothing less than the state of universal love, when altruism overrides all selfish considerations, and man lives only for others. The social order and its various classes of relationships will be meaningless. In some respects it resembles the Kingdom of God on Earth of the Christian Scriptures. This is what Confucianists call the period of Ta-T'ung or Great Communism, which, like the Millennium, is to come with the federation of man and universal peace. With this socialistic ideal before them, coming down the ages with the imprimatur of the Sages, Confucianists have always strove to leave the people as free as possible, and to introduce socialistic schemes with the object of increasing the wealth and happiness of the masses. Even in degenerate times, when Imperial governments conveniently forgot the people's privileges, no central government of China had dared to ignore the claims of the people or to deny that they were paramount. Thus the Manchus felt incumbent on the eve of abdication, to declare that the Emperor yielded to the Will of Heaven and the Voice of the People.

The ethical and theocratic Socialism of Confucius is in reality a universal religion—seeking the good of all mankind, the diverse units of which are to be knit together by the bond of love, and to be made to live in peace and happiness by means of the Golden Rule. Although it has never been thoroughly applied to practical life, yet comparatively it has achieved greater moral results than any other system of religion or morals. Consequently, during all the successive changes of rule, the Government had again and again endeavoured to introduce great socialistic schemes for the common good.

The economic policy of the statesman Kuancius (died 645 BC), resembles in many ways that contemplated by the Socialists of Europe today. It aims at state industrialism and the government manipulation of mines and certain staple trades. In 685 BC Kuancius was minister of the feudal of Ch'i. By elaborate statistical research he was able to bring to a successful issue the state operating in mining, iron-ware manufactures, and in salt-making. He further controlled the variations of exchange by issuing or buying-up money. Unfortunately the wealth and splendour which he created produced also the seeds of extravagance and decay, and, with his death, his schemes had to be abandoned.

In the succeeding periods of history, the statesman of China never forgot the great importance of the land question in social economics. Again and again the Government tried to revive the Ching-tien system in various modifications, but without success. Every time the attempt to check monopoly failed. Although Confucianists consider man as the most important factor, they had to take into consideration the part played by wealth or capital, and, from the time of Mencius, Chinese economists had disposed of the question of whether brain-workers, legislators, and inventors were entitled to equal consideration with the manual labourers. Two thousand years ago, the economics of China had satisfied all classes that in a complex civilization division of labour was indispensable, and that, in consequence, capital, brain-work and muscular work were all equally necessary. Monopoly, however, except when managed by the State in the public interests, has always been regarded by the Chinese as likely to be harmful and oppressive.

According to the "Institutes of Chou" the government should control supply and demand of commodities, and should maintain a State bank to control the money market and prevent booms and crises. Under the direction of Sang Hung-Yang of the Han dynasty the State received taxes in kind and carried on trading, thus keeping up uniform prices, buying from the cheapest and selling in the dearest markets—thus carrying out in practice the theory of English free-traders two thousand years previously.

Naturally the great merchants, and those engaged in the transport business opposed the scheme, which, however, was very successful, and which enabled the Emperor Han Wuti to expand the empire, by supplying him with all the funds he needed. But, on the death of the great financier, state trading resulted in a loss and had to be abandoned.

Nearly a century before this, the communal system had fallen into abuse and disuse. The poor sold their land, the rich bought up all the land in the market. The practice of selling the land as private property arose through the scheme of the ruler of Ts'in who in 350 BC permitted the people of adjoining states to flock into his sparsely inhabited state to buy up vacant land under exceptional conditions. Ts'in became rich and prosperous, and the practice has become prevalent to this day. Great numbers of the poor became landless, and the Government had frequently to afford measures of relief.

In AD 10 the usurper Wang Mang tried by violent measures, through banks and commercial bureaux, to maintain uniformity of prices, in order to prevent some people from becoming too rich, and to produce certain equality in the social condition of the people. Prices of goods were fixed by the local bureau, and the Government even sold things at a loss in order to maintain the official tariff. This measure was necessitated by the extortionate rents charged by the land-owners. The troubles of this period remind one of the agrarian troubles of Ireland in the last century. Wang liberated slaves, and forced the rich to give up their land, but, owing to frauds and to official corruption, these schemes brought no relief. After the fall of the Han, there was a temporary return to the Ching-tien system, and women were accorded full independence.

On the establishment of the great T'ang dynasty, the Chinese thoroughly recovered. The wealth, splendour, and glory of the dynasty were due chiefly to the genius of Liu-An, whose fiscal policy recalls that of Kuancius. Liu-An made transportation and communication easy and cheap and thus gave impetus in trade. Land was distributed on an equal basis with certain planting conditions; but the people were permitted to sell their land, and in one century the rich again monopolized the land.

Under the Sung dynasty (so justly famous for the poetry known by its name, and for the poets and the philosophers which flourished at the time) the Minister Wang An-Shih in 1069 succeeded in winning the Emperor to his side, and was able to launch upon the greatest socialistic schemes ever attempted before or since, or perhaps even in the future. He encountered bitter opposition, but, nothing daunted, he evinced great energy, invincible eloquence, and extraordinary ingenuity in elaborating his wonderful schemes. The Jesuit Fathers were struck with their marvellous grandeur and with their profound democratic import, and it has been alleged that the writings that reached France from Peking largely influenced Voltaire, D'Alembert, Diderot and Montesquieu, and inspired the Encyclopaedists with those socialistic dreams and visions that had since convulsed Europe and America, and, strange to say, are now reawakening the Chinese from their torpor of centuries.

By means of loans, advances, and exchanges, Wang proposed to control supply and demand, and by taking charge of all transportation he would regulate his profits. He devised a state monopoly of grain by advancing loans to farmers at a lucrative rate of interest.

Moreover, by a system of conscription, and by making the farmers maintain horses supplied by the State together with their food, he hoped to have an army large enough to cope with the aggression of the Mongol hordes. Besides, he started government pawn-shops for the hypothecation of goods. The merchants and the scholars strenuously opposed the great socialist, and unfortunately the great schemes of Wang came to grief, through the speculations and malpractices of the men entrusted to carry out the details of the various grandiose schemes. The collapse was not unforeseen. In any case, the attempt was the last one made in China, because the Mongols, the Mings, and the Manchus were satisfied to control the tax-gathering machinery and to leave the people to their own village and municipal autonomy. In modern China, society has for some centuries been maintained on the basis of the Confucian politics and economics, and on the stability of the social order, and the wonderful system of credit for which the people are famous all the world over. Owing to the strict observance of the law of sincerity, the Chinese are noted for their staunch adherence to definite arrangements once agreed upon. The business of China has always been carried on largely by oral contract. The same spirit prevails in their dealings with their servants, for Chinese employers voluntarily undertake to supply their employees with medical advice and medicines, and also to advance some money in case of sickness. There are besides numerous ways which a sick labourer can find funds for his unexpected expenses. As the wages is the result of mutual arrangement and bargain, there is no occasion for the workmen to strike. Chinese workmen do not think that it is reason to prevent employers from engaging those willing to work, even though they themselves consider the pay inadequate. Nevertheless the workmen generally, out of *esprit de corps*, will themselves refuse to take up work and thwart the purpose of their fellow-workers who had to be out on strike. Hitherto strikes had been engineered mainly by disaffected tradesmen against local officials, or university and college students might organize a boycott of some unpopular professor. Labourers, however, could always arrange satisfactory terms through their guilds and capitalists could well look after their interests by means of their associations.

Moreover the workmen in China have hitherto believed in the right of the individual to bargain for the price of his labour, and as Chinese foremen will take into consideration special aptitude, experience and skill, the labourers themselves will never dream of asking for a minimum wage or for an eight-hours law. With regard to compensation for injury and insurance against sickness, the employers have always voluntarily done all that humanity and charity might suggest. In the absence of such, the artisan guilds, friendly societies, and other charitable associations step in and help such unfortunate workmen. At present, just as in the future, labourers will always be able to manage satisfactory terms without appeal to law.

Dr. Sun Yat-sen in 1907 propounded the new Socialism, which reminds one of the theories of Marx and Engels. The chief proposal of Dr. Sun is to prevent monopoly in land by fixing an arbitrary limit to the amount an owner of land could make from the "unearned increment" of the value of the land. The scheme bristles with difficulties, and is of interest because it is engaging the attention of Chinese Socialists of a new school. That the expansion of European industrialism will tend to disturb the normal conditions of labour goes without saying, and unless the Government takes every precaution the people will be exploited by speculators and monopolists to the detriment of the working-classes. On his return in triumph to China in 1911, Dr. Sun Yat-sen devoted his chief attention to the question of nationalizing the trunk lines of railway. The people acquiesced in his proposals, although many had formerly opposed the same when introduced by the "Imperial" government. This clearly proved that what the people objected to was not the nationalization scheme, but the corrupt methods of the bureaucracy. In the last ten or fifteen years, socialistic groups have sprung up in China like mushrooms. The sudden contact of Chinese students with thinkers in Japan, France, America, England and Germany had a wonderfully stimulating effect upon the minds of the young men in their foreign sojourn. The majority of the students were from the middle classes. In Paris, London, New York, and Berlin, and even Tokyo, they came in contact with the lower orders of those great cosmopolitan cities, and little wonder that many of them became rabid communists, syndicalists, and socialists, and few even graduating as nihilists and anarchists. When the revolution broke out, those students with socialistic tendencies and with experience of the ways of European anarchists hastened back. All were agreed that the Empire must go. The masses had also resolved that the autocracy had lost the mandate of Heaven. At that supreme crisis Dr. Sun Yat-sen appeared in Shanghai, and all at once the discordant voices of the revolution were hushed, and he was hailed by all as the unifier of the fighting elements.

Dr. Sun Yat-sen himself is a socialist, with strong Confucian principles. He has a numerous following in America, Australia, Japan, and the Straits. He contents himself with preaching the scheme for prevention of monopoly in land and the nationalization of mines and communication. The provisional government under Dr. Sun had no leisure for any socialistic scheme. Under the conviction that Mr. Yuan Shih Kai had the confidence of the modern army of China, the provisional government and the Assembly of Deputies agreed to elect him as provisional President, and with the advent of Mr. Yuan and the resignation of Dr. Sun Yat-sen, the socialistic members of the Assemblies came into immediate contact and conflict with the more conservative members that came out of their hiding. It was quite obvious that the diverse factions that had united for the destruction of the Imperial autocracy could not work harmoniously. Foremost was the moderate party, mostly men trained in Japan. Dr. Sun Yat-sen is the titular head. The socialistic schemes to which they are committed are very modified and mild forms of Socialism. On the other hand the extreme party of Jacobins represent the anarchistic elements and those who desire to uproot Confucian ideas and destroy all forms of government, to introduce universal suffrage, and to give absolute equality to women. It has been difficult to ascertain any definite constructive schemes out of the verbiage of their angry dithyrambs against the existing order. They are so outspoken, and so violent in their ways and methods, that had their numbers been at all in proportion to the energy exhibited, China would have witnessed during the last year all the horrors of the Terror, which disgraced and degraded the great French Revolution. Fortunately they were greatly outnumbered by moderate men, who were contented with small beginnings, and who had no urgent desire to revolutionize society by martial law.

Between the two extremes there are societies representing all degrees and forms of Socialism, and the great works of the European writers are being studied both in translation and in the original. Unfortunately undue stress has been given to the view of Rousseau on social equality, and a purely mechanical interpretation has been adopted on the Spencerian theory of survival of the fittest, so that, amongst the socialist circles, liberty, equality and struggle for existence are being used in a purely metaphysical sense without historical ballast or scientific safeguards. Owing mainly to the carelessness of translators, out-of-date works are translated. Montesquieu's *L'Esprit des Lois* and Rousseau's *Contrat Social* are regarded as modern textbooks, whilst Huxley's "Essay on Evolution" serves as a guide to Darwinism. *The Wealth of Nations* is a new work in Chinese. But the really dangerous works are the essays and articles issued by the socialist and anarchist societies. These are freely translated, and are circulated among all classes.

The introduction of Nihilistic ideas amongst Chinese revolutionists resulted in the bomb-throwing in Peking in 1905. Subsequently to that, assassinations and bombs became the order of the day. The bomb outrages in Canton made all candidates for the higher offices refuse the offers of the Imperial Government and in fact men had to be almost driven by threats to proceed to their posts. Hsu-Hsiling who fired upon the Manchu Governor of Shao-hing, openly declared that men like him would continue violence till the Manchus gave way. The anarchistic movement has received a temporary blow by the energetic and rapid movements of President Yuan Shih Kai's troops. The greater number of them rallied in the Yangtze valley to try conclusions with the Dictator, and had suffered the fate which they had no compunction in dealing to others. The successes of the Central Government have also put a check upon the socialistic movement in China, and especially the suppression of the Nationalist party for treason and rebellion. For the present there is a temporary truce but the germs of Western thought have been freely sown, and the future will show whether history will repeat itself once more, and the accommodating system of Confucius will absorb the socialism and industrialism of our age, or, under stress of the social, intellectual, and political convulsions, the all-sufficient religion of the Sages will break up and dissolve, and the Chinese nation will join in the race for commercial ascendency and for military and political supremacy by taking up the shibboleths of Western politicians. The struggle has already begun. On the one hand, Confucianists have striven to resuscitate the old Socialism based on ethics and the natural humanistic order as a challenge to the crude social schemes of visionaries intoxicated by the poisons of Nihilism, Syndicalism and Anarchism. On the other hand, all orders of Christian communities, and the Socialists of the modern European schools, are bent upon destroying the Confucian culture, the great bulwark of purely Chinese institutions and the ubiquitous obstacle to innovations and disorder. The history of the past, however, justifies the presumption that the Chinese culture will yet weather the storm and that out of the chaos it will rise up phoenix-like thoroughly rejuvenated.

IV

Studying "the Malays" and their Religion

22

"LATAH"

11 September 1897
by *D.J. Galloway*

Editors' Note

The search for the "Real Malay" long engaged European visitors and officials in the Peninsula and wider region. Among the Society's members, these discussions gave particular focus to anthropological concerns around the culture and mindset of the Malays, which centred on a series of deficiencies related to factors of environment, culture and genetics perceived by European thought to be found in the community. One such study is found in the account of *latah*, a nervous disorder, presented to the Society by D.J. Galloway in 1897 and responded to by H.N. Ridley.[1] Galloway was a doctor and founder of the Straits Medical Association. In his 1897 paper he was concerned not only with *latah* as a medical condition, but also with *latah's* connection to the prevailing ideas of race and the culture of the Malays. Galloway argued that the Malays possessed attributes that were "chiefly mental" which isolated them from the other races of the Peninsula. The Malay, he noted, whilst hiding under a "mask of impassivity, of stoical deference", possessed a "sentient personality" and a "high degree of responsiveness to impulses outside him". *Latah* was thus seen to result from an increased susceptibility to external stimuli and from a lack of ability to repress instincts. The cause of this condition, he suggested, was the lack of education, which prevented subjects "from arranging and inhibiting [their] ideas". Ridley, in his criticism, noted that the spread of education and "contact with a higher civilization" was making *latah* difficult to find in the towns. This suggested to him that with modernization under British rule, *latah* would gradually die out. At the same time he conceded: "[A]t present our knowledge of psychics is really small, and of its relationship to the structure of the nervous system we know almost nothing".

It is with the painful consciousness that I come before this Society with an unfinished essay,—unfinished in every respect, in thought, in language, and in actuality (in so far that I have not been able to touch upon Amok),—that I beg your indulgence to the many shortcomings therein contained, on the score of having been able to give only a few minutes at a time to the consideration of the subject of *latah*, these few minutes being at the end of a day's hard work, when neither mind nor body was in a condition to deal with abstruse subjects requiring concentrated attention. I hope my critic and the members will deal gently with me on these grounds, as well as upon those of the difficulty of the subject in hand.

The references to *latah* in literature are many, but detailed descriptions of that state are exceedingly rare; in fact, the only description which we possess is that by the late Mr. O'Brien. References to *latah* are to be found in a number of medical dictionaries, in Moll's *Hypnotism*, in Swettenham's and in Clifford's books, as well as in most Malay dictionaries.

It is defined in the *Lexicon of the New Sydenham Society of Medicine and the Allied Sciences* as "the Malay name under which a form of religious hysteria is known in Java. There is a rapid ejaculation of inarticulate sounds and a succession of involuntary movements, with temporary loss of consciousness; in the intervals of the paroxysms the mind is unaffected. The disorder is propagated by imitation, and it is not infrequently simulated." So much for the *Lexicon*. Moll states it to be a minor form of hypnotism, i.e., fascination, and O'Brien seems to be of the same mode of thinking; but not any one of these fully covers the phenomena as we are accustomed to see them, for the obvious reason that the term *latah* covers a number of widely different states, incapable of classification under any but the most general term. For a description of this disorder I will adhere to that of Mr. O'Brien, as it is the embodiment of much intimate experience of Malays by an exact and keen observer, who possessed the strength of mind to be content with a simple narration of facts as he observed them, without any of the conjectural embroidery so often superimposed on very slender data indeed. It is chiefly for the latter reason that I use his description as better than any I could possibly give, as had I attempted a description of such a disease some bias would surely have crept in, and could scarcely be avoided by one whose profession, above all others, brings him in daily contact with all manner of mental obliquities.

I will use O'Brien's description, but not his classification. He says: "The Malay acceptation of the term is very wide. It includes all persons of a peculiarly nervous organisation, ranging from those who, from their mental constitution, seem absolutely subservient to the will of others, down to those who appear merely of a peculiarly excitable temperament."

Yet, while it is freely granted that there are "*latahs*" who fill every grade from the merely nervous to the nearly idiotic, it is convenient, for the discussion of the different phases, to attempt a classification. Before doing so, however, it would be well to discuss the "personal equation" in the matter. This Society settled, beyond any shadow of doubt, at last meeting, that the Malay was originally an Irishman (sic); but whatever their origin racially may have been, they possess attributes, chiefly mental, which isolate him from the races by which he is surrounded and among whom he mixes. He is eminently a lovable personality. With the circumstances of air, temperature, climate, and soil,—in fact, the environment,—which have all had a share in the making of the man, I have little to do, only so far as it has produced a happy-go-lucky, hopelessly improvident individual, who allows nothing to interfere with his ease, and allow him time to study his own sensations. For the Malay is much given to introspection and ruminating over events which are past.

So lightly does this environment press upon him that a little labour of the lightest kind suffices to supply his daily wants, leaving much time for leisure, which he usually employs in some way which does not involve muscular exertion. Thus gossiping, gaming, tale-telling are indulged in when companions are at hand, but when alone he will sit for hours in a day-dream until roused by some other person. This is a condition which of itself is worthy of study. Whether it is simply a mental rumination of what he has perceived at some previous time, whether an analysis of his own personal sensations, or whether a succession of those sub-sensations which are constantly entering our being, scarcely reaching our consciousness, i.e., day-dreaming proper, I am unable, without observation, to say. Yet this is a state with much bearing on our subject of tonight, especially that part of it which relates to Amok. Under a mask of impassivity, of stoical deference, the Malay hides an acutely sentient personality; keen to appreciate humour, sensitive to praise or blame, especially the latter, responsive to the moods of his visitor, and in constant "rapport" with all around him, the outcome of all this being a high degree of responsiveness to impulses outside him.

Most writers who have in their works touched on *latah* agree in some rather important points. They all agree that it is in some degree hereditary, that it is most common in women, and that it is very rare, if not absent, in children. With all these I am glad to agree, but must point out that, although *latah* is not found in childhood, other conditions of which *latah* is the development or consequence are very common.

As may be inferred from what has been said, I am inclined to believe *latah* to be a phase of activity implanted in an essentially neurotic character. We are all prepared to admit that insanity begets insanity, but we are not prepared to prove that one type of insanity produces the same type in the offspring,—that mania will beget mania, dementia, etc.,—but rather that one type of insanity may beget any one of the many types included in that term. So is *latah*. While *latah* may not beget *latah*, it is often found mixed up in the same family with persons of peculiarly neurotic constitution, who occupy the no-man's-land between sanity and insanity. All observations in civilized races tend to show that this type of constitution is peculiarly transmissible to offspring in some of its many manifestations, and I feel sure that, given time and opportunity, it would not be difficult to prove the *latah* to be a member of a neurotic family. Although I am far from putting forward the following instances as absolutely proving this assertion, they may be taken for what they are worth. In one family was a *latah* son and a very hysterical sister, while the father of both was a person who, while quite able to take care of himself, had a decided "want", as we say in Scotland. In a second family the father was intensely *latah*, a son was a "paroxysmal" drunkard, and two daughters were much subject to mock epileptic fits, hystero-epilepsy as it is sometimes wrongly termed. A third family had a *latah* mother; one of the daughters was a somnambulist; two of the sons, although assisted frequently to obtain good and permanent situations could never be kept in any of them beyond a few weeks, were decidedly born to be of the "loafer" class, unable to fix their attention for any length of time on anything; and one of the youngest children was a congenital idiot. I have recollections of another case, but cannot affirm the exact particulars.

Although using the simile of insanity to illustrate what I meant by heredity, I am of the same opinion as O'Brien when he states that the Orang Latah and Orang Gila are very distinct individuals even to the Malay mind. Having thus prepared the ground, it is advisable to venture upon a definition of the word *latah*. The following seems to me to be as far as we can go in the present state of our knowledge—"A neurosis, characterised by increased susceptibility to external suggestion, whether that be direct (psychic)—i.e., by commands, actions, advice—or indirect, i.e., through hypnosis."

I have above attempted to show that *latah* is a type of neurosis, and further to strengthen this statement I may point out that suggestion (i.e., where the excitations which impel the will to activity do not proceed from the individual's own brain, but from the brain of another) could not act so violently upon a healthy human being. It can only do so in a condition of morbid sensibility.

I will discuss, in the first instance, a class of cases which are mentioned by O'Brien in Class A, and also in the second, third, and fourth sections of Class C, and a further development of these cases which it has been my good fortune to have a chance of observing, but which, so far as I know, has not hitherto been described. To follow O'Brien's description (for I cannot hope to improve upon it)—"In this class (Class A) I would place those subjects who appear to be affected merely by such excess of nervous sensibility as is exemplified by starting unduly at the sound of an unexpected and loud noise, or at the sight of an unexpected and distressing or alarming incident. So far it might be said that, under parallel circumstances, a similar exhibition may be expected from any unit of any nation of the human race. But, having observed Malay *latahs* on numberless occasions under the above circumstances, I have noticed two peculiarities which seem to differentiate the mental shock which they undergo from that which Europeans experience under like conditions."

"Firstly, their irresistible impulse seems to be to strike out at the nearest object, animate or inanimate, and, secondly, their involuntary exclamation is always characterised by what I must call obscenity."

Section B (again I take Mr. O'Brien's description). "A Malay woman, of respectable position and exceedingly respectable age, was introduced to me some time ago as a strong *latah* subject. I talked to her for at least ten minutes without perceiving anything abnormal in her conduct or conversation. Suddenly her introducer threw off his coat, to my horror my venerable guest sprang to her feet and tore off her *kabayah*. My entreaties came too late to prevent her continuing the same course with the rest of her garments, and in thirty seconds from her seizure the paroxysm seemed to be over. What struck me most in this unsavoury performance was the woman's wild rage against the instigator of the outrage. She kept on calling him an abandoned pig, and imploring me to kill him, all the while she was reducing herself to a state of nudity. One more instance. I have met a man several times lately who is a very strong *latah* subject. He is a cook on board a local steamer, and is naturally (alas for human nature!) the butt of all the crew, who daily, almost hourly, exercise the clumsy wit—the wit of sailors plus Orientals—at his expense. All this skylarking had a tragical ending one day. This cook was dandling his child forward one day; one of the crew came and stood before him with a billet of wood in his arms, which he began nursing in the same way as the *latah* was nursing his baby. Presently he began tossing the billet up to the awning, and the cook tossed his child up also, time for time. At last the sailor opened his hands wide apart and let the wood fall on the deck, and the cook immediately spread out his hands away from the descending child, which never moved after striking the boards."

Section C. The sole example of this class which I have ever seen was a very old woman, reputed to be over 100 years old, who had been strongly *latah* all her life. It was stated to me by her son that she had several times been induced to do exactly the same as O'Brien's "respectable lady", but that for a number of years this had ceased. The explanation was not far to seek. The old lady was blind, both eyes being cataractous; but her hearing was fairly good, and impulses finding their way by that channel were responded to at once. Thus during our interview we were several times interrupted by the crowing of a cock, which was imitated by her, and once also by the striking of a clock, which was also fairly imitated.

There are one or two practical considerations as regards the subjects of this particular phase of *latah* which might throw some light on the matter. It may be noted that—

(1) most of the sufferers are women;
(2) all of them belonged to the uneducated classes;
(3) any one can direct the latah movements, and every one seems to have equal power, i.e., unlimited.
(4) These classes are merely ones of degree and not of kind, the one passing into the other with advancing age or under other conditions which tend to disturb mental equilibrium.

The fact that most of the sufferers are women presupposes an exceedingly mobile nervous temperament, and as most of them belong to the uneducated class, we might assume that, as much of our education is acquiring the power of arranging and inhibiting our ideas, and through these our acts, that power in the class just mentioned would be weak, perhaps wanting. The statement that these classes are merely differences of degree and not of kind I know from observation. I have carefully watched a Malay woman during the last twelve years, and give briefly her history. Always a nervous, hysterical subject, she evinced no *latah* predisposition in the early years of my observation. But frequent child-bearing, illness, and a very hard struggle for existence generally, have left their mark upon her, so that now any one can, by example, induce her to fulfil any or all of the conditions described by O'Brien in his C class.

Literature is crowded with instances of irresistible impulses from within. Billod records the case of a Marchioness who would, in the course of ordinary conversation, interrupt a sentence with an unseemly or obscene epithet, addressed to, or at, someone within her range of vision in the company, and then take up the broken sentence again. The utterance of this epithet was always accompanied by a blush and a confused look, and the word was jerked out like an arrow from a bow.

Now, if such an irresistible impulsion could proceed from within, suggested only by the person entering the field of vision, and could fail to be inhibited even in a person of education, how much more likely it is that in a state of *latah*, with its heightened susceptibilities, and with a suggestion from without, pointedly directed at them, an analogous condition of things might be produced!

I would therefore incline to the belief, which I place tentatively before this Society that these cases are the result of an excess of impulsion, from within or without, accompanied from a lack of the power of inhibition; the subjects are fully conscious that they are dominated by an inner force, and irresistibly impelled to do acts which they condemn. Their intelligence remains perfectly sane, the insanity affects only their acts.

That inhibition, or rather loss of inhibitory power, plays a large part in this condition is clear. As has been before remarked, much of our education consists in the cultivation of this power. The *latah*, belonging usually as he does to a class in which the cultivation of this power is deficient, i.e., the uneducated, cannot be expected to have developed it in any great degree, so that suggestions from without at once pass into action. Further, inhibition requires time. If a person insults or injures you, the first impulse is to knock him, but before this has had time to pass into action an antagonistic state is called up which inhibits such action, the new state of consciousness suppresses the other. So far are we the children of education, so habitual has this repression of our feelings become, that the most powerful inhibitory influences may be put in action automatically, which is tantamount to saying that consciousness of action is wanting. Even if the stimulus to act be so powerful as to necessitate a conscious mental effort for its inhibition, that new state of consciousness can be called up by us in a moment of time. Not so the savage, or, for that matter, the child. Any impulse passes at once into action, in fact the action seems to be purely spinal (reflex).

But should, as sometimes happens, there be an attempt at inhibition, showing that cerebral as well as spinal centres are stimulated, the inhibitory effort arrives too late. Illustrations of this are not wanting. The ordinary class of *latah*, who strikes out whenever touched (irrespective of what he hits at), and who belongs to this class, is a very good example. The act of striking out is almost immediately followed by another gesture, an action of drawing some imaginary thing towards him: in fact, the action is physiologically antagonistic to the blow, and is the outcome of a mental state in which he seeks as it were to catch up the delivered blow and restrain it; in fact, it is simply a picture of a tardy inhibition. This second gesture is generally accompanied by an apologetic expression either of feature or of language or both. Further, while many *latah* subjects are quite without the power of resistance to impulses from without, there are many who, on a deliberate or repeated attempt being made to impel them, can resist—sometimes successfully, sometimes only for a few minutes—the influence of suggestion. I have often seen the experimenter utterly fail on a second attempt. The only explanation I have to offer is that the *latah* was already on his guard, being in a state of expectation. It would thus seem reasonable to assume that the mental error here was an inability to call up the antagonistic state sufficiently rapidly to inhibit the result of the suggestion.

Class II. The second class which I propose to take up is well described by O'Brien thus: "I have more than once met with river boatmen who, when the word '*Buoya*' (alligator) was mentioned, even in the course of casual conversation after camping for the night, would drop whatever they might have in their hands and retire cowering to the cover of the nearest '*kajang*.' I have inquired into every case of this description which came under my notice, and in no case could I learn that the man had any special reason for his terror in the way of a personal experience. His friends explained that he was *latah*, and that to them explained everything. On one occasion, after a curious exhibition of this description, I shot an alligator on the bank next morning. The *latah* was the first to approach the saurian. Against my earnest entreaties he proceeded to pull the creature about, and finally forced its mouth open with a piece of firewood. His persecutors, his fellow-boatmen, stood at a respectful distance.

"An hour afterwards, as he was poling up the river, one of the crew called out to this man '*Buoya*'. He at once dropped his pole, gave vent to a most disgusting exclamation, and jumped into the river—an act which showed that his morbid terror was quite unconnected with what might be supposed to be its exciting cause. More than one man has implored me not to mention the word '*harimau*', and more than one have gone nearly insane with terror when the word '*ular*' (snake) was spoken at him.

"In each case of this description, my Malay companions solved my perplexity, at times very great, by saying '*Dia latah, Tuan*'.

"Similar cases must be familiar to many who read this Journal (*Asiatic Society*), but the man who became limp and nerveless with terror at the mention of the word '*buoya*' and who afterwards was the first to handle a '*buoya*', of whose death no one was assured, presents a mental contradiction of which I await the explanation.

"I may add that a '*pawang*' who exhibited extreme distress at my mention of the word 'tiger' was one of the few men I have met out here who habitually passed nights in the jungle alone. There was no question here of the superstitious reverence which Malays have for this animal, or of their dislike to have it called by its regular name. The man's fear was *latah*, and his friends, though apparently much amused, told me that this was his peculiarity, and I was careful not to offend again.

"With regard to snakes, perhaps the horror with which these sufferers hear the word is more marked still.

"Such cases, however, as I say, must be familiar to most readers of these pages. The class of cases in which those afflicted are led to believe in the actual presence of a reptile, where the sane only see a bit of string or a piece of rotan, belong to another—the fourth—division of my subject."

I quote this last paragraph as written, but disagree with the remark which relegates them to another class.

This condition of intense fear may be looked upon variously, as one of the phases of dual consciousness, as a state of light hypnosis. It might appear at first sight that a lapse of consciousness occurred, lending colour to the hypnotic theory, but such is not really the case. In all the instances I have seen, there was no loss of memory; everything was perfectly remembered, and the unfortunate victim begs the often unwitting, experimenter not to make use of the word again.

The differences between this state and that just described are obvious. In the preceding, an action or command pointedly directed at the subject is the cause of the action; in this form of *latah* some particular word, always the name of some wild beast or other loathsome or dreaded thing, even though quite unintentionally used, has the power to produce this state of abject terror. This condition is unique in psychology. Its nearest analogue is monomania, but in monomania the subject has quite a clear concept of the matter on which he is insane. Not so in this form of *latah*. No memory picture arises from the mention of the dreaded word, no perception results. This is fully proved by the facts: related by O'Brien. The word "*buoya*" raised in this unfortunate man's mind no image of an alligator,—at least no fear of alligators—plunging as he did at once into the river, which, as all rivers in the Malay Peninsula are, was probably alive with alligators, and his subsequent behaviour with the recently shot animal. The stimulus raised in his mind only the memory of a previous condition of intense fear, and it went no further. On each occasion of calling up the mental state some strenuous effort had been made to escape from or arrest the danger, hence the tendency of the stimulus to pass at once into action.

Nor can I believe that this has always been the whole train of events. It seems impossible that a state of such intense terror can be invariably brought about by the same stimulus, and that stimulus a word, without there having been at some time a distinct perception called up. In other words, I believe this condition to be one which, as I shall attempt to show, has been developed upon other states of mind of a simpler kind.

To trace this development I must go back to childhood. It is not at all uncommon to see, if you watch a number of Malay boys at school, that one or more of them are, owing to some peculiarity, the butt of the others, and on them is expended the clumsy boyish wit of their fellows. The kind of entertainment to which these unfortunates contribute is usually somewhat as follows. Some imp takes a billet of wood, a school-book bag, in fact anything of size sufficient; begins stroking and patting it, calling it tiger, alligator, and some kindred word, and brings his actions prominently before the boy he is experimenting on. This induces a state of terror in the boy, and I have satisfied myself, in one instance at least, that the boy actually perceives the animal mentioned by his tormentor. This you may say is hypnotism. It may be; in any case we are quite sure of our ground when we call it a delusion—an illusion of the senses. Note that to produce this. it was necessary to suggest both by word and act—that both the sense of sight and hearing were made to receive a stimulus. There is always in a normal mind the possibility of correcting an illusion, but in this condition (*latah*) we are not dealing with a normal mind, but with the disequilibrated mental processes of a neuropath.

The effect of any emotional excitement is to give a preternatural vividness to the ideas which are its excitants, and there can be no doubt that, by repeated stimulation of the senses, the impulse becomes more and more powerful, the amount of actual impression necessary to transform the mental image into an illusory perception becomes less, until a mind strongly possessed by one kind of image will tend to project this image outwards, without regard to actual external circumstances. We thus reach the stage of hallucination, i.e., a sense of impression may result without there being any physical stimulus, the imaginative impulse having gained in force relatively to the present impression, until the amount of actual impression becomes evanescent.

But we might go even further. When a shock of fright disturbs the mind, a violent and widespread molecular commotion disturbs the working of the higher nerve regions (Mercier). Now, by repeated induction of this condition of fear, I have striven to show that the smallest excitant, the mere mention of the word in ordinary conversation, produces the result, the excitant being reduced thus to a minimum. It is quite within reason that as, according to the laws of nervous action, repeated stimulation of any nervous tract—a stimulation of high intensity as we have just seen—will leave this tract more permeable to subsequent stimulations—will, in fact, leave this tract in such a state of high tension, that, like a galvanometer to electric currents, it will quiver to the smallest stimulus and respond in an intense degree. Thus, I am inclined to believe that in the final stage of this type of *latah* there is never formed any concept of the animal named, the only image called up being the image in the memory of a previous condition of intense fear.

To sum up this type of *latah*, I would say that, beginning as hypnotism with suggestion, it goes on until it reaches the state described in the last paragraph, which may also be accounted for by hypnotism. The dangers of a hypnosis repeatedly induced are the increased tendency to hypnosis, heightened susceptibility to suggestion in the waking state, and the danger of his accepting external suggestions even without hypnosis. It is this too great susceptibility to hypnosis which in some degree explains this class of *latah*, inasmuch as the means by which the hypnosis is attained are not considered, but only the idea of an earlier hypnosis is vividly recalled.

Class III. As described by O'Brien: "In 1875 at Kuala Lumpur I met a young Malay who was of material assistance to our party in pulling our boat across a narrow watershed into The Sureting. His comrades told me the man was *latah*, but I could see nothing in his conduct or conversation which was not perfectly rational. Some twenty-four hours after making his acquaintance, one night we let off a signalling rocket for the amusement of those who had given us assistance. None of those present had ever seen a rocket before. I was preparing to fire a second rocket myself, when the *latah* pushed me violently aside, snatched the torch from my hand, fired the rocket, and fell down on his face, making an unintelligible noise, to all appearance the expression of fear. I was somewhat startled, such rudeness and violence being foreign to the Malay character. When I sought an explanation from the bystanders I was informed laconically '*latah*, Tuan'. Next morning when I met this man I found him perfectly rational and perfectly respectful. I saw him standing alone on the bank as we put off down-stream, and I waved my hand to him. To my surprise he began waving his hand frantically in return, and continued to do so till I lost sight of him at the first bend of the river. I had begun to whistle an air. He also began whistling. His imitative faculty did not quite lead him to an imitation of the tune, but the fact of an up-country Malay's whistling at all is sufficiently remarkable."

This is purely and simply hypnotism. When we think of the circumstances of the case it is not to be wondered at. Here is a white man, seen probably for the first time by the natives; the condition of expectation and close attention all tended towards increased susceptibility to hypnotism. When, added to that, was the sudden loud report of the rocket being fired, a completely favourable state to hypnotism is established. The effects of a loud noise on a readily hypnotizable individual are so much a matter of common knowledge that it seems only necessary to record some of the classical instances. There is the interesting case of a girl, who had often been hypnotized by loud noises, who went to a drawer to appropriate some photographs out of it. The casual beating of a gong threw her into a cataleptic state, so that she stood motionless in the act of carrying out her theft and was so discovered (Moll). It is in fact a common way of inducing hypnosis—not only the sudden stimulation of the auditory sense, but also the use of a sudden stimulation of sight, as in using the Drummond light to induce hypnosis.

If any doubt remains as to the hypnosis, that is removed by O'Brien's narration of the whistling episode. Without doubt O'Brien was "the" man in the world for this *latah*; a complete rapport had been established between them, and O'Brien's every action would be imitated by him.

Especially well known in hypnosis are the phenomena of imitative speech and song. Berger says that hypnotics will repeat everything that is said before them like phonographs, even what is said in foreign languages is repeated with some exactness. Braid relates that a hypnotized girl once imitated some of the songs of the famous Jenny Lind perfectly, which she was perfectly incapable of doing in the waking state, and Braid attributes this feat to the delicacy of hearing and of the muscular sense in hypnosis.

I have practically finished with this subject, but I feel that some explanation of the condition of intense nervousness into which a *latah* is thrown by the hypnotizer is required.

Its cause is threefold. There is first the nervousness induced by repeated hypnoses, especially when suggestions of an exciting nature have been made. Secondly, by the hypnosis having been induced against their will. Thirdly, by the suggestion never having been terminated or done away with before waking the subject. All these tend to augment and perpetuate the susceptibility, until any person or even any thing may put in action or direct the acts of a *latah*.

CRITICISM

by Henry N. Ridley

In writing this criticism of the Essayist's thoughtful and suggestive paper, I, like himself, must plead want of time to do full justice to it. The paper was put into my hands less than a week ago, so that, from one cause and another, I have had but one or two evenings to devote to it, and I have consequently not had any opportunity of referring to certain literature which I should have liked to do. Excellent as the paper is, I could have wished to have heard accounts of cases other than those in the classical essay of O'Brien, from which the Essayist has drawn most of his facts. In a subject of this nature one can hardly have too many examples to illustrate it, and one might be tempted to imagine that the deductions would have been improved had a large series of cases been studied and described. The definition of *latah* in the Lexicon quoted, full of blunders as it is, serves to show how very little is generally known of the phenomenon, and how important it is, therefore, that further facts should be collected.

Latah, as described in the essay, certainly covers a very wide area. The Essayist mentions three classes. The first and last, what one may call imitative *latah*, have something in common; the second, a therophobic one, has, it seems to me, as little to do with the other two as any two psychic phenomena can possibly have. In fact, the word as it is defined in the essay covers nearly all the peculiar nervous disorders of the Malays.

The imitative *latah* is the most peculiarly Malayan phenomenon. Its great interest lies in the close resemblance to certain hypnotic states, and many cases would pass as ordinary hypnosis, were it not that the attack commences without any passes or other methods of inducing the hypnotic sleep, and also that the patient is quite conscious of the absurdity of his actions.

I do not say that were we to prove that this *latah* was hypnosis or modified hypnosis we should know much more about it. We know as yet so little about the causes and physiology of hypnosis that all we should have done would be to have classified the phenomenon, so as to be able to study it along with hypnosis.

The ordinary methods of hypnotizing are probably well known to all here. The subject is induced to enter a peculiar stage intermediate between sleeping and waking, in which suggestions, however absurd, are readily adopted. In *latah* cases the subject apparently needs no preparation, the suggestion producing of itself an instantaneous effect. The inhibitory action which would naturally prevent the suggestion from being carried out is in abeyance immediately.

I have seen one hypnotic phenomenon which to some extent resembles certain of these *latah* cases. A boy had been hypnotized by a man we will call A, and another, B, made a few hypnotic passes over him before he was aroused from the hypnotic sleep. He was then aroused, and found to be in a state of what would undoubtedly be classed as *latah* by a Malay. He exactly imitated every action of A, however absurd, only exaggerating it, as in the case of O'Brien's respectable lady. How far he was conscious of what he was really doing is obscure, but he never remonstrated or made any objection, nor attempted to stop it.

The fact that a *latah* person can sometimes refuse to accept the suggestion—that is to say, can of his own will put the inhibitory mechanism of his nervous system into action—would suggest that in other cases the mere suddenness of an unexpected action or noise acts quite as strongly on him as the longer hypnotic passes or other processes by which a subject is hypnotized, and puts the inhibitory mechanism out of gear at once.

It is rather remarkable that *latah* symptoms do not ever seem to occur in lunatics. If one assumes as a working hypothesis that there is in the nervous system an inhibitory centre which checks impulsive action on suggestion, it is rather remarkable that this inhibitory centre does not sometimes fail to work in cases of nervous disease. And in studying the phenomenon from this point of view, a merely tentative one, I regret that the Essayist did not give us the benefit of the bias of his profession, which, by copying O'Brien's work, he seems to have tried to avoid.

The second class of so-called *latah*, that illustrated by the fear of animals, etc., though sufficiently curious, seems to have parallels in other races. As I have pointed out, it has very little in common with the other phenomenon. There are two points; in this fear of animals which are notable, the violent panic called up by the word and the peculiar action of the crocodile-fearing man who rushes at the animal in spite of his fear of its name. The Essayist compares the whole phenomenon with monomania, but says that in this case the subject has a clear concept of the matter on which he is insane; but the facts related by Mr. O'Brien as to his jumping into the water regardless of crocodiles and rushing at the dead one prove that no memory picture is called up. I should certainly have thought exactly the reverse. To take the first point, the panic at the name "*buaya*" or "*rimau*": it is inconceivable that the mere letters would produce this; e.g., a *rimau*-fearing individual would not be panic-stricken if you said "*limau*" or "remove", or any similar word. Unless he thought you said "tiger" he would surely not be alarmed. This seems to me to be endorsed by the statement that it is boatmen who are afraid of the crocodile, jungle men who are scared at the tiger—the animals they are most likely to come in contact with.

The Malay is certainly often exceedingly nervous about certain things, the touch or approach of which makes him shudder all over. On one occasion I had a caterpillar of a Death's-head moth on a leaf in my hand, and while walking with Mr. Hervey, of Malacca, we approached his syce. The syce was horrified at the caterpillar and shuddered violently, and was almost hysterical when it was brought near him. He knew the thing was only a caterpillar and quite harmless, but evidently felt somehow it was dreadfully uncanny. Another man I was out with on one occasion suddenly in going through some bushes gave a wild leap to one side and remained shivering as if he had had a severe shock. I thought he had trodden on a poisonous snake, but no, he had merely stepped near some excrement. It took him a considerable time to recover the shock. If men are so horribly scared at such trivial things as these, it is quite conceivable that the idea of the beast which is most likely to kill them in their ordinary pursuits suddenly brought to their minds is very likely to scare them more.

The second point in this phenomenon is the frantic way in which the crocodile-fearer jumped into the water and rushed at the dead crocodile. The first action mentioned is natural enough. A man thoroughly scared simply dashes wildly away. He does not wait to think out whether he is jumping out of the frying-pan into the fire. The idea of crocodile is that it is near him in the boat; he wildly springs out. This kind of thing occurs in all panics. When he rushed at the saurian he illustrated a not unknown phenomenon, even among Europeans. How many people has one met who always declare that if they go up a precipitous height, say a church tower, they always feel inclined to jump over, the dread of falling tempting them to do exactly the thing they dread most. Other cases are the person who can never stand over a deep pool without jumping in; and another class of the same phenomenon is that of the nurse who was very much attached to the child she had charge of, but begged for it to be taken away, as she never saw its bare skin without wanting to stick a knife into it. Her mistress treated this as ridiculous, and she killed the child. I believe other instances of this peculiar nervous state are mentioned in Carpenter's *Mental Physiology*. I should therefore class the second section of the *latah* as monomania, but a more rational form of it, because in most cases of monomania the cause of the scare is either an impossibility or at the least highly improbable.

The "personal equation" of the Malay as described by the Essayist calls for some criticism. It is true that in many respects he is very dreamy and sensitive. (One would scarcely say, however, he was keen to appreciate humour. I think he is the least so by far of any race I have ever met, and this has been remarked by many others.) He lives in a world peopled not only by dangerous wild beasts, but by even worse dream figures, demons, which he usually meets with in his dreams at night, and which are as real to him as the tigers and snakes. And this seems to me to be the only nervous peculiarity of the race, if, indeed, it is confined to the race. And this makes it all the more remarkable that the two subjects proposed for the paper, *latah* and *amok*, are almost absolutely peculiar to this race. It is true that there are imitations of both phenomena in races thrown in contact with them, and *amok*-like phenomena do occur in even more distant races, but otherwise these phenomena are confined to Malays. Furthermore,—but this wants more careful testing than I can give it,—it seems that both *latah* and *amok* are disappearing.

I have been told by Malays that to find *latah* one must go up country; there are not any in the towns. This suggests, as does the difficulty nowadays of finding *latahs*, that contact with a higher civilization, and the spread of education, is killing it out, which indeed is what one might expect.

At present our knowledge of psychics is really small, and of its relationship to the structure of the nervous system we know almost nothing, and any contribution to the study of so intricate a subject like that of the Essayist is therefore highly welcome.

Note

1. For contemporaneous accounts of *latah* see, W. Gilmore Ellis, "Latah: A Mental Malady of the Malays", *Journal of Mental Science* 43, no. 180 (January 1897): 32–40; Swettenham, *Malay Sketches*, Chapter IX; H.A. O'Brien, "Latah", *Journal of the Straits Branch of the Royal Asiatic Society* 11 (1883): 143–53.

23

CHRISTIANITY AND MOHAMMEDANISM

Essay

12 February 1895
by *Rev. G.M. Reith*

Editors' Note

Discussions of religion in the Society were driven by the missionaries and religious ministers who held membership. One such figure was G.M. Reith, a Presbyterian minister, who left Singapore in 1896.[1] Reith—a representative of a more liberal tendency in the church—would reflect in his 1895 essay on two contemporary discussions in missionary circles in the 1890s. The first was the relationship between Christianity and Islam, and the second was the role of proselytization in the colony. Reith's liberalism was evident in the way in which his understanding of religion was couched in Darwinian terminology and defined by man's struggle against his environment. His identification of religious belief with the category of race allowed him to trace the monotheisms of the Middle East to a shared racial heritage, differentiated only by the "*aber-glaube*" (extra-beliefs) which had developed at a later stage. This argument allowed for Reith to disassociate himself from the hostility towards Islam amongst members of the missionary community.[2] By moving beyond the *"aber-glaube"* he proposed that a dialogue could take place between Christianity and Islam that did not have as its end the ideas of religious supremacy or salvation, but a shared liberal idea of progress.

A similar liberal tendency also informed Reith's views on proselytization of the Muslims of the colony. Opposing the missionary focus upon conversion, Reith argued that the focus of missionaries should be on building up a critical intellectual spirit amongst the Malays. This could mirror the critical re-adjustment which had occurred in Christianity. Increasing the spirit of inquiry could help Muslims uncover the "vital principle of faith which is common to the three great religions of the world". Reith's piece nevertheless generated heated debate in the pages of *The Free Press*, with supporters in *The Free Press* defending his position. Dissatisfaction from his congregation and missionaries eventually saw Reith being dismissed from his post.[3]

Let me first define the scope and limits of this essay, the title of which suggests a subject of apparently unlimited extent.

In the first place, it is my intention, in comparing these two great faiths, to deal almost exclusively with their primitive forms, to compare them as they came from the minds of their respective founders; for it hardly needs to be said that the form, and perhaps also the spirit, of both systems have undergone a very great change in the course of time—more so in the case of Christianity than in the case of Mohammedanism, its junior by seven centuries.

In the second place, it shall be my endeavour to describe the forces at work in the origin and development of both systems. Thus, the object of the essay being to present not so much history as a philosophy of history, I shall avoid crowding it with details, as far as possible.

Religion in general may be defined as man's philosophy of his struggle with his environment. As his conception of the nature of his environment varies, so will his religion. No inquiry need here be made into the ultimate origin of the religious sense in man, and of its particular manifestations. It may have sprung, as some assert, from a primeval phallic worship; or, according to others, from a more general nature worship; or from the veneration of tribal ancestors; or perhaps, as I am inclined to think, from an unconscious combination of all three. But the solution of this problem is foreign to our purpose, because, by the time that the great historical religions took a step in advance of contemporary heathenism, heathenism itself had completely forgotten its primeval origin; had various crude, fanciful, and mythical ways of explaining its own growth; and certainly did not worship the phallus, nature, or the ancestor as such, but as the manifestation of hidden and mysterious powers behind them. I would say in passing, however, that the theory which refers all religious phenomena to solar, sidereal, and zodiacal myths, once much in vogue, will soon be given up by all rational men. Ernest de Bunsen, for example, thinks he can account for the rise of Judaism, Zoroastrianism, Christianity, and Mohammedanism by the constellations of the Virgin and the Serpent. But this system of astrological mythology applied to the sacred books of the East is as futile as would be the attempt to reduce these books to a series of mystical chess problems, as futile as Donelly's attempt to read a great cryptogram into Shakespeare's plays. Such a theory implies more ingenuity in the mind of primeval man than in the mind of the modern wiseacre who finds him out.

The three religions that have most powerfully influenced the thought and destiny of man, Judaism, Christianity, and Mohammedanism, have a common ancestry, and a strong family likeness. They have sprung from one race, and it might almost be said that they speak one language. They are fundamentally one; their differences are due to the *aber-glaube* (or extra-belief) which has grown like moss and lichen on all three, and it may be confidently predicted that when, by the combined force of civilization, education, and culture, these extra-beliefs are swept away, the Christian, the Jew, and the Muslim will begin to wonder why, being so fundamentally agreed, they have permitted superficial differences to separate them so long, and to work so much hostility between them.

The area in which this trinity of religions arose is a strip of fertile country that skirts the Syro-Arabian Desert; the two *foci* or *nuclei*, Jerusalem and Mecca, being hardly 800 miles apart. Into those regions, in prehistoric times, there poured wave after wave of Shemitic tribes, the cradle of whose race was probably in Bactria, dispossessing the aborigines, whom we know in some cases to have been troglodytes or cave-dwellers (called Horites in Genesis). These tribes, entering the southern land at various periods, were at first pastoral and nomadic, but, in time most of them became settled, agricultural, and, on the coast, mercantile. Though of the same blood for the most part, the tribes were independent of and generally hostile to one another; an embryonic national sentiment appeared from time to time in the settled districts (invariably produced by danger from the neighbouring tribes), but even in the case of western Palestine, where that sentiment was strongest, we notice also well-marked lines of cleavage between the tribes—so much so that the kingdom of Solomon could not hold together after his death. In Arabia, the want of cohesion amongst the tribes was, and is, even more striking. Mohammed created a temporary national and religious sentiment, which raised Arabia to the first rank amongst the world powers of the ninth century; but the want of tribal cohesion has again made itself apparent, and if it were not for that, the decrepit government of the Turk could not hold Arabia for another twenty-four hours.

And as all these tribes were of one race (or nearly so), we may take it for granted that their religion was of one type; and indeed investigation shows that it was so. The idolatrous practices at Mecca which Mohammed attacked bore a striking resemblance to those which the prophets of Israel denounced in the name of Jehovah. In fact, when Mohammed borrows from those prophets—which some urge against him as a reproach, as if he were a dishonest plagiarist—he does so because their words were exactly suited to the circumstances of his own time. In the words of the late Professor W. Robertson Smith, whose premature and lamented death is the greatest loss British scholarship has suffered in this half-century:

> The whole history of Israel is unintelligible if we suppose that the heathenism against which the Prophets contended was a thing altogether alien to the religious traditions of the Hebrews. In principle there was all the difference in the world between the faith of Isaiah and that of an

idolater. But the difference in principle, which seems so clear to us, was not clear to the average Judean, and the reason of this was that it was obscured by the great similarity in many important points of religious tradition and ritual practice (W.R. Smith, "Religion of the Semites", p. 4).

Though the Shemitic religions were of one type, the variations within the limits of the type were considerable, for many reasons, but the general characteristics of these can be described in a few sentences.

1. First of all they were polytheistic, with a marked tendency to become monolatrous, and ultimately monotheistic. Monolatry, as distinguished from monotheism, is the exclusive worship of one god out of many. Amongst the settled tribes, the deity thus exclusively worshipped was the tribal god, while amongst the nomadic tribes a number of gods were acknowledged, but special veneration was paid to the mysterious desert divinity, called El by the ancient Hebrews, who is unquestionably the religious ancestor of the Mohammedan Allah.

2. Another characteristic of the Shemitic religions was the universal practice of circumcision, "which was originally a preliminary to marriage, and so a ceremony of introduction to the full prerogative of manhood", and gradually acquired religious significance. The Hebrew account of its institution in the time of Abraham, as a special mark of the Jehovah-worshipper, is to be taken, like all such accounts, as fanciful and entirely unhistorical.

3. Sacrifice, both human and animal, was a characteristic of Shemitic religions. In Arabia, human sacrifice continued till the dawn of Islam. It is recorded that Abdul-Muttalib, Mohammed's grandfather, was on the point of sacrificing his son, Abdullah, the prophet's father, but consulting the oracle at the Kaaba he was informed that the gods were graciously pleased to accept a hundred camels instead. The price of blood, money or *wehrgeld*, was thenceforth fixed at 100 camels. The barbarous practice of killing female infants (usually by burying them alive) widely prevailed, the cause of which no doubt was that, while male children grew up to be fighters, women were an encumbrance in war and wandering. The custom continued in Arabia till Mohammed put it down with a strong hand.

4. One last characteristic was a superstitious belief in the sanctity of special places, trees, stones, and wells, where gods were supposed to reside and to give oracles; but in regard to these it should be remembered that such superstitions flourished amongst the settled tribes rather than amongst the nomads, and that the veneration they paid to the sacred spots was, in very many cases, an inheritance from the races they had dispossessed. All of those sanctuaries are *foci* of Christianity and Mohammedanism, the two chief being Jerusalem and Mecca, where the original objects of worship were sacred stones, supposed to be meteoric. Solomon built a temple over the sacred stone on Mount Moriah; it is now in the hands of the Mohammedan, and is deposited under the dome of the Mosque of Omar. Abraham and Ishmael, according to Arabian tradition, built the Kaaba over the sacred stone at Mecca. Both sanctuaries became kiblahs—that is to say, points towards which the faithful turned in prayer. (Mohammed at first, to please the Jews, made Jerusalem his kiblah. The hostility of the Jews moved him to revert to the ancient Arabian kiblah, Mecca.) Round these and other sanctuaries established amongst the settled tribes there grew up a pantheon, a priesthood, and a ritual, which varied with the different tribes, and yet, rising naturally out of traditional beliefs and customs, were not so diversified as to obscure the fact of their common origin and their close relationship.

A comparison of Christianity and Mohammedanism without a reference to the history of Judaism is impossible. Christianity has been very appropriately described as universalized Judaism; Mohammedanism may be described in very much the same terms, though it was not, like Christianity, an offshoot of Judaism. The necessity, then, of a brief survey of the development of Judaism is apparent.

The earliest reliable traditions we possess about the religious history of Israel are contained in the Book of Judges. There is no tribal cohesion; there is no unity of worship; there is no recognized priesthood, no central sanctuary. Every man did that which was right in his own eyes; every tribe was a law to itself, and a terror to its neighbours. Frequent incursions of the trans-Jordanic tribes on the east, and the encroachments of the Philistines, a race which had settled on the coast for commercial purposes chiefly, aided in the development of a national sentiment in Israel to the extent of forcing into existence a strong and united monarchy for a short time (less than a century probably), but when the Philistines were finally crushed and the eastern tribes taught to respect the armies of Israel, the monarchy fell to pieces again; old lines of cleavage between the tribes became visible again, and ultimately the divided tribes fell an easy prey to the Assyrians and the Chaldeans. The return of the Jews from the Babylonian exile was by no means a national return; as Professor Wellhausen says, they went into exile a nation, and returned a religious sect. (Wellhausen: "Prolegomena to the History of Israel.")

It may be said that the Jews had no national sentiment till they had ceased to be a nation. Such is a brief outline of Jewish political history till the restoration under Cyrus. Their religious history is not unlike it. There was neither unity nor cohesion in their religion; there was no attempt to secure it, till the eighth century BC, after the fall of Samaria (722 BC).

Jehovah-worship had waged a successful war against the seductive and licentious Baal-worship of the Phoenicians in the days of Elijah, but the Jehovah-worship of the Israelites before the exile was not in any sense the worship that was established in the second temple, and flourished in the days of Christ. Israel—orthodox Israel—was monolatrous till the exile, but idolatrous also. Jehovah was worshipped as the national god; he had many sanctuaries all over the land; his image was a bullock, and round it stood Baalim and Asheroth; there was a sporadic and unorganized priesthood throughout the country, there was no stereotyped ritual. With the fall of Samaria came the opportunity of the Jerusalem priesthood, by that time a large, well-organized, and powerful body. They demanded a suppression of all provincial sanctuaries, and the subordination of the local priests and Levites to the Jerusalem hierarchy. They secured royal cooperation in most cases, and their endeavour after religious unity and centralization was in the main successful, though not wholly so. The people's affections could not be weaned from the ancient sanctuaries in a short time. Then came the fall of Jerusalem, and the seventy years' captivity, at the end of which time there returned to Jerusalem a religious sect, with a cut-and-dry ritual, an organized hierarchy, anti-idolatrous, and, as the custodians of the traditions of a past golden age, fanatically patriotic. There were now no difficulties in the way of a centralized worship, beyond the refusal of the Samaritans, whose kiblah was Mount Gerizim, to acknowledge the superior sanctity of Jerusalem; no difficulties in the way of a stereotyped ritual, claiming both a divine origin and the sanction of antiquity; there was now no provincial priesthood, except the Samaritan, to dispute the claims of the Jerusalem hierarchy; the ancient sanctuaries were well-nigh deserted, or frequented by those in whom the returned Jews recognized no kinship.

I have left unmentioned till now one of the most peculiar characteristics of the Jehovah-religion—the influence of the Prophets. Those that have left traces of their activity in the Old Testament appear invariably as critics of existing religious ideas and practices. At first they are seen to be simply monolatrous, protesting against the worship of foreign deities. In preference to Jehovah. They stood between the people and the licentious cult of Baal and Astarte, for example, and their influence is traceable in the puritan character of the Jewish race. Then they became anti-idolatrous, and condemned image-worship and its accompaniments. Then they became monotheistic, anti-sacerdotal, and the champions of a purely spiritual religion. The last of the Old Testament prophets, Malachi, is vehemently anti-sacerdotal, but through-out the prophetic development, from first to last, the idea that what Jehovah required of his people was righteousness was kept well to the front. In short, the prophetic religion is summed up in the well-known words of Micah: "What doth Jehovah require of thee, but to do justly, and to love mercy, and to walk humbly with thy God?" (Micah VI. 8.)

I ask your special attention to this, for reasons that will appear in the sequel.

The opposition between the prophetic and sacerdotal religions was forgotten long before the birth of Christ. The opposing elements were woven together into a wide and highly-coloured fabric of tradition, but, though an external unity was preserved, there was an underlying diversity of opinion and practice, and apparently the life of the old religion had been smothered. But it was not dead; only sleeping. John the Baptist revived the prophetic office in its crudest form, Jesus of Nazareth followed him with methods sounder and more refined. They renewed the prophetic struggle against tradition and sacerdotalism, with what tragic results to themselves we all know. The dream of Jesus was a catholic Judaism, stripped of the frivolities of tradition and the inanities of ritual—in fact, his aim was to universalize the prophetic religion. The basis of that religion was the inwardness and sincerity described by Micah in the words already quoted. It was a religion not for the Jews only, but for all mankind. The Father in Heaven needed no ceremonial worship; the kiblah of the true worshipper was to be neither Jerusalem nor Mount Gerizim, but his own heart. Jesus founded no church, instituted no ceremonies, laid down no rules for worship, ordained no priests, created no theology beyond what is implied in the Fatherhood of God and the Brotherhood of Man. He simply unveiled true religion to his followers. Of course Christianity has undergone many changes since then. St. Paul caught the catholic idea in Christ's teaching, but added Rabbinical subtleties of his own, which Church Fathers and theologians have used to make confusing worse confounded; Buddhist ideas, filtering their way from the East through Gnosticism,—such ideas as Trinity and Incarnation, for example,—influenced Church Councils in the formulation of their dogmas; sacerdotalism of a half-pagan half-Jewish complexion crept in again, so that the Christianity of three-fourths of Christendom today is merely a civilized paganism.

Now let us turn to Mohammed. What has been said will enable us to travel more rapidly over the ground that is still to be covered. He accomplished in his own person for religion in Arabia what all the prophets from Elijah to Jesus of Nazareth accomplished for Judaism; but the way was prepared for Mohammed by the fact that both Judaism and Christianity had penetrated into Arabia before his time, had made not a few converts amongst the tribes, and were in other ways exerting an influence on the popular mind that tended to the disintegration of the ancient paganism of the country. Without the unconscious assistance of these forces, Mohammed could not have broken down the idolatry of Mecca. I shall not weary you with many details of the Arabian prophet's life; its principal events are no doubt familiar to us all. He belonged to the famous tribe of the Kuraish, which at the time of his birth (AD 570) held the government of Mecca and the custody of the sanctuary there. His grandfather, Abdul-Muttalib, "enjoyed rank and consideration as the foremost chief of Mecca" (Sir W. Muir, "Life of Mohammed,"

p. 4). The first five years of his life were spent with the Bani Sad, a tribe of Bedouins. He was a delicate child; signs of epilepsy showed themselves early, "but in other respects", as Sir William Muir says, his constitution was rendered robust and his character free and independent by those five years with the Bani Sad. At any rate, his speech was thus formed after one of the purest models of the beautiful language of the Peninsula, and it was his pride in after days to say: "Verily I am the most perfect Arab amongst you; my descent is from the Kuraish and my tongue is the tongue of the Bani Sad." (Sir W. Muir, "Life of Mohammed", p. 7)

The religious influences that surrounded Mohammed were, on the one hand, the idolatrous worship of the Kaaba, and, on the other hand, echoes from the Jewish and Christian faiths. These, however they came to him,—there are many traditions on the subject,—must have profoundly influenced him. He made at least two expeditions into Christian Syria, one as a child, and the other as a young man, in charge of a caravan belonging to the rich widow Khadija, who afterwards married him. Every page of the Koran reflects his disgust at the travesty of Christianity he saw in Syria. Side by side with a profound reverence for Jesus of Nazareth, we find an equally profound contempt for the Christians, and a bitter hostility to the men who had prostituted their religion to vain janglings, frivolous theosophic speculation, and half-pagan ritual. Like Celsus, he was impressed with the intellectual levity of the Christians; and not less so with the spiritual dullness of the Jews. Always of a meditative temperament, Mohammed was in the habit of retiring annually to Mount Hira (now called the Mount of Light), where he spent days and nights in prayer and anxious thought. We trace in the earlier chapters of the Koran his intense struggles after light, which were at last rewarded by his discovery of the principles of Islam. Let it be remembered that Islam is in no sense the invention of Mohammed. He did not profess to be the founder of a new religion, he was but the expounder of the true religion. His aim was to seize, and to present in an intelligible form to his countrymen, the religious truth to which the world had never been without a witness, and of which he felt himself to be the heaven-appointed witness for his own time. His mission, as he conceived it, was to carry on the work of the seven great prophets of the past—Adam, Abraham, Ishmael, Isaac, Jacob, Moses, and Jesus. (The influence of both Jewish and Christian tradition, and of Shemitic tradition generally, is traceable in this list of prophets.) The unity of God, the sin of idolatry, the corruption of contemporary Christianity and Judaism, the immortality of the soul, and the apportionment of rewards and punishments for the deeds done in the body, were some of the ideas prominent in his mind, but the foundation of his religious thought was Islam—the reverent and obedient submission to the will of Allah the merciful and compassionate. In other words—"What doth God require of thee, but to do justly, and to love mercy, and to walk humbly with thy God?"

Mohammed was in his fortieth year when the thoughts with which he was to inspire the world took definite shape in his mind. He was an illiterate man, could neither read nor write, but he had the soul of a poet and the persuasive tongue of the orator. At first he sought no converts beyond his own household; but as years rolled on, the sense of his destiny to preach a universal faith deepened in him, and he came forth publicly as the Apostle of Allah. Then his troubles began. He made many converts, and more enemies; for the Kuraish, seeing their vested interests threatened by his successes, instituted a violent persecution of the faithful. They could not listen to teaching which was equivalent, they said, to calling "their gods idols, and their ancestors fools". A large body of the Prophet's followers fled to Abyssinia by his advice. To add to his troubles, Khadija, his dearly-loved wife and first convert, died, and he was reduced to extreme poverty. The persecution in Mecca became so fierce that, notwithstanding the protection of his uncle Abu-Talib, he was obliged to fly for safety to Yathrel, which ever afterwards bore the name of Medina-un-nabi (the city of the Prophet), or, more shortly, Medina. This was the Hijra or Flight, the Year One of the Mohammedan era (AD 622). In this safe retreat, Mohammed executed the offices of a prophet and of a king. The purely religious period of his life was over, and the administrative and military period opened. His first achievements in Medina were the organization of the new religion, and the establishment of a sound municipal government. At first he conciliated and received help from the Jews, but it is one of the characteristics of that singular people to make trouble wherever they settle, and Mohammed suffered much from their hostility and treachery in the end. Then began a war with the Kuraish—nominally a war against the enemies of Islam, really an attempted revenge on the Kuraish, and an evidence of Mohammed's desire to get back to Mecca, and to carry out his reforms in the very sanctuary of Arabia itself. This he accomplished, after a series of battles in which victory inclined now to one side and now to another. He entered Mecca in the year AD 630, and purged the temple of idolatry. "Sorrowfully the idolaters stood around", writes a Mohammedan historian, "and watched the downfall of the images they worshipped. And then dawned upon them the truth, when they heard the old voice at which they were wont to scoff and jeer, crying, as he struck down the idols, 'Truth is come and falsehood vanisheth, verily falsehood is evanescent'." (Syed Ameer AH, "Spirit of Islam", p. 193.) Mohammed soon received the submission of all Arabia, and did on the larger scale for the country what he had done on a smaller scale in Medina. Previous to his capture of Mecca, he had conceived the idea of a universal theocratic empire, with himself and his successors as Allah's viceregents. He wrote to the Roman Emperor, Heraclius, to the Kings of Persia and Abyssinia, the Viceroy of Egypt and others, demanding their submission to the true faith. How very nearly Mohammed's idea was fulfilled, within less than a century after the Hijra, is well known. Mohammed died at Medina in the year 632, amid public distress and mourning that have perhaps no parallel in history. Omar, one of his fathers-in-law, and afterwards third Khalif, would not be persuaded that he was dead, and endeavoured to make the people disbelieve the evidence of their senses, and believe him still alive. Abu-bekr, another father-in-law of the Prophet, and first Khalif, was more rational in his grief, and addressed the people in these memorable words: "Whoever among you has served Mohammed, let him know that Mohammed is dead; but he who has served the God of Mohammed, let him continue in His service, for He is still alive, and never dies."

The character of the Prophet has been variously estimated, but the old idea, once much in vogue in Christendom, that he was an impostor, a deceiver, a false prophet, an agent of Satan, has disappeared from the minds of all rational men. The Christian world now takes a juster view of the noble work Mohammed did for humanity, and recognizes that he is in no way responsible for the objectionable features of the religion called by his name. Perhaps the best-known estimate of Mohammed's character and work is that of Thomas Carlyle. But it is an idealization, and is as unlike the real Mohammed as Raphael's Madonna is unlike the real Virgin Mary. Both are beautiful; both command our admiration; but they are idealizations, not history. I quote a Christian critic's estimate of his character, and a Mohammedan's estimate of his work. "A man of Mohammed's extraordinary powers and gifts", says Emmanuel Deutsch, "is not to be judged by a modern commonplace standard; the manners and morals of his own time must also be taken into consideration. He was at times deceitful, cunning, revengeful, cowardly, addicted to sensuality and even a murderer" (I may say, I think this somewhat overdrawn); "yet not only his public station as prophet, preacher, and prince, but also his private character, his amiability, his faithfulness towards friends, his tenderness towards his family, and the frequent readiness to forgive an enemy must be taken into consideration, besides the extreme simplicity of his domestic life; he lived, when already in full power, in a miserable hut, mended his own clothes, and freed all his slaves. And, to do him full justice, his melancholic temperament, his nervousness, which often bordered on frenzy and brought him to the brink of suicide, and his poetic temperament must not be forgotten. Altogether his mind contained the strangest mixture of right and wrong, of truth and error... Take him all in all, the history of humanity has seen few more earnest, noble, and sincere 'prophet', men irresistibly impelled by an inner power to admonish and to teach, and to utter austere and sublime truths, the full purport of which is often unknown to themselves."

"His life", says Syed Ameer Ali, "is the noblest record of a work nobly and faithfully performed. He infused vitality into a dormant people; he consolidated a congeries of warring tribes into a nation inspired into action by the hope of everlasting life; he concentrated into a focus all the fragmentary and broken lights which had ever fallen on the heart of man. Such was his work, and he performed it with an enthusiasm and fervour which admitted no compromise, conceived no halting, allowed no fear of consequences; with a singleness of purpose which thought of no self. The religion of divine unity preached on the shores of Galilee had given place to the worship of an incarnate God; the old worship of a female deity had revived among those who professed the creed of the Master of Nazareth. The Recluse of Hira, the unlettered philosopher,—born among a nation of unyielding idolaters,—impressed ineffaceably the unity of God and the equality of men upon the minds of the nations who once heard his voice. His 'democratic thunder' was the signal for the uprise of the human intellect against the tyranny of priests and rulers. In that world of wrangling creeds and oppressive institutions, when the human soul was crushed under the weight of unintelligible dogmas and the human body trampled under the tyranny of vested interests, he broke down the barriers of caste and exclusive privileges. He swept away with his breath the cobwebs which self-interest had woven in the path of man to God" (Syed Ameer Ali: "Spirit of Islam", p. 212). These two views present a very different character of the Prophet than that which once held the mind of Christendom, that he was a combination of the religious charlatan and the political adventurer.

With the subsequent development of Islam this essay has no concern. The interference of ancient fathers, theologians, and tradition-mongers with its primitive simplicity has distorted and caricatured it, as a similar process has done for Christianity. Side by side with the Koran and of equal authority with it is the Sunna, "a mass of traditions and oral laws" collected and sanctioned as authoritative about the 200th year after the Hijra. The Sunnites accept the whole of it, while the Shiites, who do not recognize the legitimacy of the first three Khalifs, Abu Bekr, Omar, and Othman, reject everything connected with these three men. According to the Shiites, the first Khalif de-jure (though the fourth de-facto) was Ali, son of Abu Talib. Ali was thus the prophet's first cousin, and married his daughter Fatima.

Islam is divided into two parts—Iman, or Belief, and Din, or Practice, which includes prayer, almsgiving, fasting, and pilgrimage. Even Mohammed's extraordinary influence could not have broken the Arabs from their immemorial custom of pilgrimage to Mecca, and he very wisely did not attempt it, but turned the pagan survival into a solemn religious duty. Many other heathen practices were preserved for the same reason.

The place assigned to Jesus of Nazareth by primitive Mohammedanism is worthy of remark. I have said Mohammed's veneration for Christ was profound. He calls him the Messiah, the Spirit of God, while he calls himself merely the Apostle or Prophet of God. He did not believe the doctrine of the Trinity and the Incarnation, and the other theological subtleties of the Western Church, but neither did the Eastern Church of his time—that part, at least, with which he came most in contact. He seems to have contemplated an ultimate union between Christianity and Mohammedanism. He prophesied the second advent of Jesus, which was to be preceded by the appearance of another prophet or Mahdi, and of the Mohammedan Antichrist Dejjal, who was to be slain by Jesus at Lud. He foretold that the return of Christ would secure a world-wide adoption of Islam. Islam must not be taken as exactly synonymous with Mohammedanism; the word as used by the Prophet means the essence of the teaching of all the Apostles of God in the past, and therefore the teaching of Jesus as well as his own. Observe that Mohammed did not dream of his own return to complete his work or to witness his final triumph. The place of honour he assigned to Christ in his prophecy of the last days shows that he regarded himself not as a rival, but merely as a successor of Christ, and the introducer of Islam to his countrymen.

The popular Christian objections to Mohammedanism are chiefly four. It is alleged, first, that Islam encourages slavery; secondly, that it countenances polygamy, and keeps women in a degraded position; thirdly, that it is a religion that relies on the sword, intolerant and cruel; and fourthly, that in its highest teachings it contains nothing that is not either explicit or implicit in Christianity, and is therefore unnecessary. A few words of comment on these objections.

1. And first, I strongly doubt whether primitive Mohammedanism encouraged slavery. Both by precept and by example the Prophet encouraged the manumission of slaves. By embracing Islam a slave became the religious and civil, if not quite the social, equal of his master. The Koran lays down many excellent rules for mitigating the severity of servitude. Mohammed found the institution in existence, an integral part of the social framework, such as it was, and, as Syed Ameer Ali says, "It is abundantly clear that the legislator himself looked upon the custom as temporary in its nature, and held that its extinction was sure

to be achieved by the progress of ideas and change of circumstances." (Syed Ameer Ali: "Spirit of Islam", p. 376.)

We cannot forget that Christendom has only lately blotted the last traces of slavery out of its statute books.

2. Polygamy also was an institution before Mohammed's time—a very ancient and very widespread social arrangement. Before Mohammed's time polygamy had become almost promiscuity, and the position of a woman was that of a slave. The Prophet restricted polygamy, by allowing a man to have no more than four wives, and by putting an end to temporary and conditional unions. As for the status of women, far from having suffered by the introduction of Islam, their condition was greatly ameliorated by it. Mohammed placed women "on a footing of perfect equality with men in the exercise of all legal powers and functions" (Syed Ameer Ali: op. cit, p. 326). There was a Married Women's Property Act in all Mohammedan countries twelve centuries before Christian England did that justice to women.

3. Carlyle, in his well-known essay, has effectually disposed of the objection against Mohammedanism on the ground of its being a religion of the sword; "If we take this", he says, "for an argument of the truth or falsehood of a religion, there is a radical mistake in it. The sword indeed; but where will you get your sword? Every new opinion, at its starting, is precisely in a minority of one. ... On the whole", he continues, "a thing will propagate itself as it can. We do not find of the Christian religion, either, that it always disdained the sword when it had got one. Charlemagne's conversion of the Saxons was not by preaching. I care little about the sword; I will allow a thing to struggle for itself in this world with any sword or tongue or implement it has, or can lay hold of. We will let it preach and pamphleteer and fight, and to the uttermost bestir itself, and do, beak and claws, whatsoever is in it; very sure that it will in the long-run conquer nothing which does not deserve to be conquered. What is better than itself cannot be put away, but only what is worse" ("Heroes and Hero-worship"). In regard to the intolerant cruelty alleged against Mohammedanism, we must bear in mind that Islam cannot be held responsible for the excesses of its representatives. The policy of the early Mohammedans towards conquered peoples was to offer them Islam first of all. If they accepted it, they

received full rights and privileges as citizens, and were put on a footing of perfect equality with their conquerors. The *Kitabi*—or men of the book-religions, Zoroastrians, Jews, and Christians—received protection, and were allowed to practise their religion unmolested on payment of a small tax, but they did not receive full rights of citizenship with the faithful. It was only against idolaters that the Prophet's first followers pursued a course of remorseless hostility.

4. It is perfectly true that there is nothing original in Mohammedanism, but it must be remembered that Islam did not claim to be new. It is perfectly true that there is nothing good in Mohammedanism which is not either explicit or implicit in Christianity, but that is not the real point. The question is, was there any means of communicating the sublime and elevating truths of Islam (using the word in its widest sense) to the people of Arabia without producing it in a new form? The Islam of Judaism and Christianity was smothered, buried under a heap of foolish traditions and more foolish ritual. The light of both was obscured by the dust raised by angry controversialists. Islam had to be re-discovered and represented to men; and that was the achievement of Mohammed.

To my mind the chief weakness of Mohammedanism is its unexpansiveness. It has left itself no scope for a healthy development; it is weighted down, as Christianity would have been had it not been for St. Paul, by the practice of circumcision and the pilgrimage obligation. The Mohammedan view of the founder of our religion is that Jesus was a dreamer, while Mohammed was a practical man, who worked into a system what Jesus had only vaguely given to the world as ideas. But it is precisely that reduction of the ideal to a detailed and stereotyped system that was the reason of the immediate successes of Mohammedanism, and also the reason of its future impotence. It did not allow for growth and changed conditions.

A great part of the Koran and the Sunna is occupied with what I may call a negative criticism of Christianity. The Mohammedans have been all along more eager to build defences against Christianity and so-called Christian doctrine than to seek common ground; and the Christians have been equally zealous in returning the compliment. This has done good; it has saved Mohammedanism from several extravagances and follies into which Christianity has fallen, and of which Mussulman writers do not fail to remind us. Mohammed, for one thing, would long ago have been deified by his followers, had it not been for this negative criticism of Christianity which pervades Moslem teaching, and one of whose strongest points is the blasphemy of making Jesus equal with God, and raising his mother to heaven under the title of the Mother of God.

What is wanted, both for Christianity and Mohammedanism, is the rise of a sound historical criticism, for once again the world is in need of the rediscovery of Islam. Our age has seen the beginning of a critical re-adjustment in regard to Christianity; its results are rapidly filtering their way into the popular mind, though there is still much to be accomplished. We must look for, and where possible assist in, the wakening of the critical spirit amongst the Mohammedans themselves.

No Christian can fairly criticize and estimate Mohammed's work and influence. I conceive that the duty of the Christian missionary in Mohammedan countries is not so much to substitute Christianity for Mohammedanism, and not at all to denounce Mohammed as a false prophet, but to rouse a spirit of inquiry and to instil the principles of true criticism, in order that the Mohammedans themselves may be enabled to rediscover Islam—the vital principle of faith which is common to the three great religions of the world.

Notes

1. "The Rev G.M. Reith", *The Singapore Free Press and Mercantile Advertiser*, 3 March 1896.
2. Robert Hunt, "Interreligious Conflict and Compromise in Late 19th and Early 20th Century Singapore", *Sejarah: Journal of the Department of History* 4, no. 4 (1996).
3. Ibid., p. 71.

24

OUR DUTY TO THE MALAYS

President's Introductory Address

13 April 1901

by *C.W.S. Kynnersley*

Editors' Note

Administrative discussions around British obligations to protect and uplift the Malays were important themes throughout the essays of the Society. This would contribute towards a discourse and, more importantly, a doctrine of protection which would become enshrined in post-colonial policies of race and immigration as well as in the formation of an independent Malaya. This discourse was evident in C.W.S. Kynnersley's essay in 1901. Kynnersley was a British colonial administrator who joined the Straits Settlements civil service in 1872 and in 1901 was serving as the acting Colonial Secretary of the Straits Settlements. Kynnersley's essay, like broader colonial discourses, emphasized the underdevelopment of the Malays, as well as the failure of British policy to protect and uplift them through education and development. This reinforced, for Kynnersley, his concern in a British obligation to modernize and reform the Malays. Highlighting those states where the Malays had remained in the majority, he noted their ability under British guidance to govern themselves and develop their states. For this to be achieved, he argued for British policy to create the conditions for their growth. Central to this was a need to make provision for Malays in the civil service and to limit the employment of immigrant communities. Debates over the issues he raised continued to be significant in the Straits Settlements and Malay States for a long time after Kynnersley's essay.[1]

Being called on this evening to deliver an Introductory Address, I must in the first place crave the indulgence of members of this Society. I am aware that in past years the Society has enjoyed the privilege of listening to addresses from those who have so worthily filled the office of President. When at our last meeting I expressed the regret which we all felt at the departure of our learned and genial President, who was deeply interested in the work of the Society, I was fully sensible of the honour you were doing to me in asking me to act in his place. It is, I think, wisely provided in our Rules that the papers to be read are not confined to subjects which can properly be called Philosophical. A glance at our syllabus will show what a diversity of subjects are proposed for discussion. As President I am relieved of the pleasing duty of preparing essays as food for critics, and I presume I am privileged to address you tonight on any subject without fear of outspoken criticism. Unfortunately the time which has elapsed since our last meeting has been a particularly busy one for me. The visit of Their Royal Highnesses to Singapore has entailed of late a very considerable amount of work in connection with arrangements for their reception, and I may say that I have not found any time for elaborating an Introductory Address for tonight.

Having had occasion the other day to visit the Malay village on Pulau Brani, it occurred to me that a paper on the present position of the Malay might not be without interest. This would deal with the Malays as we found them, and what the Government has done—or, I may say, left undone—with regard to them since. In 1872 I remember going for a picnic to Pulau Brani, where there was a small bungalow on the hill. It was in those days a peaceful and romantic spot. The only inhabitants were the aquatic Malays of the sea villages of Teluk Saga and Kampong Sinkheh. Singapore was then a growing town, but no one would then have believed that in twenty years or so this unfrequented island would present the appearance of a manufacturing town, with tall chimneys pouring out volumes of smoke, and that the bulk of the world's tin would find its way thither. Beneath the shadow of those tall chimneys, the emblem of commercial enterprise, the primitive Malay villages remain unchanged by time. The huts clustered together are perched on the shelving mud bank, and the villages, which to the eye of a Municipal Health Officer would seem to be a most pestilential place, are swept by the sea, with its recurring tides, more effectually than any town was cleansed by mortal scavengers. Here the Malay has been left severely alone, and revels in the conditions which are most dear to him. Dirty wells serve for bathing and drinking purposes alike. No Inspector of Nuisances visits the place to enforce by-laws, nor has the Government ever tried to enforce Western ideas in this very typical Malay Settlement.

A stranger landing in Singapore naturally expects, from what he has read or heard of the capital of Malaya, to see numbers of Malays. He looks in vain. He may traverse many streets and scarcely see a true Malay. The shops are kept by Chinese and Indians, and the dense crowds in the streets are mainly Chinese. In the middle of the Esplanade stands a statue erected in honour of Sir Stamford Raffles, the Founder of Singapore and the friend of the Malays. How far have the dreams and aspirations of this truly great man been fulfilled? What have his successors done for the Malays? What has become of the noble race of Sultan Hussein Mahomed Shah, the ancient ruler of the country? By the first Treaty of 1819, all we obtained was the right to establish a factory or trading station, of which the boundaries were seaward Tanjong Katong and Tanjong Malang, where Fort Palmer stands, and landward as far as a cannon-shot. It was specially provided that people residing within the kampongs of the Sultan and Temonggong were not to be under the Resident. Gardens and plantations existing or to be made were to be at the disposal of the Temonggong as heretofore. Every Monday at ten o'clock the Sultan, the Temonggong, and the Resident were to meet at the Rumah Bechara. Every captain, or head of a caste, and all Penghulus of kampongs and villages, were to attend and report occurrences. Before leaving Singapore in 1823. Raffles drew up rules. To compensate them for loss of profits on monopolies, duties, etc. a monthly payment was to be made to the Sultan and Temonggong. With the exception of the land appropriate to their Highnesses for their respective establishments, all land within the island and islands immediately adjacent was to be at the disposal of the British Government. Their Highnesses were excused from attendance at the Court House, but were always entitled to a seat on the bench. In all cases the ceremonies of religion and marriages, rules of inheritance, laws and customs of the Malays were to be respected. By the later Treaty of 1824, the Sultan and Temonggong ceded in full sovereignty the island of Singapore and islands within ten miles of the coast in return for a lump sum and a monthly stipend. The East India Company agreed to treat with all the honours, respect, and courtesy belonging to their rank and station the Sultan and Temonggong whenever they resided in or visited Singapore. In 1855, Sultan Ali Iskandar Shah, the son of Sultan Hussain, ceded the whole of the territory of Johore, except Muar, to the Temonggong Daing Ibrahim Sri Maharajah, Sultan Ali was to receive $500 a month. It is within the memory of some of us how the Temonggong Abubakar was, in consideration of assistance rendered to the Government, recognized by us as Maharaja of Johore, and subsequently as Sultan. Of our treatment of Sultan Ali it is difficult to use words strong enough. Our protege the so-styled Maharaja of Johore was, with the active connivance of the British Government, allowed to seize Muar, and the Sultan's descendants have been allowed to shift for themselves in Singapore.

What Raffles would have thought of his successors in their dealings with the Malays of Singapore can easily be imagined. What has led to their practical effacement in Singapore, the ancient maritime capital of the race? The Indian officials who succeeded him had little sympathy with Malaya. Their language and customs were unknown to most of the officials. Chinese in increasing numbers continued to pour into the place, and gradually colonized the island. The padi-fields which formerly existed were gradually absorbed, and now scarcely a blade of padi is to be seen on the island. The jungle was allowed to be cleared indiscriminately, and the districts came to be known by Chinese names. Along the coast, it is true, some Malay villages have survived, but the Government has cared little for them, beyond providing police stations and schools. The town became a Chinese town, the Malays being gradually ousted from their land.

Raffles was anxious that the sons of the Sultan and Temonggong should be sent to Calcutta to be educated, but as they refused, he determined to found a college here, to combine the object of educating the higher classes of the native population, and at the same time affording instruction to the Officers of the Company in the native languages, and of facilitating more general researches into the history, condition, and resources of the adjoining countries. It was to be a great Central College for the whole of Malaya. The Institution which bears his name was endowed with land, which, had it been retained, would have yielded now sufficient funds to carry out the designs of the Founder. Apathy on the part of the Trustees, and short-sightedness, or something worse, on the part of the Government of the day, robbed the Institution of its land, and the consequence is that, instead of having at the present day a great college providing for higher education, and specially for the education of the better class of Malays, we have a school which certainly does not fulfil the intention of the Founder.

Of course it may be argued that if the Malays have been effaced it is their own fault, but if we see what they are capable of in other places, we cannot, I think, acquit the Government of blame in the matter. The Government of Johore may not be a model one in every respect, but anyone who has had occasion to visit Johore must be struck at the great advance which has been made of late years. Some of the officials are most able men. The small territory of Muar, on the borders of Malacca, is really a model Settlement. The officials are all Malays, and it is highly creditable to the government of the district that such improvements should have been carried out. The *Malay Mail* lately drew a striking contrast between Selangor, where the Malay has been allowed to go to the wall, and the town of Bandar Maharani in Muar. The town is, it is stated, larger than any town in Selangor, except

Kuala Lumpur. There is a nice *padang*, surrounded by chains linked to granite pillars. There is a magnificent galvanized-iron market. There are stand-pipes in the street, and water is laid on to the houses. There is a European doctor. The streets and roads are excellent. The police are smart and well set-up. The post office is clean and attractive. A large export trade is done. A miniature railway (2 cents a mile) runs into the Agricultural district. Fine Government launches run up the river. There are all the usual government buildings, such as Custom-house, Court, and Land Office, as well as a fine Residency, nearly all the subordinates on the railway—such as drivers, guards, clerks, and porters are Malays. What do we see when we reach Selangor? Where are the Malays? We see a host of officials, all imported. It is a happy hunting-ground for Tamils from Ceylon and Southern India. The Malay is of no account. The capital is a Chinese mining town, and Malays are few and far between. The Resident-General, who has done so much for Malays, attempted to start a Malay village, but, from what I have heard of it, it is at the best a very artificial settlement, and is not likely to succeed.

In Kedah, a purely Malay country, we again see what can be made of the natives if left to themselves. At Alor Star are fine Government Offices, including a Court, Land Office, and Treasury, where public business is carried on the model of our Departments. There is even an *offis preksa kira-kira*, presided over by an Auditor-General, who, as far as I could ascertain, has something like a sinecure. All the officials and staff are Malays, and most of the Heads of Departments are more or less connected with the Royal family. This is quite sufficient to show that our system of importing or employing clerks, surveyors, and other subordinates who do not belong to the country is unnecessary. Surely it is the duty of the Government of the Straits Settlements, and more so of the Government of the Federated Malay States, to train up Malay youths so that they may be fitted to fill all the subordinate positions in the service. It is also incumbent on them to provide an Institution where a good education may be offered to the sons of Rajas and Malays of good birth, to fit them to take a leading part in the Government of the State.

We have a lot of lost ground to make up, but it is not too late to make what amends we can for the shortcomings of the past. Let us not be unmindful of the high and noble aims of the great Founder of Singapore, who, were he alive today, would denounce laissez-aller policy of his successors, and plead for the Malay race whom he loved so well.

Note

1. Yeo Kim Wah, "The Grooming of an Elite: Malay Administrators in the Federated Malay States, 1903–1941", *Journal of Southeast Asian Studies*, vol. 11, no. 2 (1980): 287–319.

25

THE FUTURE OF THE MALAY RACE

Essay

13 September 1902
by *H.N. Ridley*

Editors' Note

Unlike Kynnersley's 1901 essay, Ridley's essay on the future of the Malay race offered a more pessimistic outlook for the Malays. Ridley, informed by his social Darwinism, argued that the Malays lacked the racial character to prevent subsumption by immigrant races, in particular the Chinese. He foresaw the Malay race intermixing with the Chinese and disappearing as they were integrated within a more dominant Chinese race. At the same time, he argued that two trends may delay this subsumption. The first was the presence of Islam as a differentiating factor between the Malays and Chinese, and the other was the presence of the British who may for some time artificially protect the Malays from external competition. In response Hanitsch, a botanist, Curator of the Raffles Library and Museum, and a colleague of Ridley, argued, against Ridley, that the long-term protection of the Malay race might be possible, but only on the basis of the restriction of immigration and through a system of education which would build upon existing trades and protect the current state of Malay society. To justify ongoing British protection of the Malays, Hanitsch noted:

> The Malay is in many ways so childlike that for a long time he will require careful training and nurturing. If we left him alone, and all Europeans took passage for home today, I really believe he would turn tomorrow again into the bloodthirsty pirate he was before. But duly taken care of for some generations to come—and I don't think ever any native race required more careful handling—I believe that the Malays would have a bright and prosperous future before them.

I take the title, the Future of the Malay Race, to refer to the distant future of the race—its final end, if ended it should be before the great globe and all that it inherits shall dissolve—and therefore I will attempt to study the probable end of the race. At the present time I think it is clear that the Malays are increasing in number, at least in the Peninsula, although successful reproduction of the race is not large, Malays have comparatively small families, and are losing a considerable number of children very young. This, however, is due to carelessness and ignorance in bringing up, and is being gradually remedied by contact with Europeans civilization, where the sanitary measures, better medicines, etc. are saving the lives which some years ago would have been lost early. We may take it, then, that for a considerable period the Malays will rather increase than decrease in numbers; and this will continue till competition on the part of other races begins to make itself felt; and should these races prove more fertile and more energetic, the struggle must end in the disappearance of the weaker race.

The number of races of which practically all members have disappeared is evidently very large, and the greater number having vanished in prehistoric times, we can only guess at the causes of the disappearance of them. Now, there are two ways in which races become extinct: one is absolute extermination, and the other absorption into a more virile race. Cases of absolute extermination are, I believe, very rare in the history of nations, and in fact, seem only to have occurred in islands, such as Tasmania, and probably Easter Island; for in almost every other case traces of intermixture of the vanishing race with the conquering race occur for long after the disappearance of the last purebred individual. In cases, rare enough, where the conquering race will not readily mix with the native population, as in Australia and North America, cases of mixture do occur. The causes of absolute extermination are war and indiscriminate slaughter, the introduction of new diseases, and the dispossessing of the best parts of the land by the invaders, so that the natives are reduced by starvation, till they are so few that they gradually cease to breed, and so vanish. This state of affairs is hardly likely to occur again, though it is not so many years since the Tasmanian race disappeared entirely in this manner. The absorption of the Malays into another and more powerful race is in all probability their ultimate destiny.

And here I may call attention to the fact that the Malays themselves have undoubtedly absorbed other vanished and vanishing races. In Patani, and the islands round Singapore, and indeed in Singapore itself, there are many Malays who have a considerable admixture of Semang and Sakai blood. In fact the Malays in these parts seem to have absorbed the old aboriginal race. The Orang Selitar, formerly the race possessing Singapore and the islands to the south, are reduced to a very small number of individuals, but Malays are often to be met with all around Singapore who have obvious traces of this curly-haired dark race. The race which formerly inhabited the Peninsula, and used the stone axes which occur so widely scattered over the country, were probably absorbed by the Sakais, as no trace except the worked stones is to be found of them, and they disappeared before the Malays invaded the Peninsula. And as these races have disappeared or are disappearing, so I believe the Malay race will eventually disappear.

Hitherto the Malays have formed the peasantry of their country; and in saying this I am including under the Malays the Javanese, Sundanese, and others of the Malay races in the Peninsula and Archipelago. They have never been to any extent a commercial nor mining race. Fishing and agricultural work on a small scale is all that they have ever done. Having no ambition of becoming millionaires like the Chinaman, and having simple, easily satisfied wants, they have nothing to vain by making money, and prefer to live from hand to mouth. Should they by chance become rich, they either throw the money away themselves or their children do so after their death. Such a race cannot compete against energetic, ambitious peoples, as the Chinese, Arabs, or any of the Indian tribes who are invading the Malay regions. The Dutch, it is true, have kept back the invasion of alien races by laws, but it is improbable that this check will last for any very great period, and there is no such check in English territory.

But it may be said that, as the strain of competition is felt, the Malays will improve their character and meet the wave so as to hold their own. I doubt very much that there has ever been a nation which has really modified its characteristics in such respects. You may improve the thorn and thistle in various rays by cultivation, but you will never get them to produce figs or grapes: thorns and thistles they will remain. The most noticeable example of this is the case of the Negro population of the United States. This race has the greatest opportunities of being civilized and developed of any native race in the world. The Negroes have been removed from their uncivilized African surroundings, and have been brought up in close contact with a European race for generations, educated and Christianized, yet they still remain savages with a thin veneer of imitation civilization.

To go into the question of the persistence of national character and the ways in which it may be modified would be too long a subject for this essay, and would only be a side issue anyway. To make it short I would call attention to the fact that the Malay race has shown less indication to develop on the lines of a higher civilization than most of the surrounding nations who are invading his domains and competing with him.

A native peasantry must, I think, always be present in tropical regions, though it is just possible that Europeans may eventually so improve methods of life in hot countries that they themselves supply a tropical peasantry, a dream of Zola's for the regeneration of France,— but it is improbable. The European poor cannot live as economically as a native race, because of their luxurious and wasteful habits. They cannot compete with an Oriental race, hence the necessity for the anti-alien laws of Africa and North America. The future peasantry of the Malay region will, I think, not be Malays. From the fishing industry and agriculture they are being ousted by the Chinese. The mines and a great part of commerce are in the hands of the Chinese. The Malay is too proud to enter domestic service. He excels, in fact, in nothing which will enable him to hold his own against the Chinaman or Indian. His many good qualities avail not in the struggle for existence, while his indolence and want of ambition are serious drawbacks. The day for such a race is drawing to its close. It will be, however, many years before the strain of the competition is felt in the many islands of the Archipelago. The Chinaman does not appear to be able to push his way through Malay countries except under European protection. In Dutch-owned countries he is, and may be for a long time, kept out; but the energy and persistence of the race will eventually overcome, and the peasantry of the Archipelago will probably become in a large measure Chinese. No doubt the Indian races will play a considerable part in the struggle for the position, but they for the most part are inferior to the Malays in almost everything, and may be ignored. They can never form a peasantry.

There are several factors which will delay the absorption of these dark-skinned races into the Chinese. The Mohammedan religion, and consequent dislike of the Malays to the Chinese, will doubtless protract the struggle; but it is already not rare to find Chinese marrying Malay women, and in this case, the children are apt to become Chinese in customs and religion. Many of the Chinese customs again, especially that of returning to China and not settling down in the country of their adaptation, militate against their forming a settled peasantry; but this is really dying out, and we may expect that, after probably a long lapse of time, we may have an agricultural peasantry composed of the Chinese race with a very large admixture of Malayan and Indian blood. The absorption of the Malay race will doubtless take some centuries, and many changes may take place, which will delay or hasten the action. Western developments may modify the whole course of progression—developments of which we have not the least idea at the present; but as the Malay races are concerned, all historical evidence seems to show that such a race as that before us will be absorbed by the more ambitious and energetic one.

Criticism
by R. Hantisch

If a number of people meet to discuss the future of anything, it generally implies that that future is in a precarious condition. Some years ago, for instance, when the political horizon of France looked rather cloudy, I was put down to read a paper on the future of that interesting country. But I made my mind up to act as cloud-shifter, taking the brightest possible view; and whether it was a case of *post hoc* or *propter hoc*—i.e., whether I simply read the future correctly or whether my prophecies acted as a tonic on the nervous system of France—in any case things look bright enough today there.

With regard to the future of the Malay race, I will repeat my experiment and act as cloud-shifter, trusting my prophecies may come true, no matter whether *post hoc* or *propter hoc*. The Essayist, however, has, right from the beginning, taken a gloomy view of the matter. He assumes the title of the paper to refer to the final end of the race, when what is left of it becomes absorbed by the Chinese, who, by then, will have already absorbed the Hindoos, and form a vast agricultural peasantry spreading over the whole Malay region. We almost see the last pure Malay, who had probably been Syce at Government House, Singapore, exhibited at the Trimillenary World's Fair in Chicago, duly adorned with *baju*, *sarong*, and *kris*, all made in Birmingham, and running *amok* to order.

Left to themselves, I think one might safely predict that the Malays would practically remain as they are now. The conditions of their life and their own personal characteristics are such as would ensure perpetual continuity. With practically no change in the climate, with a sufficient supply of food obtainable without great effort, with an easy-going temperament, there would be little struggle for existence to cause any change. But the Malays have not by any means been left to themselves in the past, and are not likely to be so in the future. The geography of the lands they inhabit is against this: they are scattered over a vast area, chiefly of islands, the unsurpassed richness of which cannot fail to attract people from other lands not so favoured by nature. The Arabs, the Hindoos, Chinese, and Europeans, have all been attracted by the wealth of the Malay region—all have come either to trade or to settle permanently. All, of course, have left and are leaving traces of their occupancy upon the land, and upon the minds and manners of the people, and in order to enable us to imagine the future of the Malay race, we must consider the influence of foreign races upon the Malays in the past.

The influence of the Arabs upon the Malays was discussed some years ago before this Society by Mr. Blagden, who showed that it began long before the Christian era, but that it gained real power only with the establishment of the Mohammedan religion. Although they came to the East in the first instance only as traders, after "the pepper of Malabar, the gems of Ceylon, the spices of the Archipelago, and the Silk of China", still they brought pandits or religious teachers with them, and the conversion to Islam seems to have taken place quite peacefully, so different from the establishment of that religion in countries to the Northwest of Arabia. But besides religion, religious laws, written characters, and a few Arab words, the Malay took nothing else from the Arabs; their life remained otherwise unchanged, and, it is not likely that the Arabs will in future have any further influence upon the Malays.

The influence of the people of Southern India upon the Malays was discussed about two years ago by Mr. O'Sullivan. The testimony of language alone shows that the Hindoos had more influence upon the social life of the Malays than the Arabs: whilst words borrowed from the Arabic have reference to religion only, those taken from the Hindoos refer to daily life, and words like *kapal* (ship), *kedi* (shop), *gedong* (storehouse), *peti* (box), etc. are pure Tamil. But, independent of this, we know from architectural remains in Sumatra, and especially Java, that the Hindoos had established a civilization here long before the advent of Mohammedanisn. It is probable that the intercourse between Tamils and Malays declined as soon as the latter had embraced Islam, and notwithstanding the large number of Indians in this colony and the Malay Peninsula, I think their influence upon the Malays is very slight, and that, unless circumstances alter very much, Malays will have little to fear from Tamil influence. According to the last census the Malay population of the colony was 215,058, against 57,150 Tamils—i.e. nearly four times as many Malays as Tamils; and this proportion is still more favourable to the Malays when we consider that with them the sexes are about equal (107,911 males and 107,147 females), whilst amongst the Tamils there are nearly three times as many males as females. In the Malay States, Perak, Selangor and Pahang the number of Malays is nearly five times as great as the Tamils, viz. 255,569 against 52,685, and the disproportion of the sexes amongst the Tamils is still more marked there than in the Straits Settlements.

We may now consider the influence of the Europeans upon the Malays. This, began with the conquest of Malacca by the Portuguese under Albuquerque (1511), followed by the Dutch and English; and I think it is a matter of congratulation for the Malays that they have been converted to Islam before the first Europeans set foot here. Look at the way the natives of other continents have withered before the Europeans, with their alcoholism and all sorts of imported diseases; those of Australia and Africa are practically exterminated; those of Africa have suffered frightfully; and that the races of Asia and the Malay Archipelago have escaped that influence is probably due to the fact that they had strong moral and religious backbone before the Europeans arrived. Thanks to the civilization which the Malays had already obtained through Arab and Tamil influence, their coming into contact with higher civilization, that of the Europeans, has been less of a shock than it would have been otherwise, and I think it cannot be doubted today the European influence upon the Malay is mainly beneficial. Internecine warfare and piracy have stopped; the sanitary surroundings have improved; the Malay has found many additional ways of making a livelihood besides fishing, agriculture and piracy; and all this tends to increase the Malay population. Mentally this horizon has been widened by European intercourse, and certainly I think we can say that morally he is not a worse man than he was before. The European has not come into competition with him in any way; and it is doubtful, too, whether this will ever be so. The Essayist says that there must always be a native peasantry in tropical regions, and that the European poor cannot compete with the natives, "because of their luxurious and wasteful habits". Certainly many Europeans at home are poor, or have become so, because of their luxurious and wasteful habits, and it would never do to dump down the occupants of a European workhouse here and to expect them to make anything of the land. But does not Europe contain millions of poor and hardworking peasantry, who do not understand what luxury is—people who have never had anything to waste? I have little doubt that, if the experiment were worth the expense, such people could be brought out here and have an easier life as peasants than at home, if not in the low-lying countries, then on the vast high-lying regions of the Malay Peninsula, Sumatra, etc. On Maxwell's Hill, Perak, at an elevation of 3,000 feet, a dairy farm flourishes and splendid vegetables are grown, and I should think that tropical life at such an altitude would, for many European peasants, be quite as suitable and much more enjoyable than life at home. Still, even if successful, such European colonizing would not seriously interfere with the Malays. But if the European out here cannot be said to compete with the Malay, it is different with the European at home, who by importing his cheap imitations of sarongs, krisses, etc. has nearly succeeded in killing, the little Malay art there was.

Much more serious seems the influence which the Chinese are likely to have upon the Malays. I do not know of any direct evidence as to when the Chinese first made their appearance in this part of the world. There must have been commercial intercourse between the Chinese and Malays for many centuries. John Crawfurd mentions that some old Chinese coins were dug up in 1827 from the ruins of an ancient settlement in Singapore, said to have been founded in 1160 and destroyed by the Javanese in 1252. These coins were deposited in the Museum of the Royal Asiatic Society, and bear the names of emperors whose deaths correspond with the years 967, 1067, and 1085 AD.

When Albuquerque took Malacca (1511) he found Chinese junks lying in the roads, and Barbosa, a Portuguese historian of that time, gives a detailed account of their trading. He also describes the manners and customs of the Chinese, states that they speak a language like German (that is, a guttural one) and describes them as wearing shoes and stockings like the Germans. (I suppose that means that amongst the Europeans of his time the Germans were the only ones civilized enough to wear shoes and stockings.) Still there seems to be no evidence that the Chinese settled permanently in or near Malacca before the arrival of the Europeans; it would naturally be after the country had become civilized and safe enough that they would begin to settle here. It seems to have been different in Northwest Borneo, where there exist many traditions of ancient Chinese settlements. In fact some of the races there, e.g. the Dusuns, are by some writers said to be a mixture of Malays and Chinese. If this should be the, case, I should say no to any intermarriage of Chinese and Malays. I had occasion once to live for four weeks amongst the Dusuns and although they were quite a good-natured people, I was not sorry to leave them, as they seemed to have adopted none of the good and all of the bad qualities of the two races.

At the present day it may certainly seem as if the Malays were likely to get swamped altogether by the Chinese in this colony and the Malay Peninsula. According to the last census this colony contains 282,000 Chinese, against 215,000 Malays; Selangor has more than twice as many Chinese Malays, viz. 108,000 as against 40,000; in Perak, too, the Chinese preponderate (149,000 against 141,000). In Pahang only are the Malays greatly in the majority (73,462 Malays against 8,695 Chinese). Even in Johore (whence, however, the figures are not quite reliable) the Chinese number about 150,000 against only about 50,000 Malays and Javanese. But, as in the case of the Tamils, the preponderance of the Chinese is much less serious when closely examined; for, whilst in this colony and the Malay Peninsula there is a healthy equality of the sexes amongst the Malays, the male Chinese population of the Straits Settlements outnumbers the female by more than three to one, in Selangor by more than eight to one, in Perak nearly ten to one, and in Pahang by seventeen to one.

Naturally the birth-rate, and, what is even more striking, the death-rate, tell a similar tale. During last quarter (April to June 1902) the number of births amongst the Malays of the colony (who number about 215,000) was 2,248, against 2,091 deaths—showing, therefore, a natural increase of 157. Amongst the Chinese (numbering 281,922) the number of births was 1,255, against 5,232 deaths—i.e. a natural decrease of 3,977, their death-rate being three times as heavy as that of the Malays.

Do these figures not mean that, if the present enormous immigration of the Chinese were to stop for any reason, they would, within a generation or less, be absolutely outnumbered by the Malays? And who is to guarantee that this immigration is to continue indefinitely? Let the tin mines of the Peninsula become exhausted, or let better paying mines be discovered anywhere else in the world, or let the Russians take it into their heads to turn the flood of Chinese emigrants into Siberia, and the Peninsula would become as much Malay as it ever was before.

The question of the future of the Malay race, therefore turns mainly on the question of the future of the Chinese race in these parts and the encouragement given by Government to Chinese immigration. This immigration has so far, I suppose, been necessary, as without it, and with the small number of Malays available, any opening up of the country would have been impossible. This, however, should not be carried so far that the Malay is ousted from his native land. And this brings me to the last part of my paper, viz. our duty to the Malay.

Most of you will remember the excellent presidential address which Mr. Kynnersley read before this Society at the beginning of last session, entitled "Our Duty to the Malay," and I only need to remind you of a few of its chief points. He asks what has become of the ideals and aspirations of Sir Stamford Raffles, and points out that in Singapore, owing to the indifference of the Indian officials who followed Raffles, the Malay has been practically effaced by the Chinese, and that in the Native States, especially Selangor, the subordinate offices are the happy hunting-ground of Tamils from Ceylon and Southern India. In contrast hereto he tells what the Malay can do when he is given a chance, and describes Muar in Johore, for instance, as quite a model settlement. The officials there are all Malays; the town is beautifully laid out, with good Government offices, a nice market-place, water laid on to the houses, a railway leading to the agricultural districts, and so forth. Similarly in Kedah, at Alor Star, the Government offices are all occupied by Malays, and things conducted on the model of this Colony, apparently in a most efficient way.

There would, then, I think, be two ways of helping the Malay: first indirectly, by regulating the immigration of other Asiatic races, that the Malay should have a first chance in the labour market; and, secondly, directly, by educating the Malay. By education I certainly do not mean cramming the Malay boys and girls with a variety of subjects after European pattern. The first thing to be done would be to keep alive any sort of art or industry in which the Malay excels, and not allow it to be killed by importing cheap imitations. A step in the right direction has been taken in Perak, where early last year a Committee was appointed to enquire into the "best methods of resuscitating Malayan Art Industries, such as those connected with metal-work, wood-carving, pottery, weaving, etc., many of which, owing to the competition of European machine-made articles, are in danger of dying out". The report states that "H.H. the Sultan of Perak has taken a keen interest in this movement from the first, and has personally presided at every meeting of the Committee, whose members comprise some of the most important Malay chiefs in Perak, as well as European officials specially interested in the subject. The recommendations of the Committee have been adopted by Government, and provision has been made for erecting a building at Kuala Kangsar in which boys and girls can be trained", etc. (J.P. Rodger, British Resident, "Administration Report for 1901", Perak Government Gazette, 18.7.1902, p. 14.)

Again, the establishment of a Malay College, first planned by Raffles, for the training of the sons of Rajahs and the boys of the better classes altogether, so as to fit them for service in the government of their own country, would be the crowning step in the education of the Malay.

The Malay is in many ways so childlike that for a long time he will require careful training and nurturing. If we left him alone, and all Europeans took passage for home today, I really believe he would turn tomorrow again into the bloodthirsty pirate he was before. But duly taken care of for some generations to come—and I don't think ever any native race required more careful handling—I believe that the Malays would have a bright and prosperous future before them.

26

THE INFLUENCE OF MODERN CIVILIZATION ON THE MALAY

Essay

8 January 1909
by *Rev. W. Murray*

Editors' Note

Questions of the modernization of the Malays were also raised in a discussion in the Society begun by Rev W. Murray's "The Influence of Modern Civilization on the Malay" and responded by David Bishop. In Murray's piece, which provided the standard characterization of the Malays by Europeans of that period, Murray rooted their character not only in the effects of climate. He also attributed it to the nature of the pre-colonial system of governance which had left the Malays "unambitious and lazy". The British presence had been able in part to counteract this by providing a system of peace and law and order which had been able to effect external changes in the Malays. This, he argued, could be translated into internal changes that would modify the Malay from "a pirate and warrior ... into a lover of peace and order". This image which Murray expressed in terms of the domestication and taming of the Malay character did not, however, suggest for his critic, Bishop, that the Malays would modernize fully. In his view the Malay character and nature would require their continued dependence on British tutelage as "the Malay has been slow to adopt Western ideas and manners". Arguing that, despite exceptions, the Malay is "conservative and suspicious of innovations, unambitious and unprogressive", he noted that "[t]he great majority of the Malay lads in school are deplorably devoid of ambition, and seem only to desire to get along with as little trouble and as little exertion of brain-power as possible. The forces of heredity are apparently too strong."

If the Committee of the Society, in fixing the subject of this paper, contemplated the Malay in widest sense of the word—that is, as a race peopling not only the Malay Archipelago generally so called, but also Formosa, the Philippines, Madagascar, and South Africa—it proposed a subject far greater than I can possibly deal with. Even in the narrowest sense of the Malay resident at our doors, I am afraid that all I can offer is an essay somewhat disjointed and incomplete.

As for what is meant by modern civilization, there may also be difference of opinion. The Mohammedan religion, when it spread over this part of the world about the tenth or eleventh centuries, brought civilization of a kind, to which the epithet "modern" may be applied in comparison with the ancient history of the Malays, which reaches into an unknown past. Or the influence of the Portuguese, some centuries later, might also from a similar standpoint be called modern, although there are some who, remembering the tyranny and bloodshed which characterized it, would scarcely call it civilization. Later, the Dutch have acquired influence, which still remains a dominant factor over vast numbers of Malays. And later still has come that British influence, with which we as individuals and as a community are, in varying degrees, a part. I presume that by modern civilization, for the purpose of this debate, we mean the last century—a period in which the West has proved remarkable for social, political, scientific and industrial progress; and a civilization which has had influence over the people of these parts since the colony was founded, and over the Malays of the Peninsula since they were brought under British protection a generation ago.

So far as British political influence goes, we find it exerted in various degrees over the Malays of these parts. We have Malays under the British flag, born and bred under it like other citizens of the Empire; Malays under their own native rulers, yet not only under British protection but controlled by British officials in British methods; Malays under an independent native ruler, whose training and ambitions are towards what is British; Malays under the patronage and protection of Siam, yet so situated on the frontiers of the British Empire, that Western civilization is felt in a real, though to a very limited extent. Possibly in the Dutch East Indies there may be found the same variety in the relations of the Malay to the Dutch power, as there is found in the Malay Peninsula with regard to the Malay and the British power. With this subject I am not familiar. As might be expected, the results of modern civilization on the Malay in such circumstances are variable in their extent. The tourist may find a Malay who to all appearance, except in colour, is European; and a Malay who is little changed from the condition of his ancestors many centuries ago; and an immense variety of Malays, influenced by modern civilization, coming between these two extremes.

The first and more patent effect of modern civilization has been to preserve and increase the Malay race. Numerically speaking, there seems to be little chance of the Malay dying out, as some races have died out on the advent of some new and progressive power among them. On the contrary, in the Dutch East Indies the increase of the native population is described as remarkable. And although British influence in the Malay Peninsula is not of such long standing as to provide safe statistics, yet it can hardly be doubted that the same increase of Malays is taking place with us. In olden days when the Malays of the Peninsula were in a chronic state of intertribal warfare, the victims of debt-slavery and other systems of oppression, the country was very sparsely populated, compared with what it is now under settled government, steady and peaceful employment, and better feeding. What the traveller of fifty years ago saw was ramshackle kampongs at distant intervals on the riverbanks, with miles of jungle stretching round them, into which even the natives seldom penetrated. Now, he can see shiningly verdant padi-fields as far as the eye can reach, and Malay villages almost innumerable.

The Malay population, though not quite so numerous as the Chinese, is almost certainly larger today than ever it was before.

So far as absorbing Western manners of life and thought goes, the Malay is handicapped in many respects. He has not the intelligence of the Chinese, not the cleverness of the Kling in adapting himself to new modes. By nature he is unambitious, and therefore unprogressive. The climate in which he lives is not one that offers any inducement to strenuous toil either of hand or brain; but, on the contrary, tempts rather a disinclination for work. The Malay, therefore, does not take readily to the energetic life which modern civilization implies. Moreover, the fatalism and narrowness engendered by his religion raise another barrier to progress in the Western sense. In disposition, further, he is so conservative that he will cling to the ills he has, even when he knows them to be ills, rather than follow the improvements that are yet untried, especially when these improvements come from the West. Swettenham in his book on British Malaya says that centuries of misgovernment have created a habit of suspicion towards every innovation; and cites, in illustration of this, that when the whole system of debt-slavery was abolished, a certain number of the manumitted received the news of their freedom with regret. To all these must be added the unfortunate impression the Malay had of the white man. In the book just referred by the author, writing with a unique experience of the Malay says—"Thirty years ago very few of the Malays of the Peninsula had ever seen a white man, and the popular impression was that they were people with loud voices, indifferent manners, and worse customs; that they habitually used bad language in their conversation, and not infrequently drank to intoxication"—failings which are specially abhorrent to the Malay mind.

However, it can hardly but be expected that a longer and more thorough acquaintance with what modern civilization really means will somewhat alter those elements in his nature which hinder the operation of its influence. He may have grown unambitious and lazy, not altogether from the effect of the climate, but because of the system under which for centuries he and his ancestors live—a system of vassalage from which the learned that nothing he could make was his own. Now, under a better regime, the spirit of his life may change accordingly. The religious prejudice he feels may be due to the superficial and fanatical way in which he holds Mohammedanism; and when he comes to realize the value of the essential element in religion, that prejudice may pass away. Then, also, it can hardly but be that his first impressions of the white man will undergo a change. It is a law of human nature that alien races start with enmity and misrepresentation of each other, and then come to recognize common interests and the reality of human brotherhood. And even now, the Malay's experience of government by western notions, based on justice and humane principles, is having its effect in destroying the old attitude of suspicion. Indeed, there are few Malays, if any, who having lived under the regime of the foreigner for any considerable time would turn back in preference to the old order of administration. But I will say more of this later.

The casual observer cannot fail to see traces of the transformation which modern civilization is making slowly and steadily on Malay life. It is not so long ago that every Malay was a bare-footed wanderer over rude jungle tracks; now thousands of them wear canvas or leather shoes on beautifully macadamized roads. Half a century ago the Malay of the Peninsula never moved about except with kris, spear, sword or gun at his side; now he carries an umbrella instead. Then even the chiefs among them inhabited a hut on piles like their neighbours, with only a more carefully wrought pattern of split bamboo on the walls to make their houses; now they build with brick and mortar, and surround their homes with well laid-out gardens and gravelled walks, a la Europeans. Once, and that not so long ago, he squatted on a mat upon the floor, as his ancestors a century ago had done; now he has chairs, tables, iron bedsteads, and general house furnishings of European pattern and manufacture. Even his clothing feels the white man's influence and when the Malay wishes to appear to advantage in the eyes of the foreigner, it is in coat and trousers instead of sarong and baju.

These are merely external changes, and yet they show an influence and work. They may be due—and in many cases doubtless are due—to the mere instinct of imitation of or respect for what they recognize as superior power. Yet the changes are voluntary and not forced, and, though merely in the sphere of the external, suggest operations that lie deeper; because, almost invariably, changes in the outward circumstances of life, if they do not arise from changes in the spirit of a people, lead to those changes in the spirit being made.

Nor are we without evidence that the Malay character is being modified. Before modern civilization appeared on the scene, the system of native government of which the Malay had experience was rotten. Blackmailing was rampant; extravagant taxation and tolls destroyed industry. Rape, jealousy and covetousness kept the people in continual unrest. Forced labour and debt-slavery laid a heavy hand upon the whole population. The poor man's only safety was to sink every instinct that made him a man and hand himself over as chattel to some feudal over-lord. Force was right; and every stranger was an enemy. Now, however, that peace and order based on justice have been established amongst them by the white man; now that life and property are protected, now that a regular and equitable collection of revenue has been introduced; and now that the whole system of gaining profit and advantage by oppression has been struck at the roots; we find that the Malay, once so famed as pirate and warrior, settles down into a lover of peace and order. The old predatory instinct has gone; or at least, lies dormant, awaiting an occasion when it may display itself on behalf of some just cause. The old excited passion which we commonly call "running amuck" is not now heard of except in the rare sense of individual and civil justice replacing, under the influence of western civilization, the old instinct of uncontrolled revenge. The same movement towards refinement may be illustrated by the passing away of the old savage recreations of cockfighting, bull and tiger baiting, and such like—things which now belong only to the life untouched by civilization.

On the other hand, there are things for which the Malay has little cause to be grateful to modern civilization. Native art and industry belong to these things. The native-woven cloth with its strange patterns and brilliant colours, strong and durable; the work in metal and pottery ware are being driven out even from the Malay markets by the cheap machine-made wares of the West. As a hand-worker the Malay suffers, as our own hand-workers have had to suffer in this age of steam and machinery. In an age when time-saving and labour-saving apparatus is the great desideratum, it is not likely that attempts made to revive and encourage native crafts will be at all permanent. The Malay in these things must go to the wall. His niche in the economy of the human race must be found somewhere else. There is no evidence yet to show that the old aggressive and hardy nature of the pirate and voyager has made a field for itself among the commercial enterprises of modern civilization. The Malay, however, is a born agriculturalist and fisherman, and so long as men live on the fruit of the earth and the fish of the sea, he may still find a place, though a humble one, on the order of modern civilization; and still enjoy his innocent amusement of riddles, songs, chess and football without fear of disturbance from any western vandalism.

To conclude this short and rather cursory treatment of an interesting subject: the Malay under the domination of modern civilization is not the stubborn, cruel and rapacious man known to Europeans of old as the pirate seeking what he may devour; but he is quiet, polite, easy-going, ready to fill a humble niche, and accommodate himself as best he can, uncomplainingly, to the ways of stronger races. Civilization works on him slowly in charges external and internal, but it has not inspired him with a spirit of self-confidence or self-help. He is not likely to be exterminated by the nations of the West, but rather to increase under their influence. He recognizes that power lies not with number, but with methods, in the progress of the world; and so is satisfied to show himself amenable to the influence, dependent on the prestige and imitative of the fashions of a race more vigorous than his own.

Criticism
by David A. Bishop

Mr Murray is right in restricting the scope of his discussion to the influence of more strictly modern civilization on the Malays resident in the colony and the adjacent states. To have dealt with the subject in its wider aspects would have been a task of somewhat gigantic proportions, and an adequate discussion on these lines would occupy much more time than we have at our disposal.

We have before us, then, an examination of the effect of the introduction of the Western civilization of the nineteenth century on the Malay's life, thought, and character.

The first point dealt with—viz: the increase in population—affords little ground for discussion. The Malay has not, as have so many other native races in many parts of the world, disappeared before the onward march of modern civilization. Possibly this is due to the fact that the introduction of western ideas has been more gradual than in other cases, and the Malay has had better opportunities of assimilating these, and of slowly adapting himself, in a measure at least, to modern methods of life and industry. The wise policy adopted by the British rulers in dealing with the Malays, and the undoubted benefits derived from a settled Government and just laws, have been instrumental in preserving the Malay race and in contributing to its continued increase and development. The histories of all nations afford instances of similar results following on the establishment of law and order by a wise and just government.

As regards the degree in which the Malay has adopted the manners of life and thought of the West, there must inevitably be difference of opinion. One man's experience may bring him in contact with Malays who are well-educated, according to Western standards, and who are apparently in all points European in manner of life and thought; another's may bring him in contact with Malays who are apparently wholly unaffected by modern civilization. As the Essayist points out, there are necessarily varieties in type, but, on the whole, one must agree with him that the Malay has been slow to adopt Western ideas and manners. He is "conservative and suspicious of innovations, unambitious and unprogressive". Of course, there are exceptions. The more enlightened have been ready to adapt themselves to modern conditions of life. Some have been roused to ambition, and are eager to bring themselves into line with the European: but coming in contact, as I do, with representatives of the rising generation, I am afraid I find little justification for joining issue with the Essayist on this point. The great majority of the Malay lads in school are deplorably devoid of ambition, and seem only to desire to get along with as little trouble and as little exertion of brain-power as possible. The forces of heredity are apparently too strong.

How far this is due to climate conditions, and how far due to the cruel and oppressive systems of government which prevailed for so long it is difficult to estimate, but I think, with the Essayist, that the latter has had the greater influence. When a man knows that he will not be permitted to enjoy the fruits of his industry, and that death will, as likely as not, be the reward for any attempt to raise to place and power, there is little inducement for him to be industrious or ambitious. The indolence and improvidence and lack of ambition bred by the system have become characteristics of the race. Modern civilization and the necessity for greater exertion which the keen competition in the modern business world entails have not yet prevailed to root out this natural indolence and easy-going contentment of the Malay. Give him enough to feed and clothe him and he is content. He would enjoy the blessings which modern civilization in the shape of settled government and just laws brings him, but he will have none of the rush and hurry, the hard work, the worry, the responsibilities which accompany its march.

In other respects the character of the Malay has changed considerably, and the Essayist would have us believe that the change is wholly an improvement. One is scarcely prepared to admit that in its entirety. True, the Malay is no longer "the cruel, rapacious man" formerly known to the European, but is, "quiet, polite, easy-going, ready to fill a humble place". We all rejoice that the pirates are practically extinct, that gang robberies (by Malays, at least) and murders and open oppression are more or less things of the past, and we welcome the conversion of these pirates and robbers, murderers and oppressors, into peace-loving, law-abiding citizens. But has there not, with all this improvement, been a deterioration in character? Where is that energy and strength and force of character which marked the Malay of former days? That energy and force of character were misdirected perhaps, but still these are qualities which call forth our admiration—the qualities which, after all, redeemed the character of the Malay. The ordinary, Malay of today, as compared with his ancestors, suggests the poor, tame, spiritless lion born and bred in a cage at the zoo, contrasted with the grand and noble animal which has never suffered bondage. True, we would prefer to meet with the zoo specimen—but which do we admire the more? Meaner qualities have replaced the grander, and the modern Malay is less simple, less sincere, less trustworthy, less noble than his ancestors. That, at least, is my opinion, based on my experience of the present and my reading of the past. This is, perhaps, after all, a transition stage, and when, in the course of time, the Malay is roused from his indolence and lethargy, these nobler qualities may again develop.

The Essayist has not touched upon the question of how far the Malay has adopted the vices of the West. Generally speaking, native races are quick to imitate the vices of the dominant white race, and slow to imitate their virtues. The Malays have perhaps suffered less in this respect than some other races. Their religion, in a measure, protects them from one of the most degrading vices, but the effect of modern civilization on native races in general is to loosen the bonds of their religion and so to remove restraints. Signs are not lacking of this effect on the Malays, with the result that spirit drinking, for instance—abhorred of the faithful—is becoming quite common. My experience has not been very extensive, but it has been sufficient to confirm me in the opinion that the Malay of today is more irreligious and less moral than his predecessors—that modern civilization, in fact, has produced a deterioration in his character, from a strictly moral point of view.

27

MOSLEM INFLUENCE ON THE MALAY RACE

Essay

12 September 1912
by *Rev. W.G. Shellabear*

Editors' Note

The engagement of the Society with missionary thinking on the native population can be found in two contributions by W.G. Shellabear in the 1910s: "Moslem Influence on the Malay Race" and "Mohammedanism, As Revealed in Its Literature".[1] As Robert Hunt has argued, Shellabear was central to the re-evaluation of the role of Islam in Malay society, challenging assumptions of Islam as a mere veneer over Malay society, and arguing for the need for missionaries to understand the true nature of Malay society, and to contribute towards the modernization and development of the Malays as part of the colony.[2]

Yet whilst his assessment of the role of Islam differed from the majority missionary opinion of the time, the fundamental thrust still assumed a strong opposition between the values of Islam and those of European thought. Although Shellabear provided a more prominent role for Islam in the development of Malay society, at the same time he saw its civilizing role as limited compared for example to earlier Hindu influence. In doing so, Shellabear would take up an Orientalist focus upon language and texts[3] to better understand the Malays, which would also be prominent in his subsequent essay "Mohammedanism, As Revealed in Its Literature". This approach was one which Tan Teck Soon would criticize for its focus on textualism as opposed to living culture.

Shellabear argued that comparing the list of Malay words derived from Arabic and those derived from Sanskrit, it was obvious that Hinduism was "by far the more effective civilising agency". Later in the same essay he would argue that the influence of Islam on the Malays was largely restricted to the sphere of religion, and to terminology for books and writing, but not for the language of government and commerce where the adoption of words from European and Chinese languages suggested that "the Chinese and European peoples have done infinitely more than the Arabs to give the Malays the fruits of civilization". Central to his analysis was the role played by the British Government which, when ending the essay, he concluded:

> I would suggest that what Islam *has* failed to do for the Malay race, Christian civilization, as represented by the British Government and British commercial enterprise, has already gone far to *accomplish*.

Shellabear, a missionary, in arguing this, was also acknowledging that it was not through conversion but through the policy of the British Empire that development was being delivered.

Shellabear's essays are also important for the contemporary reflections they would provide on the role of Islam in the development of a modern nationalist identity among the Malays. Arguing that for the Malays "Islam is not so much a religion as a nationality"—in effect identifying Malay *bangsa* with Islam—he highlighted the influence of Turkish nationalism and the development of an Islamic public sphere in the colony that was in contact with Islamic writings from the Middle East and South Asia.[4]

In dealing with the subject I purpose to confine myself as far as possible to the Malays of the Peninsula and adjacent islands who speak what we call the Malay language, and shall not refer to other branches of the

Malay race except for the purpose of elucidating the influence of Islam upon the Malays.

In order to appreciate the influence of the religion which they now profess, and of the people who brought it to them, it is necessary first of all to make some inquiry into the condition of the Malay people before they adopted it.

A very interesting paper was written for this Society by Mr. Wilkinson in 1897 on the Religion of the Malays before Mohammedanism, in which he comes to the conclusion that they originally held a primitive polytheism, the remains of which we have today in their belief in spirits and sacred places and people (*kramat*), and in the incantations still used by their *pawangs* or medicine-men.

Skeat in his *Malay Magic*, which appeared about three years later, has collected a vast amount of most interesting material for the study of the folklore of the Malays in its bearing upon their ideas as to the spirit world, a careful study of which, and a comparison with the folklore of other divisions of the Malay race, such as the Javanese, Sundanese, Achinese, Bataks, Rejangs, Lampongs, and the people of Menangkabau, ought to throw a good deal of light upon the primitive beliefs of the Malays, and the extent to which they were influenced by Hinduism. For the purpose of the present paper it is quite impossible, and I think unnecessary, to go into this very obscure subject, for it may probably be taken for granted that the primitive religion of the Malays was practically identical with that of those tribes of Sumatra which are still heathen.

I think it may also be taken for granted that the Peninsula Malays originally came from Sumatra, not because it is so stated in the mythical account of the origin of their race contained in the *Sejarah Melayu*, but for reasons which are admirably stated by the justly celebrated John Crawfurd in his *Descriptive Dictionary of the Indian Islands*. From the investigations of Crawfurd, and the more recent information accumulated by others, I think it may safely be inferred that wherever the Malay race as a whole may have come from, it is pretty certain that that branch of the race which speaks the Malay language is and always has been essentially a maritime people. The extraordinary wealth of the language in nautical terms, and the wide distribution of the people everywhere along the sea-coast of the entire Archipelago, go far to establish that statement. It was recorded, however, by De Barros, nearly four centuries ago, that the Malay language was then spoken by three distinct classes, namely, the *orang laut* or Sea gypsies, who lived by fishing and robbing, the civilized Malays, who lived by trade and cultivation, and thirdly the uncivilized tribes of the interior of Sumatra between Jambi and Palembang. Crawfurd says that these three classes had existed for two and a half centuries before the time of De Barros, and we all know that they exist still, although here in Singapore the *orang laut*, who were a distinct class twenty-five years ago, are gradually becoming absorbed in the neighbourhood of the town. They, however, were probably not Malays, but a small band of Sakais. Now, as Crawfurd says, it is probable that we may never be able to determine precisely where these Malay-speaking peoples originally came from, but it is not so difficult to decide what were the sources of Malay civilization, for it is manifestly impossible for any race to attain any considerable degree of civilization except where there is sufficient fertility of soil to admit of their congregating in such numbers as to form communities in which trade, commerce, and skill in various arts and industries would have an opportunity to develop.

In the early centuries of the Christian era there appear to have been two great centres in Sumatra where the Malay-speaking people lived in considerable numbers, and where they attained a high degree of civilization as compared with the other Sumatran tribes. These latter spoke different languages, and, not being maritime races, were confined to certain districts in the interior of the island. The Southern centre of civilization was the valley of the Palembang river. In the nineteenth century Palembang was already a flourishing city, and we learn from Chinese records that the country produced rattans, coconuts, rice, ivory, camphor, cotton, cloth, and other articles of commerce. Their capital was a fortified city, and the people lived in scattered villages outside the town, but in case of war they assembled and elected a chief to lead them, providing their own arms and supplies. Moreover we learn from the same Chinese sources that the kings of Palembang used the Sanskrit character in their writings, and had seals instead of signing their names. There is no doubt that the people of

Palembang owed their advance in civilization to the Javanese. As might be expected with a maritime people, civilizing influences soon began to spread from Palembang. The mythical account in the *Sejarah Melayu* of the establishment of a new kingdom at Singapore, then known as Tamasak, by a prince of the royal house of Palembang, is probably founded on fact. The date of this expedition is fixed by Mr. Wilkinson in the middle of the fourteenth century, but it might easily have taken place much earlier, for there are evidences of the presence of Javanese influences at Jambi and Kampar and other places in that neighbourhood at a much earlier date. The date of the destruction of Tamasak by Javanese from Majapahit is supposed by Mr Blagden to have taken place about the year 1377, and the refugees from Tamasak are stated to have established themselves at Malacca, and founded a new kingdom there, but it is quite probable that Malacca may have existed as a trading centre long before that time.

The northern centre of civilization, where there were Malay-speaking tribes in even greater numbers than in the Palembang hinterland, was the Menangkabau country in central Sumatra, on the upper waters of the Siak, Kampar, and Indragiri Rivers. A hundred years ago Sir Stamford Raffles visited this district, and thus described it:

> As far as the eye could distinctly trace, was one continued scene of cultivation, interspersed with innumerable towns and villages, shaded by the coconut and other fruit-trees. I may safely say that this view equalled anything I ever saw in Java. The scenery is more majestic and grand, population equally dense, cultivation equally rich.

The prosperity of this region dates back many centuries. Javanese inscriptions discovered in that neighbourhood show that a powerful Hindu kingdom existed there in the seventh century of the Christian era. The great assistance which the Menangkabau Malays received from the Javanese in developing their own civilization is shown not merely by the presence of the monuments which they have left, but even more clearly by the names of many places in that region, many of which are of Javanese origin, while others are a mixture of Javanese and Sanskrit. There appears to be no doubt that the Menangkabau Malays attained a high degree of civilization hundreds of years before they adopted the Mohammedan religion. As to the influence of this powerful Menangkabau kingdom upon the Malays of the entire seaboard of Sumatra 400 years ago, when Europeans first came to the East Indies, Marsden gives numerous quotations from the earliest writers, from which it appears that at that time great quantities of gold were shipped from Menangkaban down the Jambi River, and exchanged for cotton goods and other merchandise at Malacca, and the weapons manufactured in Menangkabau from iron, which was smelted locally, were considered the best in the East. From time immemorial all the Malay princes of the coast towns have acknowledged the supreme authority of the rulers of Menangkabau, whom they believed to be descended from the Sang Sipurba of the *Sejarah Melayu*; and while the petty kings on the sea-coast were constantly at war with one another, the rulers of Menangkabau were perfectly safe from attack in the remote interior, and, living in a much more populous country, had undoubtedly far larger forces at their command. Even as late as the year 1615 when the Sultan of Acheen sent a letter to King James I of England Menangkabau appears to have been looked upon as centre of the Malay universe, for, after giving a list of the Malay Kingdoms on the East of Sumatra as far south as Indragiri, he proceeds to enumerate the kingdoms on the West coast of Sumatra, commencing at the North, and concludes with Palembang and Jambi although they are of course on the East Coast.

By what has been said above in regard to Palembang and Menangkabau as centres of civilization of the Malays. I do not wish to imply that there were no other influences at work. It is not to be supposed that the trade and commerce of the Archipelago was confined to one or two important places. On the contrary it is probable that Hindu traders had carried on an extensive trade with Acheen and other ports of Sumatra, especially along the west coast, even before the Hindu religion became established in Java. The local carrying trade was all in the hands of the Malays and Javanese who collected the produce of the Archipelago and brought it to the ports from which it was shipped in the large Indian vessels, and hence the Tamil word for ship, *kapal*, became incorporated into the Malay language. It is also remarkable that some of the products though indigenous to the islands, came to be known by Sanskrit names such as camphor, aloes wood, and nutmeg. Even at the time when the Portuguese first visited Malacca, in 1511, they found many great Indian merchants from the Coromandel Coast established there, and trading in such products of the islands as camphor, benzoin, pepper, cloves, nutmegs, gold, and tin. Of these, benzoin and tin, which were peculiar to the Malay Archipelago, were named as being found in the seaports of India in the first century of the Christian era, so it is almost certain that the trade between India and the East Indies had been carried on for more than a thousand years before Mohammedanism gained any headway.

In order to estimate the influence of Hinduism and the Hindus upon the Malays, Maxwell in his *Manual of the Malay Language* has given classified lists of some of the Sanskrit words which have become incorporated in Malay. It must, however, be remembered that the majority of these words probably came into Malay through the Javanese, which is shown by the fact that corrupt forms of Sanskrit words in the Javanese have been copied in the Malay. Maxwell begins by saying that without the admixture of Sanskrit words the aboriginal Malay would be the poor vocabulary of men hardly raised above savage life, and expressing only the physical objects surrounding men leading a primitive life in the jungle, and all that has to do with their food, dwellings, agriculture, fishing, hunting, and domestic affairs. Sanskrit words are employed by them in describing many of the incidents of commerce, most of the metals and precious stones, the pomp and ceremony of royalty, terms for government and courts of law, for the use of the elephant, and the more formidable weapons, tools and implements. Divisions of time and astronomical terms are expressed by Sanskrit words, and also some parts of the human body, and the feelings and emotions of the human mind, and many abstract ideas, religious terms, and the names of trees, plants, and flowers, many of which are used in the worship of the Hindus.

It is not to be supposed that the Malays were introduced to all the things mentioned above at one and the same time, or even within a period of one or two centuries. The introduction of trade and commerce, and of the arts of civilization, was very gradual, and was spread over many centuries of intercourse with the people of Java and India. As Maxwell suggests, the centres of Hindu influence were probably the kingdoms established first in Java and afterwards at Palembang, Menangkabau, Acheen, Pasai, Jambi. Indragiri, Haru, Malacca, and elsewhere. At the seats of Hindu government there would be religious teachers and priests familiar with the sacred books, and the art of writing in the Javanese or some other modification of the Sanskrit character would gradually spread through the influence of trade. From the fact that the word for "read" (*bacha*) is of Sanskrit origin—we must not infer that the art of writing was unknown in Sumatra before the coming of the Hindu, for no less than three distinct systems of writing which were invented by Sumatran tribes before the Hindu era have survived up to the present time, and the word for write (*tulis*) is a native word. It would be no more erroneous to suppose that the art of writing was introduced by the Arabs because the words now used for pen, ink, and paper came from them. The fact is that the aboriginal tribes of Sumatra have written with a stylus on *lontar* leaves, on books made of bark, and on the smooth surface of the bamboo, before the Sanskrit or Arabic characters were brought to the country, as we can see today among the heathen Bataks. It is also pretty certain that they had attained by their own ingenuity considerable skill in weaving; and in the smelting of iron and the manufacture of steel weapons. In the manufacture of metal work, and of mats and baskets and pottery, they probably did not learn very much from the Hindus; in carpentry they may have adopted one or two additional tools such as the saw (*gergaji*), but neither Hindu nor Arab could teach the Malay anything in the art of boat-building. The most powerful influence of Hindu civilization on the Malay-speaking people of Sumatra appears to have been in matters of government and social life, in trade and commerce, and the art of expressing themselves in abstract terms. It is in these respects that the Malay rose in the scale of civilization far above the tribes of the interior of Sumatra, who did not come into contact with the Hinduism of Java or with the trade of India in the sea-coast towns.

From what has been said above, it will be seen that at the time when the Malays began to be influenced by Mohammedanism they were already living in highly developed communities in two populous districts, in Southern and Central Sumatra, of which the centres were Palembang and Menangkabau. They were also firmly established under less powerful rulers in a number of important trading towns on the coast of Sumatra and the Malay Peninsula. And they were engaged in trading operations which took them as far as Borneo, Celebes, and the Spice Islands.

That there were considerable differences between the Palembang and Menangkabau Malays in Hindu times is clearly brought out by Mr. Wilkinson in his paper on Malay law, in which he shows that there are two absolutely distinct Schools of Malay traditional law, namely the *adat témènggong*, which came from Palembang and is the foundation of the *adat* of Perak and Johore, and the *adat perpateh*, which came from Menangkabau and is met with in Naning and the Negri Sembilan. He says, however, that although there is apparently a great difference between the patriarchal and autocratic *adat* of Perak and the matriarchal and democratic *adat* of Negri Sembilan, the real differences between the two are largely superficial, and are connected with the way the law is administered rather than with the actual law itself. He thinks that they had a common origin, and the *adat témènggong* "simply represents the old Menangkabau Jurisprudence—the true law of the Malays—in a state of disintegration after many centuries of exposure to the Influence of Hindu despotism (in Palembang) and Moslem law". Be that as it may, the Malays of Palembang and Menangkabau were certainly one race, and though the dialect of Menangkabau differs considerably from what we know as the Malay language, there is no doubt that the Malays of the seacoast from Acheen in the north to Palembang in the south all spoke one and the same language which documentary evidence proves to have undergone practically no change whatever since the year 1600.

The first of the Malay kingdoms to become Moslem was probably Acheen, which had long been exposed to the influence of Indian Mohammedan traders, who settled there in great numbers. In their own annals the date of the conversion of the Achinese is given as the year 1206 of our era. Arab traders had visited the Far East in pre-Mohammedan times, but it was not until the Persian Gulf and the trade route to Western India fell into the hands of the Arabs that they began to establish trading settlements in these regions. In an interesting paper read before this Society in 1896, Mr. Blagden states that in an account given by Ibn Muhal-hal about AD 941 of a port called Qalah, which was reached after passing the Nicobar and Andaman Isles, he speaks of it as containing the mines of "the lead called Qala'i, which is found in no part of the world except Qalah"—Qala'i being the Persian and Hindustani for tin. This port was then described as being subject to the great King (Maharaja) of Java, or Zabai, which was the name by which the Arabs knew Sumatra. Mr. Blagden supposes that in Western and Northern Sumatra a population of mixed Arab and native blood had been growing up from the seventh and eighth centuries, and that after Acheen the next places to adopt the new religion were Barus, Lambri (near Acheen), Pasai and Perlak in Northern Sumatra. He dismisses the native accounts of their own conversion to Islam as purely mythical, and supposes, "that what really happened was that in one State after another Arabs and their descendants, by their intellectual powers, their wealth, and their general superiority in civilisation to the natives, acquired strong personal influence at the native courts and amongst the mass of the people, and eventually succeeded, quite peaceably, in getting, Mohammedanism established as the religion of the State".

In 1346 the great Arabian traveller Ibn Battuta visited Samudra (Pasai), which was then the most powerful State in Northern Sumatra and gave its name to the whole island. He found the king a zealous Moslem, surrounded by a court which included learned theologians and doctors of Mohammedan law. He mentions the existence of heathen States in the Archipelago at that time. The King of Pasai at the time of Ibn Battuta's visit was Maliku 'l-thahir, the son of the first Mohammedan ruler of Pasai, Maliku 'l-Saleh, both of whom are mentioned in *Sejarah Melayu*. The kings of Malacca probably did not accept the Moslem faith until some years later than the kings of Pasai, perhaps about the year 1400. Dr. C. Snouck Hurgronje states that Ibn Battuta praises the King of Pasai on account of the Holy wars which he carried on against the heathen in the interior of Sumatra. This Statement is most interesting, as suggesting the methods by which the early converts to Islam enriched themselves, and popularized the new religion in those very early days. There can be no doubt that the Arabs did much to encourage the Malay taste for piratical expeditions. Sir Stamford Raffles writes in his history of Java as follows: "The Arab

Shaikhs and Sayids, whatever doctrines they failed to inculcate, never neglected to enforce the merit of plundering and massacring the infidel; an abominable tenet, which has tended more than any other doctrine of the Kor'an to the propagation of this religion." He further states that, at the time he wrote, the Malay chiefs were constantly engaged in warlike and piratical expeditions, with the approbation of the Arab traders, in which they made slaves of all captives, and the survivors of the crews of vessels which fell into their hands, who were disposed of by sale at the nearest market to the Chinese and Arab traders, and formerly the Dutch! Many of the Arab trading vessels at that time were almost exclusively manned by the slaves of the owner, and their crews were recruited by receiving presents of slaves, or, if that should fail, by kidnapping the natives, He adds that the practice of piracy was at that time "an evil so extensive and formidable that it can be put down by the strong hand alone". Those who have read Abdullah's *Autobiography* will remember that his description of Malay piracy fully confirms the above account given by Raffles. In Africa the Moslems are of course the principal agents in what remains of the slave trade.

One of the earliest records which we have of the conditions which obtained among the Malays under Mohammedan rule is in connection with the first voyages of the ships of the British East India Company. Sir James Lancaster came to Acheen with a squadron of four merchantships in 1602, bringing with him a Jew to interpret for him through the medium of the Arabic language. There are still extant two letters of authority to trade in the countries subject to Acheen, which were given to the leaders of the squadron. They are written in Malay, and one of them is dated 1011 of the Mohammedan era, which is the year AD 1602. These letters are preserved in the Bodleian Library at Oxford, and are believed to be the oldest Malay MSS in existence. Another equally interesting letter preserved in the same collection has been referred to above, namely the letter sent by the Sultan of Acheen in 1615 to King James I. From these documents it is evident that the Malay language as spoken at Acheen in those days was practically identical with the Malay spoken in the Southern part of the Peninsula today. The spelling follows more strictly the principles of Arabic orthography than the modern spelling of the Malays, and the Sanskrit words are spelt in a way which shows that their correct pronunciation was better understood at that time. These letters are printed in No. 30 of the *Journal of the Straits Branch of the Royal Asiatic Society*. The Sultan in his letter to King James claims to have authority over the kings of all the Malay States in Sumatra and on the Malay Peninsula, but he refuses permission to the English people to trade in Tiku and Priaman, on the ground that these places were so far away that he would be unable to protect them if they should be molested. So he insists upon their trading only in Acheen.

The Malay kingdoms enumerated in this letter include ten places on the West coast of Sumatra, and seventeen on the East. It is noticeable that no Malay Kingdom on the Peninsula is mentioned, except Perak and Pahang, and that no reference is made to Menangkabau. There is no doubt whatever that at that time the Mohammedan religion had been adapted by the rulers of all these Malay kingdoms.

The following description of the Sultan of Acheen and his court is taken by Crawfurd from the narrative of a voyage made in 1673, "The King of Achin is a proper gallant man of warre, of thirty-two years, of middle size, full of spirit, strong by sea and land; his country populous; his elephants many, whereof we say one hundred sixty or one hundred eighty at a time. His gallies and frigates carry in them very good brasse ordnance, demi-cannon, culverine, Sakar, Minion, etc., etc., His building is stately and spacious, though not strong; his court at Achen pleasant, having a goodly branch of the main river about and through his palace, which branch he cut and brought, six or eight miles off, in twenty days while we continued at Achen."

At this time the whole foreign trade of the neighbouring States seems to have been attracted at Acheen, perhaps owing to the enmity of the Portuguese which drove the trade away from Malacca. In 1688 the prosperity of Acheen is thus described by Dampier:—Ten to twelve junks came yearly from China, and there were usually from ten to thirteen ships of various nations in the roads. The town consisted of 7,000 or 8,000 houses, and English, Dutch, Portuguese, Chinese, and Indian merchants were established there. The city had no walls and not even a ditch around it. There were a great many mosques with tile roofs. These favourable conditions, however, did not last long, and when Marsden wrote his history of Sumatra, Acheen had ceased to be "the great mart of Eastern commodities". With the adoption of the Mohammedan religion, and perhaps under the influence of the Arab traders, the rulers in most of the Malay ports appear, from the statements of Raffles and Marsden, to have assumed trading monopolies, Raffles says that there is no trace of such monopolies in the hereditary customs of the Malays, and that the practice might have been copied from the monopoly regulations of the Dutch. "Where this system has been fully carried into effect", he adds, "it has generally succeeded effectually in repressing industry and commercial enterprise." Thus the personal greed of the Mohammedan rulers proved a hindrance to the development of the countries over which they ruled.

Judging by the words of Arabic origin which have come into general use among the Malays, the influence of Islam has been almost exclusively confined to religion and those cognate branches of science which among Moslems are considered as a part of their religion. In the absence of definite historical data, the evidence of language is the only reliable test. When the list of Malay words of Arabic origin is compared with those derived from the Sanskrit it is at once seen that Hinduism was by far the more effective civilizing agency. Excluding words intimately connected with religion and religious ceremonies, perhaps the largest class of common Arabic words which have come into the Malay language are those connected with books and the art of writing, such as the words for pen, ink, paper, book, writing, slate, history, dictionary, poetry, science, etc. If the question be asked how the Malays came to adopt the Arabic character instead of the Sanskrit, the answer is not far to seek. The Arabs brought with them a sacred book, the use of which was not confined, as in the case of the Hindus, to a priestly caste, for among the Moslems it is expected of every man who would make any pretense of being religious that he should read the Koran for himself in the original Arabic. This requirement leads to the establishment of Koran schools in all Moslem lands, and the fees paid for instruction in the reading of the Koran is the chief means of support for the Mecca pilgrims on their return from the Hajj. Having learnt to read the Koran in his youth, it is a comparatively simple matter for a Malay to learn to read and write his own language, if he has any ambition to do so. Unfortunately, however, the tendency of the teachers of Islam is to discourage the use of the vernaculars of their converts. This is conspicuously the case among the Bataks at the present time, and Abdullah in his autobiography shows very clearly that it was the same among the Malays a hundred years ago, and that the general spread of vernacular education since his day is due not to Moslem influence, but to the efforts of Raffles and other British officers. Even at the present day, however, a very large proportion of Malays who can read the Koran in Arabic (without of course understanding a word of it) are quite unable to read their own language. In recent years a number of Arabic works on the Mohammedan religion have been translated into Malay. The work of translation has for the most part been done at Mecca and Cairo by Javanese, whose knowledge of Malay was manifestly very imperfect. The style of composition does not appeal to the Malays of the Peninsula, and I understand there is a wider sale for such literature in the Dutch Indies than in British Malaya. The catalogue of a Singapore Malay bookseller contains over 130 titles of such works.

Another important class of words which the Arabs have introduced into the Malay language are those referring to Malay rulers and their government. For instance we have Arabic words for sultan, throne, subject, decree, land, judge, law-court, council, royal drum, etc. Some of these words, however, have simply replaced Sanskrit words formerly in use, or which continue to be used as duplicates. In his paper on Malay law, Mr. Wilkinson says that, before British authority supplanted it, the Malays had three distinct and absolutely irreconcilable systems of law, namely the traditional systems of Menangkabau and Palembang and the Moslem law. Of these the first is democratic, and in Mr. Wilkinson's opinion claims "great merit as a system of law; it was just, it was humane, it tolerated no delay in criminal matters, it secured compensation for the injured; it never brutalized or degraded a first offender." The autocratic system which is associated with the name Palembang appears to have opened the way for a good deal of tyranny, and resulted in the exaction of heavy fines, the enslavement of offenders, and the cruel punishment of any man who dared to gainsay the Malay prince or to disregard his commands. Of the theocratic Moslem law Mr. Wilkinson says that it "was, in its way, even more unsatisfactory than the *adat temenggong*, it multiplied offences intolerably. Cock-fighting, opium-smoking, gambling, illicit intercourse, irregular attendance at Mosque, and even such technicalities as wearing the wrong kind of clothing, and beating gongs at weddings, are liable to be severely punished under Mohammedan law."

As compared with the Sanskrit, it is remarkable how few of the Arabic words which have become incorporated in the Malay language have anything to do with the common everyday life of the people. I do not recall any words connected with industrial pursuits, or with trade and commerce, except those already mentioned which have to do with the art of writing. In connection with funerals we have a number of words, such as death, corpse, grave, bier, tomb, besides the Persian word for tombstone. Circumcision, marriage, and divorce have given half-a-dozen words, and it is perhaps significant that we have in Malay the Arabic words for beggar, almsgiving, and poor, and the Persian *bakshish*; even to this day mendicant Arabs pay regular visits to the Malay villages, and I believe are never sent away empty.

It may perhaps be said that it is hardly fair to compare the influence of the Arabic with the Sanskrit on the Malay language, because when Moslems came to the Malays they found their language fairly well supplied with the terms necessary to civilization, thanks to the previous Hindu influence. A glance, however, at the comparatively short list of words which the Malays have adopted from Portuguese, Hindustani, Chinese, English, and Dutch since Moslem influence was at its height is, I think, sufficient to show that in material things and in practical ways the Chinese and European peoples have done infinitely more than the Arabs to give the Malays the fruits of civilization.

Turning to the question of family life and the relation of the sexes, we find that among the Malays the women enjoy more freedom than in other Moslem lands, and that there is less polygamy and divorce. I think I am also right in saying that, as compared with Egypt, Arabia, and Persia, the Malays are remarkably free from gross immorality, and that unnatural vice is practically non-existent. The only Malay version of the Arabian Nights has fortunately been translated from the English of Lane's expurgated edition and not from the vile Arabic original, but there are other Arabian works which, though they appear in the name of religion, have a most demoralizing tendency. The manuscript of a Malay translation of such a book was brought to the Mission Press many years ago, but I refused to print it owing to the filthy details of sexual intercourse which it contained. Shortly afterwards I was informed that a native printer had been fined $25 by a magistrate for publishing this very book, and that the whole edition had been confiscated and destroyed by the police. That the Malays have to a great extent escaped the corrupting influences of legalized polygamy and indiscriminate divorce is undoubtedly due to the high ideals of family life which they held under the matriarchal system of Menangkabau, which has been referred to above. Neither the degrading ideas about women taught by the Hindus, nor the loosening of the ties of family life through the teachings of Islam, have entirely obliterated the traces of a better conception of the marriage tie. Nevertheless there is much unhappiness among the women, owing to the increasing prevalence of divorce, especially in the towns, and where Moslem influence is strongest.

In estimating the influence of Islam upon the Malays we must not lose sight of the fact that to their way of thinking Islam is not so much a religion as a nationality. If a Mohammedan is asked what is his *bangsa* (nationality), he will probably answer "Islam", whether he be a Pathan, a Tamil, or a Malay. When the heathen Bataks become Moslems they are unwilling to acknowledge their own nationality, but call themselves Malays, so that amongst them Malay and Islam are synonymous terms. To become a Mohammedan means to the Batak to enlist in a great worldwide brotherhood, which raises his social position, and puts him on an equality with those whom he believes to be the most enlightened of Asiatics; and in fact the neophyte is carefully taught that Islam is the great world power, and that the Sultan of Stambul is the greatest ruler in Europe, to whom all the Christian nations are subject, and send ambassadors to his court! Even the Malays have a most exalted idea of the importance of Turkey as a world power. For months past the Malay newspapers have devoted practically all their space to the war in the Balkans, and have written leading articles on the subject *ad nauseam*. Even the enlightened editor of the *Utusan*

Melayu seems to think that it is impossible to interest the Malays in anything outside of Islam. The pilgrimage to Mecca undoubtedly has a powerful influence on the consolidation of the Moslem brotherhood. Mecca is looked upon as the centre of the world's civilization; the journey is undertaken with enthusiasm, and the departing voyagers are the heroes of the hour. On his return the pilgrim is already famous, and has an assured position among his own people. He has been in touch with the Pan-Islam movement, has seen the crowds of pilgrims of all nations, and is more convinced than ever that Islam is the one religion for the whole earth, and that, though the Christian white man is now in the ascendancy, the time will come when the Sultan of Stambul will lead the hosts of Islam to Victory, and sweep all other religions off the face of the earth. No one can read the Malay newspapers of Singapore without seeing that the Pan-Islam movement is bearing fruit even here, though not so noticeably as in the Dutch Indies. A new word for civilization (*tamadun*), which is of course of Arabic origin, has come into use, and appears on almost every page of each newspaper. At present an interesting discussion is in progress as to whether football is compatible with *tamadun*. It probably is not. For, as the editor of the *Nracha* points out, the serious thing is that the enthusiasm of the Malay youth for football matches has decreased the attendance at funerals! To the orthodox Moslem the serious business of life is the regular and proper performance of religious rites and ceremonies, which to us are mere trivialities, and yet consume so much time that it is impossible for any strict Mohammedan to fulfil all the duties of his religion, including purifications, prayers, feasts, fasts, etc, and at the same time give satisfaction to employers who expect their employees to do a whole day's work. The fact is that the excessive ritual of Islam is inimical to industrial progress. In these days of keen competition it is impossible for a Moslem to succeed in business, or even in football, without neglecting some of his religious duties.

When we come to ask ourselves the question, wherein have the Malays benefitted as a race by their adoption of the Mohammedan religion? Is it by no means easy to point to any advance in material prosperity or in civilization which can be attributed to Moslem influence, except the one matter of the widespread knowledge of the Arabic character and the art of reading the Koran, and I think even there we must be careful not to put too high a value upon the elevating influence of the mechanical repetition of strange sounds in an unknown tongue. As regards the development of the resources of the country in which they lived, it appears to me that, after the advent of Islam, the Malays did even less than they did before, owing to the paralyzing influence of piracy and the holy war. The increase of trade at such ports as Malacca and Acheen, before the arrival of the European merchants, seems to have been due to the Hindus and Chinese rather than to the Arabs. The opening up of the mines on the Peninsula was begun by the Chinese, and has been principally in their hands ever since. I can find no evidence that the Arabs have taught the Malays to produce any commodities necessary to their existence or well-being, or that they have bettered their condition as regards agriculture, fishing, or any other industries. From Mohammedan Tamils a few Malays in the towns have probably learnt something of business methods; this seems to be implied by Abdullah's account of the conditions in Malacca at the beginning of the eighteenth century; but the Tamils keep so strictly to business in the towns, and seem to have had so little to do with the spread of Islam, that I doubt whether they have had much influence upon the Malays, who are so essentially a rural people. Mohammedan law, in the opinion of those well qualified to form judgment, has not only failed to improve the lot of the Malays, but is in many respects inferior to the previous system of matriarchal government. In religion Islam has encouraged and perpetuated superstition, the fear of evil spirits, and the bondage of magic by giving the old beliefs new names. Heathen shrines are now called *kramats*, and animistic magic is known as *ilmu* or *hikmat*. Magic arts are now taught as a part of Islam; only the names of God and Mohamed and some of the Jewish prophets have been added to the old formulae. Even the pilgrims to Mecca return with specially sacred charms from Arabia, and the very names of God are made into a talisman. Islam has not merely failed to conquer the primitive animism of the Malays—it has never seriously made the attempt.

In conclusion, I would suggest that what Islam has failed to do for the Malay race, Christian civilization, as represented by the British

Government and British commercial enterprise, has already gone far to accomplish. The country is being rapidly opened up, by better means of communications; even justice is meted out to all; better conditions are being introduced among the people and in all their surroundings; causes of disease are being removed; real education in their own language and the elements of correct information are being given to all classes, and as a result it is to be hoped that ignorance and the unhappiness which results there from will gradually decrease. The devout Moslem still looks to Stambul, Cairo, and Mecca for information and inspiration, but the common people are setting new ideals of life in the vernacular schools and from "the teachers who rub shoulders with the white man on the football field of the Training College at Malacca". The best hope for the future of the Malay lies in the fact that he appreciates even justice, and the sincerity and earnestness of the men to whom he willingly resigns the supreme authority in the management and further development of what was once actually, and is still nominally, his own country. He has vision enough to see who are his best friends, and as long as he continues to trust the white man rather than the Arab, the country and the people will continue to make real progress in civilization.

CRITICISM

by J.L. Humphreys

The syllabus of the Society for the year shows that this criticism was originally to have been made by Mr. R.J. Farrer. His departure on what is generally known as a well-earned holiday made it necessary to delegate the duty to me; and no one regrets more than I do that his absence deprives us of a paper that his varied experience and special knowledge of Malays would have made particularly interesting. Perhaps I may be allowed to say, however, that several conversations with Mr. Farrer in the past have taught me that his general views on the subject of the essay are substantially in agreement with my own; but those who know him will know the wealth of illustration that we have lost by his absence.

I take it that the idea of the Founders of this Society, in making an Essay and a Criticism of that Essay the basis of our evening's meeting, was to provide two adverse aspects of the question under discussion, on the sound principle that the best method for arriving at the truth on any subject is not to listen to the pronouncement of some oracular person supposed to be impartial, but to hear the matter debated with great bias and some heat on both sides. This excellent principle no doubt underlies the procedure of our Courts of Law, though perhaps our legal members will not admit it; and the same idea is seen at work, *Si parva licet componere magnis*, in the minute-papers of the Secretariat. I am confirmed in this idea by a study of the recent publication of the Society, *Noctes Orientales*, where the hostile attitude of the Essayists and their Critics is evident. Tonight, however, I find myself in this difficulty, that I am, unfortunately, in considerable agreement with the substance of the excellent paper to which I have just listened. And I feel that, at the risk of the charge of basely betraying the trust of hostility imposed on me by my position as Critic, I shall be compelled to assent to many of the Essayist's propositions, and enter, like any Balkan State, into alliance with the enemy.

The Essay consisted largely of a summary of Malay history: the Essayist showed the great measure of civilization attained by the Malay Kingdoms of Palembang and Menangkabau under Hindu and Javanese influences traced the coming of the Arabs and the stages of conversion to Muhammadanism, and sketched the Arabic influence in the Malay language, in family life, and in the modern growth of a sense of Islamic nationality. And here, if I may he allowed to say so, I must confess to a slight feeling of disappointment with the Essayist. He is, as we know, a distinguished missionary as well as a Malay scholar; and I had hoped that the subject of his Essay would have given him an opportunity for dealing with the influence of Muhammadanism as a religion rather than as a civilizing agency; that he would, in fact, have written for us more as a missionary than as scholar, have told us more of spiritual and less of temporal changes. And if I have to criticize the Essay, it is generally on these grounds, that the Essayist has not given us what his special and peculiar qualifications give us a right to demand. I find fault with what he has left unsaid rather than with what he has said. Perhaps the dissension which is to follow may persuade him to remedy in his reply the omission of which I now complain.

With the Essayist's scholarly historical sketch of the pre-Muhammadan Malays there will be little dispute. The subject is an obscure one; but there is a general agreement on the main points of the story; viz: that the Malay race of the Peninsula is of Mongolian Tibeto-Annam stock, and descended through Cis-Himalayan regions to the Archipelago, mixing with and overwhelming the aborigines in successive waves of migration; that this race spread from the islands to the Peninsula, and that it is indebted to Hindu influence for most of its civilization.

When the Muhammadan conversion began, Malays were already established in civilized communities on the islands and the mainland. In one of his papers on Malay subjects Mr. Wilkinson classified their political developments into (1) river-states, such as those of Perak, Pahang, and Trengganu today, (2) trading or piratical states, such as the old Malaka, Johor, Brunei, or Riau, and (3) inland matriarchal states, such as the states of Menangkabau and her offshoots the Negri Sembilan of the Peninsula.

Hindu influence, as shown by the language, had given the Malays commerce, several industries, wet-rice cultivation, and, in all probability, royal institutions. They lived as agricultural communities inland, and as fishing, trading, and piratical communities on the rivers and sea-hoards.

The political development and the state of manners of the Malay States of those times find a close parallel in the Greek States of the Mycenaean age and the Trojan war. The stories in the *Malay Annals* remind one constantly: of the incidents of the Homeric poems, and of the pictures of the Greek chiefs and fighting men and their retainers, of the fishermen and peasants of early Hellas. The Annals have even their Paris in Hang Nadim of Malaka who carries off Tun Tija, the Helen of Pahang. A particularly close parallel is seen in the semi-feudal condition of the fighting chiefs. Some of you may know the drinking song of Hybrias the Cretan that begins:

My wealth is here,
The sword and spear,
The breast-defending shield;

With this I plough,
With this I sow,
With this I reap the field.

There is the perfect spirit of the Malay fighting man.

I will not press the parallel, but I will draw attention to one point as a commentary on a remark of the Essayist, namely the phenomenon of piracy as common to both civilizations. The Essayist has pointed to piracy as one of the evil results of Arab influence, and has quoted so great an authority as Sir Stamford Raffles in support of this charge. With all respect I should, suggest that piracy should rather be regarded as a natural feature of life among maritime peoples in an archipelago, where the use of weapons is developed.

I will remind you of the well-known passage in the Odyssey, quoted by Thucydides in the introduction to his history, to illustrate the manners of primitive Greece. Telemachus goes to Pylos and Sparta, and when he lands is asked the polite question: "Are you a trader, or a pirate, such as roam the wine-dark seas, bearing woe to men of alien lands?" As Thucydides points out, this question conveyed no reproach to the person addressed; it was the natural form of introduction between strangers in those days.

I know of no passage in any Malay work that suggests that Malay piracy was ever carried on in the name of religion. The Arabs seem to have been unjustly blamed for it; it should be regarded as a constant phenomenon among high-spirited maritime nations of a certain stage of civilization: a taste common to Viking, Greek freebooter and the Malay fighting men of Swettenham's and Clifford's stories.

To such communities and to such men came the Arabs; not as conquerors but as traders, by the sea routes from the Red Sea and the Persian Gulf. Keen traders, clever courtiers, strong personalities, never bringing their own women abroad, but intermarrying with the people they traded with, they gradually won over the Malay States to Muhammadanism. With ancient civilizations, such as the Hindu, the Cingalese, and the Chinese, they made slow or little progress. But with the Malays they found an inferior religion, a mixture of primitive animism and nature-worship with Hindu mythology, and they succeeded by the inherent superiority of their creed, and by their own persistence.

Such a pioneer was the famous Arab traveller of the fourteenth century, Ibn Batuta, referred to by the Essayist, who made conversions and marriages in a score of places in Asia and Africa, in the course of journeys that have been computed at 75,000 miles. This type is now in its decline. In some Malay States of today, in which a capacity for strong drink and midnight revels is the surest path to royal favour, it is still the Arab who best adapts himself to the local conditions, and obtains his reward in lucrative billets, in admission to the Bar, or in Government contracts. After a century or two of this Arabic influence there came the discovery of the route round the Cape of Good Hope, and with it the Portuguese, Dutch, and English merchants. The *Malay Annals* give us a vivid picture of the Malay State of Malaka as they found it, and of the Malays of those days. There is a famous passage in a manuscript of the sixteenth century attributed to Magellan. It describes the Malaka Malays:

> They have very well made men and likewise the women. They are of a brown colour and go bare from the waist upwards, and from that downwards cover themselves with silk and cotton cloth; and they wear short jackets of scarlet cloth and silk, and carry daggers in their waists wrought with rich inlaid work: these they call querix.
>
> And the women dress in wraps of silk stuffs, and short skirts, much adorned with gold and jewellery, and have long beautiful hair. They live in large houses and have gardens and orchards and pools of water.
>
> These Moors, who are called Malays, are very polished people and gentlemen, musical, gallant and well-proportioned.

"Very polished people and gentlemen, musical, gallant and well-proportioned." Can these words be altered or amended as a description of the real Malay as we know him today? The Malay of those days was, as he is today, a dignified and self-respecting man above all things—a Muhammadan afterwards, high-spirited, quick to resent an insult, and keenly humorous. He mocked the Arab teacher in the *Annals* for his bad pronunciation; when the first Portuguese came he thought them "white Bengalis"; and when their Captain put a gold chain round the neck of the Bendahara, he would have stabbed him for such clumsy ignorance, but the Bendahara said "Let be, he knows not proper manners."

Such was the Malay of the sixteenth century, what of the Malay of the ninteenth with five centuries of Muhammadanism behind him? Of the three types of Malay States the trading and piratical state has almost gone: under European influences Riau, Brunei, Johor, have turned to other things, the river-states of the Peninsula are flourishing exceedingly, and we still have the matriarchal communities of Negri Sembilan. It is in these last two types that we shall best study the changes in the Malay. How has Muhammadanism affected him as a man? Has he changed his character? I think the change has been very small. There is a verse in Mr. Kipling's book *Traffics and Discoveries*, called "Poseidon's Law". Its purport is that the nautical man of all ages has been compelled by the very nature of his occupation to observe perfect truth at sea, since no fiction can deceive the winds and waves; but that when he comes ashore a natural reaction sets in, and he proceeds to revenge himself on his long enforced veracity by stories whose magnificent disregard for truth has become proverbial. Ships and their construction have changed from the days of triremes:

"Where twice two hundred blades bit white, the twin propellers ply";

but the sea stories of today are what they have always been, and
"the robust and brass-bound man,
he has not changed at all."

Perhaps this is what we may say of the Malay—he has not changed at all. We find him in the sixteenth century a high-spirited man, half-child, musical and gallant, fond of sport and women, and such he is today. Muhammadanism gave him a creed and a body of law. But a whole volume of Mr Skeat proves how little the primitive animism and superstitions of Malays have weakened, and how widely they still underlie the surface of Malay Muhammadanism. And all who have studied the communities of Negri Sembilan, or that great book *Acheh and the Achinese*, know how small an inroad religious law has made on matriarchal and tribal customs.

The Essayist has said that Muhammadanism encouraged superstitions and merely gave new names to old heresies. With this statement I entirely disagree; they are still stronger than the new creed in spite of the open protests of Muhammadan priests and teachers. A few illustrations of the persistence of primitive beliefs may be of interest. A few years ago, when stationed in a certain district of Malacca; I was called to decide a question of right of way in a Kampong at the far end of the district, and on visiting the place found a house completely blockaded by the obstruction of all the ways of approach. Inquiries disclosed the fact that the occupiers were a young couple who had eloped and had been married by the Penghulu, and that the blockade was instituted by the girl's family in order to reduce them to reason and compel a divorce. The complete story was this, as told me by many Malays with little variation.

Some sixteen years before a bright light was observed in the sky above a certain house in that part and continued nightly for three months. The lady of the house then gave birth to a girl child. When she was vaccinated, it was noticed that her blood was white. Her parents owned about an acre of rice-land, and one day her mother expressed the fond wish that the land would yield one thousand *"gantang"* of rice; four hundred would be an excellent crop. When the harvest came, to the astonishment of the district, the land yielded a thousand *"gantang"*. It was then realized that the child had supernatural powers, and they were shown in the miraculous fulfilment of many vows made before her or in her name. People came from all over Malacca and even from Negri Sembilan and Selangor to make vows before her, and to bring offerings after their fulfilment; especially after the rice harvest, when for weeks there would be constant strings of bullock carts bringing grateful presents with gifts of money or kind. In short, the girl became a *"Kramat hidup"*, a sacred person, a living shrine.

This had gone on for fifteen years, and the family was now very rich indeed, as riches went there, in houses, rice-fields, and bullock carts. A shrine was built for her, shaped all too like a Muhammadan *"Surau"*, where she sat on a raised platform beneath a mosquito curtain, and granted or denied the prayers of her petitioners.

But one day a party came in bullock carts, with drums and gongs, to pay a vow and make a holiday in the paying of it, as Malays do. Among the party was a handsome boy of good family. He and the girl, the *"Kramat hidup"*, fell in love at sight, and one night fled to a house near by the house now barricaded. The Penghulu of the Kampong had the good sense to marry them, and to protect them from the vengeance of the girl's indignant family; who, like the masters of the damsel of Philippi possessed with a spirit of divination, converted by St. Paul, seeing that the hope of their gains was gone, were prepared to go to any lengths to recover the girl and be rid of the undesirable lover. After some litigation, both criminal and civil, the matter was settled, and before I left the district I had the satisfaction of seeing the girl and her husband fairly well reconciled to her family, and in occupation of a respectable piece of land, part of the proceeds of her supernatural powers. I heard many tales of the extraordinary results of vows made in her name; there was no question whatever of the implicit belief in her sacred character held by many thousands of Malays. She was always addressed as "Dato' Kramat" even by the oldest and most venerable men in the district. It may be imagined that a *"Kramat hidup"* is a very desirable possession, I have heard of two attempts to establish them. On one occasion Mr. Marriott, when district officer there, was informed that a woman had given birth to two eggs. He went to the place, and with considerable foresight took a medical officer with him, who, greatly to the disgust of the family of the lady, and to the disappointment of a crowd of credulous rustics who had gathered to gape on the new marvel, at once pronounced the eggs to be the offspring, one of a hen, and the other of a duck.

Here are primitive beliefs that five centuries of Muhammadanism have been powerless to weaken. Other such beliefs are the rice-planting superstitions, when Imam and Pawang, priest and medicine-man, go down together to the fields to drive out the earth spirits. Anyone who has hunted or shot with Malays will recollect many others; they are as common to educated Malays as to peasants and fisherman. In a Native State in which I was once stationed the prince in charge of the district devoted Friday, our weekly holiday, not to prayer, but to sports; and when a deer was killed he would himself go through the ceremony of *"buang badi"*, casting out the mischief from the carcase, stroking it with leaves and repeating the charm:

"It is not I that casts out the mischief,
It is the angel Michael that casts out the mischief.
I know the origin of the mischief"..., and so on.

So much for Malay beliefs. The same is true of law. Every book written on Menangkabau or Negri Sembilan testifies to the survival of matriarchal law and of the system of exogamic tribes. The husband marries into the tribe of his wife, lives in her house, and becomes a portion of the property of her tribe, an essentially monogamous relation. Muhammadan law and legalized polygamy have proved powerless against the *adat*, the tribal custom. In 1874 H.H. the Sultan of Johor went to Rembau and made great mock of the men of Rembau for their monogamy. But twenty years later Mr. Hale, the district officer, reported that there were only three men in Rembau with more than one wife. There are more today. But they are generally policemen. And their exceptional behaviour has been charitably attributed by Messrs. Parr and Mackray in their work on Rembau to their frequent change of abode, rather than to any strength of religious conviction. That Muhammadan Law should be so powerless against the *adat*, in a matter in which a town Malay is not slow to avail himself of his privileges, is a highly significant phenomenon.

The Essayist has mentioned the Islamic movement in the towns here, but I do not understand that he takes it very seriously. Agitation for a public holiday on Hari Raya, for the encouragement of Malay industries, or for the concession to unwilling gaol-birds of the somewhat doubtful privilege of a month of fasting, are its modern manifestations; but Pan-Islamism does not and will not rouse Malays. The late Sultan of Johor once visited Constantinople, and there was much talk of progress and Pan-Islamism, but he is not recorded to have brought away anything more notable than a decoration bestowed by the Sultan of Turkey, and some charming Circassian ladies.

In conclusion, then, the Malay is a sane and genuine Muhammadan, but no bigot and no fanatic. From Islam as a religion he has obtained a noble creed, an enlightened form of monotheism, and sound habits of personal cleanliness. By it he has been saved from the destruction by alcoholism that so often has followed in the wake of Christianity. From Islam as a political force he has obtained a sense of nationality, and the personal dignity that belongs to a member of the greatest democracy in the world. The Essayist has charged Muhammadanism with the insignificant economic progress of the Malay race as compared with rapid development under British influence, but I suggest that he has failed to show any true relation of cause and effect to justify the charge.

I think a fair verdict on Moslem influence on the Malay race must be that it has operated almost wholly for good and not for evil; and that the influence has been widely spread but not deep. The Malay spirit now is what it was in the fifteenth and sixteenth centuries: Malay literature, folklore, domestic life, art and science are what they have always been but little: perhaps, like the robust and brass-bound mariner, "he has not changed at all".

Notes

1. Robert Hunt, "The Legacy of William Shellabear", *International Bulletin of Missionary Research* (January 2002): 28–31.
2. Ibid., pp. 28–31.
3. Edward Said, *Orientalism* (New York, USA: Vintage Books, 1994), p. 321.
4. Anthony Milner, *The Invention of Politics in Colonial Malaya* (Cambridge: Cambridge University Press, 2002), chapters 6 and 7.

28

MOHAMMEDANISM, AS REVEALED IN ITS LITERATURE

Essay
7 May 1915
by *Rev. W.G. Shellabear*

To judge of a religion from its literature is not perhaps entirely satisfactory, for there are influences which cannot be expressed in writing, and can only be gauged from their results on the lives of individuals, and on the progress and social condition of races. The investigation which is before us tonight has, however, the advantage of that accuracy which attaches to documentary evidence. In regard to those statements which are found in the works which Islam has produced in such abundance there can be no mistakes, except the bare possibility of errors of translation, which in these days of intensive linguistic studies are not liable to be frequent or important. The liability to pass an unfair judgment on Mohammedanism from a study of its literature is therefore confined to misinterpretations of the text, or to a one-sided selection of the works to be studied, or an unfair selection of extracts from those works. It will therefore be my endeavour to consider Mohammedan literature from many different points of view, and to take as great a variety of works as possible under review, in the hope that we may obtain as broad a view as possible of the teaching of Islam.

In the first place it seems obvious that we should devote a good deal of attention to the Koran itself, after which I propose to consider the main teachings of the Koran, the Traditions, and other current Moslem literature on certain fundamental subjects, such as the doctrine of God, the universe, science, the future life, sociology etc., in order to show the influence of their literature upon the Mohammedans themselves.

The Arabian prophet left nothing to his followers in his own writing. Moslem authorities are not even agreed as to whether he was able to read and write. It is quite certain, however, that the Koran is his own composition either written down by his amannenses, or immediately committed to memory and afterwards recited from time to time at public worship. The commentator Bukhari states that it was not until about a year after Mohammed's death that the Koran was first collected as a whole. Subsequently it was found that differences were creeping into the text, and the Caliph Uthman ordered a friend of Mohammed named Zaid to make a recension of the work, and copies of this were sent to every part of the country, after which every other volume or sheet of the Koran was ordered to be burnt. Thus in regard to the sacred book of Islam all difficulties as to textual criticism have been eliminated, and we may assume that the Koran as it now stands is substantially as it was given to his followers by Mohammed, though there is some evidence that certain verses were omitted from Zaid's recension.

When we come to a study of the subject matter of the Koran, we find that it consists of 114 chapters or Suras of varying length, arranged without any system, unless it be that the longest chapters are placed first. This arrangement roughly inverts the chronological order of the chapters, those which were given first being for the most part brief, and the longest being the latest in order of time. In order to study the Koran in connection with the life of Mohammed, and to appreciate the gradual development of his religious system in the mind of the prophet himself, it is advisable to use a translation such as Rodwell's, in which the chapters follow a chronological arrangement, which is based partly upon the definite statements made in the Mohammedan traditions in regard to the time and place of revelation of the various chapters, and partly from a consideration of the subject-matter as connected with events in the life of Mohammed.

In contrasting the style and subject-matter of the chapters in the earlier, middle, and later periods, Rodwell says that in the first fifty chapters the poetical element predominates, with "a deep appreciation of the beauty of natural objects: brief, fragmentary, and impassioned utterances; denunciations of woe and punishment, expressed for the most part in lines of extreme brevity". These short chapters, burning with religious fervour, have in all ages had a deep influence on oriental races. As Mohammed became more prominent as a religious leader, the chapters become more prosaic, and (to quote from Rodwell again)

> the descriptions of natural objects, of the judgment, of heaven and hell, make way for gradually increasing historic statements, first from Jewish, and subsequently from Christian histories ... He who at Mecca is the admonisher and persuader, at Medina is the legislator and the warrior, who dictates obedience, and uses other weapons than the pen of the poet and the scribe.

It is exceedingly difficult for a European to appreciate the high estimate placed by the Arabs upon the literary style of the Koran. The eloquence and beauty of the poetry are considered by them to be but little short of miraculous, and the prose has remained the standard of classical purity ever since. Poetry of some excellence had been written before the time of Mohammed, and it is said that Arabic scholars generally admit that the golden age of Arabic poetry was immediately preceding or contemporaneous with him. Mohammed himself repudiated the idea of being a poet, and, emancipating himself from the fetters of metre, adopted a rhymed and rhythmical prose, in which the clauses are balanced and cadenced by a varying rhyme. The Arabs call this kind of poetry *saj'a*, and to the Malays it is known as *gurindam*. Several examples of the *gurindam* are to be found in the Malay Riddles published a few years ago by Guru Sleiman of Malacca. Captain Burton, the great Arabic scholar, says that "the Arabic is a language in which, like Italian, it is almost impossible *not* to rhyme." An attempt to imitate in English the imperfect rhyme of the Arabic he admits to be full of difficulty, but he gives the following version of the opening chapter of the Koran, known as the *Fatthah*:

1. In the name of Allah, the Merciful, the Compassionate!
2. Praise be to Allah, who the three worlds made.
3. The Merciful, the Compassionate.
4. The King of the day of Fate!
5. Thee alone do we worship, and of Thee alone do we ask aid.
6. Guide us to the path that is straight—
7. The path of those to whom thy love is great,
   Not those on whom is hate,
   Nor they that deviate. Amen.

To our ears there is no charm in this kind of jingle, but the Oriental delights in the reading of these verses with the peculiar intonation with which we are all familiar.

As a favourable specimen of the best style of the Koran the 91st Sura has often been selected. I here give Rodwell's translation of the first ten verses:

By the Sun and his noonday brightness!
By the Moon when she followeth him!
By the Day when it revealeth his glory!
By the Night when it enshroudeth him!
By the Heaven and Him who built it!
By the Earth and Him who spread it forth!
By a soul and Him who balanced it.
And breathed into it its wickedness and its piety,
Blessed now is he who hath kept it pure,
And undone is he who hath corrupted it.

After listening to these two examples of the poetry of the Koran you will perhaps be surprised, as I am, that the great German poet Goethe accords it such high commendation as the following:

> However often we turn to it, at first disgusting us each time afresh, it soon attracts, astounds, and in the end enforces our reverence... Its style, in accordance with its contents and aim, is stern, grand, terrible—ever and anon truly sublime... Thus this book will go on exercising through all ages a most potent influence.

Sale, in the Preliminary Discourse preceding his well-known translation, gives the following appreciation of the literary merits of Mohammed's work:

> The style of the Koran is generally beautiful and fluent, especially where it imitates the prophetic manner, and Scripture phrases. It is concise, and often obscure, adorned with bold figures after the Eastern taste, enlivened with florid and sententious expressions, and in many places, especially where the majesty and attributes of God are described, sublime and magnificent.

Mr. Stanley Lane Poole, in the introduction to Lane's *Selections from the Koran*, is even more favourable in his estimate, as follows:

> In the Suras revealed at Mecca, Mohammed has but one theme—God: and one object—to draw his people away from their idols and bring them to the feet of that God. He tells them of Him in glowing language, that comes from the heart's white heat. He points to the glories of nature, and tells them these are God's works. With all the brilliant imagery of the Arab, he tries to show them what God is, to convince them of His power and His wisdom and His justice. The Suras of this period are short, for they are pitched in too high a key to be long sustained. The language has the ring of poetry, though no part of the Koran complies with the demands of Arab metre. The sentences are short and full of half-restrained energy, yet with a musical cadence. The thought is often only half expressed; one feels the speaker has essayed a thing beyond words, and has suddenly discovered the impotence of language, and broken off with the sentence unfinished.

As regards the later portions of the Koran, however, the same writer says:

> In the Suras of the second period we begin to trace the decline of the prophet's eloquence... We feel we have fallen the whole depth from poetry to prose, and the matter of the prose is not so superlative as to give us amends for the loss of the poetic thought of the earlier time and the musical fall of the sentences. In the Suras of the Medina period these faults reach their climax... The earliest Mecca revelations are those which contain what is highest in a great religion and what was purest in a great man.

I think we must come to the conclusion that a proper appreciation of the poetic beauties of the Koran is only possible to those who are thoroughly familiar with the original language, and in estimating the effect of the constant reading of their sacred book upon the minds of the Moslems of these lands it must not be forgotten that with rare exceptions the Malays are almost wholly ignorant of the meaning of what they read. Consequently it seems probable that the enthusiasm with which they intone these verses in an unknown tongue is aroused by a sense of the sacredness of the volume, heightened by the reverence with which they are taught to handle it and to prepare for the reading by the most careful and scrupulous ablutions. There is also, no doubt, a feeling of pride and self-satisfaction in having mastered the difficult task of producing the unfamiliar sounds, which requires long practice and no small exercise of the memory in order to attain a result which will call forth the approbation of the admiring group of listeners.

Turning now from the earlier chapters of the Koran, which are wholly the creation of Mohammed's own genius, and to a large extent the expression of his own ideas, we come to those Suras containing historical matter, which the investigations of learned orientalists have shown to be based upon the Talmud and other traditional elements of Jewish history, and also upon certain apocryphal and spurious Christian books, as well as upon the writings of the Zoroastrians.

The close connection between the Koran and the Jewish traditions and Christian legends was pointed out by Sale nearly two hundred years ago, when his translation of the Koran was first published. A recent work, however, by Dr. St. Clair Tisdall, entitled *The Original Sources of the Koran*, has gone into this matter in great detail, showing not only that the narratives in the Koran, which differ very materially from those in the canonical Scriptures, are almost identical with the legends in the Targunis and apocryphal books, but also that Mohammed borrowed ideas, legends, and religious rites from many different quarters.

The Western mind marvels at the credulity of the founder of Islam in accepting as true all the marvellous myths and legends which he has incorporated in the Koran, but the fact that they are almost universally accepted as true by his followers even to the present day indicates that Mohammed knew what would be likely to appeal to the hearts of his people. In fact we are confronted with this strange phenomenon—that the more fanciful and improbable the story may be, the more tenaciously is it believed, and by so much the greater is the miracle conceived to be.

Take, for instance, the story of the Night Journey, or Miraj in which Mohammed is supposed to have ascended to heaven, and to have been introduced by the angel Gabriel to the Hebrew prophets. Adam being located in the first heaven, John and Jesus in the second, and so forth, until he met Abraham in the seventh heaven. Afterwards in God's court he is said to have obtained for his followers the privilege of a reduction in the numbers of prayers to be said each day from fifty down to five, the number which is now obligatory. The only reference to this miraculous journey in the Koran is as follows: "Praise be to Him who caused His servant to journey by night from the Sacred Mosque to the Farther Mosque, whose enclosure we have blessed, that we might show him of our signs." The story has, however, been greatly expanded and embellished in the Traditions, and there has been added a vision of the four rivers of Paradise and of a tree called the Lotus of the Boundary. Some Arab writers have regarded this journey as a mere vision, but the vast majority of Mohammedans accept it as literally true. Dr. Tisdall tells us that the story is in the main based upon the account of the ascension of a young Zoroastrian priest named Arta Viraf, recorded in the reign of a Persian king some 400 years before the time of Mohammed. In this "Book of Arta Viraf" it is said that "his spirit ascended into the heavens under the guidance of an archangel named Sarosh, and passed from one storey to another, gradually ascending until he reached the presence of Ormazd, the Good God of the Zoroastrians. We are also told that in the Sanskrit there are similar tales, such as the journey of Arjuna through the heavens, where he saw the heavenly palace of Indra. Similar legends are found in certain Christian apocryphal works, telling how Paul ascended to the heavens and saw the four rivers of Paradise, and how the Archangel Michael descended and took Abraham up in a cherubic chariot, which appears to be the counterpart of the animal called Burak, "smaller than a mule and taller than a donkey, and white," on which the Traditions state that Mohammed was seated.

In the Koran descriptions of Paradise and Hell there are also many things which can be traced back to Persian and Hindu origins. The word "Paradise" itself (*firdaus*) is a Persian word, and the black-eyed Houris and the immortal youths (*ghilman*), who are said in the Koran to wait upon those who enter Paradise, correspond to similar beings mentioned in ancient Persian legends and in the writings of the Hindus. Even the Bridge of the Dead, "finer than a hair and sharper than a sword", which stretches over the abyss of hell, and is the only way by which men may pass from earth to heaven on the judgment day, is the Persian Bridge of Chinvat reaching over hell, which the spirit of a man must cross in order to enter Paradise.

To the orthodox Moslem the idea that the Prophet borrowed the materials of his revelations from the Jews, Christians, and Zoroastrians of his time is utterly abhorrent. In the first place they contend that Mohammed could neither read nor write, and therefore it would be quite impossible for him to obtain all the information about the traditions of other races which we find incorporated in the Koran. There is, however, a good deal of evidence in the Traditions that Mohammed actually was able to write, and therefore of course could read. Moreover the errors which occur in the Koran, and the slight variations between his versions of the various legends and the originals from which he borrowed them, show very clearly that he received his information orally. Though the substance of the greater part of the historical matter in the Koran was gathered from a great variety of sources, Mohammed's extraordinary genius enabled him to adapt all this material to his own purposes, and to produce verses which his followers, being ignorant of the foundations upon which he was building, imagined to be original and direct revelations from God. It is remarkable, however, that the Koran itself tells us that his enemies said, "This Koran is a mere fraud of his own devising, and others have helped him with it who had come hither by outrage and lie. And they say, 'Tales of the ancient that he hath put in writing! and they were dictated to him morning and even.'"

In the second place, the Moslem theologians explain that the subject-matter of the Koran could not possibly have been obtained from human sources, because the Book itself was written in heaven on a "Preserved Tablet" long before the creation of the world, and was merely handed down to Mohammed piecemeal by the angel Gabriel. Dr. Tisdall points out that they will not even admit that the Psalms were written before the Koran, although it is written in the 21st Sura. "And now, since the Law was given, have we written in the Psalms, that 'my servants the righteous shall inherit the earth.'" We would naturally infer from the above quotation that the Psalms must have been written before the Koran, or they could not be quoted from: but the Moslems stick to their assertion that the Koran pre-existed on the "Preserved Tablet", which itself appears to be reminiscence of the later Jewish: that not only the Ten Commandments, but also all the books of the Old Testament and even the Talmud, were written on the two Tables of Stone which were "preserved" in the Ark of the Covenant, not in heaven as Mohammed teaches, but in the presence of God in the Tabernacle.

When we come to consider the influence of the Koran on the Malays, we must confess that the book itself as literature has practically no power to touch their lives owing to their almost universal ignorance of the Arabic language. It is true that there exists an interlinear translation of the text, the translation with the comments of Baihawi following the Arabic original verse by verse, but owing to the cost (from $5 to $7) the circulation of this book is limited, and the language is so very far from being idiomatic Malay that it is not at all readable. It is true that educated Malays frequently quote chapter and verse of the Koran in support of their opinions, and some of them will interlard their conversation to such an extent with these quotations, which they have memorized, that it is almost impossible for anyone who does not know these Arabic phrases to follow their arguments or to understand what they are driving at. Such quotations, however, are rarely, if ever, taken from the Koran itself: they come from the Malay tracts and booklets on which many teachers base their instruction, and which have an immense sale among the Malays everywhere. The number of such quotations which have any considerable currency among the Malays is probably very limited. The Koran itself is to all Mohammedans of other tongues than the Arabic a sealed book, and even the Arabs themselves, if they only know the colloquial language, must make a special study of the literary Arabic in order to understand the book.

We will now pass on to a consideration of the principal doctrines of Islam, as revealed in the Traditions, and in the current literature which we find among the Malays printed in their own language.

It is generally conceded that the great merit of the Mohammedan religion is its teaching in regard to the unity of God, and there can be no doubt that the monotheism taught by Mohammed was a great advance upon the idolatry which had existed in Arabia from a remote period. The mere fact, however, that the Moslems believe that there is only one God, and hold the very simple creed *La ilaha illa 'llah*—"there is no deity but Allah"—is not sufficient evidence of the truth of their religion. The really important question is, "What is the Mohammedan conception of the character of God?" If it be true, as the great traveller Palgrave declares, that Mohammed's system is really the Pantheism of Force, and that there is no place left for absolute good or evil,— all being ascribed to the autocratic will of the one great Agent, who has no love for his creatures, but chiefly a feeling of jealousy of them, lest they encroach upon his rights by attributing to themselves something of what is his alone,— then it could hardly be expected that the worship of such a despot would produce in the hearts of the worshippers those higher virtues which the great Christian apostle sums up in the words Faith, Hope, and Love. It would be much more natural to expect that the worshippers of such a God as Palgrave describes would be filled with pessimism and hatred and selfishness, and would have no definite ideas of an absolute standard of right and wrong apart from the letter of the law. Let us see what grounds Palgrave has for such a description of the God of Islam.

In the first place, is pantheism taught earlier in the Koran or in the other Moslem works? There is a verse in the Koran (Sura 57, verse 3) which is called the "Mother of the Attributes", and reads as follows: "He is the first and the last, the seen and the hidden." Dr. Zwemer in his recent work on *The Moslem Doctrine of God* says:

> Whether Mohammed himself intended to teach the ideas of pantheism, or had any idea of the import of these terms, does not alter the fact that they spell pantheism to many of his followers. If pantheism is the doctrine of one substance, it is taught here. God is the inside and the outside

of everything. He is the phenomena (*dhahir*) and the power behind the phenomena (*batin*). How far this teaching was carried is best seen in the celebrated Masnavi of Jalal-udin ar-Rumi, translated into English by E.H. Whinfield. He puts these words as emanating from Deity:

I am the Gospel, the Psalter, the Koran;
I am Uzza and Lat—Bel and the Dragon.
Into three-and-seventy sects is the world divided,
Yet only one God; the faithful who believe in Him and I.
Lies and truth, good, bad, hard and soft,
Knowledge, solitude, virtue, faith,
The deepest ground of hell, the highest torment of the flames,
The highest paradise,
The earth and what is therein,
The angels and the devils, spirit and man, am I.
What is the goal of speech; O tell it, Shems Tabrizi?
The goal of sense? This—The World Soul am I.

The verses which have been attributed to the German emperor, and are said to have been found in his waste paper basket, must have been made on this model:

Oh Me! Oh My! and likewise I!
Sit still my curls while I orate.
Me, I myself, the Throne, the State.
I am the earth, the moon, the sun,
All rolled in one!
Both hemispheres am I, Oh My!
The North and Southern Poles, the Milky Way, etc. etc.

From my personal knowledge of the Malays I incline to the opinion that they attribute all phenomena to God, and are to all intents and purposes pantheists. It is very certain that the Koran itself teaches that Allah is the author of evil as well as of good. I have already quoted a verse in which it is said that He breathed into the soul of man its wickedness and its piety. In many passages Allah is said to lead men astray, and in the 13th verse of the 32nd Sura he says: "Had we pleased we had certainly given to every soul its guidance. But true shall be the word which hath gone forth from me—I will surely fill hell with Jinn and men together." A passage in the Traditions goes even further in explaining the arbitrary predestination of certain individuals to eternal tortures; for, taking a mass of earth from which all mankind was to be formed, Allah is said to have thrown one half into hell, saying, "These to eternal fire, and I care not", and the other half into heaven, saying "and these to Paradise, I care not."

It has been said that Allah cares nothing for character, but only for submission. His mercy and compassion, which are so frequently referred to in the Koran, are only for those who obey him and the prophet. Dr. Zwemer says:

> Nothing is right or wrong by nature, but becomes such by the fiat of the Almighty. What Allah forbids is sin, even should he forbid what seems to the human conscience right and lawful. What Allah allows is not sin, and cannot be sin *at the time he allows it*, though it may have been before or after. One ha only to argue the matter of polygamy with any Moslem mullah to have the above statements confirmed. To the common mind there is indeed no distinction whatever between the ceremonial law and the moral; nor is it easy to find such a distinction even implied in the Koran.

He quotes the following examples from the Traditions: "The prophet, upon whom be prayers and peace, said—One dirham of usury which a man eats, knowing it to be so, is more grievous than thirty-six fornications; and whosoever has been so nourished is worthy of hell-fire." And again, "The taking of interest has seventy parts of guilt, the least of which is as if a man commits incest with his mother."

One most extraordinary feature of the Mohammedan conception of God is that Allah himself does not appear to be bound by any standard of justice. The Koran states that he punished Satan for being unwilling to worship Adam when he was created, though of course it is considered a deadly sin to worship any but God himself. One of the great Sunni theologians, named Al Ghazzali, says:

> Allah's justice is not to be compared with the justice of men. For a man may be supposed to act unjustly by invading the possession of another, but no injustice can be conceived on the part of God. It is in His power to pour down upon men torments, and if He were to do it, His justice

could not be arraigned. Yet He rewards those that worship Him for their obedience on account of his promise and benevolence, not of their merit or of necessity, since there is nothing that He can be tied to perform; nor can any injustice be supposed of Him, nor can He be under any obligation to any person whatsoever.

Perhaps the most widely circulated treatises in the Malay language are those on the Twenty Attributes of God (Sifat Dua-puloh). These are really thirteen in number, the remaining seven being the converse of numbers 7 to 13. It will be noticed that none of these are moral attributes. They are as follows: Existence, Eternity in the Past, Eternity in the Future, Freedom from Change, Self-subsistence, Unity, Power, Will, Knowledge, Hearing, Seeing, Speech, Life. As a specimen of the comments of Moslem theologians on these attributes, let us take the following on the Will of God, which gives us a view of the fatalism which is such a blight upon all Mohammedan races; the writer is named Mohammed al-Barkawi:

> He can do what He wills, and whatever He wills comes to pass. He is not obliged to act. Everything, good or evil in this world exists by His will. He wills the faith of the believer and the piety of the religious. If He were to change His will there would be neither a true believer nor a pious man. He willeth also the unbelief of the unbeliever and the irreligion of the wicked, and without that will there would neither be unbelief or irreligion. All we do we do by His will; what He willeth not does not come to pass. If one should ask why God does not will that all men should believe, we answer, "We have no right to enquire about what God wills and does. He is perfectly free to will and to do what He pleases."

It seems remarkable that the Koran, which Mohammed himself says (Sura 10, verse 38) "confirmeth what was revealed before it, and is a clearing up of the Scriptures" should give such a very inadequate and unworthy conception of the Deity. As a revelation of God the Koran has taken more than one step backwards, for in this respect it is vastly inferior to the very earliest books of the Hebrew canon, and it is not in the same category as Jesus Christ's conception of the universal fatherhood and love of God.

The ideas on cosmology and natural science to be found in Mohammedan literature are, to say the least of it, most extraordinary.

Let me give a few examples from a Malay work based on the Traditions and known as *Bustamus al-Salatin*, or *The Garden of the Sultans*, in which it is stated that the sun was made from the light of the throne of God, or according to another account form a kind of precious stone, and the moon from the light of the screen or covering of the throne. The sun is the size of the earth, and similarly the moon; if it were not so, they would not be visible in all parts of the earth! The commentators say that the sun is in the fourth heaven and the moon in the first; and the face of each of them is upwards and their backs towards the earth, and the size of the sun is three hundred times that of the earth, and the size of the moon twenty times that of the earth; and one story says that the sun is on a wheeled cart with 360 drag ropes, and with 360 angels to each drag rope to haul it. The fact that the different traditions do not agree appears to present no difficulty whatever to the Moslems. The same work continues: now on the west side of heaven there are 180 springs of black mud, the water of which boils as if in a cauldron, and similarly on the east side, and according to one story, the sun and moon both revolve incessantly, and when they revolve too much, both of them capsize in those springs, hence the eclipses. It is more generally believed, however, that when an eclipse occurs the sun or moon is attached by a dragon (*rahu*), and at that time special prayers are enjoined in the Traditions, that the heavenly bodies may be saved from the danger which threatens them. The phases of the moon are thus explained: the sun is always perfectly round, because every night it prostrates itself below the throne of God; whereas God does not permit the moon to prostrate itself except on the 14th day of the month, so from the first day of the month its light increases for joy that God permits it to worship on that night; after that its light decreases for sorrow. The meteors are said to be missiles thrown by the angels at devils who go to heaven eaves-dropping. One day the Prophet Mohammed was asked to explain thunder, and replied that it was the voice of the angel who guards the clouds, and holds in his hand a whip of fire. The seven layers of the earth were created from foam, for where the earth is it was formerly all water, and the foam of this water was collected in the place of the Kaabah or temple of God.

When the prophet was questioned as to where the foam came from, he replied, "From the waves, and the waves were made from the sea, and the sea from darkness." When he was asked what supported the earth, the prophet replied, "an ox with 4,000 heads, and there is a distance of about 500 years' journey between its heads". When asked what the ox stood on, the prophet replied, "On a rock"; and to subsequent questions he answered that the rock was on the back of a fish, and the fish on a sea the depth of which is about a thousand years' journey, and the sea is on the wind and the wind on darkness, and the darkness on hell, and hell on moisture. When asked what was under the moisture, the apostle of God answered, "O Abdullah, your question is wrong, for God Almighty alone knows what is under moisture." The amazing thing is that the credulity of the people is such that these fables are actually believed to be true by the great majority of the Malays, and I am told by Moslems of other races, though of course nowadays there are many who through having received a western education know better. It is perhaps worthy of remark that the book from which I have translated these extracts was used some time ago as a textbook in the Government vernacular schools of these Settlements.

The geography taught in this same book is equally marvellous. The waters of the earth are said to be divided into seven oceans, which include the Red Sea, Persian Gulf, and other waters around Arabia, but nothing more distant than the Indian Ocean and the "Sea of Rum" which is presumably the Mediterranean. The chief rivers of the world are the Nile, Euphrates, Saihun and Jaihun, the last of which is said to be the Ganges, and their importance consists in the fact that they flow down from heaven!

Moslem history is based principally on Jewish traditions. Confusions and anachronisms are not uncommon, such for instance as the inclusion of Alexander the Great among the prophets, and the statement that the Virgin Mary was the sister of Moses and Aaron. The horizon of Moslem historians is extremely limited, and their history, being based upon the Koran and the traditions, ends abruptly soon after the time of Mohammed. This is an example of the deadening effect of their religious system upon the intellectual life of Moslem races. The word science (*ilmu*) is used only of religious knowledge, as expressed in the Koran and the Traditions. Thus to the orthodox Mohammedan all knowledge is stereotyped, and further progress is impossible. Orthodox Mohammedan literature takes no account of anything which is not to be found either in the Koran itself, or in the Traditions, or in the comments thereon written by orthodox theologians.

An immense amount of space in all books of tradition is given to eschatology. A Malay translation in my possession devoted two chapters to the creation of the spirits of Mohammed and Adam (which to the Moslem is the correct chronological order); five chapters to various angels, with special reference to the Angel of Death; eighteen to the state of the soul when separated from the body, eight to the signs of the judgment-day, fourteen to the Judgment itself, eight to Hell, and six to Heaven. The Malays believe in such a literal resurrection of the body that a woman whom my wife took to the dentist last week was careful to inquire whether a filing could be removed in the event of her death because it would not be permissible for her to take such extraneous matter into heaven! The soul is represented as being deeply concerned as to the welfare of the body after death. The following is a free translation from the Malay: The Prophet said, "Three days after the spirit has left the body of a man, he says 'O my God, permit me to go and see my body.'—God permits him, and he comes to the grave and sees from afar, and verily blood is streaming from both nostrils and from the mouth. After prolonging weeping, he says, 'O my poor body, my beloved, do you remember all the days of your life, of sickness and sorrow and repentance.'" Then he goes away. But he again asks permission, and returns to the grave on the fifth and seventh days, and finds the body in a worse condition, but speaks to it as before. Another tradition follows, which says that the spirit of a believer haunts his house for a month to see about his property and how it is divided, and how his debts are paid, and when one month is complete he returns to his hole (*lobang*). The aim of this tradition is fairly obvious. Afterwards he similarly stays round about for a whole year, and sees who prays for his soul, and who is sorry about him; and when the year is complete his soul is lifted up to the place where all souls assemble till the day of judgment—that is, until the sound of the last trump.

Such literature as this is quite enough to account for the superstitious dread of ghosts which is characteristic of all Moslems. A recent account of the Mutiny here in Singapore tells how the body of a murdered volunteer was sufficient to guard the whole camp from the depredations of the Mohammedan mutineers.

The signs of the Day of Judgment are divided into "lesser" and "greater". The latter include the appearance of the Beast, sixty cubits high, which is to be a mixture between a bull, hog, elephant, stag, ostrich, lion, tiger, cat, ram, and camel, with the voice of an ass, and is to mark believers on their faces. Another sign is to be war with the Greeks and Romans, and the taking of Constantinople by 70,000 of the descendants of Isaac, before whom the walls will fall down when they cry, "*La ilaha illa 'llah*," there is no deity but God. Other signs will be the coming of Anti-Christ and of Jesus; the latter will accept the faith of Islam, marry and beget children, kill Anti-Christ, and at length die and be buried at Medina. Gog and Magog will oppose Jesus, and their hosts will drink the Sea of Galilee dry, but God will destroy them, and fill the earth with their carcases, and the Moslems will burn their bows, arrows, and quivers for seven years. Of course Islam has no thought of more modern weapons. Finally there is to be the coming of the Mahdi, concerning whom the Prophet said that the world would not come to an end until one of his own family and name should govern the Arabs.

In the 32nd Sura, verses 4, it is stated that the Day of Judgment will be a thousand of such years as we reckon, but in Sura 70, verse 4, the length of that day is given as fifty thousand years. The resurrection will include angels, jinns, mankind, and animals. When one of the Prophet's wives heard that men would be raised up as naked as when they were born, she asked whether the males and females would be together: to which the Prophet replied, "striking his glorious band on the shoulder of Ayesha, 'On that day all mankind will be sad, looking up to the sky with staring eyes, and standing for forty years without eating and drinking, and every one of them sweating through shame before God; some of them up to their ankles in sweat, some to the calves of their legs, some to their bellies, some to their breasts, and some up to their faces, all through waiting so long. All men will be divided into three classes, believers, hypocrites, and unbelievers; and during the period of waiting, the believers will be shaded from the heat of the sun by the shade of God's throne, but the wicked will be so tormented that they will cry, 'Lord, deliver us from this anguish, though Thou send us into hell-fire.' Finally God will appear to judge them, and some say that he will judge all creatures in half a day, but others say it will be done in less than the twinkling of an eye."

The bridge as-Sirat, along which all creatures must pass, has already been referred to. The briars and hooked thorns, with which the bridge is beset on either side, present no obstacle to the believers, who pass as swiftly as the wind, while the wicked fall headlong into hell, where they endure a great variety of tortures, with which I will not harrow your feelings.

The Mohammedan conception of seven heavens, with four rivers, and something corresponding to the tree of life, has already been spoken of in connection with the night journey of the prophet. The gates and the rivers and trees, and the food and drinks which are supplied, and many other things in heaven, are described in great detail in the Malay translation of the Traditions to which I have referred. But of course the most remarkable feature of the heaven of Mohammed is the lavish provision which is made to satisfy the sexual appetites of the faithful. The Malay version describes the *houris* (*bidadari*) as being made of saffron and perfumes from the toes to the knees, and from thence to their breasts of musk, and thence to the neck of ambergris, and from the neck upwards of camphor. Their hair is of silk, and their colour is white and green and yellow and red. Now, when men reach the gates of heaven and knock at the doors, they are met by the *houris*; and each *houri* comes out to her husband, and kisses him and says "You are my beloved and I am pleased with you, and will love you for ever." And they go into the house with their husbands, and in the house there are seventy beds, and on each bed seventy mats, and on each mat seventy *houris*, and each *houri* has seventy garments, so transparent that the plumpness of their legs is visible. The tradition continues—Now, all the men in heaven have intercourse with the *houris* and with the women who were their wives on the earth, whom God most likely causes to become virgins again; similarly when men have had connection with the women of their household they become virgins again. After describing the delicious food and drinks provided in heaven, the tradition proceeds to explain that the only secretion necessary in heaven is a kind of perspiration, which is more fragrant than musk. Moreover the people in heaven become daily more beautiful, and the males are given the strength of a hundred men, both for eating and drinking, and also for sexual intercourse, and they have connection with the *houris* as with their wives on the earth for a period, and one period of coition is 80 years; and the males have no emission of semen, neither do the women have semen.

As all Moslems are well aware that this kind of a life is promised them in heaven, it is not to be wondered at that their minds are filled with thoughts of sensual pleasure in this world also. A close acquaintance with the family life of the Malays reveals the widespread corruption of morals, which must in large measure be attributed to the prurient literature of Islam, for it is in the remote country districts, where Mohammedanism is little more than a name, that we find the purest family life. It is astonishing to what an extent the literature of Islam is tainted with gross sensuality. It is difficult to imagine anything more vile than the Arabian Nights Tales, as revealed in Burton's literal and an expurgated edition translation, alongside of which the very worst French novels are comparatively innocent. Yet I am told that these filthy stories are a faithful picture of present-day social conditions in Persia. But what shall we say when we find that the most barefaced and realistic word-pictures of the sexual act are incorporated in the religious literature of Islam with the avowed intention of instructing the votaries of that religion in the art of obtaining the maximum of sensual gratification from an act the real purpose of which, our reason tells us, is the propagation of the species and not mere lust. Such a word-picture I was surprised to find recently in a pamphlet on the attributes of God!

Some years ago, when I was managing the Mission Press, a Mohammedan religious teacher brought me a book to be printed; I found however, on examination, that it was a treatise on sexual intercourse, and explained to the customer, to his evident astonishment, that I considered it immoral, and would not print it on any account. Subsequently I was told by some of my workmen that the book had been printed at a native press but had been confiscated by the police, and that a fine had been imposed upon the printer. Probably the police are too busy now to attend to such things, for I have recently purchased for 50 cents a treatise entitled "The Laws of Coition". The descriptions contained in the book are so bald and lewd that they cannot fail to have a very demoralizing influence upon the reader. This the author seems to be well aware of, for he says that the force of the sexual act is increased by looking at other people or animals in the act of coition, and by reading books composed by the theologians to explain sexual matters, and by reading stories of those who are strong in sexual intercourse, and by listening to the voice of passionate women, for all of these inflame the sexual passion. The main object appears to be to prolong the sexual act, and Burton tells us in a note to the Arabian Nights that it is for this purpose that opium is used, to the utter destruction of the nervous system, complete impotence often resulting, which is the object of so many oriental quacks to cure.

I regret that it has been necessary to use such great plainness of speech in dealing with this aspect of Moslem literature, but unfortunately it is impossible to arrive at a proper and complete understanding of Mohammedan books without a very definite statement of the facts of the case.

If I had not already exceeded the usual limits to the length of our papers, I might have dealt with books of magic, love potions, lucky times, etc. I think, however, that what I have written is sufficient to show that the literature of Islam is not of the most elevating character. The poetry and literary elegance of the original Arabic works are lost upon the Malays and other races who do not speak the language. What remains is a confused mass of unscientific and often self-contradictory statements in regard to the phenomena of nature, elaborate instructions in regard to religious ceremonials, a great deal of miscellaneous matter which arouses and fosters ignorant superstition, and a doctrine of God which is far inferior to that of the two great religions which were not altogether unknown to the Prophet of Arabia. One can hardly resist the conclusion that a religious teacher who professed to confirm and perfect the previous revelations ought to have been able to produce something better adapted to benefit his own and other races.

CRITICISM
by Tan Teck Soon

At the outset of this criticism I think it would be but justice to myself to premise that personally I am not a Mohammedan, nor a student of Mohammedan literature in any of its branches. From the view point of the Christian missionary, as well as of a *bona fide* Mohammedan defender, I am therefore but a Philistine and an ignorant pagan and I feel myself like an advocate suddenly called upon to plead for an absent and dumb defendant without any evidence in support or justification—so cannot help sometimes assuming the function of a judge, or perhaps of a disinterested arbitrator on the several points at issue. I shall therefore refrain from discussing any of the controversial or polemical points of dispute, such as authorship, theological or doctrinal dogmas, accuracy of literary expressions, technical terminology exact interpretation, etc.

Religion, I take it, is not a mere historical survey of the progress of civilization, nor a record of its intellectual development; nor can we understand its full significance without a wider investigation into what is known as "religious dynamics"—that is, the life impulse of a civilization, the motive power which uplifts a race or individuals out of the ire into regions ethereal. To expect therefore that the literary products of a race or civilization would reveal or even adequately reflect its innate life, or its inner religious consciousness is perhaps to demand too much from its individual mental endowments. At best we can have but partial and imperfect glimpses of such revelations. With a civilization like the Indian, Chinese, Jewish or Arabian, which has evolved its own distinctive religion out of its own ethnic elements and consciousness, this method of inquiry would perhaps be justifiable. But to expect the same results from such civilizations like the Burmese, the Siamese, or the Cingalese, who have adopted Buddhism as their national religion, or from the Persian, the Turk, or the Malay, who have embraced Islam as mere converts, would perhaps be less satisfactory. With European Christianity the case, however, is somewhat different, for the mental equipment of the race being more vigorous, active, and scientifically analytical, we do possess abundant materials in the literature of its several sects to enable us to form with approximate correctness some idea as to its doctrines, dogmas and ethical aspirations and ideals. To expect from Malayan literature especially revelations as to Mohammedan beliefs and doctrines appears to me analogous to expecting the same results from Chinese converts as regards Christian tenets and dogmas. From purely Chinese opinion the literary productions and textbooks of the Taiping rebels of the last century do really express the spirit and teachings of Christianity—of course not the Christianity of European frock-coats and top-hats but from the view-point of the missionaries: then supernatural claims and worldly aspirations appear antagonistic, and so they have been repudiated as spurious. But even as regards European literature, while one, though but a foreigner, can know well enough what individuals among their authors wish one to believe, one is yet too imperfectly acquainted with their underlying motives, expectations, and private practices, as often to become perplexed, suspicious and even weary of the long winded, loftily-worded discourses upon religion which theologians and philosophers, who have apparently strayed away from the fullness of life into a mere narrow intellectualism, are pleased to claim as their pious contributions to revelation. The Essayist would have us place reliance upon the advantage of that accuracy which attaches to documentary evidence, but even in the best and most exact translations we could miss the atmosphere, the environment, the impulse and motives which actuate the writers. And the subjective attitude of the inquirer or investigator himself, whether sympathetic or otherwise, must not be overlooked. Let us therefore remember the wise, though paradoxical, admonition of the Chinese philosopher Laotze that "Truth is not confined to speech, though the use of speech is to reveal the Truth", and be charitable and cautious.

That Islam should value, cherish and venerate the Koran is to be expected. It is the chief depository of their religious life impulses, the

Logos from which the derive the transcendental forces which maintain them in their life struggles. Its intrinsic merits are of course only relative. Whether it could rival the Rig Veda and Upanishads in profundity and heights of thought, the Buddhist Tripitaka in universality of philosophy and psychology, the Tao-te-King in formal speculations, the Chinese Shus and Kings in practical ethics and morality, must be left to the verdict of investigators and students. Personally, I must confess, I am inclined to classify it, with all its excellencies, its potentialities, its imperfections and crudities in the same category as the Jewish Talmud and the Christian Bible. In this I do not think I am disparaging the latter. There may be passages in the Koran more sensual, carnal and prurient than corresponding ones in the Bible, but in my humble opinion the test should be subjective rather than objective. We should impartially investigate and interpret the attitude, the fervour, the loyalty, the devotion and veneration of worshippers towards the source of their religious life, rather than criticize the mere contents and teaching of the book they venerate. Let me illustrate this remark by a short reference to their respective God-idea.

Islam, as well as Christians, believe in an anthropomorphic and personal God. But while the attitude of the Moslem worshippers towards his deity while in his religious mood is consistently one of reverence, of awe, of submission, of resignation: that of the Christian towards his God is indefinite and scarcely understood. From personal experience I fear I am constrained to the opinion that the affective relations of modern Anglo-Saxon Protestantism to the divinity have recently changed. Freedom and equality are in modern European and American society the keynote of his relations to God. This feeling of freedom towards God has largely supplanted the duty motive which the Catechisms continue to inculcate: action in obedience to God's will or command is getting out of fashion; it is what is right and what is best which is now the favourite reason for conduct. Even a certain feeling of equality, monstrous as this may seem has passed into the attitude of the people to God; awe, reverence, worship appear only dimly, and not as frequently as is assumed in the religious consciousness of the democratic West. And whilst God may not be feared or even understood, while He is frequently not even present to the mind of his worshippers,

He remains for them the bestower of things they want, only the belief that adoration is an effective means of obtaining satisfaction has been to a very large extent forgotten. Whether as meat-purveyor, as a moral support, as a friend in need, as an object of love and affection, they use Him and pray to Him a good deal with an admirable disregard for logical consistency and with the directness and bluntness characteristic of the aggressive children of a domineering century. If He proves himself useful, His right to remain in the service of man is thereby vindicated.

In this short digression on the subjective attitude towards the God-idea, I hope I have somehow though perhaps imperfectly, hinted at the disparity between religion according to Bible and traditions and religion as the infinitely larger breath of life has made it. The discrepancies exist not only in the externals of religious life but they show themselves in the inmost consciousness of individuals, and is often a question of different hopes and different affective needs: what is "bread of life" to one is dregs to another. And the frequent logical inconsistencies, the indifference to objective truth, to rational proof in the different doctrines and dogmas, attest and affirm that the supremacy of life-impulses over the directions of the intellect is incontestable—not what is objectively real, not what is subjectively logical but that which ministers to approve needs and desires is the "religiously" true. Not God therefore, but life—more life—a higher, larger richer, more satisfying life—is in the last analysis the end of religion. The love of life at any and every level of development—or to use another phraseology, the instinct for preservation and increase—is the religious impulse. Universality may be the ultimate aim of all positive religions but each civilization must evolve its own means to arrive at such universality out of its own life impulses and resources.

CONCLUSION:

The Afterlives of the Straits Philosophical Society

In the aftermath of the First World War, the intellectual life of the colony began to change. Many of the European members would go off to fight in the war and would not return. At the same time, one of the Society's most prominent members, Lim Boon Keng would leave the colony for China in 1921. He was increasingly dissatisfied with the lack of opportunities for Straits Chinese and the British inability to treat them as free men within the British Empire.[1] As Lim would earlier argue in 1917,

> Surely this war must have taught us this lesson—that in dealing with human beings we must look at the spirit, we must look at the total of a man's character and culture, and not merely at a man's skin. ... I think, that in this colony we shall always maintain that great British spirit which we have inherited from Sir Stamford Raffles that in this colony we shall treat all men as men, not by the colour of their skin but by their character, their merits and their qualities as useful citizens.[2]

This built upon Lim's calls during the war to challenge racial discrimination within the British Empire and for the movement of colonized towards democratic self-government within a reformed Empire, as a first step towards a "federation of the world".[3] Yet Lim's belief in the promise of British Liberalism, and hope that the British Empire could transcend racial discrimination, diminished. Nor did the promise of the smooth integration of Anglicized elites within the colonial establishment realize a harmonious colonial order.

By the 1920s new challenges and claims were being made against the colonial order in Malaya, and a colony that had earlier been seen as devoid of politics was increasingly becoming politicized.[4] The earlier decades of the Society had seen a more tranquil political climate in the colony in which questions of colonial policy could be openly debated in a more non-partisan manner. In the aftermath of the war, questions of the future of Malaya became more urgent, and a new series of claims emerged which challenged the stability of the old order with stronger rhetoric.

Replacing Lim Boon Keng on the Legislative Council, a young Tan Cheng Lock would continue Lim's liberal critique of the British Empire by advocating for the political development of British Malaya. Calling for increases in the number of non-Europeans on the Legislative Council and for a system of direct elections, alongside other demands, which sought to challenge the subordinate status of Anglicized non-Europeans in the colony, he articulated political positions which would anticipate the concerns of a later generation of Malayan nationalists.

> Our ultimate political goal ... should be a united self-governing British Malaya, with a Federal Government and Parliament for the whole of it, ... I think it high time that we commence to take action towards forging the surest and strongest link of that united Malaya by fostering and creating a true Malayan spirit and consciousness amongst its people to the complete elimination of the racial or communal feeling. We should aim at building up a Malayan community with a Malayan consciousness closely united with the British Empire.[5]

At the same time, the colonial administrative order was increasingly being challenged. The First World War brought new claims for representation in the colony's civil service which challenged the colour bar instituted in 1904 to prevent, particularly Indian civil servants, being sent to Malaya. By the 1920s the British had not only removed this colour bar in the Malay states but more importantly, began to respond to pressure to open up the administrative service to the Malays.[6]

Key to this process of grooming an elite Malay administrative service was the development of Sultan Idris Teacher Training College and the Kuala Kangsar Malay College. The former was where a generation of

Malay teachers would be trained and where questions of the history and the identity of the Malay race would be disseminated; whilst the latter would provide the training ground for a new generation of Malay civil servants that would eventually take over the country's administrative service from the colonial government.[7] Both of these institutions would be the spaces in which a modern nationalist discourse would develop among the Malays in the 1920s and 1930s.

The increasing assertiveness by British colonial officials to take up pro-Malay policy positions—building upon the discourse on race found in the papers of the Society—continued unabated in the 1930s. In the 1930s Sandra Khor Manickam has noted a "divergence from British race discourse and a movement towards a Malay-centred colonial discourse"[8] in which British concerns with race were mixed with questions of Islam and pre-colonial themes of Malay identity. This reflected an emerging discourse on race which has similarities with the earlier Straits Chinese discourse, one which adopted European categories of race in a way that challenged a European focus on supremacy. Such a discourse may be seen to provide a foundation for the development and modernization of the Malays, and for the emergence of a Malay national identity.

In reading Malay texts from the period Manickam has highlighted how Malay intellectuals in the 1920s would point to racialized assumptions of Malay laziness and feudal backwardness as arguments for the necessary development of the Malays. She has highlighted what she describes as "exhortation-type writings"[9] in which the Malays would not only be encouraged to improve and modernize but were also enjoined to be opposed to other groups—Indians, Chinese and Europeans—who were seen as preventing the progress of the Malays. This development in Malay political consciousness, to a great extent, is an extension of the colonial ethnography found in many of the Society papers which identified the Malays as "sons of the soil" and provided a racial definition of Malayness which "entrenched them as the privileged race in the Malay Peninsula".[10] Such a discourse would go on to dominate Malay mainstream consciousness and thinking until well past the 1920s and 1930s. And it continues to resonate today.[11]

The question of race remained central also to non-Malay thought in the post-Straits Philosophical Society period, with many of the arguments made by the Straits Chinese in the Society taken up by a later generation. Chua Ai Lin's work has highlighted the *Malayan Tribune* and other Anglophone newspapers established by non-European elites in Malaya, including Lim Boon Keng, as spaces in which questions of nation and race were being discussed.[12] Chua has noted the way in which such discussions concerned not only British understandings of race and nation but also sought to import Indian and Chinese discussions of race, as part of a broader engagement of the colonial and non-European world with Western thought.

Integral to the discourse among Chinese participants was a widely accepted identification of race and culture, in which racial definitions of Chineseness reflected assumptions around conformity to Chinese culture. This contrasted with the dual identity outlook of the Straits Chinese who managed both Chinese and colonial identities. One example was the establishment by the Singapore Indian community of a Sun Yat-sen memorial school in 1929, which provoked a member of the Chinese community writing in the *Malayan Tribune* to object to the use of Sun Yat-sen's name. The writer argued that "we have every right and monopoly over things that are our own, and it is our duty to see that nothing is taken from us without our consent".[13] This argument along racial lines—that members of the Indian community should choose figures from their own community—may have been a minority view. However, whilst other writers disagreed with such narrow ethnic definitions of identity, we can discern the beginnings of racial compartmentalization in the development of political life in Malaya.

Central to early debates was also the question of racial mixing in the dynamics of a Malayan identity. As discussions of Malayan nationhood became more animated in the 1930s, particularly amongst non-Malays, they came to focus on the racial basis for this nation, as well as the question of whether or not the mixing and intermarriage of Malayans could form the basis for a homogenous Malayan community. As Chua notes, whilst there emerged some support for such inter-communal mixing, many remained opposed to the breaking down of established racial barriers, seeing in miscegenation the watering down of the races. In Chua's view, the fear of miscegenation "placed limits on the direction a uniquely 'Malayan' identity could take in the future".[14]

This would emerge as particularly evident in the debates led by Tan Cheng Lock over Malayanization in the Legislative Assembly in the 1930s. Moving beyond the narrow confines of the Straits Chinese Tan would advocate for the welfare of Chinese labourers following the Wall Street Crash in 1929. Tan had then emerged as a strident voice for the Chinese community in Malaya and the development of a Chinese Malayan identity.[15] When Clementi called for an educational focus on the Malay language Tan not only argued that the British were discriminating against the Chinese language and other vernacular languages in Malaya, he would also object to attempts to homogenize the population of Malaya, particularly through mixing with the Malays. As Tan stated:

> I hope and presume that the term "Malayanisation" does not at all imply that the Government has the least intention in view, however remote, ultimately to attempt the mixing ethnologically of the various races living in Malaya, so that the product of this race mixture will be a homogenous amalgamation of the component races in whom the Malay characteristics will predominate ... my aged grandmother used to relate to me, when I was a child, how the Chinese born of Malay mothers or with a strong Malay admixture revealed such dire physical and moral depravity that they "never in virtue's ways did take delight" but spent their days exclusively in cock-fighting, kite flying and other frivolous and harmful past times ... The causes must have been due both to environment and heredity."[16]

In arguing this Tan was recalling the arguments of Lim Boon Keng around the harmfulness of the Malayan climate and the mixing with Malay blood which required, for Lim, the re-sinicization of the Chinese in Malaya. For Tan it now entailed the freedom to maintain elements of Chinese culture within a Malayan nation.

This and other similar lines of racial thinking in the 1920s and 1930s clearly influenced the reasoning and development of post-war nationalism. The larger discourse on race and identity that emerged as important to Malay nationalism in the 1920s and 1930s would become central to Malay politics with the formation of the United Malays National Organisation. Similarly, it would become important to Malayan Chinese political development through the conservative

Malayan Chinese Association. In Singapore, this discourse on race would take a different path but it would also filter into the colony's politics and internal political development, although less intensely and more peripherally. What we can see is that the concerns around race, climate, the body and development discussed in the Society continued to resonate in the political life of the post-colonial state, despite the fact that the Society itself had long disappeared from the intellectual life of the Peninsula.

It is not surprising that the subject matter of racial difference, eugenics and racial improvement, which were an important part of the Society's discussions, were taken up by two of Malaysia and Singapore's most prominent political leaders—Mahathir Mohamad and Lee Kuan Yew. Mahathir's *Malay Dilemma* has been central in reproducing ideas of race in post-colonial Malaysia through singling out biological characteristics as well as the character and personality of particular racial communities to explain social and economic differences.[17] His reasoning was based not just on colonial ideas of Malayness but also in terms of narrower and more controversial European understandings of race, particularly in reference to Jewish people. As David Henley has noted Mahathir's position that hybridity and mixing would produce improvements in the Malay community reflected a very particular racial understanding.[18] Mahathir would also argue that the Chinese remained racially strong due to their custom of marrying outside of clans, unlike the "pure-bred" rural Malay who, as he explained, practised intra-breeding and therefore remained racially "weak", leading to backwardness, laziness and underdevelopment. Similarly, he would note that the Malay phenomenon of high birth rates, caused by early marriage and a refusal of celibacy, ensured that poor and disabled Malays were able to "survive, reproduce and propagate their species. The cumulative effect of this can be left to the imagination."[19] This explanation, which rehashed earlier discussions in the Society on heredity and the survival of fittest, led Mahathir to posit a continual decline in the quality of the Malays. Mahathir's solution was firstly a call for urbanization and secondly a focus on the Malays' economic standing. Although Mahathir's views did not develop into a fully-fledged programme of eugenics in Malaysia, such sentiments contributed to the underpinnings of the New Economic Policy and provided support for the main objective of his premiership which centred on the role of the state in uplifting and developing the Malays.[20]

It has been pointed out also that Lee Kuan Yew was "increasingly enamoured of the kind of racist eugenic theories that were popular in Edwardian England".[21] Sunil Amrith has noted that Lee in the 1960s had argued in eugenic terms, suggesting that in any society five per cent of the population would be more endowed than the rest and should therefore rule in the interests of all.[22] So too would Lee worry in 1969 that "free education and subsidised housing lead to a situation where the less economically productive people in the community are reproducing themselves at rates higher than the rest".[23] This formed part of a programme of family planning and population management which sought to improve the quality of Singapore's population. In 1984 this led to the introduction of the Graduate Mothers' Scheme which sought to encourage the reproduction of Singapore's elite. As Amrith notes, this later became enshrined in the government's approach to immigration policy and foreign workers—something evident also in Malaysia.[24] The continuing legacy of social Darwinism to Lee's thought was also evident in a 1994 interview with *Foreign Affairs*, when he would argue that: "Genes cannot be created, right? Unless you start tinkering with it, as they may be able to do one day. But the culture you can tinker with. It's slow to change, but it can be changed—by experience—otherwise human beings will not survive. If a certain habit does not help survival, well, you must quickly unlearn that habit."[25]

As with Mahathir, Lee's policies did not amount to a fully-fledged programme of eugenics, but they did share with Mahathir a view that it was the responsibility of the post-colonial state to develop society, biologically and culturally, and to prevent processes of racial degeneration and underdevelopment. The association between race and the state which fixated the post-colonial state in Malaysia and Singapore suggested that its central role was the development of the society over which it governed. This focus on race and development is perhaps the most striking outgrowth of the Society's discourse. This has resulted not simply in reinforcing a racial sense of identity and bringing about racial division. It has also prevented non-racial forms of identity and of belonging from taking root. It is with the passage of time, and through reflecting back upon the Society papers, that we can see more clearly the lasting legacy of colonial rule and post-colonial racial policy and practice in Malaysia and Singapore today.

Notes

1. Daniel P.S. Goh, "Unofficial Contentions: The Postcoloniality of Straits Chinese Political Discourse in the Straits Settlements Legislative Council", *Journal of Southeast Asian Studies* 41, no. 3 (2010): 500–1.
2. Legislative Council Proceedings, 22 October 1917, p. 122.
3. Lim Boon Keng, "Race and Empire with Special Reference to British Malaya", in *The Great War from a Confucian Point of View, and Kindred Topics, Being Lectures Delivered during 1914–1917* (Singapore: Straits Albion Press, 1917), p. 115; Lim Boon Keng, "The Race Question in Colonial Administration", *The Straits Chinese Magazine* ix, no. 1 (March 1905).
4. Chua Ai Lin, "Imperial Subjects, Straits Citizens: Anglophone Asians and the Struggle for Political Rights in Inter-War Singapore", in *Paths Not Taken: Political Pluralism in Post-war Singapore*, edited by Michael Barr and Carl Trocki (Singapore: NUS Press, 2008), p. 18.
5. Tan Cheng Lock quoted in K.G. Tregonning, "Tan Cheng Lock: A Malayan Nationalist", *Journal of Southeast Asian Studies* 10, no. 1 (1979): 30–31.
6. Yeo Kim Wah, "The Grooming of an Elite: Malay Administrators in the Federated Malay States, 1903–1941", *Journal of Southeast Asian Studies* 11, no. 2 (1980): 300–1.
7. Ibid., p. 1.
8. Sandra Khor Manickam, "Common Ground: Race and the Colonial Universe in British Malaya", *Journal of Southeast Asian Studies* 40, no. 3 (2009): 601.
9. Ibid., p. 603.
10. Ibid., p. 604.
11. Lim Teck Ghee, "Malay Middle Class at a Crossroads", *The Sun*, 18 August 2019.
12. Chua Ai Lin, "Nation, Race, and Language: Discussing Transnational Identities in Colonial Singapore, circa 1930", *Modern Asian Studies* 46, no. 2 (2012): 283–302.
13. Ibid., p. 294.
14. Ibid., p. 302.
15. K.G. Tregonning, "Tan Cheng Lock: A Malayan Nationalist", *Journal of Southeast Asian Studies* 10, no. 1 (1979): 30–31.
16. Legislative Council Proceedings, 12 February 1934, p. 1.
17. Mahathir Mohamad, *The Malay Dilemma* (Singapore: Marshall Cavendish, 2008).

18. David Henley, "Hybridity and Indigeneity in Malaya, 1900–70", in *Belonging across the Bay of Bengal: Religious Rites, Colonial Migrations, National Rights* (London: Bloomsbury Academic, 2017), pp. 181–92.
19. Mahathir, *The Malaya Dilemma*, p. 29.
20. See Lim Teck Ghee, "Dr M's 'Malay Dilemma' Misshaping Race Discourse", *Malaysiakini*, 1 August 2020.
21. Joe Studwell, *Asian Godfathers: Money and Power in Hong Kong and South East Asia* (London: Profile Books, 2008).
22. Sunil S. Amrith, "Eugenics in Postcolonial Southeast Asia", in *Oxford Handbook of the History of Eugenics*, edited by Alison Bashford and Philippa Levine (Oxford: Oxford University Press, 2010), p. 308.
23. Ibid., p. 310.
24. Ibid., p. 309.
25. Fook Kwang Han, Warren Fernandez and Sumiko Tan, *Lee Kuan Yew: The Man and His Ideas* (Singapore: Marshall Cavendish, 2015).

INDEX

A
Abubakar, Temonggong, 359
Acheh and the Achinese, 408
Adam, J. Collyer, 275
Adam, John, 275
adat perpateh, 393
adat téménggong, 393, 399
Aitken, James, 25–26, 212–13, 224
Akkads of Babylon, 97, 99
alcohol, as narcotic, 263–70, 274–75
alcoholism, 275–76, 286, 370, 411
Alexander the Great, 427
Alfred, King, 166
Al Ghazzali, 424
Ali Iskandar Shah, Sultan, 359
Allison, J.M., 234, 244
America, and immigration, 118–19
amok, 320, 322, 337, 368
Amrith, Sunil, 443
ancestral worship, 23, 193–94
Anecdotal History of Singapore, 199
Angel of Death, 428
Anglo-Chinese College, 27
Anglo-Indian race, 65
Anglo-Saxon race, 60, 101, 303, 435
animism, 402, 406, 408
"anthropologist-as-legislator", 11, 15
Anti-Christ, 429
anti-opium movement, 148, 157, 262–63, 269
Anti-Opium Society, 26, 148, 263
Arab community, 189, 195, 393–94
Arabian Nights, 399, 431–32
Arab traders, 363, 395, 397
Ark of the Covenant, 421
Aryan, 95, 97, 100, 119
asceticism, 105–6
Asiatic Society, 328
Assembly of Deputies, 313
Autobiography, 395

B
Baba, 259, 262, 293
    degeneration of, 29–30, 33
    Singapore, of, 292

Straits-born, 235, 242, 254
see also Chinese; Straits Chinese
Baba Mission, 19
Banishment Ordinance, 176
Barlow & Co, 234
Barton, Henry, 205
Bengal Asiatic Society, 191
Bengal Civil Service, 51
Bengal Tenancy Act, 52
Best, Captain, 205
Bible, 69, 90, 96, 435–36
Biggs, J.N., 5
Bintang Timor, 31
Birch, 11
Bishop, David, 17, 375–76, 381
Blackburn Commercial Mission, 241
Bland, R.N., 3
Blundell, Governor, 22, 189
Bodleian Library, 395
Bonser, John W., 2–3, 53
"Book of Arta Viraf", 419
Book of Judges, 343
Boshier, Carol Ann, 2
Botanical Gardens, 3
Bourne, Consul, 241
Boys Brigade, 19
Brahmanism, 95–96
Brahmo-Somaj, 66
bribery, 55, 143, 166, 216–19, 228, 251, 285
Bridge of the Dead, 420
Bright Celestials, 27
British Board of Trade, 234
British Empire, 153, 377
 English law in, 188
 loyalty to, 22, 27, 255
 racial discrimination, within the, 29, 437–38
 role of, 21, 31–32
British India, 149
British intervention, 10–11
British Malaya, 227, 378
British Malaya, 165, 438
 Chinese in, 181, 278, 281, 289, 293
 corruption in, 228
 intellectual culture in, 6, 35
 languages spoken in, 220
 penal district, within, 186
 reformation of, 213, 224
 translation work, and, 398
Brooke, Gilbert E., 5, 12, 25, 79–80, 103, 129
Buddhism, 96, 434
Buddhist Tripitaka, 435
Burgess, P.J., 5
Burma Research Society, 2
Bustamus al-Salatin, 426

C

Caldecott, Andrew, 4, 34
Campbell, J.G., 263, 273
Cannon of Rites, 307
Canon Law, 193
Cantonese, 282–83, 301
Carlyle, Thomas, 350, 353
Carpenter, Mary, 174
Central College, 360
Chamber of Commerce, 221, 283, 297
Chartered Bank, 300
Chatterjee, Partha, 8, 31
China
 imports from, 242–43
 social order in, 311
 war with Japan, 295

Chinese
- birth-rate, in Malaya, 372–73
- British Malaya, in, 181, 278, 281, 289, 293
- colonial order and the, 26–30
- criminals, 161, 180–81
- education and, 254–56, 259–60
- Federated Malay States, in, 195–97, 301–2
- immigration, 180, 279–80
- law, 22–23, 189, 193–96
- Malacca, in, 280, 282, 287, 372
- Malaya, in, 278–79, 292–93, 299–302, 305, 440–41
- Malay Archipelago, in, 280, 286, 296
- migrants, in Singapore, 22, 132–33, 141, 162–63, 188–89
- nationalism, 26–28, 30, 234, 278
- prejudice against, 285
- riot, 151, 180, 284
- Straits Settlements, in, 184, 301–3, 372
- succession, and, 194
- trade, and, 133, 234–36, 240–42, 244–45, 280
- *see also* Baba; Straits Chinese

Chinese Advisory Board, 215, 285
Chinese Crisis from Within, The, 292
Chinese Malayan identity, 441
Chinese Philomathic Society, 26
"Chinese problem", 22, 128
Chinese Protectorate, 165, 197, 255
- Contagious Diseases Ordinance (CDO), and, 128
- establishment of, 24
- role of, 184, 200, 215

Ching-tien, style of, 307–8, 310

Choo Kia Peng, 26
"Chou-li", 307
Chou period, 307
Christianity, 92, 281
- changes in, 346
- corruption of, 347–48
- Europe, ruled in, 60
- Islam, compares with, 20–21, 338–40, 343, 352, 354–55, 411, 434–35
- Mohammedanism, compares with, 352–55
- morality, and, 142–43
- origin, 96, 98

Christian Scriptures, 307
Chua Ai Lin, 440
citizenship, 60, 354
Civil Procedure Code, 223
civil service, 17–18, 51, 85–86, 159, 227, 356–57, 438
clan association (*kongsi*), 22
Clifford, Hugh, 11, 15–16
Clive, Lord, 51
Cocos Islands murder, 204
Code Napoleon, 189
Code of Manu, 191
Coke upon Littleton, 112
Collyer, W.R., 3, 5, 13, 25, 58, 93, 198
"colonial difference", 21
colonial hegemony, 2
colonization, 56, 78, 117
colony, governing the, 21–26
Common Law, 189
communism, 45, 306–7
community, category of, 8–9
Confucianism, 26, 29–30, 255, 293, 297–98, 305–6

Confucius, 85, 166, 255, 306–8, 314
conscription, 310
Contagious Diseases Ordinance (CDO), 127–29, 135–42, 147
Contract Act, 191
Contrat Social, 314
Cook, J.A.B., 148
coolie trade, 22–23
Cooper, Frederick, 7
copper coins, 242
Cornwallis, Lord, 52
corruption, 183, 216–19, 228, 310, 348, 431
Court, formation of, 200
Court of Judicature, 207
Court of Justice, 201, 206
Court of Quarter Sessions, 209
Courts of Bengal, 190
Crawfurd, John, 43, 371, 396
    British subjects, and, 201–3, 207
    "enlightened" approach, and, 12
    gambling-farm, and, 210
    Malay origin, and, 387–88
creole, 28
crimes, violent, 174, 180
criminal class, 56, 76, 160–61, 167, 170–72, 174
Criminal Investigation, 275
Criminal Procedure Code, 223
Crown Agents, 224, 229
Crown Colony, 10
culture system, in Java, 47–49, 51
customary law, 9, 23, 188–89

D

Daily Advertiser, 27, 80
Daing Ibrahim, Temonggong, 359

Dangerous Societies Suppression Ordinance, 23–24
Darwinian evolution, 8, 15, 20, 338
Darwinism
    guide to, 314
    influence of, 10, 34, 71
    race, and, 79, 279, 363
    legacy of, 443
Day of Judgment, 428–29
death penalty, 161
debt-slavery, 11, 377–78, 380
demon-worship, 96
Descriptive Dictionary of the Indian Islands, 387
Deutsch, Emmanuel, 350
Doran, Christine, 29
Du Cane, Edmund, 171
Duke of Chou, 307
Dutch Cultivation System, 43
Dutch East India Company, 45
Dutch East Indies, 377
Dutch rule, over Java, 44–57

E

Eastern art, 68
Eastern School, 19
East India Company, 199, 202–5, 359, 395
ecclesiasticism, 98
"educated criminal, the", 84
education
    China, in, 85–6, 90–92
    Chinese, and, 254–56, 259–60
    lower classes, and, 79–84, 89–91
    Malay, and, 79–80, 227, 257–58, 374
"Education Act", 84
Education Commission Report, 259–60

Egyptians, 96
Elizabeth, Queen, 109
"embourgeoisiement", 7
Emerson, C., 5
Emerson, Rupert, 44
Encyclopaedia Britannica, 81
English Civil Procedure, 223
English law, 23, 44, 188–93, 195, 200
"enumerated communities", 9
"Essay on Evolution", 314
eugenics, 8, 442–43
Eurasian, 66, 120, 132, 254
European art, 67–68
European, as dominant community, 248–50
European education, 81–82
Europeanization, 33, 279, 286, 288

F
Factory Acts, 192
family planning, 443
farm system, 150, 152, 156
Farquhar, Major, 200
Farrer, R.J., 403
Fatalism, 425
Fatthah, 416
Fécondité, 77
Federated Malay States
  Chinese in, 195–97, 301–2
  improvements, 225–26, 229
  judicial system in, 213, 223–24
  Malays in, 215, 227, 361
  success of, 291
  Tamils in, 216, 220
"federation of the world", 437
feudalism, 15
feudal system, 83, 87, 90, 307
filial piety, 163, 166

First World War, 34, 437–38
forced labour, 45–47, 52
Foreign Affairs, 443
Fortnightly Review, 242
Freemason, 153
Free Press, The, 339
French law, 189
French Revolution, 313
Frost, Mark, 10
Fukien dialect, 282
Fukienese, 282
"fuzzy communities", 9

G
Galloway, D.J.
  climatic influence, and, 121
  essay on *latah*, and, 15, 319
  medical doctor, 2, 5, 127
  monogamy, observations on, 144–46
  opium trade, and, 148–49, 263
  sexual disease, paper on, 24–25, 128–29, 140–42
Galton, Francis, 8
Gambier and Pepper Society, 238
gambling
  extortion, as a means of, 281
  vice, as, 163, 170, 179, 183, 200, 209, 217, 237, 399
gambling-farm, 210
Garden of the Sultans, The, 426
General Hospital, 223, 229
Girl Slavery, 137
globalization, 6
Gnosticism, 346
God-idea, 435–36
God of Fertility, 97
Goethe, 416

Goh, Daniel P.S., 15
Goh Kitmoh, 295
Government of India, 22, 154–55, 157, 206
Government Scholarship, 229
Graduate Mothers' Scheme, 443
Grand Jury, 207–11
"Great Study", 250
Greek education, 82
Gross, Hans, 275
Guthrie Scholarship, 27

H

Hainanese, 237, 282
Hakka, 282–83
Han dynasty, 309–10
Hanitsch, R., 5, 18, 368
Han Wuti, 309
Harcourt, William, 48
Hardie, Keir, 114
Hare, G.F., 196
Harper, Tim, 6
Hart, Robert, 242
Hastings, Warren, 190, 192, 196
Haviland, G., 2, 127, 129, 140
heathenism, 92, 340–41
Henley, David, 442
Henry, Prince, 61
higher education, 83, 360
Hinduism, 20, 30, 98, 190, 386–87, 391–92, 397
Hobsbawm, 7
Hokkien, 130, 180, 218–20, 235, 301
holy war, 402
Hongkong Medical School, 294
House of Commons, 136
Hsu-Hsiling, 314
Huang Hing, 296

Hullett, R.W., 3, 5
human race, evolution of, 73–74, 94–95
Humphreys, J.L., 403
Hunt, Robert, 20, 385
Hurgronje, C. Snouck, 394
Hussein Mahomed Shah, Sultan, 358–59
hybrid identities, 30–34
Hylam, 130, 133, 180, 218, 282
hypnotism, 320, 330–32

I

Ibn Battuta, 394, 407
Ibn Muhal-hal, 394
"idle-rich", 287
illiteracy, 255
Immigration Ordinances, 192
imperialism, 6–9
Impey, Elijah, 206
indentured labour, 216
India, law in, 191
Indian Civil Procedure, 223
Indian Mutiny of 1857, 43
individualism, 72, 307
industrialism, 308, 312, 314
infantile mortality, 221–22
"Infantilism", 139
Institutes of Hindu Law, 191
"Institutes of the Government of the Chou Dynasty", 307, 309
Introduction to the Study of the Law Administered in the Colony of the Straits Settlements, 23, 188
Islam, 64, 418, 439
    Christianity, compares with, 20–21, 338–40, 343, 352, 354–55, 411, 434–35

conversion to, 369–70
Day of Judgment, and, 428–29
differentiating factor, as, 18
doctrines of, 19, 422
literature, and, 413–14, 431–32
Malay, influence over, 385–87, 393–94, 397, 400–402
parts of, 351
slavery, and, 352–53
see also Mohammedanism
Islamic law, 22
Island of Singapore, cession of, 200

J

"Jacobins", 305, 313
jail system, 170
James I, King, 206, 390, 395–96
Japan, war with China, 295
Java
    culture system, 47–49, 51
    Dutch rule, under, 44–57
    Raffles reforms in, 44–47
Java, or How to Manage a Colony, 51
Jawi Pekan, 254
Jawi Peranakan, 3, 31
Jehovah, 344–45
Jesuit Fathers, 310
Jesus of Nazareth, 345–48, 352, 354–55, 425, 429
Jinrikisha Ordinance, 169
John, Prester, 66
John the Baptist, 345
"Jonesia Asoka", 191
Jones, William, 191, 196
Journal of the Straits Branch of the Royal Asiatic Society, 396
Judaism, 340, 343, 346, 348, 354

K

kangchu (river lord), 237–39
Kang You Wei, 10, 292, 295–96, 300
Kaviraj, Sudipta, 9
'keris', 104, 115
Khoo Siokwan, 295
Kingdom of God on Earth, 307
Kinghorn, Captain, 300
King of England, 206
King of Pasai, 394
King of Siam, 100
Kipling, Rudyard, 68, 94, 100, 114, 251, 408
Kitabi (men of the book), 354
Knight, Arthur, 2, 5, 24, 153, 212–13, 224, 256
kongsi (clan association), 22
Koran, 191, 347, 425
    holy books, as one of, 434–35
    literary style of the, 414–18
    Malay, and, 402, 418, 421, 427–28
    Night Journey, reference to, 419
    pantheism, and, 422–3
    Paradise and Hell, descriptions of, 420, 424, 429–31
    piracy, and, 395
    schools, 397–98
    slavery, and, 352
    Sunna, and, 351, 354
"Kramat hidup", 409–10
Kuala Kangsar Malay College, 438
Kuancius, 308, 310
Kuangsu, Emperor, 295
Kuomintang, 27, 292
Kynnersley, C.W.S.
    career of, 159, 356
    prison system, paper on, 25, 177, 179–85

Straits Philosophical Society, member of, 3–4, 12, 17
Malays, and reformation, 356–57, 363, 373

L

Labour Ordinances, 192
Lamont, Archibald, 19
Lamont, Arthur, 27, 148
Lamont, J.A., 2
Lancaster, James, 395
Land of the Midnight Sun, 117
land-tax, 52, 237
Laotze, 434
latah, 15
    definition of, 323, 333
    description of, 320–22
    hypnosis, as, 334
    nervous disorder, as, 319, 323–26, 333
Latin race, 77
Laws, 82
"Laws of Coition, The", 432
Lee Kuan Yew, 442–43
Legislative Council, 215–16, 228, 234, 438, 441
Lei Juanhung, 297
Lellington, Gregory, 205
L'Esprit des Lois, 314
Lewis, Su Lin, 2
Lexicon of the New Sydenham Society of Medicine and the Allied Sciences, 320
Liang Chichao, 295
liberalism, 5, 7, 28, 34, 44, 103, 338
    critique of, 12–14
Light, Captain, 203–4
Li-Ki, 307

Lim Boon Keng, 148, 233
    Chinese in Malaya, essay on, 278–79, 292–93, 299–302, 305, 440–41
    opium and alcohol, on, 262–63, 273–74, 276
    perspectives, on issues, 26–30, 33
    Straits Chinese Magazine (SCM), co-founded by, 6
    Straits Philosophical Society, member of, 3, 5, 27, 34, 437–38
Lim Neesoon, 296
Lin, Commissioner, 269
Lind, Jenny, 332
lingua franca, 283, 298
Literary History of India, 66
Liu-An, 310
"lock hospitals", 127
Long Depression, 7
Low, Hugh, 11
Loyalist Association, 295
Luther, Martin, 83, 90
Lu Xun, 293

M

Macaulay, Zachary, 63, 90
Mackenzie, Colin, 46
Mahathir Mohamad, 442–43
Maine, Henry, 9
Malacca, 214, 335, 360, 409
    agricultural show, 258
    Chinese in, 280, 282, 287, 372
    conquest of, 370–72, 391
    Eurasians, in, 254
    importations, and, 242
    kings of, 394
    landowners of, 53

mukim regulations in, 33, 279, 291
opium shops in, 156
plantations in, 236–37
Straits Settlements, as part of, 207
trading centre, as, 389–91, 402
Malaya
   Chinese birth-rate, in, 372–73
   Chinese immigrants in, 280–82, 286–88, 298, 301–3
   nationalism in, 31, 34–35, 438–39, 441
Malayan Art Industries, 374
Malayan Chinese Association, 442
Malayan identity, 440
Malayanization, 441
Malay Annals, see *Sejarah Melayu*
Malayan Tribune, 440
Malay Archipelago, 43, 283
   Chinese in, 280, 286, 296
   natives of, 370, 376
   trading in, 391
Malay Archipelago, The, 43
Malay College, 374
Malay Dilemma, 442
Malay literary forms, 31
Malay Magic, 387
Malay Mail, 360
Malay Peninsula, and colonial thought, 10–12
Malay race
   attributes, 99, 110, 321–22, 378
   birth-rate, 372–73, 442
   civilization, 388–91
   education for, 79–80, 227, 257–58, 374
   employment, and, 214–15, 227–28
   extinction, possible, 364–66, 368
   Federated Malay States, in, 215, 227, 361
   foreign races, influence of, and, 369–72, 376
   identity, 439
   Islam, influence of, 386–87, 393–94, 397, 400–402
   kingdoms, 393, 396, 404
   Koran, and, 402, 418, 421, 427–28
   land reservation, 44
   language, 219–20, 386–88, 390, 397–99, 404, 425, 441
   law, 200–202, 393
   lazy, 44, 122, 248, 253, 375, 378, 439, 442
   lingua franca, 283
   Menangkabau, 389–90, 393, 400
   modern civilization, effect on, 378–83
   natives of the soil, as, 213, 226–27, 252, 439
   opium, and, 270–71
   origin of, 387–88, 405
   peasantry, 365–67, 371
   population, 253, 370, 378, 382
   protection of the, 363–64, 376–77
   Raffles, and, 358–60, 373–74, 389, 397–98
   reformation, and, 356–57, 363, 373
   religion, and, 18–21
   sixteenth century, in, 407–8
   study of, 14–21, 321, 356
   sultanate, 11
   superstitions, and, 408–10, 429
   systems of writing, 392

Malaysia Advocate, 31
Maliku 'l-Saleh, 394
Maliku 'l-thahir, 394
Mamdani, Mahmood, 9
Manchu dynasty, 293–94, 298, 300, 303
Mandarin, as *lingua franca*, 298
Manickam, Sandra Khor, 71, 439
Mantena, Karuna, 9
Manual of the Malay Language, 391
Married Women's Property Act, 353
martial law, 204–5, 313
Max Havelaar, 48, 50, 56
Maxwell, Benson, 192
Maxwell, William, 12
McKillop, J., 3
Mecca
    idolatrous practices at, 341, 346
    Mohammed, prophet and, 348–49, 415, 417
    pilgrimage to, 351, 397, 401–3
    sacred spots, one of, 340, 343
    translation works in, 398
Medical College, 220
medicine-man, 214
medievalism, 15
Menangkabau Malays, 389–90, 393, 400
Mencius, 307–8
Mental Physiology, 336
Methodist Publishing House, 6, 19
"middling" classes, 28
Mill, John Stuart, 9, 12, 104–5, 108–13
mining industry, 239–40
Miraj, 419
Mission Press, 400, 431
model farm, 248, 254, 258

Mohammed al-Barkawi, 425
Mohammedanism, 431
    ancestry, common, 339–40, 343
    Christianity, compares with, 352–55
    civilization before, 369, 387, 391
    conversion to, 122
    influence of, 253, 379, 392, 404, 408
    intermarrying, and, 406
    origin of, 96
    State religion, as, 394
    see also Islam
"Mohammedanism, As Revealed in Its Literature", 385–86
Mohammedan Marriage Ordinance, 189, 195
Mohammed, prophet, 341–42, 346–55, 414, 418–19, 426–27
    Mecca, and, 348–49, 415, 417
Money, J.W.B., 43, 49–50
Mongol race, 92, 97, 99–102, 310, 311, 405
monogamy, 131–32, 138, 144–46, 253, 411
monomania, 329, 335–36
monotheism, 338, 342, 411, 422
moral maxims, 166
Morgan, John, 202–3
Moslem Doctrine of God, The, 422
"Moslem Influence on the Malay Race", 385
mother-tongue, 80–81, 90, 220
Muar, as model settlement, 373
Muhammadanism, *see* Mohammedanism
Muir, William, 346, 347
mukim regulations in Malacca, 33, 279, 291

Müller, Max, 95
Municipal Commission, 215
Municipal Council, 216, 228
Municipal Ordinance, 175
Munshi Othman, 19
Murray, W., 5, 16, 18–19, 116, 263, 375, 381
Museum of the Royal Asiatic Society, 371

N

Napier, Walter J., 3, 12, 23, 43, 188
nationalism, 7–8
    Chinese, 26–28, 30, 234, 278
    Malaya, in, 31, 34–35, 438–39, 441
    Turkish, 21, 386
native law, 190–92
natives of the soil, 213, 226–27, 252, 439
Native States Service, 227
natural selection, 143
Netherlands Trading Society, 48
New Economic Policy, 442
"New Imperialism", and race, 6–10
nicotine, 276
Night Journey, 419
nihilism, 314–15
Noctes Orientales, 6, 34, 159, 404
Nracha, 401

O

Odyssey, 406
Old Testament, 96, 345, 421
Old World, 76
Ong Siang, 303
opium, 21, 159, 215
    alcohol, and, 262–63, 273–74, 276
    anti-opium movement, 148, 157, 262–63, 269
    consumption, 28, 150–52, 163, 180, 183, 210, 272–73, 399
    Malay, and, 270–71
    narcotics, as, 264–8, 277
    problem, 148–50
    revenue, 153–56, 200, 269, 288
    shops, 156
    suppliers, 240
    trade, 25, 148–49, 155, 157, 262, 269
    use for, 432
Opium Commission, 263
oral contract, 311
orang laut, 388
Orang Selitar, 365
Ordinances of Manu, The, 191
Original Sources of the Koran, The, 418
origin of species, 102

P

paganism, 346
Paget, James, 135
pantheism, 422–23
Paris Municipal Ordinance, 136
Pax Romana, 60
Peck, F.C., 4–5
Penal Code, 176, 185
penal system, 160
Penang, 19, 159, 173, 204, 261, 296
    inhabitants, 227, 282
    opium shops in, 156
    plantation, 236
    population, 192
    rehabilitation centre, 263
    revenue, from opium, 154–55

Straits Philosophical Society,
    members in, 3–4
Supreme Court, 208
uninhabited, 203
Penang Free School, 260
Penang Philosophical Society, 3–4
Penang Riots, 23
Pennefather, Lieutenant-Colonel, 5
pepper monopoly, 46
Perak War, 11
Persian Bridge of Chinvat, 420
Peter the Great, 295
Petit Jury, 211
phallic worship, 340
Philippines, Chinese in, 288–89
philosophical school, 96
Pickering, William, 24, 285
"Pidgin English", 299
pilgrimage, to Mecca, 351, 397, 401–3
piracy, 45, 192, 207, 213, 370, 395, 402, 406
Plato, 82, 91–92
pleasures, merits of, 106–9
plural society, 32, 247
Po-Leung-Kuk, 165, 184
Police Court, 162, 169, 217, 285
political identity, 27, 31
polygamy, 254, 352–53, 399–400, 411, 424
polytheism, 387
Poole, Stanley Lane, 417
Port Tarascon, 77
"Poseidon's Law", 408
poverty, 162–64, 192, 272, 348
Presbyterian Church, 2
"Preserved Tablet", 420–21
Prince of Wales Island, 192, 207

Principles of Heredity, 275
prison discipline, 168, 172, 179, 183, 185–86
Prison of Weltevrede, The, 56
prison system, 25, 177, 179–85
private education, 255
Privy Council, 193, 195
prostitution, 136, 138, 140–42, 145–47, 200–201, 218–19
Protector of Chinese, *see* Chinese Protectorate

Q

Qing dynasty, 292
Queen's Scholarship, 26, 212, 260, 301–2

R

race
    concept of, 8
    Darwinism, and, 79, 279, 363
race-based thinking, 72
races in Singapore, 129–31, 442
racial compartmentalization, 440
racial discrimination, 29, 437–38
racial mixing, and, 33, 72, 93, 116
racial prejudice, 284
"racial problem", 22
racial superiority, 28
racism, 14
Raffles College Union, 4, 34
Raffles Institution, 26–27, 208
Raffles Library and Museum, 127, 363
Raffles, Stamford, 19, 406, 437
    charter, for religion, 281–82
    Enlightenment ideas, and, 12, 61
    equality before law, and, 198–203, 207

gambling, against, 209–10
Java, reforms in, 44–47, 394–95
Malay race, and, 358–60, 373–74, 389, 397–98
"race", and concept of, 8
Rajah of Kedah, 203
Rankin, H.F., 5
"Real Malay", 319
Reformation, 83, 87, 90, 105, 113
Reformatories Ordinance, 168
Registrar of Societies, 24
Regulation Act of 1773, 206
Reid, Archdall, 275–76
Reith, G., 2–3, 19–20, 24–25, 140, 148–49, 153
Reith, G.M., 292, 338–39
Report of the Educational Commission, 255
Republic, 82
Ridley, Henry N., 15, 25, 71, 159
    Darwinist approach, 14, 17–18, 79, 129, 363
    latah, and, 319–20
    liberal approach, 44
    racial mixing, and, 33, 72, 93, 116
    Straits Philosophical Society, member of, 3, 5–6, 12
    Utilitarianism, and, 103–4
Rig Veda, 435
Ritchie, Major, 5
river lord (*kangchu*), 237–39
Roberts, J.H., 293, 299
Roman Dutch law, 189
Rome, ancient, 60
Royal Commission on Opium, 275
Runciman, W.M., 14, 116

S
Salisbury, Edward, 71
Sampo, Chinese eunuch, 280–81
Sang Hung-Yang, 309
Sang Sipurba, 390
Sankey, Lieutenant-Colonel, 5
Sanskrit, 20, 191, 386, 388–92, 395, 397–99, 419
Sanskrit Vedas, 95
Sarawak Museum, 127
sea gypsies, 388
"Sea of Rum", 427
sea village, 357
"second-class improvements", 225
Second World War, 154
secret society, 23–24, 165, 183, 208, 283, 294, 296
Sejarah Melayu, 387, 389–90, 394, 405, 407
Selections from the Koran, 417
self-government, Chinese system of, 23, 189
sex trade, 23–25, 127–29, 148, 159
sexual disease, 24–25, 128–29, 140–42
sexual morality, 135, 143–44
Shao-hing, 314
Shelford, T., 3
Shellabear, W.G., 12, 19–21, 148, 263, 385–86, 413
Siam Society, 2
Sia, T.B., 300
Singapore
    Baba, of, 292
    Chinese migrants, and, 22, 132–33, 141, 162–63, 188–89
    death-rate of, 222
    opium shops in, 156
    pineapple industry, 239
    races in, 129–31, 442
    sea village, 357

Singapore Anti-Opium Society, 263
Singapore Chinese Educational Institute, 27, 80
Singapore Club, 5
Singapore Free Press, 4, 273
Singapore New Year Regatta, 214
Singapore Philosophical Society, 34
Skeat, William Walter, 12, 19
slavery, 107, 110
    debt-, 11, 377–78, 380
    indentured labour and, 216
    Islam, and, 352–53
    philosophy, and, 96
    suppression of, 213
Smith, Arthur, 283
Smith, W. Robertson, 341
social inequality, 306
socialism, 10, 30, 293, 296, 298, 305–8, 312–14
Socialistic Utopia, 297
Society for the Acquisition of General Knowledge in Bengal, 2
sociology, 8, 129, 140, 414
Socrates, 82
Song Ong Siang, 26, 212
"Son of Heaven", 255
Spencer, Herbert, 8, 12, 79–80
Spiritual Empire of the Church, 60
S.S.Arratoon Apcar, 300
Stanley, H.M., 61
statesmanship, 250, 253
Still, A.W., 3
Stoler, Laura Ann, 7
Straits Chinese, 1, 34, 248
    anti-opium cause and, 262
    children of, 259–61
    community, 282
    Confucianism, and, 293
    conservative, 298
    hybrid identity, and, 30–32, 439–41
    indigenous race, as, 130–32
    infant mortality and, 222
    intellectuals, 25–30, 233
    modernization amongst, 21
    opportunities for, 437
    see also Baba; Chinese
Straits Chinese British Association, 27
Straits Chinese Herald (*Surat Khabar Peranakan*), 31
Straits Chinese Magazine (*SCM*), 6, 26–30, 262, 303
Straits Medical Association, 127, 319
Straits Philosophical Society (Society), 244, 256, 304
    Chinese immigrants, and, 22–25
    colonial thought, and, 10–12, 35
    establishment, 1
    Malays, study of, 15–21, 321, 356
    members, 2–6, 26–27, 34, 233, 248, 279, 437
    missionaries in, 263, 338, 385
    papers presented, 30, 33, 43, 71–72, 103–4, 116, 127–28, 141, 148–49, 159–60, 188, 234, 247, 262, 293, 305, 319–20, 375–76, 387, 393, 403–4, 438–40, 443–44
    post-colonial state and, 442
    Presidential Address, 93, 198, 292, 357, 373
    role of, 12–14
    themes and concepts, 28
Straits Settlements, 2–3, 198, 213, 356–57
    Chinese in, 184, 301–3, 372

Contagious Diseases Ordinance
   (CDO), in, 127, 139
   judiciary in, 207, 223
   Crown Colony, as, 10, 199
   death, causes of, 284
   Indian labourers in, 220, 370
   Malays, and, 215, 361
   opium problem in, 148–50
   opium revenue in, 153–54, 269
   population, 192
   unoccupied, declared as, 23, 188
   urban life in, 21–22, 25
Straits Settlements Civil Service, 159
Straits Settlements Legislative
   Council, 292
Straits Times, 3
Straits Trading Company, 3
Straits Volunteer Corps, 27
Sudds, John, 204
Suez Canal, 10
Sultan Idris Teacher Training
   College, 438
Sultan of Acheen, 390, 395–96
Sultan of Johor, 411
Sultan of Perak, 374
Sultan of Stambul, 400–401
Sultan of Turkey, 411
Summary Jurisdiction Ordinance, 175
Sung dynasty, 310
Sunna, 351, 354
Sun Yat Sen, 27, 292, 294–97, 300,
   312–13
Sun Yat-sen memorial school, 440
superstitions, Malay and, 408–10, 429
Supreme Court, 203, 206, 208
Surat Khabar Peranakan (Straits
   Chinese Herald), 31

"survival of the fittest", 8, 14, 72, 75,
   78, 442
Swettenham, A., 295
Swettenham, Frank, 11, 15, 227
Swettenham, J.A., 11
"Sworn Brotherhood", 296
Syed Ameer Ali, 350, 352
Syed Hussein Alatas, 15
syphilis, 139, 146
System der Kriminalistik, 275
systems of writing, 392

T

Tabernacle, 421
Tables of Stone, 421
Tagore, Rabindranath, 10
Taiping movement, 294
Talmud, 418, 421, 435
Tamil
   education, 229
   employment, 228, 361, 373
   Federated Malay States, in, 216,
      220
   gender disproportion, 131–32,
      372
   influence of, 369–70, 390
   labour, 236
   language, 219–20
   Mohammedan, as, 400, 402
   standard of, 213, 215
Tan Cheng Lock, 438, 441
Tan Chulam, 295
Tang dynasty, 280, 310
Tan Teck Soon, 19, 244, 386
   anti-opium movement, and, 148
   death, 34
   educational credentials, 26–27

education, support for, 247–48, 303
social reform, and, 28–29, 32–33, 80, 160
Straits Philosophical Society, member of, 3, 5, 233
Tan Tock Seng Hospital, 208
Tao-te-King, 435
Ta-T'ung, 307
Ten Commandments, 421
Teochew, 130, 180, 218–19, 237, 282
Teo Enghock, 295
theocracy, 294
theology, 1, 82, 346
Thien Nan Shin Pao, newspaper, 27
Thomas, G.E. Venning, 5, 12–13, 104, 112
tin trade, 10, 241
Tisdall, St. Clair, 418–19, 421
toll collection, 11
Tongmenghui, 27, 292
trade guilds, 90, 242
Traffics and Discoveries, 408
Treaty of 1819, 358
Treaty of 1824, 359
Triad Brotherhood, 294
Tso Ping-lug, 296, 300
Tunanjihpao, 295
Turkish nationalism, 21, 386
Twenty Attributes of God (*Sifat Duapuloh*), 425

U

United Malays National Organisation, 441
Universal Peace movement, 294
Universal Races Congress, 29

Upanishads, 435
Uthman, Caliph, 414
utilitarianism, 9, 12–13, 103–6, 108, 110–13, 115
Utusan Melayu, 400–401
"urban problem", 22

V

Van Den Bosch, General, 47
Varley, Henry, 156
venereal disease, 133, 139, 141–42, 147
vernacular school, 227, 252, 257–58, 398, 403, 427
violent crimes, 174, 180
Virgin and the Serpent, 340
Virgin Mary, 427

W

Wallace, Alfred Russel, 43
Wall Street Crash, 441
Wang An-Shih, 310
Wang Chingwai, 296
Wang Mang, 309
Warren, Charles, 3
Wealth of Nations, The, 314
Western Europe, developments in, 97–98
Whinfield, E.H., 423
Wilberforce, William, 63
Wilkinson, R.J., 19, 252, 387, 398, 405
witchcraft, 206, 214
Wu Lien-the, 263
Wu Sankuei, 294
Wu Yueh, 296

X
Xiamen University, 34

Y
Yin Suat Chuan, 263
Young Bengal movement, 2

youth offenders, 167–68, 170, 172–73, 176
Yuan Shihkai, 299, 313–14

Z
Zoroastrianism, 340, 354, 418–20